BLACK MERCURIES

BLACK MERCURIES

African American Athletes, Race, and the Modern Olympic Games

David K. Wiggins
Kevin B. Witherspoon
Mark Dyreson

ROWMAN & LITTLEFIELD

Lanham • Boulder • New York • London

Published by Rowman & Littlefield
An imprint of The Rowman & Littlefield Publishing Group, Inc.
4501 Forbes Boulevard, Suite 200, Lanham, Maryland 20706
www.rowman.com

86-90 Paul Street, London EC2A 4NE, United Kingdom

British Library Cataloguing in Publication Information Available

Library of Congress Cataloging-in-Publication Data

Names: Wiggins, David Kenneth, 1951- author. | Witherspoon, Kevin B.,
   author. | Dyreson, Mark, 1959- author.
Title: Black mercuries : African American athletes, race, and the modern
   Olympic games / David K. Wiggins, Kevin B. Witherspoon, and Mark S.
   Dyreson
Description: Lanham, Maryland : Rowman & Littlefield, [2023] | Includes
   bibliographical references and index. | Summary: "This book chronicles
   the struggles and triumphs of African American athletes in the Modern
   Olympic Games, from 1896 through the 2020 Tokyo Games. It explores the
   lives and careers of both legendary and little-known Black Olympians as
   they sought to honor themselves, their race, and their nation on the
   world stage"—Provided by publisher.
Identifiers: LCCN 2022023330 (print) | LCCN 2022023331 (ebook) | ISBN
   9781538152836 (Cloth : acid-free paper) | ISBN 9781538152843 (epub)
Subjects: LCSH: Olympic athletes—History. | African American
   athletes—History. | Racism in sports. | Sports and globalization. |
   Sports—Sociological aspects.
Classification: LCC GV721.5 .W455 2023 (print) | LCC GV721.5 (ebook) |
   DDC 796.4809—dc23/eng/20220811
LC record available at https://lccn.loc.gov/2022023330
LC ebook record available at https://lccn.loc.gov/2022023331

To William J. Baker, superb storyteller and matchless biographer of Jesse Owens—and mentor and friend to each of the authors; to Edwin Bancroft Henderson, the original historian of Black Mercuries; and to John Apostal Lucas, passionate compiler of Olympic chronicles

CONTENTS

FOREWORD

In 1983, as a fledgling curator at the yet-to-be-built California African American museum, I was tasked to create a major, inaugural exhibition and write a catalogue that chronicled the impact and the history of Black Olympians as part of the Olympic Arts Festival that accompanied the 1984 Los Angeles Games. I never imagined how much that experience, including interviewing more than two dozen Olympians, would shape my career and how examining the Black presence in the American Olympic movement would dramatically alter my understanding of the paradox that was at the heart of the intersection of sport and race: how did athleticism, Olympic triumphs and an international stage become weapons in the struggle for freedom and fairness in America? And how did these athletes handle the burden of race and racism during and after the Olympic games? And did Olympic glory translate to lasting racial change? In essence, was America made better by the achievements and struggles of Black athletes that unfolded in the global cauldron of visibility that are the Olympic games?

In a year of interviewing and engaging Black Olympians, I realized that though they shared the bond of race, their experiences and their memories were shaped by educational, gender, generational, and political differences. I remember sitting on the front porch of a home in Teaneck, New Jersey, interviewing Cheryl Toussaint, a silver medalist in the 1972 Munich Olympics. She spoke of her excitement at reaching the pinnacle of amateur athletics. But our conversation quickly moved from a discussion of her

Olympic experience to her memories of the Munich massacre where eleven Israeli athletes and coaches were murdered by members of the Black September faction of the Palestine Liberation Organization. As she spoke about the pain of that moment, she tightly held her newborn baby. She seemed to hold her child even closer as she swayed, and as she expressed her horror and her frustrations that the Olympics continued despite the tragedy rather than honoring and acknowledging their deaths by ending the athletic competition. From that moment I knew that story of the Black Olympian transcended fleetness and medals.

Later that year I interviewed Mack Robinson who broke an Olympic record in the Berlin Olympics of 1936 but finished behind Jesse Owens to capture a silver medal. The older brother of Jackie Robinson, Mack was never able to translate his athletic achievements to post Olympic success. I was struck by how angry he was that he "was forced" into menial jobs in his hometown of Pasadena, while his brother was lauded for his pioneering efforts that led to the re-integration of baseball. Though proud of his Olympic experiences, Mack Robinson believed his role as one of eighteen Black athletes in Berlin, who garnered fourteen medals and destroyed Hitler's myth of Aryan superiority, had been overlooked or undervalued. To Robinson, his Olympic experience changed little, for himself and for the country. Yet his Berlin teammate John Woodruff believed that winning gold in the 800 meters contributed mightily towards, or at least foreshadowed, the changing racial landscape in Post War America.

I then spent time with Alice Coachman and Audrey "Mickey" Patterson, the first Black women to win Olympic medals competing in the London Games in 1948, whose conversations reinforced the notion that Olympic excellence translated to improved race relations. I traveled to Albany, Georgia to interview Alice Coachman, the first African American woman to win Olympic gold. She insisted we walk through the fields near her home. I struggled to keep up with her as I ruined my best pair of shoes walking through the red clay, trying to ensure that my cassette recorder could capture at least the sense of the conversation. She recalled with pride that both she and Mickey Patterson felt they were representing Tydie Ann Pickett and Louise Stokes, the first Black women to make the Olympic team in 1932 but who were not allowed to participate in the games due to their race, a decision made by the American coaches. And that their participation in 1948, their victories, marked a leap forward for Black women. As I spoke with Mickey Patterson at a stadium near her home in San Diego, it was clear that she was proud of what she accomplished but there was also a sense that there were strong racial tensions that surfaced during the

Atlantic crossing on the ocean liner the SS America. She recalled that the racial attitudes of Jim Crow America were present on the SS America. And she intimated that some of the nine Black women on the team faced sexual harassment but despite my prodding she would not share the details. Her conversation emphasized the double burden of being Black and female in post-war America.

Despite the willingness of some athletes to meet with me, many, especially more recent Olympians, were more reluctant. Some of the Black Olympians were concerned that their efforts would continue to be undervalued or that someone would profit off their struggles and stories. Barbara Ferrell, a gifted sprinter who participated in the 1968 Olympics in Mexico City, agreed to host a meeting where I could speak to many of the athletes who participated in the Olympic competitions of the 1960s and 1970s. When I arrived at her home in Inglewood, there were forty Olympians seated in a semi-circle and a single, lone chair for me. I explained that this would be in an inaugural exhibition of the only state funded museum (at that time) dedicated to African American history, an exhibition that would give their stories greater visibility as part of the Los Angeles games. After speaking for an hour, I seemed no closer to gaining any support for the museum. As I tired, about to give up, John Carlos, famed and tarred by his Black power protest in 1968, said I had an accent and was I from New Jersey. I nodded yes, and Carlos then said, "If he is from Newark, New Jersey, we can trust him." And from that support from John Carlos, the California African American Museum was able to open an exhibition entitled "The Black Olympian: The African American in the Olympic Games," which launched an important museum that garnered visibility and acclaim as the world's attention turned to the summer Olympics in Los Angeles in 1984.

Twenty years later I was tasked to lead a team to create the Smithsonian's National Museum of African American History and Culture. As we wrestled with the potential content, I never forgot how important and how illustrative the history of the Black Olympian is to our understanding of the impact of race in America. So as we developed an exhibition on the role of the intersection of race and sports, we decided that the lens into that subject should be the history of African Americans in the Olympics. And what better marker than to have all the visitors engage a large statue based on the photograph of John Carlos and Tommie Smith displaying a Black power salute on the medal stand during the playing of the national anthem that included sprinter Peter Norman who wore a badge supporting Smith and Carlos, and who was ostracized in his native Australia for his role in the protest.

The history of the African American in the Olympic games is finally getting the scholarly treatment worthy of this history. *Black Mercuries: African American Athletes, Race, and the Modern Olympic Games* reveals the central role that race has played in shaping both the modern Olympics and the character of modern America. Race has cast a shadow over the Olympic games and that shadow is brilliantly and exhaustively researched and interpreted in *Black Mercuries*.

Lonnie G. Bunch III
Founding Director, National Museum of
African American History and Culture
Secretary of the Smithsonian Institution

ACKNOWLEDGMENTS

Chronicling the stories and experiences of Black Mercuries in the modern Olympic games was a team effort and a meaningful and enjoyable journey in all respects.

David Wiggins wishes to thank JoDee Dyreson for her superb editing of the manuscript and ability to link together the differing styles of three academics. Thanks also to Chris Elzey for his careful reading of portions of the manuscript and cogent suggestions and recommendations that contributed to a much better product. Lastly, thanks and appreciation to Kevin Witherspoon and Mark Dyreson for agreeing to be a part of this project and providing their unparalleled expertise concerning the interconnection among race, sport, and the Olympic experience.

Mark Dyreson wishes to thank JoDee Dyreson for her close and detailed editing of the manuscript and Dave Wiggins and Kevin Witherspoon for serving as co-authors and generously sharing their knowledge of the experiences of African American athletes in the Olympic games.

Kevin Witherspoon wishes to thank Mark Dyreson and David Wiggins for their peerless scholarship, deep reservoir of knowledge, and most importantly for their patience, support, and good humor. Thanks to JoDee Dyreson for her exquisite editing of the work, and to other preliminary readers who offered their comments. Thanks to my mentors, Bill Baker and James P. Jones, who both passed away as this work was in progress but whose influence is evident on every page. Thanks to Lander University and the Lander

University Foundation for its support of my research and this project in particular. Thanks to the group of Lander University students who assisted with my research: Aaliyah Day, Austin Greer, Cameron Pate Addie, Abigail Piper, Matthew Shepherd, Jessi Vinson, and especially Macy Gault. Finally, there are not words enough to express my gratitude to my wife Jacky, and kids Lexi and Andrew, who keep me going on the toughest days.

INTRODUCTION

In his highly popular and frequently cited *Rome 1960: The Olympics That Changed the World*, David Maraniss wrote that Rafer Johnson, the iconic African American decathlon champion and the first flag-bearer for the American team, "refused to feel manipulated, yet he could not escape the burden of carrying other people's expectations and dealing with their contradictory demands. He was aware . . . of the irony of representing a nation that treated people of color like second-class citizens, but he also felt that he could advance the cause most effectively by doing what he did best, which was to excel at his sport and comport himself with dignity."[1] This assessment of Johnson could easily be replicated for the majority of African American athletes who have competed in the modern Olympic games down through the years. Most of them have been content with letting their athletic accomplishments do the talking, believing they could do more to bring honor to themselves, to their race, and to their nation by triumphing in their respective sports on the world stage. The recognition that they served as representational figures fueled their desire to achieve greatness in the most famous of all mega-sporting events while at once adding to the burden they already felt as members of a race who throughout the history of the United States have been marginalized and experienced some of the worst forms of discrimination. As to whether their athletic achievements in the Olympic games improved race relations and brought more people from diverse backgrounds closer together is difficult to assess, but victorious

African American athletes in the biggest sporting event on earth have generated enormous attention and brought many of them fame if not fortune.

With that said, when one explores the experiences of African Americans in the Olympic games it becomes quite clear that you cannot divorce those experiences from what has taken place in sport more generally and on the world stage. The stories we share of *Black Mercuries* indicate very clearly that the United States government and sporting bodies used African American athletes at various times as part of their propaganda efforts and, in turn, African American athletes understood that one of the most effective ways to point out the racial inequities and discrimination in this country is to disrupt in some way the sacred institution of sport. And nothing was more sacred than the Olympic games. African American athletes have, since their first appearances in the Olympics, served both to promote visions of racial harmony and to signal enduring racial disparities. This was certainly apparent during the Cold War period when the United States government employed famous African American Olympians as ambassadors in an effort to convince the world that this country was living up to its principles as a democratic society characterized by freedom of opportunity and racial harmony. Conversely, at the height of the civil rights movement Tommie Smith and John Carlos startled the world with their protest on the medal stand ceremony in 1968 in Mexico City in an effort to make visible the continued racial inequality and discrimination in the United States. The post–civil rights era has seen nothing approaching the controversial Smith and Carlos Black gloved salute and accompanying attention it drew, but there has been an increasing willingness more recently on the part of African American Olympians to speak out about racially discriminatory practices and other inequities in sport and the larger society as a result of the Black Lives Matter movement, police brutality, and an assortment of other issues.

Our intention in *Black Mercuries* is to delineate the differing athletic paths of African American Olympians and how they impacted the games as well as reflected and shaped larger historical, social, and cultural trends. We also trace the career trajectory of the relatively few and largely unknown Black coaches and other support personnel that have been involved in the Olympic games. In the process of doing so, and not unexpectedly, we have been reminded that African American Olympians have not been immune to the racialist thinking and discriminatory practices experienced by other members of their race. Superior athletic skills, while admired and respected and acknowledged, did not always shield African American Olympians from the racial tropes and insensitivity sometimes spewed by fellow athletes, spectators, the media, and many others. The racial realities of American culture are also largely responsible for the relatively limited number of sports engaged in by African American athletes in Olympic competition. In the earliest games, African American athletes were largely confined to track and field, always one of the premier and most publicized sports in the Olympics. Over time, African American athletes have gradually found their way into an increasing number of Olympic sports ranging from swimming and basketball to fencing and wrestling, but much more still needs to be done to ensure that they are given the opportunity, encouraged, and provided the support system necessary to expand the competitive activities available to them. Not only have African American athletes continued to be underrepresented in certain sports in Olympic competition but have largely found their way into the games after first training and participating in intercollegiate sport at predominantly white universities. Although a select number of African American Olympians have emanated from Historically Black Colleges and Universities (HBCUs), the most notable example being the long and decorated line of Olympians—mostly women—to come out of Tennessee State University, an overwhelming number of them had received their training and participated in sport at predominantly white universities. Such institutions had the resources to recruit the very best Black athletes, some of them foreign-born with citizenship in other countries, in an effort to realize institutional prestige and enhance their university brands and popularity. This pattern, which will certainly be impacted by the increasing number of professional athletes participating in the games, was noticeable from the beginning of Black American participation in the Olympics. In the first half-century of American Olympic history, from 1904 through the 1930s, every one of the more than forty Black athletes who made an American team emanated from predominantly white institutions rather than an HBCU—with one exception, a single athlete who hailed from Morgan College (today's Morgan State University). Recent levels of participation make clear that this pattern will probably continue to exist in the foreseeable future.

In addition to this pattern of participation, we have been reminded in the course of putting together *Black Mercuries* that an increasing number of African American women athletes have found enormous success in Olympic competition. Although still not shielded from discriminatory practices and unequal media coverage, the impact of Title IX (notwithstanding the fact it has been particularly beneficial for white women athletes) and increased professionalization and continued fights for gender equality have proved helpful in attracting, training, and honing the talents of physically gifted African American women athletes for Olympic competition. They are still largely found in basketball and track and field, but there have been a very select number of African American women athletes over the more recent past who have distinguished themselves in such white dominated sports as swimming, volleyball, fencing, boxing, wrestling, and soccer. Just like their male counterparts, African American women Olympians have had little to no participation in rowing (a notable exception being Anita De Frantz), golf, handball, cycling, table tennis, sailing, kayaking, or equestrian events, an indication that much work needs to be done to fully incorporate them in a full range of sports. Be that as it may, we have also been reminded that African American women Olympians, medalists as well as non-medalists and similar to their male counterparts, have experienced diverse post-athletic careers, some failing to find much personal and professional success and others flourishing in a variety of different ways. Not surprisingly, the decided differences in the post-athletic lives of African American women Olympians, again like their male counterparts, resulted from numerous factors, some of them controllable and others not.

We have also been reminded in the course of completing this book, which took place during the 2022 games in Beijing, how much more prominent Black athletes have become in the winter Olympics. Because of space limitations, however, we devote our attention to the experiences of African American athletes in the summer games and will leave the story of African American athletes in the winter Olympics to other historians. This does not mean the experiences of Black winter Olympians are not important, interesting, and consequential. On the contrary, the full story of Black winter Olympians needs to be explored by historians and sport studies scholars. The exploration of figure skater Debi Thomas's Olympic career should be undertaken as well as that of Shani Davis, the speed skater from Chicago who captured gold medals in both the 1,000 and 1,500 meters in Torino in 2006 and duplicated the same feat four years later in Vancouver. And, of course, we are well aware of the increasing number of African American men and women who have represented the United States on bobsleigh teams in more recent winter Olympic history. Not unexpected considering the premium placed on speed and power in the sport, many of these athletes have been drawn from track and field and football. Included among this group was Willie Davenport, the great hurdler who competed in bobsleighing at the 1980 games in Lake Placid to become the first African American to participate in a winter Olympics, Heisman Trophy–winner Herschel Walker who placed seventh in the two-man bobsleigh in Albert-ville in 1992, and Vonetta Flowers, an outstanding college sprinter and long jumper who became the first African American to win a gold medal in the winter Olympics when she teamed with Jill Bakken to capture the two-woman bobsleigh title in Salt Lake City in 2002. An outlier in many ways among African American bobsleigh competitors was Elena Myers, a softball player at George Washington University, who captured a combined total of five medals (three silver, two bronze) over the course of the 2010 Vancouver, 2014 Sochi, 2018 Pyeongchang, and 2022 Beijing Olympic games.

Finally, we were reminded while completing *Black Mercuries* just how many African American Olympians participated in the games but the relatively small percentage of those whose names resonate with even the most rabid followers of sport and African American history and culture. While such luminaries from the Olympic games as Jesse Owens, Rafer Johnson, Wilma Rudolph, Michael Johnson, Carl Lewis, Florence Griffith Joyner, Jackie Joyner-Kersee, Sugar Ray Leonard, and Simone Biles are well known to the sporting public, many others who have participated and realized success in the world's most important mega-sporting event have been lost from historical memory. The myriad reasons for this fact are too numerous to mention here but suffice it to say far too many accomplished African American Olympians throughout history have gone unnoticed and not received the attention their sporting successes and other achievements deserve. Although it is not our intent to assess the participation of each and every African American who has participated in the Olympics, we trust the following pages will provide interesting and insightful stories not only of legendary Black Olympians but also many of those who have failed to receive their just due for their outstanding performances in the games. We regret there is not space enough in this volume to fully examine the lives and stories of these lesser-known Olympians. Nonetheless, we hope this book furnishes a more complete picture of the modern Olympic games while at once providing needed insights into how and why some athletes, irrespective of race, are accorded iconic status and others are forgotten and left out of historical accounts. For the three of us, that would be accomplishment enough.

I

PIONEERING BLACK MERCURIES

African American Olympians, 1896–1920

The winged foot of Mercury, the ancient Roman messenger god who symbolized speed, blazed across the American landscape in the late nineteenth and early twentieth centuries, heralding the rise of the fashionable new sport of track and field athletics. Sewn onto jerseys, featured in the logos of athletic clubs, and employed to advertise meets, winged feet became the emblems of the sport. American sportswriters in that era regularly employed the folklore of Mercury, and occasionally his classical Greek progenitor Hermes, to adorn their accounts of athletic prowess on the track and in the field. The 1896 recreation of a modern Olympics made Mercury's winged-foot iconography even more popular. Most of the American athletes the press glorified in this era as Olympic "Mercuries" were white. Occasionally, the media mentioned Black embodiments of the messenger god, as a reporter in the *Indianapolis Freeman* did in 1916 when identifying three potential American Olympic medalists as a "Black Mercury trio."[1]

As the modern Olympic movement took root in the United States between 1896 and 1920, it was like so many other American institutions, an overwhelmingly white establishment. At best, it permitted African Americans to inhabit its margins, an occasional Black Mercury flashing among legions of white Hermes. American color lines drawn by both custom and by law ran through Olympic sport, including track and field. A uniformly white cadre led by Princeton University history professor William Milligan Sloane, the journalist Caspar Whitney, and Amateur Athletic Union (AAU) chieftain

James Edward Sullivan, served as the American leaders on the International Olympic Committee (IOC). Uniformly white American athletic leaders selected U.S. Olympics squads drawn from uniformly white pools of athletes.

Almost uniformly white. Here and there Black athletes in the 1890s found niches on intercollegiate track teams and on AAU club sides. William Tecumseh Sherman Jackson of Amherst College, Napoleon Marshall of Harvard University, and Spencer Dickerson of the University of Chicago figured prominently in intercollegiate track meets. George Coleman Poage starred on the University of Wisconsin's track team and ran for the Milwaukee Athletic Club in the early 1900s. In 1904 Poage became, by most accounts, the first African American Olympian and medalist when at the Games of the IIIrd Olympiad in St. Louis he earned bronze medals in both the 200-meter hurdles (a now extinct distance) and the 400-meter hurdles. Edwin Bancroft Henderson, one of the earliest chroniclers of Black athletes, dubbed this generation the "pioneers" who laid the foundation on which the "wonder works" of later Black Olympians such as Jesse Owens were built.[2]

Among those "pioneers" was a Philadelphian by the name of William H. "Billy" Morris, a middle-distance runner who became a mentor to generations of Black athletes. Later in his career, Morris "made" several Olympic teams by serving as the official trainer during the 1920s and 1930s for several U.S. Olympic track and field contingents. From his Olympic trainer's post Morris attended to several of Henderson's later "wonder work[er]s," including Owens. While still running competitively in the 1890s and 1900s, Morris competed against early white Olympians, even before Poage laid his claim as the first Black Olympian in American history. Morris' biography as an "almost" Olympian reveals just how difficult it was for Black athletes to find their way from the margins onto American Olympic teams in the early history of the revived games.

PIONEERING BLACKNESS: THE BILLY MORRIS STORY

In the late nineteenth century, Billy Morris rose to national prominence in the quarter-mile, half-mile, and mile runs. In 1890 Morris entered the AAU national championship meet held in Washington, D.C., then a city segregated not only by custom but by law. In Washington Morris wore the colors of the interracial Young Men's Christian Association (YMCA) Athletic Club of Philadelphia. He finished third in both the half-mile and mile races, the first Black athlete to place in the top three at an AAU national championship meet.

His placings at the AAU nationals and victories in multiple regional meets stirred the Black press to promote his feats. The *Cleveland Gazette* identified him as a "champion half-mile sprinter" who had been born in Richmond, Virginia, shortly after the Civil War.[3] His family migrated to Philadelphia, a city that in that era had the nation's largest African American community. In 1888, he took a job as a messenger and a janitor for the Real Estate Investment Company. While running a communiqué through downtown Philadelphia for his employer, Morris spied a picture of Lon Myers, the great Jewish American sprinter of the late nineteenth century, in the window of a Philadelphia newspaper office.

Enamored of becoming a famous track star like Myers, Morris faced the reality that he had to work full time to help support his parents and many siblings. Running messages through the streets of Philadelphia for his employer built his stamina. In the evenings after long days on the job he trained at the Philadelphia YMCA at 15th Street and Chestnut, an institution that allowed Black as well as white patrons. The intense running paid off as Morris blossomed into one of the nation's leading middle-distance runners.

As his running career flourished, the white press as well as the Black media chronicled his feats. Morris entered the amateur division in every race he could find. He ran in the periodic "picnic games," the rowdy contests sponsored by unions at holiday celebrations that featured abundant food and adult beverages as well as athletic competitions. He won races staged by ethnic clubs such as Philadelphia's Caledonian Club for patrons of Scottish heritage and the city's Hibernian Club for those of Irish descent. He represented Philadelphia in competitions against runners from urban rivals including New York City, Washington, and Baltimore. He toed the mark in international contests against British harriers. Morris regularly faced fellow Philadelphians in local meets sponsored by the amateur athletic clubs that sprang up throughout the city, including the Dorian Club—a collective of athletes from the University of Pennsylvania, known colloquially as Penn. Though Morris never had the chance to go to college, he regularly ran against the top collegians on the club circuit. Morris raced against and frequently beat athletes from Penn, Princeton, and other elite schools.

The first American Olympic contingent, which easily conquered its track and field rivals at the inaugural modern games in Athens in 1896, drew its membership from the very athletes against whom Morris regularly competed. That team was comprised not of champions selected from an open trial but instead from a group of Princeton athletes and a couple of their colleagues from the Boston Athletic Association (BAA), a prominent AAU club. Princeton history professor Sloane, the original American member of the IOC, circulated the invitation among this small group. This collection of college and club athletes who went to Athens were not top-tier competitors in the United States, with the exception of AAU quarter-mile national champion Thomas Burke of Boston University and the BAA. The original American Olympic "team" ventured to Athens at Sloane's request as a sort of "study abroad" spring semester project—the Athens track and field meet took place in April. In spite of their mostly mediocre talent, the American squad dominated the 1896 Olympic contests.

Had Billy Morris been among the club men who made the trek to Athens, his standard time in the half-mile would have easily beaten the 2:11 that Australian Edwin Flack turned in to win that event at the first modern Olympics. Morris routinely ran the half-mile under two minutes, and since no American entered the 800-meter race (a distance a bit shorter than the standard Anglo-American 880-yard "half mile") in Athens, Morris could easily have added to the many prizes the Americans took home.

As a national amateur contender for the Philadelphia YMCA, Morris would also have fit in well with the American Olympic squad for the 1900 Paris games. Once again, the American entry at the Olympics was comprised not of an officially selected group from a national trial but by a collection of amateur athletes who were sponsored by their colleges or clubs. Morris, who consistently placed well in major American meets and ran for a prominent club, seemed a solid contender for the 1900 American Olympic squad.

A gaggle of athletes from Philadelphia made the Olympic trip to Paris in 1900, most of them members of the track team from Penn. The contingent from Penn earned ten Olympic crowns, took eight second prizes, and three third prizes in Paris—the IOC would not begin awarding gold, silver, and bronze medals at the games until 1904 in St. Louis. Morris knew the Penn Olympic stars quite well, as in 1896 he began an apprenticeship as a part-time "rubber" (or a trainer in modern parlance) for Penn's track team. A protégé of Penn's legendary trainer Michael "Mike" Murphy who led the university's Olympic contingent in Paris, Morris thrived in his new post. However, getting paid to train athletes as he did at Penn made him by the standards of the complicated amateur rubric of that era a potential professional and thus open to challenges to his eligibility for the Olympics. In 1897 Morris cemented his transition from amateur to professional status when he accepted cash awards of $10 for winning the half-mile and $6 for a second-place finish in the mile in a Philadelphia Caledonia Club meet.

Morris' turn to professionalism ruled him out as a competitor for the 1900 Olympics or future games. However, Morris would eventually "make" the American Olympic team in a different role. While at Penn, Morris worked with the leaders of U.S. Olympic track and field teams, not only Mike Murphy, but also Lawson Robertson who served as an assistant and head Olympic track and field coach for 1912 until 1936. In 1920 Robertson tabbed Morris as the lead trainer for the U.S. Olympic track and field team, a post Morris helmed through the 1936 Berlin Olympics. From his trainer's post Morris would witness DeHart Hubbard win the long jump at the 1928 Olympics to become the first African American to garner an individual gold medal. Morris would watch African Americans Eddie Tolan take gold in the 100-meters and 200-meters dashes and Edward Gordon earn gold in the long jump at the 1932 Olympics. Morris would stand on the floor of Olympic Stadium in Berlin and bear witness as Owens and a host of other African Americans runners and jumpers stunned the world in 1936.

Though Henderson's 1939 chronicle did not mention Billy Morris as one of the Black "pioneers" in American sport, the Philadelphian deserves inclusion on that list. In the more than half-century that spanned his career as an athlete and trainer in American track and field, Morris witnessed an increasing number of Black Mercuries move from the margins to center stage on American Olympic track and field teams. In his youthful days on the track Morris competed with a handful of other Black club and intercollegiate track and field athletes as one of the lone representatives of his race during the final decade of the nineteenth century, as the 1896 Supreme Court decision of *Plessy versus Ferguson* cemented legal segregation in much of the American South, and custom and habit allowed color lines to flourish in every other nook and cranny of the nation. Had he maintained his amateur standing for a bit longer, he might have been the first African American Olympian. As it turned out, he became one of the longest tenured Black Olympians as a staff member rather than as an athlete.

As the modern Olympic movement emerged and expanded in the 1890s and early 1900s, 90 percent of the nation's African Americans lived in the South where the rapidly expanding shadows of Jim Crow prevented them from any opportunities to appear on the world's most important sporting stage. Like Morris, the first African American Olympians came from the growing number of families who made the trek out of the post–Civil War South to new lives and new opportunities north or west of the Mason-Dixon line. They grew up enmeshed in white educational and recreational institutions that offered at least a few opportunities to the most gifted Black athletes. Customary segregation and deeply held racial stereotypes certainly limited their horizons, but as avatars of the "talented tenth"—as the era's foremost advocate of African American rights, W. E. B. Du Bois, dubbed the leading edge of Black aspirations for equity and inclusion beyond the segregated fortress of white supremacy in the South, they overcame enormous obstacles to represent not only their nation but also their race in international Olympic arenas.

These pioneers, to use Henderson's term, represented undeniably Black anomalies to white dominion in the early history of American engagement in the modern Olympics. In 1904, a Black American would compete in the Olympics for the first time. The Games of the IIIrd Olympiad were the first held outside of Europe and the first hosted by the United States. They took place in a city that stood at the confluence of American regional and racial divides. St. Louis served as the meeting ground of the South, the West, and the North, an urban hub in which legal segregation thrived but which also aspired to appear as an enclave of more progressive racial sensibilities to its economic partners beyond the ex-Confederate South. After a battle with more internationally renowned American urban centers such as New York, Philadelphia, and Chicago, St. Louis won hosting duties because it was also the site for the 1904 World's Fair, formally known as the Louisiana Purchase Exposition, which incorporated the Olympics into its panoply of glittering exhibits. When he lined up at the starting line for a hurdles race, George Coleman Poage became the first Black American Olympian.

UNDENIABLE BLACKNESS: THE GEORGE COLEMAN POAGE STORY

Born in 1880 about 100 miles from St. Louis in Hannibal, Missouri, Poage was the son of former enslaved peoples, James Poage and Annie Coleman Poage. His father labored as a tanner while his mother labored as a domestic worker. In 1884, the family migrated to La Crosse, Wisconsin, where the Poages took positions on the estate of Albert Pettibone, a local lumber baron. Tragedy struck soon after when his sister Lulu Belle in 1887 and then his father James in 1888 succumbed to tuberculosis. His mother took George and his surviving sister to live at the Albert Clark Easton and Lucian Frederick Easton estate where Annie helmed the domestic staff. The Eastons, Yale University alumni who earned fortunes in railroads and finance, encouraged the educational development of the surviving Poage children. George, one of the few Black students at La Crosse High, proved an outstanding student and dominated the sprints on the track, setting Wisconsin prep records in the 50-yard and 100-yard dashes.

Supported by the Eastons, Poage in 1899 enrolled at the University of Wisconsin. At Wisconsin, as in high school, Poage was one of a handful of Black students. He thrived, once again, in this white institution of higher education. The eminent American historian Frederick Jackson Turner mentored Poage in his academic studies. Poage earned plaudits for his oratorical and choral skills. He also stood out in track. He joined the varsity squad in 1901 and routinely placed highly in the Western Conference (now the Big 10) championships, specializing in the quarter-mile race and the hurdles. Earning a Bachelor of Letters degree in 1903, his senior yearbook entry touted his "matchless swiftness."[4]

George Coleman Poage, the first Black Olympian, approaches the finish line of the 200-meter hurdles race at the 1904 Olympics in St. Louis. Poage is approaching the hurdle, trailing a competitor gliding over a hurdle just in front of him. Poage earned the bronze medal in the event and also won a bronze medal in the 400-meter hurdles, the first Olympic medals for an African American competitor. *Photograph from the Louisiana Purchase Exposition Collection: Olympic Games, Jesse Tarbox Beals Photographs, Olympic Games, 1904: Hurdle and Relay Races, Missouri Historical Society, St. Louis, Missouri.*

After his graduation, the Wisconsin track coaches hired Poage as a "rubber," like Billie Morris at Penn. The prestigious Milwaukee Athletic Club (MAC) tapped him for membership, the first Black athlete to receive that honor. Wearing the MAC colors at the 1903 AAU national junior championships, Poage won the 220-yard hurdles and finished second in the 100-yard dash. His points helped the MAC to claim the junior national title. He enrolled in graduate school at Wisconsin and took several history courses, though he did not complete a degree. His graduate student status extended his Western Conference athletic eligibility, and his post as a "rubber" did not disqualify him from amateur events as it had seemed to reclassify Morris in Philadelphia—a distinction that betrayed the frequently mystifying boundaries of amateurism during the era. In the spring of 1904 Poage became the first Black champion in "Big Ten" track history when he won both the quarter-mile sprint and the 220-yard hurdles. Later that year Poage joined the MAC contingent bound for the St. Louis Olympics.

The white media covering the St. Louis games invariably stressed Poage's Blackness. In the pre-Olympic predictions and in the coverage of his races, Poage appeared as the "colored sprinter," the "colored man," the "colored runner," the "negro," and the "colored boy."[5] The "official report" of the 1904 Olympics labeled Poage the "the only colored man to compete in the games."[6] The report distinguished Poage as an "official" competitor, in spite of devoting some attention to the "unofficial" participation of two Black South Africans in the marathon race. Henderson's early compendium, *The Negro in Sport*, identified Poage as the "first Negro track and field entrant in the Olympics," as well as a "remarkable hurdler and quarter-miler."[7]

In St. Louis Poage won bronze medals in the 200-meter and 400-meter hurdles. Poage's performances helped his MAC secure a third-place finish behind the New York Athletic Club (NYAC) and the Chicago Athletic Association in the Olympian contest for AAU club supremacy—two national powerhouses notorious for excluding Black athletes from their rosters. In accounts of Poage's feats decades later, he sometimes emerged as a harbinger of racial integration. Assertions that the 1904 Olympics contributed to racial integration, however, simply do not match the realities of the racism and segregation that suffused St. Louis in that era. Poage stood as an example of a limited experiment in desegregation, establishing an Olympic bulwark in American mythology as one site where Black pioneers from the margins pushed back against color lines.

Both the St. Louis games and the St. Louis fair were in fact segregated in all sorts of ways beyond the confines of the stadium in which Poage sprinted. While local fair leaders offered tidbits of racially egalitarian rhetoric, the realities of racial intercourse at the Louisiana Purchase Exposition did not match the flowery hyperbole. Still, at least one African American athlete and perhaps two took part for the first time in the Olympic Games, staged at David R. Francis Stadium, named after the exposition's leader and located on the then segregated campus of Washington University. George Coleman Poage's mentor in the history department at the University of Wisconsin, Frederick Jackson Turner, gave pioneers the leading role in the American epic in his paradigm-shifting theory of the role of the frontier in American history. In 1904 in St. Louis, his student Poage played a pioneering role in an American saga of color lines at an exposition devoted to the heritage of the frontier.

Scholars have generally regarded Poage's St. Louis debut as the first appearance of an African American athlete at the Olympics. The physician Charles J. P. Lucas who compiled the official contemporary chronicle of the St. Louis games clearly identified Poage as the "only colored man to compete in the games."[8] An eyewitness account from Dr. Lucas, so deeply involved in the meet that he served as the attending physician for the winner of the marathon race, seems to offer a definitive view on the matter. However, a mystery remains about whether Poage had a Black teammate.

UNCERTAIN BLACKNESS: THE ENIGMA OF JOSEPH STADLER

Since 1904 claims that another African American competed and, like Poage, earned medals, in this case a silver as well as a bronze, have periodically cropped up. If that athlete were indeed Black, he would stand as the first African American Olympic silver medalist in history and as Poage's racial compatriot on the roster of first African American participants. Joseph Stadler represented Cleveland's Franklin Athletic Club at the St. Louis Olympic carnival. What is not in doubt about Stadler's Olympic moment is that competing in now-extinct forms of Olympic leaping, the standing high jump and the three standing jumps (also known as the "standing triple jump"), Stadler took the silver medal in the standing high jump and the bronze medal in the three standing jumps. What is in doubt is Stadler's racial identity. In the media previews of the St. Louis Olympics, a handful of newspaper stories in white dailies identified Stadler as a "colored athlete" from Cleveland.[9] Beyond that quartet of stories, not a single other contemporary account from the St. Louis Olympics nor from Stadler's record in other meets ever labeled him as "colored," or a "Negro," or "dusky," or any other appellation common to that era to signify his racial identity. The two leading white dailies from his hometown in Cleveland, the *Plain Dealer* and the *Leader*, and from the city's African American newspaper, the *Cleveland Gazette*, do not reference Stadler's Blackness.

For the next six decades any mention of Stadler as a pioneering Black Olympian competing alongside Poage disappears from the historical record. Stadler first reappears as a Black Olympian in the 1960s, an era in which interest in chronicling Black history surged. In the 1966 *American Negro Reference Book* and the 1969 *Chronological History of the Negro in America*, Stadler materializes alongside a misspelled "Poag" on the 1904 American Olympic roster. However, the encyclopedists do not credit him with his silver or bronze medals. "Joseph Stadler, a Negro athlete from Cleveland, Ohio, competed in the standing broad jump, but did not place," reads both entries.[10] Neither of these blurbs offers any documentation for Stadler's racial heritage nor any explanation about where the information originated, a pattern that continued thereafter.

Stadler once again reappears as a Black Olympian in 1984, when for the first time since 1904 the summer Olympics returned to the United States. For the eightieth anniversary of the St. Louis Olympics, the *St. Louis Post-Dispatch* in its glossy *Sunday Magazine* section ran a retrospective on the 1904 games by local sports expert John McGuire that noted Stadler was identified as Black in contemporary newspapers in St. Louis. Still, McGuire admitted that Stadler's racial identity remained murky. "Apparently, his race is still a matter of debate," the St. Louis journalist observed.[11] Not only in hometown reminiscences about St. Louis but also in previews and promotions of the 1984 Olympics, renewed interest in Stadler placed him alongside Poage on the roster of America's original Black Olympians. Stadler made it into the 1984 *Guinness Book of Records* alongside a correctly spelled Poage. The compendium of popular "facts" identified Stadler as one of the first Blacks on an American team and as the silver medalist in the standing high jump.

Since the 1980s Stadler has more regularly resurfaced as Poage's Black teammate. An entry on Stadler in a 1991 compendium, *Black Olympian Medalists*, reports that "little is known about this early Black Olympian."[12] Bill Mallon, a careful compiler of statistics and anecdotes on the early Olympics, supported the claim that Stadler is the first African American Olympic silver medalist in his 2003 entry on the "Olympic Games" in a reference work on *African Americans in Sports*.[13] In *America's First Olympics* (2005), George Matthews also asserts that Stadler was Black. "Scholars, researching Cleveland newspapers, discovered many years later that Joseph Stadler was an African American," Matthews insists, labeling the absence of his racial identity in most accounts from 1904 "a mystery." Matthews contends that both Stadler and Poage "deserve dual recognition as the first African-American medal winners."[14] One of the most thorough historians of the African American experience in turn-of-the-century sport, Gregory Bond, also affirms Stadler's Blackness. Bond maintains "both Poage and Stadler became the first African Americans to earn Olympic medals."[15] Twenty-first-century litanies of African American "firsts" at the Olympics in the popular media have followed these scholarly leads and tabbed Stadler as a co-star with Poage in breaking the Olympic color line at St. Louis in 1904 as well as anointing the Cleveland jumper as the first Black silver medalist.

In spite of the claims since the 1960s in Olympic encyclopedias and monographs, the historical evidence for Stadler's "Blackness" remains sparse. In decades of poring over first microfilm and later digital news-paper accounts of the original American Olympics, we have yet to find stories in the St. Louis, Cleveland, or Chicago press that identify Stadler as Black. The four articles we have come across that put Stadler in the "col-ored" category in the *Philadelphia Inquirer* and *Louisville Courier-Journal* were almost certainly written by the same un-bylined correspondent, given the nearly exact syntax match in the accounts. A pre-Olympic article in the white *Cleveland Leader* before Stadler set off for St. Louis depicts the "champion track athlete of the Franklin Athletic Club" bound for St. Louis along with his trainer and teammate Everett Barnes, listing Stadler's many record-setting performances in Cleveland meets. A photograph of Stadler and Barnes clad in the track uniforms of the Franklin Athletic Club accompanies the text. While the dangers of reading racial identity from photographs has been well documented, Stadler appears to be white in the photo, and the *Leader*'s text does not offer any racial designation.[16]

In spite of the claims by other scholars, our searches of newspapers that covered Stadler's Olympic feats and post-Olympic life have not uncovered any new stories that shed more light on his racial identity. Not a single article in the early twentieth-century Cleveland press implies that Stadler was Black. Cleveland's African American newspaper, the *Gazette*, never ran a story on Stadler. Beyond the four articles previewing the 1904 games, no other contemporaneous account identifies Stadler as Black. In that era both Black journalists and white reporters almost invariably identified the racial identities of those whom they covered—for quite different reasons. Certainly, white observers were not in the habit of letting suspected Black Americans "pass" as white. Was Stadler "passing" in 1904, and after a brief slip in a couple of newspaper articles did he manage to recreate his camouflage and resume his white existence? Given the limited evidence, an absolute answer cannot be offered. The preponderance of the circumstantial evidence indicates Stadler was white and was simply misidentified in a few accounts previewing the 1904 Olympics.

The incorporation of Stadler into the pantheon of African American Olympians dates primarily from the buildup for the 1984 Los Angeles Olympics, an event that sparked celebrations of African American heritage in the Olympics and reintroduced the first indisputably Black Olympian in American history, George Poage, to the public. In St. Louis in the late twentieth century and the early twenty-first century, the media cheered Poage's 1904 participation in the Olympics as a progressive moment of "integration" in the city's history. In fact, it should be more properly understood as a flash of desegregation, a transitory alteration of a color line in a city that was deeply segregated by both law and custom. While the World's Fair organizers admitted Black visitors to the exposition, they kept segregated boundaries intact in much of the exposition's spaces even as they allowed Poage to run on the track at David R. Francis Stadium at Washington University—the normally segregated arena that housed the St. Louis Olympics.

UNDAUNTED BLACKNESS: THE JOHN BAXTER TAYLOR STORY

In St. Louis at the 1904 Olympics Poage became the first African American participant and medalist in history. In 1908 at the London Olympics John Baxter Taylor became the first Black gold medalist in U.S. history. Taylor rose to national prominence under the tutelage of "Billy" Morris and the rest of the staff at the University of Pennsylvania who prepped Taylor for Olympic glory. Taylor, born in 1882 in the nation's capital in Washington, moved to Philadelphia with his family during his childhood. His family settled into a house a few blocks from the Penn campus. A standout in track in his new city, he captained the team at Central High School. After graduating in 1901, he spent a year at Philadelphia's Brown Preparatory School and then matriculated at Penn in 1903. A standout in the classroom as well as on the track, Taylor spent two years in Penn's Wharton School and then switched to the School of Veterinary Medicine, where he completed a doctorate in 1908.

On the track, Taylor became one of the best quarter-milers in the world. A mainstay on Penn's dominating teams from 1903 to 1908, he set numerous records and won intercollegiate national championships in 1904 and 1907. Early in his Penn career, in the summer of 1904, he made an international tour of England and France, dominating his European rivals. In 1907, Taylor earned intercollegiate crowns indoors and outdoors and also became the first African American to win an AAU national championship. Taylor earned his AAU title at an unlikely venue, in the heart of the Jim Crow South in the town that many knew from its fame as the first permanent settlement in English North America—Jamestown, Virginia.

The 1907 championship in Jamestown marked the first time that the AAU held its top track and field meet in the ex-Confederate South, though the event had been staged in segregated cities in border regions—Washington, D.C. in 1890 and St. Louis in 1904. The AAU had permitted African Americans to compete in both of those legally segregated cities. In Jamestown the AAU championships again found a home at a world's fair as it had for the 1904 Louisiana Purchase Exposition. The 1907 Jamestown Exposition heralding the 300th anniversary of permanent English settlement in North America housed the AAU event. Staged by commercial leaders in nearby Norfolk who wanted to showcase the economic promise of the "new South," the Jamestown fair offered a few amenities for African Americans. The U.S. government spent $100,000 to construct a "Negro Building" that promoters promised would showcase the Black experience from slavery to the present.

The AAU made certain that African Americans would be permitted not only in the "Negro Building" but also in the track and field competitions as they refused in spite of local pressure to draw a color line in their games. The meet drew the nation's leading athletes and the sporting press to the miasmic hamlet of Jamestown. Reporters depicted the contests as a titanic struggle between the AAU's top squads, especially between New York's City's many clubs and their rivals from newer metropolises in the vast "West," from Chicago and Milwaukee to San Francisco and Seattle.

Taylor went to Jamestown as part of Greater New York Irish American Athletic Club's (IAAC) contingent and returned home the first Black AAU champion. White newspapers from the South mentioned Taylor by name and identified him as an AAU champion but did not identify his racial classification. White newspapers beyond the South mentioned his race but, with a few exceptions, offered little comment on the significance of the location of his triumph, even though Taylor's Jamestown appearance aroused animosity from ardent segregationists. AAU clubs from Richmond and Norfolk withdrew rather than face Taylor on the track. After Taylor's triumph, rumors swirled that the AAU was in fact considering drawing color lines in future championships, especially against Taylor. The *Indianapolis Freeman* assured readers that these stories were groundless. "To a man the A.A.U. officials laughed at the story, and on all sides it was voted as being

John Baxter Taylor (far left: gold medal in the medley relay) poses in London with his fellow American gold medalists from the 1908 Olympics, Ray Ewry (center: winner of two gold medals in the standing high jump and standing long jump) and Melvin Sheppard (far right: winner of three gold medals in the 800-meter race, the 1,500-meter race, and with his teammate Taylor in the medley relay). *Photograph from the "Prize Winners in the Olympic Games" collection, photographs by Benjamin Stone, © National Portrait Gallery, London.*

extremely ridiculous," the *Freeman* reported. AAU sources promised that they would never concede to color lines. A "high A.A.U. authority" insisted that "'a good amateur, whether black or white, will always have the same footing in the A.A.U. field.'"[17]

The next year, in 1908, Taylor earned a spot on the American Olympic team at a tryout held in his hometown of Philadelphia. Celebrating Taylor's selection, and the broader ethnic and racial tapestry of the American Olympians, the *Outlook* depicted a team comprised of "Anglo-Saxon, Teuton, Slav, Celt, Black Ethiopian, and red Indian."[18] Taylor, in *Outlook*'s jaded racial parlance, represented the "Black Ethiopian" of the squad, while the Hopi Lewis Tewanima and the Tuscarora Franklin Pierce Mount Pleasant, teammates from the Carlisle Indian School, comprised the indigenous American contingent.

In London Taylor overcame the challenge of a disappointing outcome in the 400-meter final to become the first African American to win a gold medal. His Olympic crown came as he ran the 400-meter leg in the medley relay, a now defunct event in which the first two contestants ran 200-meter segments, the third contestant ran 400 meters, and the anchor leg ran 800 meters. Taylor's team included three of his white teammates from American schools and clubs, William Hamilton and Nate Cartmell of Penn, who ran the first two 200-meter legs and Melvin Sheppard who anchored the victory on the 800-meter leg and who was on teams with Taylor at Brown Prep and with the IAAC. Taylor ran a blistering third leg to put the American team in a commanding position. His old Brown Prep teammate Sheppard secured the victory with two blazing final laps to secure the gold medal.

That triumph provided some solace for Taylor after a controversial finish of the 400-meters final. Anglo-American hostilities that plagued the entire Olympics boiled over in this gold medal race. Four runners contested the single lap of the track for Olympic glory, three Americans and one Briton. Charging a heinous foul, British umpires literally pulled Taylor off the track toward the end of race. Taylor had a penchant for coming from behind in the final stretch, and his supporters believed he had been poised to win the race until the officials intervened. After a protracted debate between the British officials and American coaches, the race marshals curiously decided to ban not Taylor but another American, John Carpenter, who won the disputed race, for obstructing Lieutenant Wyndham Halswelle, the British entrant in the final. The British judges ordered a re-run of the final with the three remaining contestants. The two Americans who were not disqualified, Taylor and William Robbins, refused to race under those conditions.

Halswelle ran by himself to Olympic gold, still the only "walkover" in Olympic track and field history.

Just five months after the London Olympics Taylor was dead, a victim of typhoid fever that he probably caught on the return voyage from Britain to the United States. His passing occasioned a huge outpouring of grief in Philadelphia and beyond. Even a white Southern newspaper, Georgia's *Augusta Chronicle*, lamented Taylor's demise, though the reporter forgot that in 1904 George Poage had been the first Black athlete on an American team. "Dr. Taylor was the first negro ever picked to carry the American flag on his breast in the Olympic championships, running in the 400-metre race and the relay event,"[19] noted the correspondent. Taylor's funeral drew several thousand mourners. His white Olympic teammates, comrades from the IAAC, and friends from Penn turned out en masse. The list of luminaries included a bevy of 1908 Olympic medalists, including his former Brown Prep and IAAC teammate Sheppard, a triple gold medalist who had been with Taylor on the victorious medley relay team.

Mike Murphy, the renowned trainer who had coached Taylor at Penn and on the U.S. Olympic team, blamed the quarter-miler's well-known humility and his immunity to fatigue for his death, indicating that Taylor simply ignored his symptoms for too long because he did not want to be a bother to anyone. Harry Porter, elected "president" of the 1908 American Olympic team by his fellow athletes, wrote a heartfelt letter to Taylor's parents that the press published. "As a beacon light of his race, his example of achievement in athletics, scholarship, and manhood will never wane, if indeed, it is not destined to form with that of Booker T. Washington, another inseverable link in the chain of progress that is leading the black man out of the bondage of prejudice, inequality, and ignorance into true freedom and culture," Porter proclaimed.[20] The thousands of white as well as Black mourners who gathered in the streets of Philadelphia for Taylor's funeral procession seemed to confirm Porter's proclamation.

FORGIVABLE BLACKNESS: THE HOWARD DREW STORY

Taylor's tragic demise made a repeat of his 1908 Olympic feats impossible. By the time the next Olympics took place, in Stockholm in 1912, the racial and sporting contexts in which "Black Mercuries" competed would dramatically shift. Taylor's tragic narrative of the athlete dying young took place in a context that drew thousands of whites as well as Blacks into the streets of Philadelphia to herald him as a "beacon of light" for his race, an avatar of

Booker T. Washington's gradualist doctrine of race relations. Beating white men in elemental foot races around cinder paths while thriving in white institutions of higher education as George Poage and John Taylor had, in the estimation of many African Americans and their white allies, contributed mightily to the perpetual labor required for racial reconciliation.

On December 26, 1908, in Sydney, Australia, just weeks after Taylor's funeral, a Black American pugilist named Jack Johnson defeated white Australian Tommy Burns to win the heavyweight boxing championship of the world. Johnson's seven-year reign as the globe's greatest boxer who routinely defeated white men in the primal endeavor of hand-to-hand combat as well as the persona he crafted as a celebrity outside of the ring would catapult him to a position as the most famous, and infamous, Black man in the United States during the early twentieth century. His braggadocio, his flamboyant lifestyle, his flouting of racial boundaries—in particular his public dalliances with white women—his open hostility to white racism, and his roots in the impoverished African American underclass shunned by white institutions made him a heroic figure of Black pride to some, a reviled villain to many white Americans, and a complex challenge for Black and white Americans committed to civil rights. His pummeling of "great white hopes" from 1908 to 1915 did not bring the adoring white masses into the streets who had bid farewell to John Taylor. Instead, white Americans responded to Johnson's victories by joining murderous mobs who ignited race riots in several of the nation's cities that killed and maimed Black citizens and unleashed massive destruction on Black communities. Johnson, as the documentary filmmaker Ken Burns depicted in his 2004 visual history, *Unforgivable Blackness*, came to symbolize white hostility toward African Americans.

The white categorization of Johnson as unforgivably Black helped to stifle more critical discussions of the race and bifurcated African Americans into the oversimplified categories of "agreeable" and "wicked," based largely on white judgments. Ironically, the leading Black public intellectual of the era, W. E. B. Du Bois, first coined the "unforgivable Blackness" metaphor for Johnson in the social critic's discourse on the intricacies of interracial marriage. Du Bois's efforts to broaden the horizons of American racial dialogue through examining the complexities of Johnson's resistance to white racism gained little traction in an epoch dominated by the polar bifurcation of racial narratives into simplistic tales of righteousness versus malevolence.

The American Olympic enterprise, committed to projecting a righteously plural racial and ethnic vision of the United States that united even the *Outlook*'s "Black Ethiopian" into the national tapestry, embraced Taylor as a symbol of tolerable Blackness in which his race did not exclude him from the social concoctions smelted in the melting pot. Telling, in the pages of Du Bois and the NAACP's *The Crisis*, features on Black Olympians featured far more prominently than the Black heavyweight champion of the world. Black advocates for integration and their white allies gravitated to lionizing athletes such as Poage and Taylor, African American athletes who excelled in the white world and functioned as "inseverable link[s] in the chain of progress," rather than Johnson. As the Games of the V Olympiad approached, *The Crisis* and its allies found a worthy inheritor of Poage's and Taylor's roles as pioneering Black Mercuries racing for Olympian glory and racial equality.

Springfield, Massachusetts prep star Howard Porter Drew seized the mantle. He burst onto the sprinting scene in 1911, finishing third at the AAU nationals in the 220-yard dash and winning the 100-meter dash in the junior division. Back in high school in Springfield, he competed on the 1912 indoor circuit at New York City venues, twice equaling the world record in the 70-yard dash. That summer at the U.S. Olympic trials, Drew equaled the Olympic record in the 100-meter sprint to earn a spot on the American team. Drew's selection permitted the mainstream white media to once again crow about racial inclusion as an American strength. An editorial in *The Independent*, from its antebellum origins one of the great American voices for the abolition of slavery and a consistent postbellum opponent of segregation, proclaimed that officials selected an American squad "without regard to . . . race, color, or previous condition of servitude."[21] In two articles in *Harper's Weekly*, a correspondent cheered the team as a "heterogenous gathering" that included "negroes"—a plural claim although Drew represented the sole representative of his race. The journalist added that his teammates embraced Drew and heralded that "there was no class or color distinction" in the American Olympic expedition.[22] Experts touted Drew as a gold medal favorite in both the 100-meter and 200-meter sprints in Stockholm.

Like Taylor, Poage, and Morris, Drew was born in the segregated South— in Lexington, Virginia—in 1890. The son of a Baptist preacher who decided that he wanted to raise his family outside of the shadow of Jim Crow, the family settled in New York City in 1895 and then relocated to Springfield in 1904—the year that Poage became the first African American Olympic medalist. Drew soon impressed the denizens of his new hometown, winning a quarter-mile Fourth of July race in 1905 in Springfield in his bare feet. Drew enrolled in Springfield High School in 1910 but dropped out after his first year to help support his family, just as Billy Morris had done in 1890s Philadelphia. A married father of two children who was a bit older at age twenty than the average high school student, Drew worked as a hotel bellhop and a railroad porter. He returned to school in 1911 while continuing to work and became a track and football star for Springfield High. The Black press lauded not only his athletic prowess but also his work ethic and devotion to his family, while cheering him as a gold medal favorite in Stockholm. White promoters also lauded Drew's chances. Mike Murphy, Billy Morris, and John Taylor's patron at Penn, who also served as the lead trainer for the 1912 American Olympic squad, praised Drew's talent.

In Stockholm, Drew easily won his opening heats. Unfortunately, he injured himself in the semifinal. In an account in *The Crisis*, the journal of the National Association for the Advancement of Colored People (NAACP), Drew valiantly lined up for the final in spite of his injury. "Hoping against hope that he might be able to start, Drew donned his running togs and went out to the starting post, but had to be helped back," the correspondent for *The Crisis* revealed. "It was unfortunate that the little colored boy Drew broke down," trainer Murphy lamented. "But for that unfortunate happening I believe he would have proven America's greatest sprinter," noted Murphy, even as three white Americans led by Ralph Craig whom Drew had bested in the American trials led an American sweep of the medals in the 100-meter final.[23] The *Cleveland Gazette*, that city's leading Black newspaper, concurred with Murphy's sentiments. Noting Drew regularly beat Craig in practice, the *Gazette* proclaimed "therefore safe to say that had Drew not sprained his ankle he would have brought back the world's championship for fast running from the Olympian games for the race."[24]

Though Drew injured himself and could not run in the Olympic final in Sweden, he dominated American sprinting over the next few years. Sporting the colors of the Boston Athletic Association (BAA), he won the 1912 AAU 100-yard dash title shortly after returning from Stockholm. His triumph helped the BAA to a third-place club finish behind the powerful IAAC and the NYAC. Drew also burnished his role as a Black icon by headlining athletic meets devoted to African American heritage, including a 1913 track meet held as a feature of Philadelphia's Emancipation Proclamation Exposition that celebrated the fiftieth anniversary of Abraham Lincoln's Civil War announcement that ended slavery in the seceded states. The event, organized by Penn's Billy Morris, drew not only Black athletes and spectators but many white athletes and spectators as well.

Later in 1913, Drew broke with the BAA, putting his forgivable Blackness reputation at risk by challenging a color line at the renowned Boston club. Drew refused an invitation to the BAA's 1913 indoor meet that year after he noticed a posting proclaiming that it did not permit Black members. Drew admitted that he had been personally well-treated by BAA officials when he wore their colors at meets but insisted he had to take a stand. Drew explained that the "club states specifically that it does not want Negroes, and under the conditions I think it would be foolish for me to appear as a money-making attraction for them."[25] The Black press cheered Drew's stand. A headline in the *Cleveland Gazette* proclaimed "Howard Drew Manly!" with a subhead that read, "Has Race-Respect and Race-Pride and Shows It in an Unmistakable Manner."[26] *The Crisis* also lauded Drew for his BAA stance.

After resigning from the BAA team, Drew ran in the 1913 AAU national meet representing Springfield High. He defended his 100-yard title and added the 220-yard crown. As a one-man team he led his school to a seventh-place finish against a powerful lineup of national clubs and major college squads. For the Black middle classes and elites who comprised the bulk of the NAACP membership and consumed Black media such as *The Crisis*, as well as for their white allies, Drew became in the parlance of the era, a "race hero." Drew served as a counterweight to Jack Johnson's looming intolerability in their enduring struggle to win civil rights through ceaseless adherence to the canons of respectability. The *Chicago Defender*'s editors employed Drew's successes to identify track and field as superior to pugilism as an "entering wedge" for this struggle. The *Defender*'s staff argued that in track athletics "whenever members of the race are given an opportunity they generally come away wearing champion medals."[27] Access to opportunity represented the key to racial progress in sport and every other realm in the estimation of the *Defender*'s editors, who cited the achievements of Black athletes at the Olympics and AAU meets as evidence for their contention. The editors called for major league baseball to adopt the racial sensibilities of Olympic leaders and provide African American baseball players the same level playing field that Black runners, jumpers, and throwers received in track and field. The *Indianapolis Freeman* followed the *Defender*'s lead and singled out track and field as a key realm for erasing color lines. "Unlike many other sports, track athletics offer the Negro boy, poor as he may be, an equal chance to compete and become a champion, and the colored young men are certainly making good use of the opportunity," contended the *Freeman*'s columnist. The writer pointed to Drew and the deceased Taylor as evidence for those claims, contrasting the increasing number of Black Olympians with the omnipresent color lines that kept Black players out of major league baseball.[28]

In the Black media, Drew inherited Taylor's position as a racial symbol who combined athletic and academic virtuosity. A columnist in the *Savan-*

nah Tribune, an African American newspaper in Georgia, declared: "As an athlete of the highest type, he [Taylor] brought fame and renown not only to himself but to the entire race with which he was identified." The columnist added that "Howard P. Drew is doing likewise."[29] Like Taylor, Drew aspired to academic and athletic success at the collegiate level. After graduating from Springfield High in 1913, Drew considered an offer from Brown University but decided to enroll at the University of Southern California where he thrived on the track and in the classroom as he pursued a degree in law. While at USC he prepared for the 1916 Olympics, competing in major meets in the United States and Great Britain.

Drew's travels, while supposedly a self-funding student from an economically challenged family, raised consistent questions about his amateur status—not an uncommon issue for world-class athletes in that era, Black or white. Drew conspicuously refused an offer from British promoters to appear in professional races, but one of his West Coast rivals from the University of California at Berkley made accusations that Drew took money under the table. Charges and counter-charges flew, as Drew sat out the 1914 AAU championships in the ensuing furor and then decided to quit the sport. He dropped out of USC to return to work and support his family. The retirement proved short-lived, as Drew joined the field for the AAU nationals held in San Francisco as part of the Panama-Pacific Exposition. Injuries kept him from reclaiming his sprint titles in that meet, but he persisted as the Games of the VI Olympiad in Berlin approached. Drew began setting new records and reclaimed his status as the favorite to win the gold medal that eluded him in Stockholm in 1912. Unfortunately, World War I scuttled Drew's Olympic dreams by cancelling the Berlin games.

Had the 1916 Olympics taken place and Drew claimed the 100-meter dash gold medal and reinforced his status as the world's fastest human, he would have perhaps eclipsed even Jack Johnson in the era's racial iconography. Even though he never won an Olympic medal, Drew stood as symbolic contrast to the image of Jack Johnson. The Black press and the white media lauded the sprinter as an icon of "forgivable" Blackness. Inspired by that vision, a 1916 feature on Drew in a Black newspaper portrayed him as a superstar in both the Black and white communities. The journalist contended that Drew served as an inspiration to "colored boys" who could "follow in his footsteps" and rejoiced that with white audiences Drew's "gentlemanly qualities have everywhere made friends for him, thereby making friends for the race." In the classroom, Drew shined just as brightly, an honor-roll legal scholar who wrote for the student newspaper at USC. The journalist observed that Drew's "academic standing is that of a good and well-thinking student" who showcased mental as well as physical brilliance. In the final analysis, the biographical sketch depicted Drew as a crucial bridge between racial divides. In all of his endeavors "he reflects that he understands his brother is white, who, in turn makes a new study of his brother in black."[30]

Drew's brilliance in both sport and academics drew consistent praise from the leading journal of middle-class Black sentiment and activism, *The Crisis*. The NAACP's magazine featured him coiled at the start of a sprint, on the cover of an issue devoted to Black progress in higher education.[31] In a 1916 issue of *The Crisis*, Drew inspired a poem by Lucian B. Watkins entitled "Go!" Watkins depicted Drew firing off the starting line and winning a race, his "flying feet" signaling his status as a Black Mercury. As Drew cruised to victory, Watkins shifted the focus from Drew's individual triumph to the inspiration the sprinter offered to his fellow Black citizens. "Drew ran his race—outstripped the world—and won," Watkins cheered. "Now we resolve, O God, to win our own!"[32]

Drew himself heeded his poet's call to persevere against all obstacles. Disappointed that global war had canceled the 1916 Olympics, frustrated that injuries had scuttled his efforts to reclaim his national titles, and no longer pursuing his studies at USC, Drew's competitive fires and stellar athletic career seemed finished by the end of 1916. Instead, Drew persisted. In 1917 he enrolled at Drake University in Des Moines, Iowa, to complete his law degree. He also joined the track team at Drake, quickly returning to top form as one of the nation's best sprinters and nurturing visions of an Olympic return at the 1920 Antwerp games.

Another obstacle soon appeared. In 1918 he was drafted into the U.S. Army and became a sergeant in an all-Black unit that deployed to France. After the war ended, the military kept him in France to help organize and compete in the 1919 Inter-Allied Games, an international track and field meet intended to revive global sporting events that included all the victorious allies from the Great War including France, Great Britain, and the United States but excluded the defeated Central Powers of Germany, Austro-Hungary, and the Ottoman Empire. Though injuries kept him out of the competition, he trained American sprinters as well as appearing in promotions for the "Military Olympics."

After the war, Drew returned to Iowa and resumed his studies, graduating from Drake Law School in the spring of 1920. That summer, he made one last bid for Olympic glory. "Howard Drew, the fastest man who ever pulled on a shoe, will try to 'come back,'" applauded Jim Thorpe expectantly in his syndicated column.[33] Thorpe, the Sac and Fox athlete who in 1912 had been Drew's American Olympic teammate in Stockholm and who had been unceremoniously stripped of two gold medals by the AAU and the AOC after accusations he had violated amateur standards, had by 1920 gone on to stellar careers in professional baseball and football while also moonlighting as a sports columnist. Now medal-less like Drew, Thorpe wished his former teammate success in his final Olympic quest. Competing in the 200-meter race at the U.S. trials, Drew finished back in the pack, failing to make the American roster.

In spite of the fact that he never won an Olympic medal, Drew's commitment to respectable challenges of color lines, his relentless efforts to better himself through pursuing higher education, and his successes in white institutions including track and field and law school, marked him as a counterbalance to Jack Johnson's "unforgivable Blackness." Drew became famous among both Black and white Americans as a "world champion" like Johnson. Though he never won an Olympic medal, in races against first-rate competition he equaled the world records in both the 100-meter and 100-yard dashes. At one point, Drew held or shared every world record from 50 yards to 250 yards. In an article from the era in *Popular Science Monthly* that explored "records of the swiftest animals," Drew appeared as the ultimate example of human speed. "The greatest speed attained by any man is that of Howard P. Drew," contended the author of the cross-species comparison—although ruefully admitting to his readers that his time put Drew and humankind far behind the average speed of an antelope.[34]

THE PIONEERING BLACK MERCURIES IN PERSPECTIVE

Drew's Olympic comeback fell short, but five Black athletes made the 1920 American team. Billy Morris, who had come as close as any Black athlete before George Poage (and perhaps Joseph Stadler) to competing in the Olympics, joined the group and enjoyed his maiden Olympic voyage as a member of the U.S. staff to the Games of the VII Olympiad in Antwerp. Morris served in that trainer role for next five Olympics, linking a new generation of Black Olympians who emerged in the 1920s and the 1930s to the original tiny band of pioneers. Over the next two decades, Morris would regale a growing corps of African American Olympic stars he trained with tales of the marvelous feats of Poage, Taylor, and Drew.

The legacy of the original Black pioneers provided a foundation for the generations who followed. In spite of their small numbers, they established a record of excellence. They contributed to American claims of Olympic team triumphs over all other nations in the sporting event that by the end of the Great War had become the world's foremost athletic spectacle. The achievements of Poage, Taylor, and Drew solidified a central place in the American Olympic enterprise for African Americans as tangible data points in claims that the United States triumphed at the Olympics through a doctrine of American exceptionalism in which race, ethnicity, religion, and social class allegedly mattered less than talent, merit, perseverance, and work ethic. Though that ideal remained unrealized as Poage, Taylor, Drew, and Morris knew all too well, it nevertheless represented a significant national aspiration that helped African Americans confront color lines in Olympic sport and elsewhere in American culture. For the white leadership of American Olympic expeditions, Black faces on the roster had become necessary ingredients in their formula for promoting the U.S. team as emblematic of American exceptionalism.

That meant that the AAU and the AOC had to continue to resist the creation of color lines at the highest levels of track and field, outside of the deep South where they had ceded control of the "race question" to the ardent segregationists and white supremacists of their Southern branches who kept Black athletes out of contention in the "Dixie." In the rest of the nation, Olympic trials and regional and national meets had to remain open to Black entrants, even as other sporting arenas maintained powerful color lines that extended far beyond the borders of Jim Crow. The great migration that began during World War I saw millions of African Americans move from the South to the North and West and fueled not only industrial but also athletic production. The great migration provided opportunities for stellar performers to emerge and thrive when they would never have had those opportunities had they remained in the South. To give the most famous example, had Jesse Owens remained in his Alabama birthplace and not emigrated with his family to Ohio, he would never have competed in a single Olympic event, let alone to win four gold medals at the 1936 Berlin games.

Morris, Poage, Taylor, and Drew served as harbingers of this important dimension of the history of American sport, paving the way for later generations. Though their exodus preceded the floodtide of the great migration that began during the war, each of them moved at a young age from the South to a new home north of the Mason-Dixon line. Had their families remained in the South, they would never have had the opportunities to compete, let alone become Olympians—like the 90 percent of African Americans who remained in the South. Migration represents one of the important elements in the history of Black Olympic pioneers.

In addition to migration, the pioneering generation also demonstrated an ability to thrive in white institutions. In order to succeed, Black athletes in this era had to navigate the overwhelmingly white environments where track and field flourished—high schools, universities, and AAU clubs. Morris, Poage, Taylor, and Drew functioned as members of tiny minorities in overwhelmingly white institutions as they carved out niches as exceptions to the general patterns of racial dynamics that limited opportunities for most of their racial compatriots. Outside of the South, a few all-Black institutions promoted engagement and offered opportunities to Black track and field athletes, including metropolitan New York City AAU clubs such as the Salem-Crescent Athletic Club, the St. Christopher's Club, and the Smart Set Athletic Club, and Chicago's Frederick Douglass Center Athletic Association. These Black enterprises sprang up in response to customary color lines drawn by powerful white clubs such as the NYAC and the BAA. Historically Black colleges north of the Mason-Dixon line, Cheyney and Lincoln in Pennsylvania and Wilberforce in Ohio, began to field track teams in this era. However, none of these Black clubs or colleges yet produced elite level performers. Morris found his conduit to success via the Philadelphia YMCA club, a mainly white organization. LaCrosse High School, the University of Wisconsin, and the Milwaukee Athletic Club—white organizations—nurtured Poage's talents. The white-dominated University of Pennsylvania and the Greater New York Irish American Athletic Club cultivated Taylor's gifts. Springfield High School, the BAA, the University of Southern California, and Drake University, white organizations all, fostered Drew's development. Without at least a modicum of white patronage and white support, the Black Olympic pioneers would have been kept off the track and out of the field.

Conversely, for white audiences, the Black Mercuries' triumphs nurtured the mythologies that turned exceptional people like Morris, Poage, Taylor, and Drew into protagonists in mythical American meta-narratives that anyone who worked hard and persevered could rise above their humble origins—and could even "transcend" their racial heritages. Their pioneering triumphs obscured for their white fans the more typical experiences of Black Americans and created the illusion that anyone who "tried" hard enough and "behaved" well enough could overcome racism. That mythology remains a powerful force in twenty-first-century American culture that limits understandings of the power of systemic racism and white privilege not only in sport but in every other economic, political, and social venue.

For African American leaders in the long struggle for civil rights, and for Black communities and their white allies, the pioneering success of Morris, Poage, Taylor, and Drew beyond the track and field stadiums was every bit as important as their victories inside those arenas. Morris became not only the beloved long-time trainer for Penn and the U.S. Olympic track team but also a leader in Philadelphia's Black community who promoted youth sports and starred in musical, dramatic, and comedic shows in the city's thriving Black arts scene. Poage retired from track after the 1904 St. Louis Olympics but remained in the city as an educator in the segregated Black school system. Poage also became a patron of jazz and blues, a devotion that got him into trouble with his school board and led in 1914 to his resignation. He relocated to Chicago, taking a post as a soloist in one of the city's biggest Black churches, and launched a music career. Struggling in that difficult endeavor, he found a job in the city's post office where he enjoyed middle-class success from the 1920s through his retirement in the 1950s. Taylor, though he tragically died at just twenty-six years of age before he could launch his post-athletic career, earned a doctorate from Penn's prestigious veterinary school and no doubt would have developed a thriving practice. Drew retired from track after the 1920 Olympic trials and soon thereafter opened a law practice in Hartford, Connecticut. In 1924 he won election as a justice of the peace in Hartford. In 1928 he was appointed a night court judge for the city, the first African American in Connecticut history to serve in that role.

Their successes in white institutions of higher education, in white track clubs, and in middle-class professional endeavors that served white as well as Black communities marked Morris, Poage, Taylor, and Drew as the antitheses of the most controversial African American of their era, the boxing champion Jack Johnson. For Black communities and white supporters, the Black Olympians served as exemplars of not only physical but also intellectual successes in competition with white rivals. They represented their generation's "good Negroes" who played by the rules and met the hostility of white supremacists with even-tempered demeanors. They challenged color lines drawn against them with good manners and iron-willed grit. They served as affirmations to white and Black audiences as model citizens who assimilated to white institutions while simultaneously offering fierce but temperate resistance to white supremacy. They defied negative stereotypes and responded to white hostility and attempts to draw color lines against them with implacable resistance and impeccable manners. In contrast to the "unforgiveable Blackness" in which white America shrouded Johnson, the Olympians modeled a forgivable version of Blackness that endeared them to white allies willing to accept at least desegregation if not committed to integration. This pioneering generation of Black Olympians set a standard that would shape African American roles on U.S. Olympic teams—and expectations for the long struggle against segregation in American culture—for decades to come. They were undeniably, as Edwin Henderson asserted in his groundbreaking history of Black athletes, "pioneers" on whom the "wonder works" of the 1920s and 1930s would be built.[35]

2

BLACK MERCURIES
IN THE JAZZ AGE

From the resurrection of the Olympics in their modern version in 1896 throughout the 1920s, not a single African American Olympian competed in a sport other than track and field except for a lone boxer named Benny Ponteau who made the American team in 1920. Two Black track and field athletes joined Ponteau on the American roster at those Antwerp games. Overwhelmingly, African American athletes represented their nation as Black Mercuries in the sport symbolized by the classical god of fleet feet. In gymnastics, rowing, cycling, swimming, wrestling, weightlifting, fencing, and other Olympic disciplines, Black Olympians remained in the poignant phrasing of the mid-twentieth-century African American novelist Ralph Ellison, "invisible men,"—and "invisible women" too, as the Olympics grew more gender-inclusive beginning in the 1920s. Even in sports where African Americans thrived in other arenas during the first half of the twentieth century, such as boxing and basketball (which debuted at the 1936 Berlin Olympics), Black Olympians were at best rare but generally nonexistent in this era. Still, in spite of the profound lack of Olympic opportunities faced by most African American aspirants, the three Black athletes who went to Antwerp in 1920—a tiny fraction, just a bit more than 1 percent of the 288 competitors on the American team—represented a considerable increase in African American representation from the lone Black athletes who competed in 1904, 1908, and 1912.

Throughout the Jazz Age of the 1920s, a handful of Black athletes would make American Olympic teams. Black Olympians in that era would, as they had since the early 1900s, symbolize the evolving racial demographics, the complex patterns of segregation, and the persistent struggles for integration that confronted African Americans in a decade in which a cultural sensation that Black Americans had created and inspired—jazz—developed into a national and international phenomenon that crossed color lines and became a brand name for a global epoch.

MUSIC, SPORT, AND A BLACK "RENAISSANCE"

Music and sport sometimes intersected in Jazz Age African American culture. Jazz bands would welcome African American Olympians as they returned home from Antwerp in 1920, serenade them as they walked through the streets of Paris in 1924, and salute them as they ventured to Amsterdam in 1928. Jazz musicians and Olympic athletes served as the most visible public faces for an emerging new African American culture that during the 1920s blossomed especially in communal renaissances in New York, Chicago, and other cities. Black jazz musicians and athletes pierced the consciousness of white America from the floodtide of the great migration that began during World War I as more than a million Black citizens from the deeply segregated realms of the South trekked to new homes beyond the traditional American racial geography marked by the Mason-Dixon line. The migrants fled a burgeoning Southern racial tyranny devoted to maintaining white supremacy in a region where, before 1920, the vast majority—at least 90 percent—of African Americans lived. Migrants joined the exodus to escape post-Reconstruction Southern scourges afflicting Black communities of endemic poverty, economic servitude, political disenfranchisement, pervasive segregation, and systematic violence—most horrifically embedded in the widespread practice of lynching. Millions more followed over the next half-century.

Unsurprisingly, given those realities, not a single African American Olympian emerged from Southern institutions in the first half-century of U.S. participation in the games. While quite a few Black Olympians from this period were born in the South, like the original three from the early 1900s—George Poage, John Taylor, and Howard Drew—their families joined the internal diaspora out of "Dixie" and they grew up beyond the boundaries of Southern Jim Crow. In escaping the South, however, Black migrants realized that racism, segregation, and discrimination flourished in their new homes as well. Color lines and vitriolic prejudice limited their opportunities in these new "promised lands," just as it had in the South. Still, they found more economic opportunities, more access to political power, and more fluid ethnic boundaries at the termini of the great migration than they had experienced in the Southern "Black belts" from which they departed. Though customary segregation stung no less than its legal form, more opportunities for social mobility beckoned.

Relocated mainly to major cities in the Northeast, Midwest, and West, Black migrants transformed popular music, igniting the jazz movement and transforming other genres. Music represented just one aspect of what contemporary observers defined as a "renaissance" of Black culture, particularly in art, literature, and social criticism. Black migrants also kindled a transformation in American sport in their new homes, producing athletes who competed against and sometimes vanquished their white opponents as well as occasionally joining the rosters of white teams at every level of competition from children's playground leagues to prep contests to intercollegiate competitions to professional match-ups. Some of the new sporting opportunities remained walled-off from white America, such as the separate "Negro Leagues" that sprang up in the 1920s in professional baseball. Some of these opportunities pitted teams of Blacks against whites in interracial competitions, such as the barnstorming basketball teams like Harlem's famous "Renaissance Five." Some of these opportunities incorporated Black athletes onto white intercollegiate sports teams, such as 1920 Olympian Sol Butler's renowned multi-sport career as a star on his college's football, basketball, baseball, and track teams.

Butler and the other Black Olympians of the Jazz Age highlighted the expanded opportunities and new dynamics that the great migration created. The three Black Olympians from the 1920 American team, Ponteau, Johnson, and Butler, represented three of the most popular metropolitan destinations where African American populations increased dramatically during the Jazz Age. Ponteau boxed for the Black St. Christopher's Club in New York City's Harlem. Johnson ran for a Black team in Pittsburgh's Hill District. Butler, after living in the smaller industrial cities in Iowa and Illinois during high school and college careers, settled in the "Black Metropolis" of Chicago's Bronzeville neighborhood in the 1920s and joined a variety of both Black and interracial sports clubs.

Alongside African American musicians and literati, athletes became the avatars of the Jazz Age Black urban renaissance, even as the vast majority of the nation's Black population remained rooted in the South. Music and sport served as emblems of identity for Black communities, signaling pride in racial achievements, promoting cultural solidarity, and offering opportunities to press against color lines and push for integration. Music and sport also served the interests of leaders in white communities who wanted to promote national commitments to racial and ethnic equity and trumpet the gospel of American exceptionalism at home and abroad. In a United States becoming a global superpower, Black musical geniuses and Black Olympians promoted idealized visions of American society to domestic and international audiences. The purpose of sending American teams to the Olympics in the 1920s, according to U.S. Olympic movement leader Colonel Robert Means Thompson, was to "sell the United States to the rest of the world."[1] Having a few Black faces on American teams fit the images many white Americans wanted to export—and to consume. White American entrepreneurs and diplomats made the same arguments about exporting jazz.

PASSING THE BLACK MERCURY BATON TO SOL BUTLER

In 1919 Solomon "Sol" Butler previewed this new effort to include Black athletes in American projections of the nation's cultural power when he won the long-jump title at an international spectacle held in the European city where jazz flourished—Paris. Butler beat the world in the "Inter-Allied Games," or "Military Olympics," an American-designed spectacle signaling a postwar return to normality, celebrating the victorious allied militaries, honoring the millions who perished in the conflagration, and paving the way for the return of the Olympic Games in 1920.

Butler was born in 1895 in the deeply segregated hamlet of Kingfisher, Oklahoma, about forty miles northwest of Oklahoma City. When Sol was ten, his father, who was born into slavery, moved the family to Hutchinson, Kansas. Young Sol Butler stood out in schoolyard athletics and became a high school football and track star at Hutchison High. At the 1913 Kansas state track and field championships Butler won six events—the long jump, the shot put, the 120-yard hurdles, and three sprints—leading Hutchinson to a dominating victory. He did not completely escape color lines in Kansas. Some rival high schools refused to compete when Butler appeared, drawing color lines at football games and track meets.

In 1914 Butler followed his high school football coach to Rock Island, an industrial city on the Illinois side of the Mississippi River. The coach thought it would be easier for Butler to attract the interest of college recruiters in the sports hotbed of Rock Island than in rural Kansas. Butler starred on the

Rock Island High football team and won fame in Chicago track meets. In 1915 he broke the national interscholastic record and tied the world record in the 60-yard dash and won the AAU junior national long jump title. That feat made Butler into a worthy successor for Howard Drew in the Black press, a high-school sports phenom who served as a national vessel for African American hopes of pressing against color barriers and a member of W. E. B. DuBois' vaunted "talented tenth" of African American exemplars who thrived not only in classrooms but also in other cultural and social realms.

As his athletic reputation burgeoned, Butler attracted recruiters from the University of Illinois, Northwestern University, and the University of Chicago. He also dreamed of a collegiate future focused at the institution where DuBois had earned a BA, an MA, and a PhD—Harvard. Local boosters in his former hometown of Hutchinson, heartened by the publicity he had brought their town, hatched a plan to fund Harvard educations not only for Sol but also his brother Benjamin. He surprised everyone when he chose not Harvard, nor Chicago, nor Illinois, nor Northwestern but rather an obscure Iowa institution in a small city on the other side of the Mississippi River about seventy miles north of Rock Island. One day in downtown Rock Island while shining shoes to earn money to support his family, he encountered a Presbyterian pastor from nearby Bettendorf, Iowa. The two struck up an immediate friendship. The minister had trained for his calling at Dubuque German Theological Seminary—later the University of Dubuque. The pastor arranged entry to the school not only for Sol but also for his brother "Benny." In the fall of 1915 the Butler brothers enrolled at the tiny liberal arts school. While Benny ran the quarter-mile and relays as well as serving as the manager of the football team, Sol became a four-sport phenom—excelling in football, basketball, track and field, and baseball.

Butler's athletic exploits brought national attention to the Dubuque "Germans" as the press called the school's teams before growing anti-German sentiment during the Great War led to a switch to the Spartans. In the more innocent days before the United States entered in World War I, the press dubbed Butler the "Blue Kaiser," after the seminary's blue-and-white uniforms. In an era in which a national intercollegiate track and field championship had yet to develop, Butler showcased his athletic talents on the circuit of major amateur meets in urban centers such as New York City and Chicago, invitational collegiate relay carnivals such as the Penn Relays, and AAU national championship meets. Like Howard Drew, Butler was a featured performer who drew paying customers to national events and won dozens of medals, cups, watches, and other prizes for his performances at the highest levels of American track and field.

By the spring of 1919 as Butler won his second Penn Relays long-jump title, he had become widely acclaimed in both the Black and white press as the nation's best competitor in that event, a clear gold-medal favorite for the restoration of the Olympics following the end of the Great War. Later that spring both Sol and Ben Butler graduated from Dubuque Theological Seminary. Sol joined the army that, even though the war had ended, was deployed to France for the negotiation of the Treaty of Versailles. The U.S. military assigned the long-jumping phenom for duty at the "Military Olympics." Clearly, Butler understood he was in the army to win track meets and not to dodge artillery shells in the trenches. As he departed from Dubuque for France, a large contingent of students and citizens gathered for his send-off, which included a brass-band salute. Butler told a *Chicago Defender* correspondent on the scene to cover the event that he planned to bring back a long jump title when he returned. "Tell them in the States that I will do all in my power to win the honors for my school and country."[2]

Butler's legs in Paris backed up his boasts at the Dubuque train station. Howard Drew helped to organize the event and coached American athletes but, nearing the end of his competitive career, did not participate. Butler stepped into Drew's shoes as the former "Blue Kaiser" won the long jump with a leap that broke the U.S. record. Butler's triumph added an African American face to a U.S. team that the press described as the usual world-beating assemblage of Americans from all races, ethnicities, and social classes. A year later at the 1920 U.S. Olympic trials Butler won the long-jump contest with another record-setting performance, making him a leading medal-contender in Antwerp.

THE STARTLING EMERGENCE OF A BLACK DISTANCE RUNNER

At the same Olympic trials in which Butler earned his ticket to Belgium, the veteran Howard Drew, attempting a monumental comeback for a sprinter over the age of thirty, failed in his effort to join Butler on the roster. Butler, however, would not be the lone Black member of the American team as a little-known distance runner from Pittsburgh named Earl Johnson qualified for the 10,000-meter race. American sports fans, Black and white, knew Drew and Butler, Black Mercuries who had been in the news for years. Johnson, however, appeared to come out of nowhere to make the

American team. Still, as the sports editor of the white *Pittsburgh Gazette Times* reminded Johnson's hometown readers, "They don't make Olympic champions overnight." Johnson had been working for years to become an Olympic-caliber distance runner.[3]

Like Black Olympians before him, Johnson had migrated as a child from the Jim Crow South to the urban North. Born in 1891 in the rural Shenandoah Valley of Virginia, Johnson's family moved north of the Mason-Dixon line to the thriving industrial metropolis of Pittsburgh, Pennsylvania. At the age of ten, Johnson approached Hunter Johnston, a Black coach and trainer who worked with the University of Pittsburgh's football and track teams and had a local reputation for developing talented athletes, both Black and white. At the time Johnston trained one of the early elite Black distance runners in the United States, professional pedestrian Howard Hall, a Pittsburgh mailman who won several ultra-distance ordeals in the early twentieth century. The young Johnson idolized Hall and sought Johnston's help in developing his own endurance running prowess. Trainer Johnston thought "little Earl" too young and frail to withstand the endurance training grind and told him to wait until he was older. Johnston saw Johnson a few years later running in a race in Butler, Pennsylvania, and noted that the Pittsburgh youth had matured into a solid competitor. The young runner then went off to Morgan College in Baltimore where he ran on the track team but did not face much competition, though he did win some local races, including the 1915 *Afro-American Ledger* Marathon, a rather grand title for a five-mile race. Johnson thus continued the tradition of Black Olympians as collegians. He also became the first American Olympian to attend one of the nation's historically Black institutions, as Morgan College had originated in 1867 as an outreach of the Methodist Episcopal Church to train Black ministers to serve post-slavery African American communities. The school expanded its campus in the 1910s with a generous bequest from Pittsburgh steel-baron-turned-philanthropist Andrew Carnegie, drawing students such as Johnson from western Pennsylvania.

When Johnson returned to Pittsburgh from Morgan College, Coach Johnston decided that Johnson was ready for the rigors of endurance training. Johnston observed that his protégé would have to overcome common track stereotypes that Black athletes did not have the fortitude to run long distances. The trainer noted that at one of the first Pittsburgh meets in which he entered Johnson, one of region's leading white endurance racers badly beat his new pupil. "Some of the track officials joshed me a bit about my 'find,' saying they never had heard of a Negro runner who was good at a long distance," Johnston recalled. "I told them to give me another year's work with Johnson and I would show them a man of color who could stand the gaff and beat his fields," the Pittsburgh track guru retorted.[4]

Johnson made his first mark on the national scene while serving in the U.S. Army during World War I. Stationed at Camp Upton on Long Island, one of the major embarkation sites for the AEF to ship out to Europe, Johnson joined the base athletic club and qualified for the 1918 AAU championships. Held in that war year at the Great Lakes Naval Training Center outside of Chicago, the meet featured several powerful wartime military clubs alongside the usual roster of AAU titans including the New York Athletic Club, the Chicago Athletic Association, and San Francisco's Olympic Club. Johnson entered the five-mile race in the junior division, designated for competitors who had never before competed in an AAU national event. He surprised the experts, beating all of his white rivals as well as Black runner Lee Umble of the University of Colorado. Johnson dashed from behind almost the entire field on the final lap in a remarkable closing burst to win. The next day, he pushed the white victor in the senior five-mile race to break the American record in order to keep Johnson in second place. Though the "Spanish Flu" pandemic and an unseasonable cold front kept crowds at the Great Lakes nationals sparse, the African American press made sure to spread the word of Johnson's performances around the nation. "Earl Johnson, . . . running under the colors of Camp Upton, placed his team in first money when he furnished one of the most stirring finishes of the big five mile event," the *Chicago Defender*'s reporter covering the race marveled.[5]

Johnson's surprising emergence in endurance running made him a hot commodity among AAU clubs. While stationed at Camp Upton he joined Harlem's Salem Crescent Athletic Club. When the war ended, he mustered out of the military and returned again to Pittsburgh and trainer Johnston's care, taking a job at a new settlement house, the Morgan Memorial Community House, as a social worker helping the large numbers of African Americans flowing into Pittsburgh's thriving industrial economy as the great migration commenced. Johnson switched allegiance from Salem Crescent to the new Morgan Community House Athletic Club—a contingent helmed by Coach Johnston—donning their colors in track meets around the nation.

In 1920 he secured a spot on the American team at the U.S. Olympic trials. "Few had ever heard of him before, and therefore they thought he had been 'made' overnight, not knowing of his long-cherished ambition to be a great runner and of his many years of patient preparation," Coach Johnston revealed to the Pittsburgh media after his star pupil sewed up an Olympic berth. *Pittsburgh Gazette Times* sports editor Harry Keck depicted Johnson in the white daily as an exemplary "good Negro," a blessing of the great migration. "The crack runner has adopted community work among his own people as his life work and is employed at the Morgan Community House where he makes his home and where he also is in charge of juvenile court cases," Keck contended. "He is a clean-cut young man and immensely popular," Keck added, transforming Johnson into the "steel city's" favorite native son. "Right now all eyes are glued on Earl Johnson, the hope of the Morgan Community House—and of Pittsburgh—in the 10,000 meter run in Antwerp," Keck cheered.[6] The Black press also lauded Johnson. The "Smoky City boy's" performance in the Olympic trials, proclaimed a *Chicago Defender* reporter, made Johnson "one of the very few Race boys to represent Uncle Sam at Antwerp."[7]

The *Defender*'s "very few" Black Olympians totaled three athletes plus Billy Morris's inclusion as an official trainer. Morris made his first American team as the newly commissioned official Olympic "rubber" for the American track and field squad. "We wish him every success," cheered his hometown *Philadelphia Tribune*, one of the nation's leading Black newspapers, as Morris departed for Belgium.[8] Morris oversaw the training of two of those Black athletes, Butler and Johnson.

THE FIRST BLACK AMERICAN OLYMPIAN FROM BEYOND THE REALM OF TRACK AND FIELD

Besides Johnson and Butler, pugilist Benny Ponteau made the U.S. boxing squad. Ponteau represented a rarity in American Olympic history in the first half of the twentieth century—a Black athlete in a sport other than track and field. The Harlem-based fighter represented the Black St. Christopher Athletic Club in AAU pugilism tournaments. He earned a lightweight (135.5 pounds) berth on the team, even though he lost to white fighter Frank Cassidy in the final of the U.S. boxing trials. In that era, the U.S. team carried multiple fighters in each weight class. The 1920 team ended up with three lightweights, Ponteau, Cassidy, and Sam Mosberg, on the roster for Antwerp.

Ponteau's Olympics began on the ship to Antwerp. In a match designed to winnow the three American lightweights into two Olympic entrants, Ponteau reportedly lost a bout to Mosberg, which put the Jewish fighter from New York's East Side onto the official roster instead of the Black fighter from Harlem. More than two decades later, Mosberg himself recalled the shipboard battle for the Olympic spot. He noted that Ponteau was "a good colored fighter" but claimed, "I licked him aboard the ship and so started in Antwerp."[9] The *New York Age*, a leading Black newspaper, offered a different version of the story. The *Age*'s reporter contended that Mosberg refused to get in the ring against the Black fighter. American Olympic officials then unfairly selected Mosberg over Ponteau anyway. The *Age*'s correspondent contended Ponteau had been "robbed" of an Olympic gold medal, as Mosberg fought his unlikely path from second alternate to the Olympic crown in Antwerp—whether or not he beat Ponteau on the Atlantic crossing or bureaucrats picked him over the Black Olympian.[10]

OLYMPIAN DISAPPOINTMENT FOR THE BLACK MERCURIES

Arriving in Antwerp, Butler and Johnson shook off their sea legs and readied themselves for their events. Unfortunately, Butler's Olympic debut ended almost as quickly as Ponteau's. As an article on the front page of the *New York Times* related, "Today began badly for the American competitors in the Olympic games. In his first running broad jump Sol Butler, one of the most popular men in the contest, pulled a tendon in his leg and had to withdraw."[11] Butler's jump missed qualifying for the final by just three centimeters. Trainer Billy Morris worked feverishly on Butler's leg. After the treatment, Butler gamely tried to continue but could barely walk. "Tears ran down his cheeks when he asked for another try," reported American Olympic coach Jack Moakley. "It was splendid courage," Moakley declared. "Butler would have been willing to break his leg rather than drop out of the competition."[12]

Black newspapers lamented Butler's injury and saluted his valor. The unfortunate result, according to the *Chicago Defender*, "ruined America's chances of winning first place, as the place had already been conceded to Butler."[13] White newspapers concurred with that assessment. Two white Americans made the six-person final grouping. Carl Johnson of the United States managed a second-place finish, but Swedish leaper William Petersson won the gold medal. Hopes for an African American medal now rested entirely on Johnson's slim shoulders. "This leaves R.E. Johnson of the Morgan Community House in Pittsburgh as the only other representative of the Race at these games," noted a correspondent in the *Chicago Defender* after Butler's heartbreaking injury.[14]

Unfortunately, Johnson's Olympic debut ended almost as quickly as Butler's and Ponteau's stints. In his 10,000-meter qualifying heat Johnson cramped severely and dropped out. "I thought Earl Johnson of Pittsburgh would do better, but the pace for the trials was too hot for him," U.S. track coach Moakley dejectedly admitted.[15] Finnish endurance prodigy Paavo Nurmi took the top prize in the 10,000-meter race, one of three gold medals the "Flying Finn" earned in Antwerp.

COMING HOME—AND DISCOVERING
TWO MORE BLACK OLYMPIANS!

The trio of Black Olympians returned with the rest of the U.S. contingent to New York City where they joined a huge ticker-tape parade through Manhattan that welcomed the American team who dominated the overall medal count. Although the African American athletes had not added any medals to the world-beating bounty, they were nevertheless heralded in the African American media as racial avatars, as an article in the *New York Age* demonstrated. Columnist Theodore "Ted" Hooks lamented that not all African American athletes had received a fair opportunity to make the team. "Other Negroes," in addition to Ponteau, Butler, and Johnson, "proved themselves eligible but were overlooked by the American Olympic Committee for reasons which were never stated," Hooks protested. "Yet granting that the Olympic Committee's reasons were sufficient to keep the others off the U.S.A.'s team, we looked over our . . . [athletes] and could not help but feel cheerful."[16]

Remarkably, Hooks discovered two previously unrecognized Black athletes on the American team. He pointed to "two giant men of the American tug o' war team whose names we have been unable to learn" as the additional African American Olympians.[17] Their names were William Penn and Joseph Winston, both sergeants in the U.S. Army and veterans of the American Expeditionary Force that fought in France. Penn and Winston competed on the U.S. Army–supplied tug-of-war team in Antwerp. Before Hooks noticed them, not a single observer in the American press, white or Black, mentioned the interracial composition of the tug-of-war team. In fact, Hooks' account in the *New York Age* represents the sole mention in the American media of two Black soldiers on the army tug-of-war squad.

Hooks' discovery increased the number of Black American Olympians to five and heartened African American fans. "When we reviewed the records made by our five in contests which finally gained them recognition, we could

The U.S. tug-of-war team travels to Antwerp for the 1920 Olympics. Comprised of active-duty U.S. Army soldiers, the squad included two Black athletes, Sergeant William Penn (seventh from the left) and Sergeant Joseph Winston, far right. Originally unnoticed by both the Black press and white media, Penn and Winston were heralded by an article in the *New York Age*, an African American newspaper, when they returned from their Olympic trip. *Carleton L. Brosius Papers and Photographs, Wisconsin Veterans Museum, Madison, Wisconsin.*

not help but feel proud," Hooks maintained. "Realizing the adversities, they were compelled to face assured us of their exceptional merit," he insisted. "Furthermore, five men in the grand total of about a hundred and fifty, is not such a small percentage," Hooks concluded. "This is a white man's country," he reminded his readers.[18] In actuality, the percentage was much smaller than Hooks calculated. While six Black Olympians—including trainer Morris—were far more than the United States ever sent to a games, the total headcount of the U.S. delegation was closer to 350 than 150.

As Ponteau, Butler, Johnson, Penn, and Winston returned home after the Olympics, they anticipated another shot at medals four years later at the 1924 Paris Olympics. Penn and Winston would never get that chance as tug-of-war, on the Olympic docket since 1900, disappeared from the Olympic program after Antwerp. Ponteau gave up his Olympic eligibility in 1922 and became a professional fighter. Butler moved to Chicago, taking a post at a local YMCA to stay in shape for the 1924 Olympics. In 1922 he won the AAU national long jump title again. He also competed regularly on

football and basketball teams that played against professional players, earning investigations by and warnings from the AAU, the guardian of American
amateur standing. Realizing his Olympic window had closed and that he
could make money playing football and basketball, Butler in 1922 went to
New York City and handed in his AAU amateur card at the organization's
headquarters, beginning his career as a professional athlete.

Several early professional football clubs coveted Butler's prowess. He
played for Coach Fritz Pollard's Chicago-based Lincoln Athletic Club team
and then on the Pollard All-Stars, an all-Black touring team that featured
Pollard and Paul Robeson. Pollard, a star collegiate quarterback at Brown
University, became one of the first African Americans to play in the fledgling National Football League (NFL) that emerged in the 1920s. Butler
soon joined Pollard in the NFL, playing for a variety of teams throughout
the 1920s including a stint with the Canton (Ohio) Bulldogs squad that
featured Jim Thorpe.

Butler earned a living not only on the gridiron but also played on several
Chicago-area professional Black basketball teams, as the "Windy City"
became one of the centers of barnstorming squads. He continued to work
with the YMCA and other organizations developing the athletic talents of
young African Americans in the burgeoning Black enclave of "Bronzeville"
on Chicago's South Side, including some talented women's basketball players. Butler also wrote copiously for the *Chicago Defender* while leading the
barnstorming basketball squad that the influential Black newspaper sponsored. He later became the sports editor of the *Defender*'s rival, the *Chicago Bee*. As the Paris games approached, Butler had given up his Olympic
dreams for paychecks in basketball and football—a much less lucrative
living in the 1920s than in the twenty-first-century United States.

EARL JOHNSON MOVES TO CENTER STAGE
AMONG BLACK OLYMPIC HOPEFULS

With Butler in the professional ranks and tug o' war off the Olympic program, Earl Johnson became the only 1920 Black Olympian to return to the
1924 games. In 1921, Johnson's employer and team sponsor, the Morgan
Community House, closed its doors. Johnson found a new job and a new
sponsor at the Edgar Thomson Steel Works in North Braddock, Pennsylvania, which had been a part of Andrew Carnegie's industrial empire and then
became a linchpin in U.S. Steel's far-flung corporate colossus. Johnson took
a post as social worker for the mill that employed thousands of the African

Americans who in the 1920s joined the great migration and arrived in the Pittsburgh region.

Unlike his Black teammates from the 1920 Olympics, Johnson resisted the lure of professional athletics and committed to running in more Olympic races. By day he labored as a welfare officer overseeing the adjustment of Black employees at Edgar Thomson's sprawling works in Braddock, steering them to housing units, providing them basic social services, and setting up recreational opportunities for them. After work he logged thousands of miles training for the Paris games. Work and sport merged in his role as the organizer and star attraction of the new Edgar Thomson Steel Works Athletic Association. In one telling episode, Johnson traveled to Chicago to attend the national convention of the Urban League, a prominent civil rights group devoted to improving the lives of the Blacks migrants negotiating the transition from rural Southern life to metropolitan Northern environments. After attending the conference, he donned his Edgar Thomson jersey and won a fifteen-mile road race.

Sporting the colors of his new employer, Johnson put the steelworks' name in the national spotlight by winning races all over the United States. A profile in the *Wall Street Journal* heralded Johnson's combination of athletic prowess and professional acumen. "U.S. Steel can boast of the national five and ten-mile and cross country champion," proclaimed a story in the national financial newspaper that lauded Johnson as "a remarkable colored athlete" as well as one of the most valued of the 30,000 employees of the mammoth corporation.[19] As the *Wall Street Journal* paean highlighted, in 1921 Johnson won AAU titles at five miles, ten miles, and in cross-country. In the ten-mile contest and in the cross-country race, Finnish star Vihlo "Ville" Ritola finished second to Johnson, sparking a rivalry between the Edgar Thomson Steelworks star and the Finnish runner often referred to as "Willie" in the American press that captured national newspaper coverage. Ritola emigrated to the United States in 1913 and worked as a carpenter. His craft allowed him to build a career as an endurance racer in the United States while his Finnish citizenship allowed him to compete in the Olympics for his birthland.

Over the next few years as both runners prepared to face off in the Olympics, they traded U.S. national championships. In 1922, they faced off in several memorable contests. Johnson defended his five-mile title and defeated Ritola at the AAU championships. Ritola turned the tables on Johnson at the ten-mile AAU championship. The "Flying Finn" then defeated the "Smoky City" runner at the AAU national cross-country championship in New York City. Johnson and Ritola renewed their rivalry

Earl Johnson trains for the Olympics wearing the jersey of the Edgar Thomson Steel Works Athletic Association in the undated photograph taken in the early 1920s. Johnson not only ran for Edgar Thomson Steelworks but also worked as a welfare officer for the company assisting Black employees who flocked to the area for opportunities in the "Great Migration." *Dorsey-Turfley Family Photographs, MSP 455, Detre Library & Archives, Heinz History Center, Pittsburgh, Pennsylvania.*

in 1923, as Johnson again claimed the AAU national five-mile crown. The white *Chicago Tribune* championed Johnson's victory as providing "an exception to the rule that colored athletes are not as good in the distance and weight events as in the sprints, middle distance runs and jumps."[20] In Johnson's hometown, the Black *Pittsburgh Courier* celebrated Johnson's third straight national five-mile title as placing him among the American heroes who would "furnish the real nucleus for the 1924 Olympic team which will sail from these shores, to participate in combat with the best team from other nations."[21]

Later in 1923, Ritola rebounded and once again won the 1923 AAU titles in the ten-mile race and the cross-country race—though Johnson did not enter either of those two events. The next year, with Ritola returned to Finland to represent his homeland, Johnson dominated the selection races for spots on the American Olympic team. With a 10,000-meter track clash as well as a 10,000-meter individual and team cross-country race on the 1924 Olympic docket, Johnson dominated the American trials and prepared to take on Ritola and his fellow "Flying Finns" in Paris. The Black press touted Johnson as one of the nation's best hopes for a medal in the distance events. "America's ace in the hole for the Paris Olympic marathon of 1924 is Earl Johnston [the reporter confused Johnson's name with his coach and trainer's name], the Negro from Pittsburgh, who appears to possess all the qualifications of a great distance runner," asserted a columnist from the *Norfolk New Journal and Guide*.[22] A *Pittsburgh Courier* columnist also heralded Johnson's prospects, insisting that the Pittsburgh runner would help to "score the points really vital in bringing home the bacon."[23]

The "bacon," in this case, referred to an American victory in the overall medal count. The Black press speculated that several other track and field athletes might join Johnson on the American team, including long jumpers William DeHart Hubbard and Edward "Ned" Gourdin, decathlete and pentathlete Charles West, and sprinter Albert Washington. In the *Norfolk New Journal and Guide*, sportswriter P. Bernard Young concurred with that list, adding the name of Charles Brookins, a University of Iowa hurdler, to the roster of Black Olympic hopefuls. Young noted that while color lines excluded Blacks from most other sporting endeavors, track and field retained relatively few racial barriers. "Track athletics are the only sport in which Negroes are permitted to perform on equal terms in open competition with athletes of the Caucasian Race, and in this branch of sport they have made good," Young proclaimed.[24]

PROMOTING THE RACE VERSUS "PASSING" ON THE 1924 AMERICAN TEAM

As officials set the final roster for the 1924 American team, the African American press cheered that four, or perhaps five, or even six Black athletes made the squad, all in track and field. "Six Negroes, by virtue of their splendid showing in the final Olympic tryouts . . . sailed today on the steamship *America*," the *Norfolk New Journal and Guide* reported in the most robust count.[25] In addition to Johnson, Hubbard, Gourdin, and West, the Virginia newspaper listed two other athletes, Franklin Hussey and Charles Brookins. Perhaps the *Journal and Guide* assumed that since Hussey was born in Harlem that the prep sprinting sensation at Stuyvesant High School was African American. Hussey, however, was a well-known white runner who competed in AAU competitions for the notoriously all-white New York Athletic Club. No other press outlet beyond the *Journal and Guide* confused Hussey's racial heritage.

The racial identity of Charles Brookins proved a more complicated issue than the Hussey misidentification. Born in 1899 near Oskaloosa, Iowa, Brookins starred in high school football and track. In 1921, he enrolled at the University of Iowa where he became a sprinting sensation, winning collegiate and AAU national titles, setting world's records at multiple distances, and emerging as an Olympic medal-contender. The Olympic program did not offer the metric equivalent of his best event, the 220-yard hurdles, so Brookins made the American team in the 400-meter hurdles. As Brookins rose to become a world-class hurdler, the American media classified him as white. His selection for the U.S. Olympic team, however, ignited controversy in the African American press about his ethnic heritage. The *New York Age* contended that Brookins "has been generally considered as white, but those who know him say that he is a Negro."[26] A story on the 1924 Black Olympians in the *Norfolk New Journal and Guide* ran with the sub-headline, "A Good Athlete with Obscure Identity." The reporter noted that Brookins denied that he was Black. The Norfolk correspondent asserted that readers should ignore the controversy and celebrate the Iowa hurdler's prowess, regardless of his race. Still, the reporter could not resist from offering his own opinion on the matter, postulating that Brookins "is probably a race lad who is afraid that he will be mistreated if his identity is known."[27] A *Chicago Defender* columnist also chimed in on the debate. "Some say Charles is one of us and others show a winking eye and Charles himself denies any relationship to the sons of Ham and the children of Aunt Hagar." Having raised the question, the *Defender*'s columnist then tried to tamp down the controversy. "We will leave the identity of Charles out of the question," he demurred.[28]

The sentiment to leave the matter "out of the question" did not, however, prevail. As the Paris games approached the controversy surrounding Brookins heated up in the Black press. "There is a determined effort on the part of our papers to make Charles Brookins, world's champion hurdler, a Negro," commented W. Rollo Wilson in the *Pittsburgh Courier*. "This, to our mind, is much ado about nothing. If Brookins can be what he wants to be that should settle it," Wilson insisted, adding that the Iowa runner "is not the first and will not be the last to essay such a stunt."[29] In the *Philadelphia Tribune* J. M. Howe noted that the debate over Brookins' racial categorization had spread to the white press. "Colored persons are coming forward with the claim that the dashing champion hurdler is one of us and attempting to prove it while the *Sporting World*, white magazine, declares that the Iowan star is pure Caucasian," Howe declared. "It shouldn't be a vastly important thing, this question of this great athlete's color," Howe asserted, while fueling the dispute himself. From the Philadelphia correspondent's perspective, "if Brookins is colored he hasn't chosen to admit it so wherein lies the honor of claiming the man or his achievements?" In the very next sentence, Howe betrayed his professed neutrality and revealed his animosity toward Black athletes who "passed." "The pale colored man who chooses to cast his lot with the violators of women of his mother's race can bring neither credit nor glory to us," Howe maintained, revealing that as always in American culture, race mattered immensely.[30]

Nearly a century later, Brookins' white great-grandson offered a fascinating family history in which he detailed how his great-grandfather had "passed" as white, a family secret that endured into the twenty-first century. In excavating his family's genealogy, the great-grandson discovered that his great-great-grandfather, Charles Brookins Sr. had been born into slavery in the 1850s. After the Civil War, Brookins Sr. earned a divinity degree at Wayland Seminary in Washington, D.C., a "freedman" institution founded by the American Baptist Home Missionary Society. Brookins Sr. accepted a pastorate in Oskaloosa, where in the 1870s a large influx of Black strike-breakers into a nearby coal mine created an African American enclave. Brookins Sr. remained in Iowa for the rest of his life, becoming a well-known minister, educator, and civil rights champion in the state's small Black community. Brookins Jr. was born in 1899 into a family that the federal census bureau routinely identified as "Black" or "mulatto." Brookins Sr. the former slave and lifelong advocate for Black rights, died sometime between 1905 and 1910, when Brookins Jr. was a child. By the time he matriculated at the University of Iowa in 1921, if not earlier, the light-skinned Brookins Jr. "passed" as white. [31] While Black newspapers debated Brookins' identity intensely, the white press mostly ignored the controversy, implying acceptance of the hurdler's "whiteness" among the white majority.

PROUDLY BLACK

While Brookins' racial heritage remained opaque, a total of four unquestionably Black athletes sailed to the Paris Olympics onboard the S.S. *America*. Distance runner Johnson made his second Olympic sojourn. Long jumpers Hubbard and Gourdin and decathlete and pentathlete Charles West made their first Olympic team. Accompanying the quartet of competitors, trainer Billie Morris made his second Olympic trek, joined by Charlie Porter, another African American trainer from Syracuse University.

Edward Orval "Ned" Gourdin fit the standard pattern of Black athletes born in the Jim Crow South who found opportunities via the great migration. Originally from Jacksonville, Florida, or, as the chronicler of pioneering Black athletes Edwin B. Henderson put it, the "cracker state of Florida," Gourdin graduated in 1916 as the valedictorian of Stanton High School, the first Black school established in the state following the abolition of slavery.[32] His father, a meat-cutter by trade and part Seminole, and his mother, an African American domestic laborer, recognized their son's talents and moved to Cambridge, Massachusetts, in order for Ned to prep at the prestigious Cambridge High and Latin School in order to enroll at Harvard University. Gourdin started at Harvard in 1917, working as a postal clerk to pay tuition. He starred on Crimson track teams and thrived in the classroom. He won AAU and collegiate titles in the dashes and the pentathlon. Gourdin also set a world record in the long jump at the prestigious 1921 Harvard–Yale versus Oxford–Cambridge track meet. Gourdin earned both undergraduate and law degrees from Harvard, taking his final law exams just before the 1924 American Olympic team embarked for its Atlantic crossing.

The other two Black rookie members of the 1924 Olympic squad were Northern-born offspring of the great migration. Charles West was from Washington, Pennsylvania, where he excelled on the gridiron and earned accolades in track and field for Washington and Jefferson College. West quarterbacked the Presidents to a 1922 Rose Bowl berth where the small Pennsylvania school battled the University of California to a scoreless tie.

Acclaimed the greatest athlete in Washington and Jefferson history, West reigned as a two-time intercollegiate national pentathlon champion. The final Black member of the team, William DeHart Hubbard, was born in 1903 in Cincinnati, Ohio. He attended Frederick Douglass School and then Walnut High School where he became a national prep sensation in the long jump and the sprints. Attracted by Earl Johnson's rising renown, while still in high school Hubbard went to Pittsburgh for the summer and joined the Morgan Community House track team, working as a "redcap" porter at Union Station. Under the tutelage of Johnson's coach, Hunter Johnston, Hubbard blossomed into a long jumping prodigy. He competed for the University of Michigan, becoming the intercollegiate national champion in the long jump.

The day before the American Olympians sailed for Paris on the S.S. *America*, Hubbard sent a letter to his mother imploring her to deliver a message to his father. "Tell him I'm going to do my best to be the FIRST COLORED OLYMPIC CHAMPION."[33] Perhaps Hubbard did not know about, or had forgotten, John Baxter Taylor's gold medal in the medley relay at London in 1908. Or perhaps Hubbard meant that he dreamed of becoming the first Black to win an individual gold medal. No doubt his Black teammates harbored similar ambitions as they voyaged to Paris.

FROM DISAPPOINTING RACES AND BUREAUCRATIC HEARTBREAKS TO STRIKING GOLD IN PARIS

When the Americans arrived in Paris, Earl Johnson got the first chance at winning gold when he lined up on the track for the 10,000-meter race held on the opening day of the 1924 games. Johnson faced a heavy rain, a muddy track, and his old rival "Willie" Ritola, in the contest. Ritola got the better not only of Johnson but also of the entire field as the "flying Finn" set a world's record in the race. While Johnson finished a respectable eighth, he was nearly two minutes slower than the fleet Ritola. A disappointed reporter for the Black *Philadelphia Tribune* observed that Johnson and his "white teammates . . . were literally run into the ground" by Ritola.[34]

Charles Brookins also competed on opening day and earned a berth in the 400-meter hurdle finals. A white American won the gold medal in the event, but not the "passing" Brookins who was disqualified in the final for running out of his lane. On the same day Brookins ran afoul of the referees in the hurdles, Charles West was disqualified from the pentathlon due to paperwork mistakes on his entry form. West's defeat by bureaucrats frustrated African American reporters covering the Olympics. "We would not accuse the American team managers of deliberately making an error to keep West from competing, but we will say that it is a mighty peculiar mistake for a group of officials to make after sending in around 350 other entries," observed *Norfolk Journal and Guide* sportswriter P. Bernard Young Jr.[35]

After those initial setbacks, DeHart Hubbard delivered on the promise he had articulated in his letter to his parents by winning the long jump. Hubbard became the first African American to win an individual Olympic title. Even though he tweaked his foot and ankle in the preliminary round of the event, Billy Morris taped him securely for the final. The injured Hubbard miraculously mustered the winning jump. Hubbard's Black teammate Ned Gourdin took the silver medal in the same event. The Black press cheered Hubbard's and Gourdin's feats as major contributions to national prowess. *Chicago Defender* columnist Roscoe Simmons contended the long jumpers' triumphs changed white attitudes. "'See what our Colored boys can do,' Americans in Paris are saying with pride," Simmons declared. The journalist observed that Black audiences had a quite different view of the long jump results. "Colored boys at home feel like saying, 'See what our white people AT HOME do to us,'" noted Simmons, referring to racial discrimination in general and a resurgence of lynching during the 1920s in particular.[36]

Johnson got a chance at Olympic redemption a few days later in the individual and team cross-country race, two medal-events combined into a single competition. The brutal course led the runners over rock-strewn trails and through fields of knee-high thistles. Intense heat, over 100 degrees Fahrenheit, and suffocating humidity compounded the difficulties of the challenge. Thirty-eight runners started the race but only fifteen finished. French organizers had to send out Red Cross medics to scour the trails for runners who collapsed during the race. As in the other distance events at the 1924 Olympics, "flying Finns" took top honors. The individual star of the Paris games, Paavo Nurmi, earned the gold medal while Johnson's old nemesis Ritola took the silver. Johnson seized the bronze medal, leading his white teammates to a second-place finish in the team standings, thus earning himself an additional silver medal.

A Black press lauded Johnson's grit in the difficult conditions. "Johnson's running in defiance of the blinding attack of the terrific heat was proof of his bulldog tenacity in holding out to the end," wrote a *Chicago Defender* reporter.[37] The *Pittsburgh Courier* valorized their native son's performance. Describing Johnson seemingly without irony as a "'dark horse'" in the race, the *Courier's* report glorified the Pittsburgher's "remarkable fighting spirit." Recounting the Parisian crowd's reaction to Johnson's finish, the *Courier* observed that after the two favored Finns crossed the worsted "came the big surprise of the day. Behind these two into the stadium came an American, and a Negro. Who was he? Closer inspection revealed the fact that it was none other than R. Earl Johnson," the Pittsburgh correspondent marveled. According to the *Courier*'s story, as Johnson "finished the race, the crowds gave him a cheer which compared favorably with that given Nurmi and Ritola."[38]

While the Black press celebrated a gold medal, two silver medals, and a bronze medal earned by African American Olympians, the white media offered little comment on their accomplishments. Johnson, Hubbard, and Gourdin remained mostly "invisible" in mainstream white press accounts of the Paris games. Johnson's heroic efforts in the cross-country ordeal failed to earn him a solitary mention in any of the Olympic stories told in nationally circulated magazines aimed at white audiences. In the Black print media, the trio of medalists fared better. The *Chicago Defender* touted Hubbard as one of the greatest athletes in American history and ran a picture proudly reminding readers to "notice the Olympic shield on his breast."[39] The *Pittsburgh Courier*'s cartoonist Ted Carroll drew a panel featuring Hubbard, Gourdin, and Johnson, captioned "Our Boys in the Olympics."[40] The *Courier* saluted them in a feature story. "And playing no small part in the victory of America, three athletes of color have stood out prominently, covering their country, their race and themselves with the glory of being Olympic point-winners," declared the Pittsburgh correspondent.[41]

The *Chicago Defender*'s Simmons summed up the trio's power in framing national racial dynamics. "Be proud of your boys now showing your name abroad," Simmons insisted. "Likewise be proud of your countrymen, white, who gave them the opportunity in the U.S.A. to prepare for the Olympic," Simmons added. "Our civilized white people want to do what is right," he contended. "They long to do justice," he declared. "They have a hard time walking the rope while their uncivilized brethren jeer them from below," Simmons maintained. Simmons ended his homily with a consideration of the Olympians' contributions to the enduring American struggle for racial equity. "Sixty years ago you jumped from the bull whip. You ran from the slave driver. Today our sons jump for a prize and run for an honor while thousands cheer," Simmons stated. "Think of what you were and thank God for what you are and MAY become if you keep jumping high and run with swiftness AND endurance," the *Defender*'s renowned columnist and the nephew of Booker T. Washington cheered.[42]

HOMECOMING FOR THE PARISIAN BLACK MERCURIES

As the Black Olympians left Paris, Black newspapers reported that French girls showered them with bouquets of flowers while an African American jazz band serenaded them. The *New York Age* implored the city's Black community to honor the African American Olympians' return. "Not in the history of the Olympic games have four Negroes been on the American team before," noted the *Age*, perhaps forgetting that the 1920 team actually counted five Black members when the tug-of-war team was included in the racial calculus.[43] Responding to the entreaties, Harlem's Black communities organized a grand welcome. They even included Brookins on their list of African American Olympic honorees. Brookins, as his great-grandson later revealed, never admitted any Black heritage as he returned to the University of Iowa after the Olympics, finishing his competitive career and then joining the school's coaching staff. In Olympic retrospectives on the Paris games, the Black press continued to suggest that Brookins really belonged in the Black category in spite of his denials.

The openly Black Olympians found several routes to post-athletic success. Recruited to the fledgling NFL by the Akron Pros, Charles West instead went to medical school at Howard University. While he briefly coached the Howard football team in the 1930s, West concentrated on medicine and built an impressive career. He became a prominent physician who founded a practice in Alexandria, Virginia, where he attended to the community's health-care needs for more than a half-century. Ned Gourdin retired from athletics after Paris and put his Harvard law degree to work. He got a job in a Massachusetts legal firm, passed the federal bar exam, and enlisted in the National Guard. The Great Depression left him jobless for a bit, as not even his Harvard degree could secure a Black lawyer employment in that economic calamity. He persevered and became a leader in the Massachusetts Democratic Party. In 1936 his party's standard-bearer, President Franklin Delano Roosevelt, named Gourdin assistant U.S. attorney for the district of Massachusetts. During World War II he commanded the segregated 372nd Infantry Regiment. He joined the Massachusetts judiciary in the 1950s, and in 1958 Gourdin was appointed the first Black justice on the Massachusetts Superior Court. The following year he retired from the National Guard as a brigadier general. During the 1960s Gourdin continued his judicial career as well as taking leadership roles in the NAACP and on the U.S. Olympic Committee.

Like Gourdin and West, Earl Johnson retired from competition shortly after the Paris games. He returned to Edgar Thomson Steelworks social welfare division and resumed his communal welfare efforts. He organized sporting opportunities for Pittsburgh's Black community and also began a long career as a columnist for the city's Black newspaper, the *Courier*. Of the four—or five if Brookins is included—Black athletes who competed in Paris, only DeHart Hubbard would return for the 1928 Amsterdam Olympics. In a 1925 essay in the *Pittsburgh Courier*, Hubbard recalled his Olympic and Morgan Community House teammate Johnson as a paragon of persistence and promoter of racial equality. Hubbard noted that he learned from Johnson that track and field, especially at the Olympics, represented one of the few places in the United States and beyond where whites could not draw color lines. "We can enter any of their championship competitions, and we get as square a deal as any athlete could deserve," Hubbard insisted, a lesson he attributed to Johnson. "This then, is one place in athletics where there is no Color Line."[44] After the Paris Olympics, Black athletes seemed destined to move to the center of the American Olympic enterprise. Those hopes would prove at best wildly optimistic, as the Black contingent shrank to a mere three athletes in Amsterdam.

AMSTERDAM DISAPPOINTMENTS
FOR THE BLACK MERCURIES

In the Olympic interregnum between Paris and Amsterdam, DeHart Hubbard graduated from the University of Michigan in 1926 and returned home to Cincinnati where he found a city job providing recreational opportunities and affordable housing for the Black community. Hubbard continued to reign as the 1928 Amsterdam games approached as the world's best long jumper, setting U.S. and global records and piling up national titles. American track cognoscenti, white and Black, touted him as sure bet to defend his Olympic long jump title. He also bettered or tied world marks in the triple jump and several sprint events, making him a contender for multiple medals in Amsterdam.

Hubbard's prowess made him one of the first Black athletes to star on the new medium of radio that spurred national and international passions for sports. In his pioneering work on Black athletes, Edwin Bancroft Henderson recalled that when Hubbard jumped and ran, for the "first time the radio waves began to crackle with thrilling references by the early broadcasters to the dark lad who led his light-skinned contenders to the tape."[45] Adding to his celebrity, in 1926 to celebrate the sixtieth anniversary of the ratification of the Thirteenth Amendment to the U.S. Constitution abolishing slavery, the national Interracial Commission featured Hubbard's gold medal at Paris in an article chronicling Black achievement in the six decades since abolition. Heralded as an emblematic "New Negro" who battled representatives of all races on equal terms in international arenas, Hubbard's feat nurtured African American dreams of a grander haul of Olympic medals in 1928.

As the Amsterdam games approached, Black journalists lamented that another Black world-class athlete, Phil Edwards of New York University, decided to compete for Canada rather than the United States. A native of British Guiana, Edwards moved to New York City when he was thirteen years old and won numerous U.S. middle-distance titles. Heralded by both the Black and white press as a Black American athlete and a favorite to win the Olympic 800-meter race, Edwards declared his preference to wear a maple-leaf adorned jersey in Amsterdam. Without Edwards, only three Black athletes managed to win Olympic roster spots in the 1928 U.S. trials. Hubbard earned a long jump spot as did Edward Gordon, a young Black athlete from the University of Iowa who had just recently burst onto the long-jumping scene. An unknown teenager, John Lewis of Detroit, surprised the field and earned a place on the 400-meter relay team. Like so many of the Black Mercuries who competed in the Olympics in the first half of the twentieth century, Gordon and Lewis had been born in the South into families that joined the great migration during their childhoods. Gordon was born in Jackson, Mississippi, in 1908. His family migrated to the steel-mill magnet for Black Southerners of Gary, Indiana. Lewis was also born in 1908, in Macon, Georgia. His family settled in Detroit. The Black press noted that Lewis was a construction laborer from an impoverished family who had been funded by the Detroit YMCA in his unlikely quest to make the American Olympic team. Bunking for the tryouts at a Philadelphia YMCA, veteran Olympic trainer Billy Morris reached out to the unknown young runner and helped Lewis win his spot on the American team.

Hubbard, Gordon, Lewis, and trainer Morris sailed with the American team, arriving in Holland a week before the opening ceremonies. The African American press hoped that Hubbard could defend his Olympic long-jump title and take back his world record from his white Southern Olympic teammate, Edward Hamm of Georgia Tech University, who had just eclipsed it. "We are pulling for him to 'beat Hamm' and win first place in the Olympic broad jump," declared a *Chicago Defender* columnist.[46] Dogged by injuries, Hubbard had spent his pre-Olympic training months in Philadelphia with Olympic trainer Morris who at the Paris games had fixed Hubbard's ankle well enough for the long jumper to win the gold. Morris could not conjure the same magic at Amsterdam. A hobbled

Hubbard failed to make the long jump finals. Gordon finished in seventh place in the opening round, just out of the top six who qualified for the medal round. The white world-record holder Hamm won the gold medal for the Americans, much to the chagrin of the Black press corps. Left without African American long-jump medals to tout, some Black reporters turned Hamm's victory over the injured Hubbard into a positive sign in American race relations. W. Rollo Wilson of the *Pittsburgh Courier* lauded the "Sothron" Hamm for his public declarations of admiration for Hubbard. "It takes courage for a southern white boy to admit, voluntarily, that he got his inspiration from a Negro," Wilson observed.[47]

Compounding the long-jump disappointments, American officials scratched John Lewis from the 1,600-meter relay, ending his hopes for a medal in an event that the United States won handily. A few correspondents questioned the circumstances surrounding Lewis' removal. Without solid evidence of racial discrimination, however, the Black press raised suspicions without making firm charges. Years later Ray Barbuti, the American gold medalist in the 400-meter race who replaced Lewis on the relay team, recalled that the leader of the 1928 American Olympic expedition, General Douglas MacArthur, commanded Barbuti to take the Black runner's place. Though Barbuti protested he was still hungover from celebrating his 400-meter crown and that Lewis had been practicing for months for the opportunity, Barbuti recollected that MacArthur brushed aside his objections. The general summoned Lewis and informed him that he was benched, dissolving the youngster from Detroit into tears. Barbuti ran the anchor leg and won a second gold medal, while Lewis returned home without getting an opportunity to compete on the Olympic stage.

THE BLACK MERCURIES OF THE JAZZ AGE IN PERSPECTIVE

During the 1920s, Black Mercuries in track and field, joined by a boxer and two tug o' war titans, won multiple medals and fueled speculation that African American athletes would in the future play larger roles on American Olympic teams. Alongside Black musicians, Black Olympians became during the Jazz Age important faces of their communities to white Americans. Their depiction as portents of a brighter future for African Americans links this second generation of Black Mercuries to the pioneers of the first generation who in the first two decades of the twentieth century evoked similar sentiments. The reality of migration out of the American South also linked to first two generations. As the exodus grew larger, it became clearer that only those African Americans whose families made the trek North and West had an opportunity for Olympic glory. In spite of more than a million Blacks moving out of the South during the 1920s, by the end of the decade more than 80 percent of the nation's African American population still remained in that region. For Southern Blacks, absent a move beyond those historic boundaries, the dream of making an American Olympic team remained a mere fantasy.

The first generation of Black Mercuries had to flourish in white institutions in order to find a path to the Olympics. That remained a common experience for the Jazz Age generation as well. Most of them went to desegregated high schools, competed for white universities, and joined interracial clubs. However, a handful of Black Olympians in the 1920s developed their talents in Black institutions such a Harlem's growing list of Black AAU clubs. Pittsburgh's Earl Johnson became the first Black Olympian to emerge from a historically Black educational institution, Baltimore's Morgan College. Many of the era's Black Olympians built careers as teachers, social workers, and recreational leaders in posts that mainly served the rapidly growing urban Black communities that the great migration fueled. All three of the Black Mercuries on the 1928 American team illustrated this trend. After the Amsterdam games, Hubbard and Lewis returned to their hometowns, Cincinnati and Detroit respectively, and began long careers in municipal recreation and urban development programs targeted at Black communities. Gordon returned to the University of Iowa and built a remarkable track and field career there. He also earned his degree and moved to Lewis' Detroit where Gordon began a distinguished career as an elementary school teacher.

As the decade of the 1920s drew to a close, the future Olympic prospects of the nation's Black Mercuries seemed to have diminished a bit. African American Olympians had failed to medal in the 1920 or 1928 games, although they shined in the 1924 Olympics as Hubbard became the first individual Black gold medalist in American history. With the 1932 edition of the games slated for Los Angeles, however, their fortunes would soon be revived. The 1930s would witness the realization of the hopes and dreams that Black communities in the United States invested in their Olympian avatars. Black Mercuries would emerge who ignited the adoration not only of African American fans but even of whites. Edward Gordon would play a major role in the dawn of this "golden age" of Black Mercuries when he struck gold in California on his nation's home soil. He would be joined by a bevy of new stars who emerged from the depths of the Great Depression.

3

BLACK MERCURIES IN
THE TURBULENT 1930s

From the depths of a worldwide economic calamity and in the midst of the gathering storm clouds of a second world war, the most famous Black Olympic Mercury in the history of the modern games burst onto the global stage. "Never before in the recorded history of the oldest forms of athletic games, the track and field events, has a meteor so colorful, so wonderful in performance as Jesse Owens, ever blazed across the great athletic firmament," marveled Edwin Bancroft Henderson, the original chronicler of the nation's Black Mercuries after the American star won an unprecedented four gold medals in the sprints and jumps at the 1936 "Nazi" games.[1] Though Owens proved the brightest comet of the turbulent decade, he was not the only African American to star in the Olympics during the era. Black Olympic potential glimpsed in the previous decades bloomed in the tumultuous 1930s.

African American Olympians who returned home from the "Jazz Age" Olympics helped to prepare for the harvest. Many of them built careers serving urban Black communities. They led social welfare offices, staffed municipal parks and playground departments, and taught and coached at public schools in Pittsburgh, Cincinnati, Detroit, Chicago, Cleveland, and other cities where the Great Migration of African Americans from the South that began during World War I had dramatically increased Black populations. As the Great Depression devastated the American economy, this cadre of former Olympians who led social uplift programs faced massive challenges as unemployment wracked their communities. In the early 1930s the national jobless rate grew to 25 percent while among African Americans in the North and West it reached 50 percent and even higher as the pattern of "last hired, first fired" plagued Black workers. In the Depression-era South, where for decades millions of Blacks fled systemic economic discrimination and pervasive racial violence, migration escalated in spite of the daunting prospects of finding a decent job. Even the breadlines appearing in the nation's industrial heartland seemed a better prospect to many Black Americans than remaining in the Jim Crow South.

This Black exodus out of the South during the 1930s continued to transform sport as African American athletes who were born below the Mason-Dixon line but migrated out found opportunities on playing fields that their Southern kin—still the vast majority of the nation's Black population in spite of the shifting demographics—never enjoyed. In addition to the new influx of migrants, a first generation of Black athletes born in the North and West to parents who had made the trek from the South joined their Southern-born neighbors in desegregated competition. The rising Black stars of the 1930s were tutored by former Black Olympians including Sol Butler, DeHart Hubbard, Earl Johnson, and John Lewis who returned from Olympic stadiums to lead youth sport programs in African American communities.

During the 1930s, their pupils would win an increasing share of the medals claimed by the United States at Olympic arenas in Los Angeles and Berlin. They would be transformed by the global media into international superstars. At home and abroad, this new vanguard of Black Mercuries became the public face of African American communities across the United States, looked upon for leadership in an era of shifting economic, political, and social patterns in American race relations.

"GO OUT AND JUST SHOW THEM": THE "GREATEST GENERATION" OF BLACK OLYMPIANS

During the 1930s, Olympic trainer Billy Morris began his fifth decade at the center of American track and field from his post at the athletic colossus at the University of Pennsylvania. He offered both white and Black Americans his historic perspective on Black Mercuries amid the carnage of the Great Depression. While he paid homage to the pioneering generation of George Poage, John Baxter Taylor, and Howard Drew and their successors in the 1920s including Sol Butler, Earl Johnson, and DeHart

Hubbard, Morris contended that the Depression-era "crop of athletes are head and shoulders above the ones we have had in the past." In answering the question of why the Depression generation surpassed even the wildest expectations of their adoring boosters, he contended that the vast expansion of recreational and athletic opportunities that the Great Migration kindled played a key role in producing champions. He insisted, however, that the most important factor in their athletic brilliance was not simply this new racial demography but also the dedication of Black competitors to the struggle for racial equity. Growing up in Northern and Western communities where racism and discrimination were just as real if not as overt as in the South, the Black standouts understood that they were not merely competing to demonstrate their personal talents but to prove the virtue and value of their race to white America. Morris told a reporter for one of the nation's leading Black newspapers, the *Philadelphia Tribune*, that Black "athletes have in their subconscious minds when competing, a will to go out and 'show them.'" "Them" referred to the white Americans to whom Black Americans constantly had to prove themselves.[2]

Morris served as lead American Olympic trainer at Los Angeles in 1932 and Berlin in 1936 as Black Americans came to the forefront of the international sporting spectacles. The athletes he treated and nurtured stunned the world in the 1930s, winning multiple gold medals in track and field. They set Olympic and world records and reigned as the world's fastest humans, the appellation that the global press corps gave to the champions of the 100-meter dash. In the midst of the Great Depression, which fell more heavily on African Americans than on any other group, Black Mercuries moved from the margins to the leading roles in American Olympic dramas as well as in larger tales about racial dynamics in American culture.

Even the lily-white leadership of the American Olympic Committee (AOC) recognized the importance of including Black Mercuries in national narratives that depicted American Olympic teams as world-beating "melting pot" agglomerations that drew strength from every race, creed, and caste in the United States. The AOC during the 1930s constructed a tryout system for track and field that included a myriad of regional trials followed by semifinal qualifiers and then a final selection meet. The regional competitions took place across the United States, even in the Jim Crow South that barred interracial competition. Blocking Black Southerners from Olympic opportunities meant ignoring an enormous potential reservoir of talent, as more than 80 percent of the African American population lived there. In an attempt to remedy that problem, in 1932 the AOC slated a special meet for "Colored Schools, Universities and Colleges in the South" at Tuskegee

Institute.[3] Additionally, the AOC made sure that none of the higher-level semifinal trials or the final tryout took place at Southern sites that might exclude Black contestants. When the 1936 regional Olympic qualifying meet held in Washington, D.C., refused to accept Black athletes, the AOC announced that it would automatically advance any African American competitor excluded from those contests in the nation's capital into the next round of semifinals slated at Harvard University where color lines would not be drawn.

BLACK MERCURIES STRIVE FOR SPOTS ON THE 1932 AMERICAN OLYMPIC TEAM

In spite of the AOC's adjustments of its trials, Southern Blacks remained locked out of Olympic opportunities. The number of African American participants from other regions would increase substantially in the 1930s. In 1932 at the Los Angeles Olympics trainer Morris would work with six Black track and field athletes, only one of them a veteran of the games. After finishing seventh in the long jump at the 1928 Olympics, Ed Gordon returned to the University of Iowa where he won three straight intercollegiate national championships as well as the 1929 and 1932 AAU national titles. Gordon easily qualified for the 1932 U.S. Olympic team. Two Black sprinters also made the American squad. Ralph Metcalfe who was born in 1910 in Atlanta, Georgia, and whose family moved to Chicago, as well as Eddie Tolan, born in 1908 in Denver, Colorado, and whose family moved to Detroit, garnered even more pre-Olympic publicity than Gordon as they rose to the top rank of world-class sprinters in the early 1930s.

In addition to Gordon, Metcalfe, and Tolan, the Black press touted nearly a score of African Americans competing for spots at the U.S. trials. One correspondent predicted that at least five more of them would "surely bear the cudgel of battle well and lift the hearts of twelve million of their compatriots whose high hopes have followed them across the continent to this final test."[4] While Metcalfe, Tolan, and Gordon certainly bore the cudgel well, thrilling their 12 million Black compatriots by making the team, most of the rest of the Black contenders faltered, including some medal favorites such as University of Chicago long-jumper John Brooks, Michigan State Normal College hurdler Eugene Beatty, and Tolan's University of Michigan teammate, all-around stalwart Willis Ward. Only an unknown teenager in the high jump who would make his Olympic debut in his hometown of Los Angeles, Cornelius Johnson, managed to join the Black trio of medal favorites on the American team.

One other Black athlete, Illinois State Normal College sprinter James Johnson, initially appeared to have qualified for a position on the relay team by finishing sixth in both the 100-meter and 200-meter races. The AOC, however, altered their policies and substituted two white runners who did not even enter the 100-meter dash in the trials in place of Johnson. The Olympic bureaucrats retorted their decision was not racial but financial since the white substitutes lived in California and allegedly did not need travel funding.

The Black press did not buy the AOC's reasoning and asserted that racial calculations played a role in the decision. In the *Baltimore Afro-American*, Bill Gibson labeled Johnson's removal a "decidedly raw deal" that "double-crossed" the Black sprinter by giving his place to "TWO non-Afric fellows." Johnson was "ROBBED," Gibson charged. Gibson added 400-meter hurdler James Beatty to the list of Black athletes cheated by the AOC. Beatty had posted the fastest American time in his event for 1932 but unfortunately fell in the final of the Olympic trials and failed to cross the finish line in a four-man race for three spots on the American roster. The white winner of the race, Glenn Hardin of segregated Louisiana State University who ran for the segregated Southern Association of the AAU, was also disqualified for crossing over into the wrong lane and gliding over the wrong set of hurdles. Rather than appointing Beatty to the third spot based on his record in the event, the AOC leadership decided to dismiss the Black contestant for falling and promoted the disqualified Hardin onto the U.S. team. "And they say they're trying to pick the best men," Gibson scoffed. "PHOOEY!!"[5] Hardin would win the gold medal in the 400-meter hurdles in Los Angeles while Beatty watched from the stands.

With Johnson and Beatty out in spite of appeals, the contingent of Black men on the American team remained at four. For the first time, however, Black women represented the United States at an Olympics, bolstering the number of African Americans on the roster. Theodora "Tiyde" Pickett and Louise Stokes both qualified. Born in Chicago in 1914 to parents who migrated from the South to find factory jobs, Pickett grew up in "Bronzeville," as the thriving "Black Metropolis" section of the city was known. She developed her long-jumping skills in the city's municipal athletic program under the tutelage of University of Chicago long-jumper John Brooks. While Brooks finished fourth in the 1932 Olympic trials and failed to make the team, his star pupil Pickett did not have an opportunity to earn a place in her best event since the women's track and field program at the 1932 Olympics did not include a long jump. Pickett used her sprinter's speed to finish sixth in the 100-meter dash, earning a spot in the pool of relay runners.

Stokes, a native of Malden, Massachusetts, and also an accomplished long-jumper, took the fourth spot in the 100-meter dash at the U.S. women's trials to join Pickett in the relay pool. The daughter of a gardener and a domestic worker who had come north in the Great Migration, Stokes was like Pickett a member of the second-generation of migrants born beyond the Mason-Dixon line. She was also, like Pickett, a product of municipal and scholastic sports programs that flourished in her small industrial home-town in the greater Boston area.

In their journeys to Los Angeles, the six Black Olympians had significantly different experiences. Tolan and Metcalfe traveled by automobile and missed a large crowd of Black supporters who gathered at the train station to welcome the African American Olympians to Los Angeles. The Black fans instead cheered Edward Gordon as his train arrived. Cornelius Johnson, a Los Angeles native, made a short trip to the Olympic Village where he joined Gordon, Metcalfe, and Tolan at the Baldwin Hills complex that both the Black and white press described as a global melting pot of all races, ethnicities, and religions. Indeed, an article in the *Pittsburgh Courier*, one of the nation's leading Black newspapers, labeled the site as the "Sun-Kissed Olympic Village, Melting Pot of World."[6] Tolan and Metcalfe roomed together at the Olympic Village and fraternized with other Black Olympians, including Olympic returnees Phil Edwards of Canada and Sylvio Cator of Haiti.

The two Black women on the American team found the "melting pot" more racially combative as they traveled to the Olympics. Pickett and Stokes bunked together in a sleeping compartment of the transcontinental train junket. During the train trip, their superstar American teammate Mildred "Babe" Didrikson, a white native of segregated Texas, expressed her displeasure with the lack of a color line on the American women's team, pouring water on Pickett while she slept. Though Didrikson had a well-deserved reputation as a nasty teammate to all of her fellow athletes—white and Black—racial animus clearly motivated her attack on the Chicago teenager. In another incident, when the women's team stayed at the Brown Palace Hotel in Denver during a layover, the white women enjoyed single rooms, a sumptuous banquet honoring the team, and fawning press interviews; Pickett and Stokes were consigned to segregated quarters, required to eat their meals in their rooms, and kept away from the media.

RACIAL DICHOTOMIES IN OLYMPIC IMAGINATIONS AT THE LOS ANGELES GAMES

In the African American press, the dichotomy between the Olympics as a fortress of racial equity free of color lines or a bastion of hypocrisy revealing rigid color lines beneath Olympian platitudes appeared consistently in interpretations of what transpired in Los Angeles. Black commentators on the July 30 opening ceremonies of the Games of the Xth Olympiad celebrated that the six African Americans on the U.S. squad received a hearty welcome not just from the thousands of their fellow Black citizens in attendance but also from the tens of thousands of white fans in the capacity crowd of 105,000 at the Los Angeles Coliseum. Sub-headlines in the *Pittsburgh Courier* coverage of the opening ceremonies proclaimed "6 Bronzed Stars on Brilliant U.S. Team" and "Color Line Missing in the World Games."[7] Other Black reporters noted approvingly that athletes of African descent appeared on the rosters of other nations as well, not only Canada and Haiti but also Brazil and Argentina.

One of the leading Black sportswriters in the nation, Chester Washington of the *Pittsburgh Courier*, portrayed the Olympics as a "literal melting pot of the nations of the world." Washington rhapsodized about the Olympics as a model of racial inclusion. "In a fine spirit of understanding and amicable rivalry, black competes against white, yellow against red, and brown against brown, and the plaudits and rewards to the winners alike—regardless of color."[8]

Articles in Black newspapers also depicted the egalitarian treatment the two African American women received at the female headquarters for the spectacle, the swanky Chapman Park Hotel. Stokes and Pickett were not consigned, as they had been in Denver, to separate quarters, nor did Didrikson throw more water on them. American Olympic officials, however, quickly doused Stokes and Pickett's Olympic dreams. As practice began for the women's 4×100-meter relay, the coaches sidelined Stokes and Pickett in favor of an all-white foursome of sprinters. Two of those runners, Evelyn Furstch of Tustin, California, and Annette Rogers of Chicago, had not made the relay roster based on the U.S. Olympic trials process. "Lily-whiteism, a thing more pronounced than anything else around here on the eve of the Olympic games, threatened to oust Tydia [*sic*] Pickett and Louise Stokes from participation and put in their stead two girls who did not qualify," charged a *Chicago Defender* journalist. "This bit of back room treachery is nothing more than a sequel to the many acts of prejudice that have arisen since the athletes arrived here," the reporter continued, reviving the debates over Johnson and Beatty's treatment by the AOC.[9] In an exclusive to the Southern Black newspaper, the *Norfolk New Journal and Guide*, correspondent Gladys Jamieson exclaimed that Furtsch had failed to qualify through the official process: "Suddenly her name turns up on the program of the Games here and a colored girl, who actually QUALIFIED, was left out!"[10] When on August 7 the American women's relay team set a world record and won Olympic gold, the Black female "Mercuries" watched from the stands.

Color lines emerged in other locations at the 1932 Olympics as well. While Black athletes were accommodated at the Olympic Village, when a Los Angeles radio station tried to include a local Black entertainer in a live show staged at that site, the local Olympic staff announced that Black performers were not permitted in the Village. Color lines also restricted employment at the venue. The National Urban League, a civil rights advocacy organization for Black metropolitan communities, complained that the only Black employed at the Village was a shoe shiner and announced it was working to guarantee that Black waiters would be hired at the cafeteria. The fact that Blacks had to protest for even menial jobs at Olympic sites underscored the reality of color lines at every level of American Olympic enterprise in spite of periodic outbursts of color-blind rhetoric.

THE BLACK MERCURIES BECOME THE WORLD'S FASTEST HUMANS

Where they were permitted to compete, Black athletes flourished. On the first full day of competition, Cornelius Johnson finished in a tie with three other competitors for the top mark in the high jump. Had contemporary high jump rules been applied, Johnson would have earned a silver medal based on his number of misses. In 1932, however, the rules required a jump-off, and Johnson slipped to fourth place. Ed Gordon fared better in the long jump, soaring to the gold medal. In the 100-meter and 200-meter dashes, Tolan reversed the pre-Olympic script and beat the favored Metcalfe in both events. Metcalfe distinguished himself as well, earning a silver medal in the shorter sprint and a bronze medal in the longer one.

The two Black sprinters, or, as *Philadelphia Tribune* sports editor Randy Dixon referred to them, "two bronze statues of Mercury come to life," became instant global heroes and seized the top spots on the list of world's fastest humans.[11] Reporters in the *Pittsburgh Courier* commemorated Tolan and Metcalfe as "bronzed" and "sun-tanned" Mercuries.[12] Curiously, in the arcane policies of AOC relays in 1932, the coaches left the world's two fastest men off the 4×100 relay team. A white American foursome set a world's record in winning the gold medal. The Black press did not accuse the AOC of racial meddling in this case, since the administrators had followed their previously announced selection policies. Had American officials made a different decision, Tolan would have won his third gold medal and Metcalfe his first gold and third overall medal in the relay.

The white press depicted Tolan and Metcalfe as Olympic heroes by employing standard skin-color tropes. Grantland Rice, one of the most widely read white sports columnists in the nation, used his poetic palette to sketch the two Black Americans, depicting them bursting upon the Olympic scene like "two black bolts from the Azure of a California sky."[13] White commentators also portrayed Tolan and Metcalfe as the epitome of the "Good Negro" of the era—humble, well-mannered, and willing to tolerate their places in the American racial hierarchy without defiantly confronting racism. White reporters and fans cheered their contributions to the U.S. triumph in the overall medal count and the projection of American might and virtue through Olympian feats. However, they rarely commented on how Black Olympic victories challenged racial stereotypes and confronted the myriad color lines that embroidered the United States.

Will Rogers, the widely syndicated white humorist, provided a satiric exception to the typical pattern. "The man that brought the first 'slaves' to this country must have had these Olympic Games in mind, for these 'senegambians' have just run the white man ragged," Rogers jabbed after Tolan and Metcalfe's races. "Every winner is either an American Negro or an American white woman," Rogers jested, heralding the contributions not only of Black men but also of white women to the U.S. quest for Olympian supremacy. "Wait till we get to golf, bridge or cocktail shaking, then the American white man will come into his own," Rogers smirked.[14]

Rogers' acerbic jests touched on the challenges Black Olympians presented to racial categories and practices, a generally taboo subject in white media coverage of the Olympics. In contrast, Black media accounts made racial analyses central to their Olympic narratives. In her exclusive observations for Norfolk's *New Journal and Guide*, Gladys Jamieson noted that Tolan and Metcalfe's performances countered the stereotypes that white reporters had repeated to her, that Black athletes "haven't got the fight and grim determination to win when the going gets hard."[15]

Tolan and Metcalfe's performances earned accolades not only from journalists but also from African American civil rights crusaders. The leader of the NAACP Walter White wired: "You have by your great achievement brought honor not only to your country and yourself, but to your race as

well." White commended the Black Mercuries for shattering racist stereotypes. "'No sane man who is free from prejudice can view your magnificent
feat in its grueling demands on energy and courage and ever again think or
speak of Negroes as slothful or lacking in stamina and heart,'" White proclaimed, linking their achievements to the civil rights crusade.[16]

For their high-profile dismantling of racial stereotypes, African American correspondents made the rise of the American Black Mercuries into
the central narrative of the Los Angeles games and the key to American
dominion in the Olympic power rankings. "As the dim light fades on what
is called the greatest Olympics games in recent times which was held on
the sun-kissed shores of California, we wish to give a summary of what
Uncle Sam's dark-skinned citizens did to push the point percentage far
out in front of the other competing countries," declared Charles Bowen in
the *Atlanta Daily World*.[17] In a *New York Amsterdam World* recap of the
thrilling 100-meter dash, Thomas Anderson observed: "It was the world
against Metcalfe and Tolan on today's Olympic program." Anderson added
that the "world lost, for the two ebony twins hogged all the laurels in the
finals of the short sprint classic." Anderson contended that in leading
the United States to a medal-count victory, Tolan and Metcalfe defeated the
"Nordic universe."[18]

The Black American Olympians had a bit of help from other nations in
their battles with the "Nordic universe." Phil Edwards of Canada, adopted
once again as a member of "Colored America," won three bronze medals
in Los Angeles, earning third-place finishes in the 800-meters, the 1,500-
meters, and helping Canada to third in the 4×400-meters relay. The Black
press in the United States acclaimed not only Edwards' amazing Olympics
but also the gold medal in the heavyweight boxing division by the "giant
Black Argentine," as one Black reporter described Santiago Lovell.[19] Black
reporters also praised participants of African descent who participated but
did not earn medals.

The Black press lauded not only the speed of Black American Mercuries
and their compatriots from other nations but also their grace under pressure and their sterling characters. Black correspondents hailed Tolan and
Metcalfe in particular for embodying the Olympian ideal of sportsmanship. Metcalfe's second-place in the 100-meter dash and third-place in the
200-meter race happened under especially difficult circumstances. The
100-meter finish with Tolan was so close that it required several minutes
and an examination of the official photographs to determine the victor. Before the announcement that Tolan had triumphed, most of the crowd and
the majority of the press thought the favored Metcalfe had won. Indeed,

Ralph Metcalfe (left) and Eddie Tolan (right) share a moment after their photo-finish in the 100-meter dash at the 1932 Los Angeles Olympics. *Ralph Metcalfe Collection: The Olympic Years, 1932–1936, Department of Special Collections and University Archives, Raynor Memorial Libraries, Marquette University, Milwaukee, Wisconsin.*

even the photo-finish revealed Metcalfe had reached the worsted marking 100-meters first, but the rules at the time stipulated that the first racer to get his torso across the line was the victor. Tolan managed that feat at Los Angeles. In 1933, the international governing body for track and field changed the rules so that the victory went to the first runner who had any body part across the line—small solace for Ralph Metcalfe.

Controversy dogged Metcalfe in the 200-meter final as well. The judges erred in placing Metcalfe nearly two yards behind the rest of the finalists for the staggered start on the curve. Their mistake was not a rectifiable oversight, and Metcalfe ended up third behind Tolan and fellow white American teammate George Simpson. Press experts who reviewed the motion picture footage of the race concluded Metcalfe would have been at least second and perhaps first had he been granted the correct starting position.

The Black press cheered that the star-crossed Metcalfe bore his defeats magnificently. According to Gladys Jamieson, in the 200-meter final "Metcalfe knew of the handicap under which he was running when he toed the line, but did not say anything about it for fear he would be misunderstood for a poor sport." Jamieson added that Tolan and Metcalfe were not only teammates and Olympic Village roommates but also good friends. She believed their "friendship is the expression in practical real form of the ideal of Olympic sportsmanship."[20] Tolan himself acknowledged Metcalfe's grace in the face of devastating disappointment. Tolan admitted that despite his joy at winning two gold medals a part of him wished that his teammate could have earned gold as well. Tolan recalled that when Metcalfe's mother congratulated him on his victory after one of the races, Tolan struggled to avoid collapsing into tears. For Tolan, his friend Metcalfe epitomized the Olympic ideal.

As the Los Angeles Olympics closed, news reports chronicled the honors and celebrations that the trio of Black medalists received for their performances. The Black athletes toured Hollywood as rumors swirled of possible movie roles. Reports surfaced that vaudeville promoters had offered Tolan $1,000-a-night appearance fees. Metcalfe's name also surfaced in the vaudeville gossip. Other newspaper stories claimed that the Japanese national track team extended Tolan a high-dollar contract. For Tolan, who announced that his amateur running days were over, the entertainment gig seemed a lucrative opportunity. Tolan decided, however, that he was not relocating to either Hollywood or Tokyo but instead planned to attend medical school back in Detroit and become a doctor. Tolan's hometown of Detroit staged a huge parade for the returning hero while one of the city's leading industrial behemoths, General Motors, gave him a new automobile. A candidate for Wayne County coroner even promised that if Tolan endorsed him, the coroner would find the future medical school student a place on his staff and underwrite his professional education. Shortly after his "Motor City" homecoming parade, the governor of Michigan declared an "Eddie Tolan Day" at the Michigan State Fair. A Black newspaper reporter noted that "this kind of recognition, and honor have never been paid a member of the Negro race in all of Michigan's history, and some have said it is the first time such an honor and recognition have been bestowed upon any member of the Negro race by a governor of any state in the history of the United States."[21]

In an ironic compliment to Michigan's "Tolan Day," the white mayor of Atlanta declared September 23, 1932, "Ralph Metcalfe Day," in the city of his birth. The mayor's proclamation asked white as well as Black Atlantans to commemorate Metcalfe's Olympic feats in "such a manner as to give due recognition to the internationally known athlete who was born in Atlanta, and who, if he had remained here, would probably have been a rose 'born to blush unseen, its fragrance wasted on the desert air.'"[22] As Tolan's life unspooled, he would discover that the Atlanta mayor's lamentation about the fate of talented Black men in the United States resonated north as well as south of the Mason-Dixon line.

FROM OLYMPIC HERO TO UNEMPLOYED SYMBOL OF BLACK TRAVAILS IN THE GREAT DEPRESSION

As the parades and accolades for his Olympic feats mounted, Tolan readied himself to transition from his athletic career and pursue his ambition to become a physician. He hoped to bankroll medical school by profiting from his fame, a path none of his fellow 1932 Black teammates pursued. Fellow gold medalist Gordon did not garner the press attention that Tolan received. Gordon relocated after the Olympics to Tolan's hometown of Detroit where Gordon began a long and distinguished career as a public school teacher. Metcalfe, in the midst of his collegiate career, maintained his amateur standing by rebuffing the get-rich-quick schemes and setting his sights on winning gold medals in the next Olympics. The three Black teenagers, Johnson, Stokes, and Pickett, also worked toward a return to the next Olympics. Tolan, however, decided to translate his Olympic fame while the white-hot spotlight of national publicity shone on him, as other American Olympians such as Johnny Weissmuller, the white swimmer who became a Hollywood legend as Tarzan, had so successfully done.

Tolan faced two enormous hurdles in his quest. The economy was crumbling—and Tolan was Black. In the midst of the Great Depression even in the "Motor City" capital of American industrial might, unemployment ravaged Black workers even more than white laborers. Tolan's parents both lost their jobs before the Olympics. His half-brother Fred had a menial post with the city collecting trash. Indeed, the day Tolan arrived home from the Olympics at the downtown Detroit train station to the plaudits of thousands of adoring fans, Fred had been picking up litter just across the street. A few months after the Olympics as the double-gold-medalist endured a long stretch of unemployment that dashed his medical school dreams, Eddie acknowledged that he now regarded Fred as "'luckier than I am.' He had a job."[23]

Tolan's immediate post-Olympic life became an allegory in both the Black press and the white media for the racial disparities of the Great Depression. In spite of a college degree from a prestigious white institution—the University of Michigan—and graduate school experience—at historically Black West Virginia State University—as well as enormous Olympic fame, Tolan struggled to find gainful employment. Knowing it required giving up his amateur athletic career, Tolan teamed with African American vaudeville star Bill "Bojangles" Robinson on the entertainment circuit. He quickly found those gigs did not meet his family's financial needs nor provide an income sufficient to pursue his medical school ambitions.

As Tolan and his family descended further into poverty, he continued to receive plaudits for his Olympic feats. He finished third, much to the chagrin of Black sportswriters who asserted he should have been the top vote getter, in the Associated Press poll for best athlete of 1932 behind two whites, U.S. Open and British Open golf champion Gene Sarazen and Wimbledon and U.S. Open tennis champion Ellsworth Vines. *Pittsburgh Courier* sports editor Chester Washington blasted his colleagues for picking country-clubbers Sarazen and Vines over Tolan. "Does America forget so soon?" Washington wondered, that Tolan "brought boundless international glory" to the United States? "Is this the way the cream of the U.S. white sports writers pay a nation's debt of gratitude to the streaking bit of brown lightning which carried its shield to world renown?"[24]

In December of 1932 as unemployment reached its highest level in American history and Black joblessness more than doubled the white rate, Tolan stood in front of Detroit's political leaders to receive an embossed certificate expressing his hometown's appreciation for the glory he brought the city. Someone noticed Tolan looked a bit pensive and asked him what was wrong. Tolan hesitated in his response. Detroit Democratic Councilman Edward J. Jeffries jumped into the breach. "You can't eat gold seals, can you Eddie?" Jeffries queried. "'No, sir,' replied the 'world's fastest human,' in his precise diction," according to the *Chicago Defender* reporter who chronicled the exchange. "You see, I have no job and none of my family is working," Tolan confessed. Mayor Frank Murphy then addressed the assembly, declaring that Tolan "deserved the city's appreciation not only in words, but in deeds. His home city owes him a chance to earn a living. I shall see that he gets it."[25] The mayor promised to find a city job for the Olympic hero.

Tolan soon received several local offers of employment from Democratic officials who had just dominated the 1932 elections that swept their party's standard-bearer Franklin D. Roosevelt into the presidency and swollen the Democratic ranks at every level of government around the nation. Tolan accepted a post as a clerk in the office of the register of deeds, earning enough to at least keep his family fed and housed in the midst of the economic calamity.

Just months after he starred on the track of the Los Angeles Coliseum in a triumphal narrative of American prowess, Eddie Tolan became a leading character in stories about the devastating impact of the depression on Black Americans. This time he "starred" in tales about the struggling "last hired, first fired" legions of unemployed and underemployed Black Americans. Not only the Black media but also the white press used Tolan's plight to sketch portraits of the disparate racial impacts of the economic calamity. A widely syndicated AP story that ran in the *New York Times* and many other white newspapers chronicled how for Tolan the "heady wine of victory has turned, overnight, to vinegar."[26] Speaking from his family's home filled with his medals and trophies, Tolan explained how his accolades had failed to help his job search and how his dreams of becoming a physician had evaporated. Still, he expressed gratitude that his Democratic patrons had at least secured a file clerk job that kept his family afloat.

Tolan's woeful tale inspired one of the nation's most prominent sportswriters, John Kieran of *New York Times*, to question whether the amateur bargain was worth it for Olympic athletes. A similar commentary on Tolan's plight in a white Michigan newspaper, the collegiate daily at Tolan's alma mater in Ann Arbor, went further than Kieran ventured and pointed out that white "amateurs" could cash in on their fame while contending that the Black Olympic star was a "Victim of Race Prejudice." The *Michigan Daily* correspondent found it "a peculiar thing, but these set-backs don't seem to occur when a white athlete makes good." A white Olympic star "is slapped on the back; he appears on big-time vaudeville circuits, and draws

heavy pay-checks; he writes articles for the *Saturday Evening Post*; if nothing else, he is paid for endorsing sports equipment," observed the student
columnist. The reporter lamented that "Eddie, however, had the misfortune to be born into the 'wrong race.'" The reporter hoped that Tolan "may
someday get his chance, and earn enough money to return to college and
go through medical school." At the nadir of the Depression, in the bleak
winter of 1932–1933, "it looks very much as though another Negro, worthy
of better things, is about to be shelved for life," the *Michigan Daily* writer
acknowledged.[27]

Tolan never made it to medical school. He labored as a Detroit municipal clerk for years before finally finding in 1945 a job that at least put his
university degree and athletic acumen to work, joining his fellow Black
gold-medalist Gordon as a teacher and coach at a Detroit public school.
Gordon served as a pall-bearer for his Olympic colleague when Tolan died
too young in 1967, at age fifty-nine, of complications of diabetes. A eulogy
in Detroit's Black newspaper, the *Michigan Chronicle*, recalled Tolan's
significance. "When Eddie Tolan returned to Detroit after his victories
in the Olympic games, there was no good job waiting for him; there were
no fabulous endorsements for him or any Negro star to build his security
on," opined Frank Lett in the obituary. Tolan had to content himself with
paving the way for others, observed Lett, noting a roster of beneficiaries
of Tolan's trailblazing that ranged from Jackie Robinson and Willie Mays
to Wilt Chamberlain and Muhammad Ali. "The penalty of being a 'first' is
sometimes compensated for as you look back and realize that you helped
get the door open for others," Lett declared.[28]

Among those others for whom Tolan kicked open the door, Lett noted,
was Jesse Owens who as a high school junior in 1932 won the 100-meter
race and long jump at a regional Olympic trial in Ohio before faltering in
the semi-final selection round to the mature brilliance of Tolan, Metcalfe,
and Gordon. In the next Olympics slated for Berlin in 1936, Owens would
surpass even Tolan's marvelous Olympic accomplishments, and a host of
other Black athletes would win medals for the United States. How wide
the doors had been opened by Tolan for Owens and his fellow "black auxiliaries," as first the German press and then American reporters frequently
labeled them, would prove to be more complicated than Lett recalled in
1967 as he honored the genius of and acknowledged the challenges faced
by Eddie Tolan.

ANTICIPATING THE "NAZI OLYMPICS"

The International Olympic Committee (IOC) initially awarded the Games of the XIth Olympiad in 1931 to the Weimar Republic, a more liberal and Western regime than the Nazi Third Reich that seized power just two years later and took over the international athletic exposition. The Nazis considered pulling out of the Olympics but after witnessing the advertising marvels that the United States staged in 1932 at Los Angeles, Adolf Hitler recognized the propaganda potential inherent in the games. As the world learned about the new Nazi ideology, the 1936 Olympics became an international flashpoint for not only political but also racial and ethnic concerns. Nazi promotion of Aryan racial supremacy magnified the racial discourses that always swirled around the Olympics. Boycott movements and campaigns to relocate the 1936 games surged in many nations, including the United States.

The boycott question divided the African American community, as it did other ethnic, religious, and political groups. Some Black leaders, including Walter White of the NAACP who had hailed the contributions of Tolan, Metcalfe, and Gordon to American race relations in Los Angeles, advocated withdrawal from the "Nazi Olympics." Others, including athletes who sacrificed for years to earn Olympic roster spots, counseled that the best course of action was to show up in Berlin's Olympic Stadium and trounce Hitler's Aryan "supermen" and "superwomen." Catholic, Protestant, and Jewish groups weighed in on the pro-boycott side of the debate, as did many labor unions, political groups, and public intellectuals.

Both the pro-boycott and anti-boycott factions made for strange Olympian bedfellows. In one illuminating example, the lily-white leadership of the Southern branch of the AAU comprised mainly of Jewish and Catholic elites from New Orleans, condemned Nazi anti-Semitism and voted to boycott the Berlin games at the very same annual meeting at which they upheld white supremacy by rejecting a membership application from a Black New Orleans athletic club. Ultimately, the AOC and the AAU decided to send an Olympic team to Germany. In this climate, Black Olympians garnered more scrutiny than they had ever before received.

Not only did the attention paid to Black Olympians intensify, but the number of African Americans who made the roster surged. Eighteen Black athletes won places on the 1936 American team, including five boxers and one weight lifter, plus the legendary Billy Morris was once again appointed trainer. As usual, track and field performers made up the bulk of the African American Olympians. On the women's side, Tidye Pickett and Louise

Stokes made the U.S. roster again. With their best event, the long jump, still missing from the Olympic docket, Pickett qualified in the 80-meter hurdles. Stokes ran poorly in the 100-meter sprint qualifiers at the U.S. trials, but the AOC decided to add her veteran leadership to the relay pool.

On the men's side, Los Angeles Olympic veterans Ralph Metcalfe in the sprints and Cornelius Johnson in the high jump repeated as qualifiers. John Brooks, Pickett's coach, made the squad in the long jump in his second attempt. The sensational Jesse Owens led the American long jumper qualifiers and joined the veteran Metcalfe in the 100-meter and 200-meter dashes. Owens' Ohio State teammate David Albritton joined Johnson in the high jump. Frederick Douglass "Fritz" Pollard Jr., the son and namesake of a pioneering NFL quarterback and coach, qualified in the 110-meter hurdles. Matthew "Mack" Robinson, the older brother of a future African American sports and civil rights superstar, Jackie Robinson, made the cut in the 200-meter sprint. Archie Williams and James LuValle earned slots in the 400-meter dash, while John Woodruff earned a roster spot in the 800-meter race.

Like earlier contingents of the Black Mercuries on Olympic teams, the athletes on the 1936 U.S. squad underscored how the Great Migration had transformed American sport and society. Five of the Black Olympians had been born in the Jim Crow South and moved beyond the Mason-Dixon line as youngsters. Owens and Albritton were born in the same year, 1913, just two and a half miles apart in Alabama, and both families migrated to Cleveland. Robinson and Metcalfe were both born in Georgia. Metcalfe's family relocated to Chicago while the Robinsons moved to Southern California. LuValle was born in Texas, and his family also relocated to California. The other African American men were first-generation or second-generation descendants of ancestors who made the trek out of the South to industrial centers in other parts of the nation. Williams and Johnson were born in California. Woodruff was born and grew up in a steel mill town, Connellsville, outside of Pittsburgh. Pollard was born in Springfield, Massachusetts, the hometown of early twentieth-century Black sprinter Howard Drew, and grew up in Chicago where his father starred in professional football.

The backgrounds of 1936 Black Olympians revealed that although the AOC had offered special tryouts for athletes from historically Black institutions in the legally segregated South, the best African American athletes still came of age outside of "Dixie" in major metropolitan areas where they interacted regularly with whites in school and social situations, even as customary forms of racial segregation created color lines in their daily lives. All of the Black Olympians went to desegregated universities where a handful of Black students lived among their white classmates, including the University of California at Berkeley and the University of California at Los Angeles, Ohio State University, the University of North Dakota, Marquette University, the University of Chicago, and the University of Pittsburgh.

As in Eddie Tolan's case in 1932, the new crop of Black Mercuries came from Black families disproportionately impacted by the Great Depression as compared to their white neighbors. The father and older brothers of Jesse Owens lost their well-paying jobs in Cleveland's steel mills, and Owens considered abandoning his track career to support his family. Many of the other Black track stars and their fellow Black teammates on the boxing and weight-lifting squads faced similar decisions. They also harbored hopes, in spite of Tolan's experiences to the contrary, that they might be able to translate Olympic fame into opportunities to boost their fortunes. The global media fascination anticipating the 1936 Olympics stoked their aspirations.

The Black Olympians traversed the Atlantic onboard the S.S. *Manhattan* with their white teammates, though they roomed only with members of their own race—a reminder of color lines that shaped even desegregated arenas of American life. Both the Black press and the white media predicted that they would challenge Nazi racial stereotypes. White newspapers lauded the Black medal hopefuls by churning out the traditional "melting pot" narratives trumpeting the virtues of American pluralism. John Kieran of the *New York Times* speculated the multi-racial American squad might even "cause a change for the better in the Hitler mind." If they could not convert Hitler to racial egalitarianism, "at least the United States contingent, with its representative mixture of Protestants, Catholics and Jews and its amazing collection of great Negro athletes, should open his eyes a little," Kieran hoped.[29]

A handful of white American journalists employed the Black Olympians to challenge doctrines of white supremacy at home. An editorial by one of the nation's top journalists, Westbrook Pegler, observed that the African American Olympians challenged not only Nazi but also American versions of white supremacy. Pegler observed that "if the Olympics were held anywhere in the southern tier of American states, all athletes of the complexion" of the Black contingent "would be automatically barred."[30] Commentaries connecting Nazi racism to American Jim Crow featured more prominently in the Black press. "Judging by the actual experience of [Black] stars . . . who have run in Germany since it became Nazi, sundown members of the 1936 squad will receive treatment in Berlin that would lead to lynching in such 100 per cent American villages as Atlanta, Birmingham or New Orleans," posited one editorialist in an opinion piece widely circulated in African American newspapers by the ANP.[31] The ANP story could have mentioned Washington, D.C., in that list given the exclusion of Black competitors from the Olympic trial in the nation's capital.

TRIUMPHS AND TRIBULATIONS AT "HITLER'S GAMES"

The Black Olympians arrived to a Berlin scrubbed of anti-Semitic signage and other public displays of Aryan racial ideology as the Nazis tried to sanitize the city for the Third Reich's appearance on the global stage. According to accounts from the press, from visitors, from U.S. government and AOC officials, and from the Black athletes themselves, most Germans accorded the African American contingent a courteous welcome. At the Olympic Village and in the streets of Berlin, German fans tendered civil receptions. In the stadium the Black Olympians received the same treatment as their white teammates, polite applause mixed with occasional "raspberries"—the American term for the whistles that constituted boos in Europe. Occasional raspberries were to be expected for a U.S. squad whom the world perceived as an Olympic juggernaut almost certain to dominate the overall medal count.

As the competitions commenced after an ostentatious opening ceremony, an African American contender won an Olympic laurel for the first time in a sport other than track and field when Jack Wilson took a silver medal in the bantamweight (112 pounds) boxing division. American coaches contended that nefarious judging deprived Wilson of a gold medal. The other four Black boxers failed to earn a medal, and the Black weight lifter, John Terry, also finished out of the medals.

In track and field, Tidye Pickett became the first Black woman to participate in an Olympic race when she ran in the preliminary and semifinal rounds of the 80-meter hurdles. Alas, she broke her foot when she struck a hurdle in the semifinal, ending her Olympic dreams. Louise Stokes' dream regrettably ended the same way it had in Los Angeles as the coaches benched her for the 4×100-meter relay. She once again sat in the stands as her white teammates won the gold medal.

The Black men on the track and field team fared far better than the two women. John Brooks qualified for the semi-finals and made the seventh best long jump of the games, a respectable showing but one that failed to earn him a spot in the final six who competed in the medal round. The other nine Black men on the U.S. team each earned at least one medal in their events. Jesse Owens took the top prize in the long jump. Cornelius Johnson and David Albritton earned gold and silver medals respectively in the high jump. Fritz Pollard earned a bronze medal in the 110-meter hurdles. Archie Williams and James LuValle won gold and bronze medals respectively in the 400-meter dash. John Woodruff triumphed in the 800-meter race, while the venerable "Colored American" representing Canada Phil Edwards once again earned a bronze medal in that race. Mack Robinson sped to a silver medal in the 200-meter dash while the veteran Ralph Metcalfe, hoping to finally earn a gold medal in the 100-meter dash, once again had to settle for second place behind an American teammate.

That teammate was Jesse Owens who, in addition to the long jump and the 100-meter sprint, also won the 200-meter race. Owens earned an additional gold medal in the 4×100-meter relay, teaming with Metcalfe and two white runners. Metcalfe's first Olympic gold medal was Owens' fourth, which made the younger sprinter the most incandescent star of the 1936 Olympics both in the United States and around the world. The four medals Owens won, as well as the world record he set in the 200-meter race, the world record he anchored in the relay, and the Olympic record he set in the long jump, earned him a fan base even in Hitler's Germany.

The fact that Owens and Metcalfe ran in the 4×100-meter relay broke with U.S. Olympic precedent established at Los Angeles. In 1932, even though two Black Americans, Tolan and Metcalfe, won the top two spots in the 100-meter dash, the white Olympic coach Dean Cromwell of the University of Southern California employed fresh runners who did not compete in the 100-meter race. Cromwell's system had kept the two fastest men in the world from winning another gold medal in Los Angeles. Cromwell had also dropped James Johnson, the lone Black qualifier for the relay team, from the final foursome and installed two of his Southern California sprinters on the U.S. entry.

In Berlin, Cromwell, once again in charge of the sprint relay selections, broke precedent and included Owens and Metcalfe on the relay foursome. The coach also added two of his Southern California athletes to run with the two Black Mercuries, leaving two Jewish runners, Marty Glickman and Sam Stoller, out of the mix. Glickman and other observers contended that Cromwell and AOC officials had capitulated to Hitler's anti-Semitism by removing them from the final lineup. In the after-action AOC report, U.S. officials bristled at the accusations, insisting that anti-Semitism played no part in the selection and that they had picked the top four sprinters from the trials for the 4×100-meter lineup. Yet, in selecting the 4×400-meter relay team, Cromwell had conveniently left the two Black Americans who had won gold and bronze medals in the 400-meter sprint, Williams and LuValle, off of the U.S. team in favor of four white runners. Great Britain upset the United States in the 4×400-meter final, leaving the Americans with a disappointing silver medal in the race and depriving the "Black aux-iliaries" of two additional golden prizes. Whether or not anti-Semitism and anti-Black prejudice shaped the relay choices remains a contentious issue, but the failure to choose Williams and LuValle probably cost the United States first place in the 4×400-meter relay. Whether the inclusion of two Black men instead of two Jewish men on the 4×100-meter team offended Hitler more remains a mystery as well.

While some of the German populace marveled at the accomplishments of the African American athletes, the Third Reich's propaganda machine derided them as "Black auxiliaries," a supplementary racial force whom the United States merely employed to win a few medals. That term, used not only by the Nazis but also a variety of other European commentators, represented a double-edged condemnation that not only stereotyped Black athletes but also censured American versions of white supremacy that celebrated the use of Blacks to win Olympic medals and world wars while refusing to accord them equal citizenship. These European critiques of the "Black auxiliaries" fit into an enduring habit of European whining that the United States only won Olympic championships because they employed immigrant mercenaries—a broad term in these discourses that applied not only to European migrants but also to Americans of African descent and absurdly even to indigenous Americans such as 1936 marathoner Ellison "Tarzan" Brown, a member of the Narragansett tribe!

The "Black auxiliary" label denoted the fascist updating of this older trope condemning the racial composition of U.S. Olympic teams. American commentators in both the Black media and the white press responded by defending the multi-racial character of their team and proclaiming that the medals earned by Black Olympians signified a resounding American triumph over Hitler and his pernicious ideology. The American press swelled with stories about Hitler snubbing Owens and his African Ameri-can comrades. Actually, a more complicated reality undergirded Hitler's interactions with Olympic medalists. After the German chancellor con-gratulated a couple of German winners on the first day of the games, the IOC had chided Hitler for "politicizing" the Olympics and barred him from future public meetings with Olympian victors. Thus deprived by the IOC's mandate of that particular propaganda forum, Hitler never had to reveal whether he would have openly "snubbed" Owens and the rest of the "Black auxiliary." Initially, Owens himself made this point repeatedly in interviews with the press in Berlin. He later gave up trying to correct the media's nar-rative of the incident and turned Hitler's supposed rebuff into a standard feature of his retellings of his glory days in Berlin for decades thereafter.

THE "BLACK AUXILIARIES" AND THE RACIAL PARADOXES OF THE "NAZI OLYMPICS"

In Berlin, the Black Mercuries won more than half of the prizes that American men garnered in track and field. Their performances could not be ignored. A reporter in a Southern Black newspaper quipped that "if any of the vast throngs who filled this huge stadium left the individual track and field championships believing that Uncle Sam was a mulatto instead of a Nordic blonde on the face of performances they would have been justified."[32] Indisputably, African American athletes in 1936 took center stage at the world's biggest sporting spectacle. What their triumphs meant, however, to understandings of race both in the United States and around the world proved to be a complex and contradictory issue.

In Germany, the "Black auxiliary" were lionized as tremendous champions while simultaneously animalized as a subhuman species. Unable to portray them as completely inferior after their Olympian exploits, many Germans celebrated them as glorious but primitive physical specimens, atavistic throwbacks to the more advanced Aryan and Nordic races. German filmmaker Leni Riefenstahl's cinematic masterpiece of the "Nazi Olympics," *Olympia* (1938) showcases this schismatic representation, framing adoring portraits of Black athletic bodies interspersed with triumphal scenes of Aryan supremacy. Other European commentaries on the Black Mercuries manifested a similar schizophrenia, particularly in nations such as Great Britain and France that condemned Nazi racial ideology but nurtured their own colonial traditions espousing European racial supremacy.

Discordant interpretations erupted in the United States as well. Cromwell, the controversial coach involved in replacing Black and Jewish runners on U.S. Olympic relay teams with white Californians, clumsily explained the prowess of the Black Mercuries in pseudo-scientific terminology that differed little from Nazi interpretations. "I'll offer the opinion that the Negro athlete excels because he is closer to the primitive than the white athlete," Cromwell dithered in his famous textbook on track and field.[33] Some American scientists concurred with Cromwell's evolutionary notions. Dr. Charles Snyder, a physiologist at Johns Hopkins University, offered pseudo-scientific calculations that countered the common perceptions that Black athletes dominated the Berlin Olympics. Snyder scoffed that "when Owens was winning his wonderful races a great cry went up in the American press proclaiming that once and for all the myth of superiority of one race over another had been smashed." Recalibrating the data on a medals-per-capita basis, Snyder asserted that the racial egalitarians read the results incorrectly and that the "'great northern races'" of Europe were overwhelmingly the world's superior athletes. Predictably, Snyder utilized his findings to fulminate for restrictions against immigration from non-Nordic nations, prohibitions against interracial marriage, and a variety of other measures supported by eugenicists in the United States and in Nazi Germany.[34]

The fact that the Third Reich had upset the United States in the overall Olympic medal count fueled the chorus of white supremacist analyses from Snyder and other pseudo-scientists. A cadre of American commentators pushed back against the white supremacist claims, understanding that race is a social and not a biologic construct and arguing that the performances of the "Black auxiliaries" affirmed that American racial pluralism enhanced their nation's power and contributed to the cause of equality. Dr. William Montague Cobb, an African American scientist and a major figure in scientific debates about race, countered the pseudo-science of evolutionary racial heredity as the causal agent in African American success in particular events such as sprints and jumps. Cobb pointed out that John Woodruff's triumph in the 800-meter race—then considered an "endurance" event that favored participants of European descent—proved that social opportunity rather than racial heredity accounted for racial disparities in sport. Olympic trainer Billy Morris, himself a former 800-meter runner, argued that the theories that Black athletes were somehow biologically adapted for sprints and jumps would soon be disproven as Black athletes followed Woodruff into mastering longer distances.

Cobb and Morris subscribed to the widely held American faith that sport at its best showcased racial equality rather than racial inequality. A broad spectrum of Americans embraced that vision as they celebrated the triumphant return of the Black Mercuries from Berlin. At the traditional ticker-tape parade in New York City hailing the returning American Olympians, Mayor Fiorello La Guardia singled out the Black Olympians, proclaiming, "We are all Americans here; we have no auxiliaries in this country."[35]

Both the Black media and the white press swelled with similar sentiments. Many Americans from all races and backgrounds cheered Owens and his teammates as Black avatars who shattered pernicious racial stereotypes. An editorial in Owens' hometown Black newspaper, the *Cleveland Call and Post*, captured those visions. "'America's Negro Auxiliary' was part and parcel of the American team," the editors insisted. "They were the best answer the world could give to Hitler and his Aryan superiority stuff." The Black Mercuries proved to the world that "color plays no part in a man's ability to do any given thing," the *Call and Post* team proclaimed. "We only hope that the South will profit thereby."[36]

Jesse Owens (center) soars at the 1936 Olympic long-jump competition. Owens won one of his four gold medals in Berlin in the event. *Photograph of Jesse Owens in the long jump at the 1936 Berlin Olympics, 242-HD-125a3, National Archives Collection of Foreign Records Seized, 1675–1958, Series:Summer Olympic Games, Berlin, 8/1936–8/1936, Record Group 242, National Archives and Records Administration II, College Park, Maryland.*

The Cleveland newspaper's leaders nailed the central paradox of the racial contradictions that sprang from African American triumphs in Berlin. In shattering the "logic" of Nazi racism, the "Black auxiliary" simultaneously shined light on American racism. Their feats showcased the depth of segregation inside their own nation in which American Olympic officials had to stage separate Southern tryouts for Black athletes or offer them a free pass to the next round of trials when a qualifying meet in the nation's capital refused to let them compete because of the color of their skin. Nailing that paradox did not resolve what came to be known soon thereafter as the "American dilemma"—the malignant racial relations that excluded Blacks from the promises of American civilization. Though some observers anticipated that the "Black auxiliary" would soften the hearts and minds of even ardent Southern segregationists, systemic oppression of Black citizens did not melt away in "Dixie" in the immediate aftermath of their triumphs. Color lines remained firmly ensconced beyond the South as well, as Owens himself discovered when he returned to the United States and was forced to take the freight elevator rather than walking through the main lobby on his way to a banquet honoring his Olympian feats at New York City's Waldorf Astoria hotel.

In the short run, the brilliance of the "Black auxiliary" in Berlin generated attention about color lines and racial stereotypes but did not instantaneously eradicate racism or dissolve segregation. Ardent proponents of pseudo-scientific doctrines of white supremacy sought to explain away Black Olympic victories while dedicated champions of civil rights used their medals to further their cause. Many Americans cheered the Black Mercuries' defeat of Hitler and the Nazis while ignoring the realities of racial discrimination in their own homeland. Even some Black leaders expressed frustration that white America paid more attention to Black athletic accomplishments than to Black achievements in academia, innovation, entrepreneurship, and the arts, though they reconciled themselves with the recognition that sports captured the attention of the white masses. "For these millions, who hold the solution of the race problem in their hands, the beautiful breasting of a tape by Jesse Owens . . . carr[ies] more 'interracial education' than all the erudite philosophy ever written on race," testified the editors of *The Crisis*, the journal of the NAACP.[37] An influential Black Southern leader of "interracial education" through sport concurred, heralding the Black Olympians as the foremost "ambassadors of good will and racial understanding" in the nation.[38]

In the longer run, Black Olympians from the era served their nation as "ambassadors of good will and racial understanding" in the lengthy processes of "interracial education" that fed the enduring struggle for civil rights that continues to this day. Owens, as Tolan had in 1932, hoped to translate his Olympic fame into lucrative career opportunities as white athletes did. Though initially a bit more successful in cashing in than Tolan, Owens still found his financial horizons limited by racial barriers. He endured tours on the Black vaudeville circuit with Bill "Bojangles" Robinson and barnstorming appearances that featured demeaning races against horses. Eventually, however, as a perpetual symbol of American Olympic excellence, he translated his renown in both the Black and white communities into a well-compensated career in public relations for government agencies and corporate entities, including a stint after World War II as the foremost American Olympic goodwill ambassador in Cold War propaganda skirmishes with the Soviet Union.

Many of his fellow "Black auxiliaries" also built enduring careers beyond Olympic arenas. David Albritton and Fritz Pollard Jr. served alongside Owens in the diplomatic corps as Cold War goodwill ambassadors. Albritton was also a successful politician and was elected to the Ohio state legislature. Pollard was also a municipal recreation leader and an educator in his hometown of Chicago. Cornelius Johnson joined the U.S. Merchant Marine but tragically died young at thirty-two after contracting pneumonia on a voyage. Archie Williams and John Woodruff helped to desegregate the U.S. military. Williams served as a Tuskegee Airman during World War II and then built an Air Force career, retiring as a lieutenant colonel—one of the highest-ranking Black officers in the military during this era. Woodruff joined the U.S. Army and served in World War II and the Korean conflict, retiring as a captain and then enjoying a long career as an urban social worker. Mack Robinson struggled in the immediate aftermath of the Berlin games but eventually became a community activist and civil rights leader in Southern California. James LuValle became an academic star, earning a doctorate in chemistry from Cal Tech and becoming renowned researcher and professor. Ralph Metcalfe, second by an eyelash in the race for recognition as the world's fastest human to Tolan in 1932 and Owens in 1936, became an educator, coach, and urban recreation leader. He returned to his hometown of Chicago and entered into local politics. In 1970 he was elected to the first of his four terms representing Chicago's Southside in the U.S. House of Representatives where he became a co-founder of the Congressional Black Caucus.

FROM THE ORIGINAL BLACK MERCURIES TO THE "BLACK AUXILIARIES"

The 1936 Black Olympians, like their forebearers who had competed in the games since 1904, were children of the Great Migration who overcame a myriad of color barriers to make Olympic teams. They consistently overperformed, on the basis of their small numbers, in garnering medals for their nation. In their journeys to the Olympics, they learned how to navigate white as well as Black institutions. Most of them earned degrees from prestigious white universities. They returned from the Olympics and built careers that served Black communities, working as leaders in municipal sports programs, as teachers, as social workers, as lawyers, and as entrepreneurs.

They won appointments to the judiciary and votes to elected office at the local, state, and national levels. They led the desegregation of schools and military units, playgrounds and government agencies, courtrooms and legislatures.

Black Olympians served from their debut in 1904 through the 1936 Olympics as "ambassadors of good will and racial understanding." They would remain as emissaries of "interracial education" long after they starred in Olympic arenas, as a second global war disrupted the Olympic calendar and cancelled the 1940 and 1944 games. From Billy Morris to Jesse Owens, they continued to serve as envoys of the African American experience at the Olympics.

And, from the beginning, Morris was there. Though he never had the opportunity to compete as an athlete, he should be remembered as the original African American Olympian for training and championing both Black and white athletes from the early 1900s until 1948, when he finally retired from the University of Pennsylvania. From his posts on the Olympic team and at the athletic colossus at Penn, Morris witnessed the first five decades of modern Olympic history. He beheld the emergence of the first three generations of Black Mercuries from their beginnings to their blossoming in the pressure cooker of the "Nazi Olympics."

In an interview with the nation's oldest Black newspaper, the *Philadelphia Tribune*, shortly after he returned from Berlin, Morris delivered his historic perspective on the emergence of America's Black Mercuries. He asserted that the expanding opportunities to participate in sports offered by the Great Migration in concert with the calling to demonstrate to white Americans that their fellow Black citizens were their equals had produced several generations of Black champions. Black athletes developed a powerful spirit of perseverance from their lifetimes of proving their mettle to white America, Morris contended. Black athletes "know the breaks are against them and they steel themselves to surmount these obstacles and go on to victory," the reporter related that Morris had explained to him. "With this spiritual situation, if it may be called that, they often surpass themselves," the reporter concluded regarding Morris' explanation for the startling number of Black triumphs at the Olympics.[39] Surpassing themselves—exceeding both circumstances and expectations—served as a fitting summary of the first half century of Black American achievement at the Olympics.

4

BLACK MERCURIES AND THE DAWNING OF THE COLD WAR

Eddie Tolan and Ralph Metcalfe, the duo who took the top two spots on the medal podium in both the 100- and 200-meter sprints at the 1932 Olympics in Los Angeles, became heroes and role models for African Americans everywhere in the United States. In fact, one witness to their memorable photo-finish in the 100-meters on August 1 that year was a seven-year-old boy who would go on to Olympic greatness of his own. Malvin "Mal" Whitfield sneaked into the stadium with a group of his friends. They watched transfixed as Tolan and Metcalfe streaked to their gold/silver finish. Whitfield was mesmerized, and as he recalled later, from that moment he "knew [he] wanted to run in the Olympics."[1] Thus, unbeknownst to anyone at the time, Tolan and Metcalfe passed the torch from one generation of Olympians to the next.

Whitfield went on to become one of the most decorated—and celebrated—Olympians of the postwar era. He competed in three events in both the 1948 London Olympics and the 1952 Helsinki Olympics, winning five medals. At both Olympics, he won gold in the 800-meters, clocking exactly the same time at both games. In the ensuing decades, his work with other athletes and his sensitivity to the mounting Civil Rights struggle in the United States and abroad meant that Whitfield was never absent from the Olympic scene. As a contemporary of Jackie Robinson, he joined a generation of Black athletic barrier-breakers. In the trying decades of the 1950s and 1960s, he lent his voice to the Black athletic struggle for equality and was among the first to advocate for a boycott by Black Americans of the 1964 Tokyo Olympics, a call-to-arms that grew far more prominent with the next Olympics in 1968 in Mexico City. While he was but one of hundreds of Black Americans to compete in the Olympics in the Cold War era, perhaps no single athlete better encapsulates that period better than Mal Whitfield.

SPORTS, RACE, AND THE COLD WAR

Historians have made clear that the Cold War rivalry between the United States and the Soviet Union transcended politics and war and came to include all aspects of life, including sport. International competitions at every level took on heightened significance, as victory on the playing field came to represent broader physical, cultural, and even military superiority. American athletes squared off against Soviet and Eastern-bloc athletes in a dizzying array of exhibitions, international tours, regional meets or competitions, and international championships. Athletic competition became a metaphor for the Cold War itself, with none more significant than the Olympics.

At the same time, the heightened emphasis on sports competitions also had ramifications on the home front. Who would be allowed to participate in various sports, and under what conditions? What should our athletes do and say? How should they behave? And how should our most prominent athletes be deployed by sporting and government agencies in this international clash? Should the American government play a greater role in influencing, even dictating, how sports events, teams, and leagues were organized and run? American sporting officials and even politicians debated these and other questions often. For a nation determined to win over the "hearts and minds" of nations at the periphery of the Cold War all over the world, the depiction of happy and successful Black and female athletes became an important element of American sports diplomacy over the first few decades of the Cold War. Olympic medals were gold, silver, and bronze—not black and white—and American officials proved willing to compromise on long-standing limitations based on race or gender when America's international reputation was at stake. Thus, in the realm of Olympic sport from 1948 to 1960, a number of Black athletes, both male and female, came to be viewed as American heroes and heroines.

Even as Black Olympians achieved new heights of prominence, their position as American "heroes" proved problematic. Many Black Olympians, after enjoying the extravagances of international travel and life abroad, returned home to poverty and neglect. After competing in a realm where their exploits were objectively measured in times and distances, a realm in which they frequently were the best in the world, they came home to a segregated nation, where even a gold medalist had to ride in the back of the bus. Such stark realities posed difficult challenges for Black athletes, most of whom began their long climb to athletic greatness with little thought of how the nation and the world would view them. Sports offered an outlet for excitement, the rush of competition and victory, and for some an escape from more debilitating activities such as violence or crime. As they became Olympians, however, they were asked to wear the red, white, and blue, to carry and wave the American flag, and at times to give speeches and interviews declaring love for their country. They became "diplomats," whether formally or informally, and in the 1940s and 1950s questioning the "American way of life" was not an option for such athletes. Only later, in the growing tumult of the 1960s, could Black athletes find an outlet for protest and challenging the status quo.

"MARVELOUS MAL" WHITFIELD

The extraordinary life and athletic career of Mal Whitfield offers an ideal figure to examine when considering Black athletes in this era. Like so many other transcendent individuals, Whitfield's childhood and formative years left him uniquely suited to the roles he would later play. Born of mixed race in Texas in 1924, he was raised by his older sister in Los Angeles after both his parents died when he was young. There, he attended Thomas Jefferson High School, where he mingled freely with children of all races and backgrounds. Whitfield graduated from high school in 1943 at the height of World War II. Drafted into the armed forces, Whitfield launched a decorated military career spanning nearly ten years. He was a Tuskegee Airman during World War II and later served as a tail-gunner on twenty-seven missions during the Korean War from 1950 to 1952. From 1944 to 1950, interspersed with his military service, Whitfield also attended Ohio State University, inspired and encouraged to attend the school by its most famous track star, Jesse Owens. He became one of the top collegiate track men in the country, among the best in the 400- and 800-meters.

Whitfield headed a strong American track and field team at the 1948 London Olympics. In his strongest event, the 800-meters, he won the gold medal and set a new Olympic record of 1:49.2. He added a bronze medal in the 400-meters and ran as part of the gold-medal winning 4×400-meter relay team. Four years later, at the Helsinki Olympics in 1952, Whitfield gave a repeat performance in the 800-meters, winning gold with exactly the same time as he posted in 1948 and added a silver medal in the 4×400-meter relay.

As impressive as his Olympic achievements were, Whitfield's greatest years may well have been 1953 and 1954, between the Helsinki and Melbourne Olympics. During that period, Whitfield broke and re-broke world records in his signature race, the 800-meters, becoming a mainstay in sports pages around the country and the world. This string of record-breaking performances, along with the fact that he was "held in high regard by contestants in this country and abroad, as well as popular with fellow athletes and officials and most cooperative in assisting youngsters who request information on training," led to his recognition as the winner of the Sullivan Award in 1954.[2] He was the first African American to win this prestigious

Dean Cromwell (far left), head track coach of the University of Southern California and 1948 United States Olympic team, watches four of his top sprinters limber up on a deck of the liner *America* during the voyage to the games in England. The sprinters, from left: Mal Whitfield, Barney Ewell, Harrison Dillard, and Mel Patton. A highly successful coach known as the "maker of champions," Cromwell became controversial for his views on the reasons for Black athletic success. *Courtesy of Associated Press.*

award, given by the Amateur Athletic Union to America's top amateur athlete each year.

Throughout these years, and for decades after, the State Department
called upon Whitfield frequently to represent the United States abroad.
For State Department officials, Whitfield represented the idealized racial
vision they sought to portray abroad. Here was not only an athletic champion but also a decorated veteran of two wars. Furthermore, Whitfield, with
his background in the military and his time at Ohio State, not only demonstrated the restraint and discipline to follow orders but also was accustomed
to working in an integrated environment and under white leadership. As
described by one official, "Whitfield was in every way an outstanding representative of America."[3]

THE 1948 OLYMPICS AND A NEW
GENERATION OF BLACK MERCURIES

Mal Whitfield was but one of many African American athletes to excel in
London. A number of stars, including triple-medalist Barney Ewell and
double-medalist Harrison Dillard, joined Whitfield on the track squad. Dillard, raised in the same neighborhood of Cleveland as Jesse Owens, grew to
become one of the greatest sprinters and hurdlers of his generation. Like so
many others, his exploits on the track were interrupted by years of service
during World War II, where he saw intense action in Italy as one of the so-
called Buffalo Soldiers of the 92nd Infantry. During the war, he caught the
attention of Gen. George S. Patton, who after seeing Dillard run in an Army
competition called him "the greatest goddamn athlete I've ever seen."[4]
Dillard prevailed in the 100-meter sprint, winning the gold medal, nipping
his Black teammate Ewell at the line in the first photo-finish in Olympic
history. Ewell took the silver, and both men drove the squad taking gold in
the 4×100-meter relay. Ewell, from Pennsylvania, added a second silver in
the 200-meter sprint.

Joining Ewell and Dillard on the men's track team in London were three
other Black athletes, who took gold, bronze, and fourth place in the long
jump: Willie Steele, Herb Douglas, and Lorenzo Wright. Steele, raised in
San Diego, enjoyed a steady progression up the ranks of the nation's top
long jumpers between 1941 and 1948, interrupted by three years of decorated service in the military. In London, Steele suffered an ankle injury
and was limited to only two jumps in the long jump final, though both
jumps were long enough to secure the gold. Douglas finished third in that

competition. Raised in Pittsburgh, he represents yet another Black athlete who drew inspiration from an earlier star, in this case Ralph Metcalfe, who recruited Douglas to come south and run for Xavier University in New Orleans. There, Douglas anchored an outstanding squad, becoming the first team from a Historically Black College or University to win the 440-yard relay at the Penn Relays, among the most prestigious collegiate competitions. In London, Douglas finished third in the long jump, just five inches behind Steele's gold medal–winning mark. Lorenzo Wright of Detroit finished fourth in the long jump competition and also ran as a member of the gold medal–winning 4×100-meter relay team.

The excellence of America's Black athletes was not limited to track and field. Three African Americans competed in boxing. Horace Herring, of St. Petersburg, Florida, won a silver medal in the welterweight division. Norvel Lee of Eagle Rock, Virginia, competed in the light heavyweight division but did not medal. Cincinnati's Wallace Smith failed to medal in the lightweight division but later went on to become world champion.

In weight lifting, the London Olympics finally provided an opportunity for John Henry Davis, one of the greatest strongmen the world has ever known, to demonstrate his dominance on a global stage. Davis was undefeated in major competitions from 1938 to 1953, meaning he had already been at the top of the sport for a decade before his first Olympic appearance. Raised in Brooklyn, New York, Davis played football and competed in gymnastics and track in high school, in an era when strength training as an independent discipline was still evolving. Eventually, the legendary equipment and weight lifting magnate Bob Hoffman, owner of the York Barbell Company in York, Pennsylvania, caught wind of the schoolboy who could lift 125-pound concrete blocks with ease. Hoffman invited Davis to his lifting school in Philadelphia, and after less than a year of training Davis competed in his first national championships in 1938, at age seventeen. There, he broke world records in the press and total weight lifted. The following year, Europe descended into war, and international competitions were almost completely absent for the next seven years, as the young Davis grew into the most dominant lifter in the world.

From 1942 to 1945, Davis served in the U.S. Army in the Pacific, where he was able to train only sporadically and eventually lost more than forty-five pounds in the harsh living conditions. Though he contemplated retirement, Davis returned to lifting after his wartime service and—despite the toll of those years—within a year was again winning titles and breaking records. By 1948, Davis was again undisputedly the best in the world, and he won the gold medal in the heavyweight division at the London Olympics with relative ease. The only question about Davis' 1948 victory was that his strongest rivals were not at the Games: the Soviets. Rumors swirled about Soviet strongmen and their feats, notably Jakov Kutsenko, who claimed to be besting Davis' lifts in training. As the two began to face off in international competitions following the war, though, Kutsenko never measured up to Davis. At the 1950 World Championships, the two engaged in a captivating duel, with Davis ultimately lifting nearly 100 pounds more than his Soviet rival. Not only was Davis now regarded as the greatest lifter in the world; he was becoming an important symbol of American strength in the deepening Cold War.

DON BARKSDALE: BREAKING THE COLOR BARRIER ON THE HARDWOOD

Just one year after Jackie Robinson took the field for the Brooklyn Dodgers, breaking Major League Baseball's color barrier, Don Barksdale took the court for the U.S. national basketball team at the London Olympics, becoming the first African American to do so. In 1939, as a high schooler, Barksdale had a chance to meet Robinson, who at the time was a four-sport star at UCLA. Robinson so impressed Barksdale that the high schooler vowed that day to attend UCLA if he ever got the chance, a promise he fulfilled several years later. Barksdale began his collegiate career at Marin (CA) Community College, transferred to UCLA and played part of the 1942–1943 season before enlisting for service in World War II. After completing his wartime service, he returned to UCLA in 1945 and finished out his collegiate career.

Following his career at UCLA, Barksdale found a home in the Amateur Athletic Union (AAU) American Basketball League, joining the Oakland Bittners. He led the league in scoring in the 1947 to 1948 season and broke several racial barriers as his team traveled to different venues. This experience served him well, as Barksdale was soon to be breaking such barriers on the U.S. Olympic basketball team. Olympic basketball itself was still relatively new, having debuted as a medal sport in 1936, with an all-white U.S. team easily winning the gold medal. The process of selecting a team was still being perfected, and Barksdale navigated a confusing series of games and practices in hopes of making the team. After intense deliberation, coaches and U.S. basketball officials eventually selected Barksdale, making him the first Black player on a U.S. Olympic basketball team.

After a four-game exhibition tour through Scotland, the team began tournament play with relatively easy wins in each of its five preliminary round games. Barksdale played well and saw extensive action outside of the first game, when he did not play. Barksdale played a prominent role in the gold medal game against France, scoring a solid eight points. Overall, Barksdale was the team's third-leading scorer in the tournament, and a significant contributor in rebounding and other elements of the game. He was arguably the best all-around player on the team.

Like many Black Olympic athletes, Barksdale returned from his Olympic experience to a segregated America offering little opportunity. He returned to his role with the Oakland Bittners for three more years, while working as a beer distributor. In 1951, he accepted an offer to join the National Basketball Association (NBA), the fourth Black player in the league. In 1953, he was named the first Black all-star in the league's history. He played in the league for five years at a high level, but his place in the NBA record books might be much more noteworthy had he not lost several years of his prime to his wartime service and the segregation enforced by the league.

TIGERETTES AND TIGERBELLES: THE ASCENT OF AMERICA'S BLACK FEMALE OLYMPIANS

The heightened emphasis on sporting success in the early Cold War years after World War II presented new challenges—and opportunities—for Black female athletes, whose Olympic experience thus far had been limited to the frustrating appearances of "Tidye" Pickett and Louise Stokes in 1932 and 1936. This group of athletes enjoyed their newfound prominence in the upper echelon of athletics but also faced heightened scrutiny of their suitability as feminine and domestic role models. In some cases, Black women—even those achieving great success on the field or the track—were criticized for their muscular physiques or "unfeminine" behavior. Moreover, Black women confronted the challenge of double prejudice, marginalized for both their race and for their gender. They were expected to represent their country with pride and joy, while at once recognizing that the nation they represented did little to protect their rights, safety, and well-being at home.

Black women in the postwar years also found an opportunity to participate, and excel, in a sport that white women had largely vacated: track and field. As historian Jennifer H. Lansbury has explained, "As a result of . . . concerted opposition and public negative attention, women's track experienced a significant reversal in popularity in the U.S. during the 1930s."[5] As white women increasingly withdrew from track and field, Black women found an opportunity to compete, and succeed. Two Black women qualified for the Olympics in the 1930s, both after training in the north. In the decade after the 1936 Olympics, as the next two Games were cancelled during World War II, women's track and field flourished in the Black community, spearheaded by a number of Historically Black Colleges in the South, most notably Tuskegee Institute and later Tennessee State University.

Even as the voices against women's sport prevailed in the 1930s, there remained staunch advocates who promoted physical activity. Among them was Tuskegee Institute athletic director Cleveland Abbott, who initiated the track and field program at Tuskegee in the mid-1930s and quickly began attracting some of the nation's top athletes. The Tigerettes, as they were known, competed in the AAU national championships in 1936 for the first time, placing second. Starting the following year, the Tigerettes won both the indoor and outdoor national championships every year until 1951, save for a second-place finish in 1943. By the early 1940s, Abbott had established a track and field powerhouse at Tuskegee.

By the time the Olympics resumed in 1948, the greatest Tigerette of them all was ready to seize her opportunity, Alice Coachman. Coachman was born in Albany, Georgia, and raised in the Jim Crow South. With no access to traditional training facilities, Coachman was self-taught and self-motivated, practicing in her backyard and jumping over "bars" she fashioned for herself, cobbled together with sticks and rags. Her rough talents finally benefited from proper coaching when she joined the Madison High School track team, and her self-taught high-jump technique was refined to the form that led her to break record after record for the next decade.

As a fifteen-year-old in 1939, Coachman cleared 5'4" at the Tuskegee Relays, a jump so impressive it attracted the attention of the Tuskegee Athletic Director Abbott, who convinced Coachman to transfer to Tuskegee High School. At Tuskegee High School and later at the Tuskegee Institute, Coachman and the other young women received coaching in athletics, beauty, manners, and life skills. In so doing, Coachman grew well-equipped to become the standard-bearer not only for Black female athletic excellence but also an unprecedented role as a Black woman representing a positive expression of American womanhood and femininity. As sportswriter Sam Lacy affirmed in 1944, "[Coachman is] definitely effeminate. [She's] got charm, personality, and dimples, and she cuts a nice figure—running, walking, or standing."[6]

In London, Coachman engaged in a gripping duel in the high jump with Great Britain's Dorothy Tyler, who exchanged a series of jumps after all the other competitors had failed. Both cleared 5'6⅛" before failing at 5'7". Coachman was awarded the gold medal via the tiebreaker for fewest total misses during the competition. Joining Coachman on the U.S. track team in the 1948 London Olympics were eight other African American women. Mickey Patterson became the first African American woman to medal in the Olympics when she took the bronze in the 200-meter sprint. Theresa Manuel, the first African American woman to compete in the javelin, also participated in the 80-meter hurdles and the 440 relay. Others on the team included two other high jumpers who did not medal, Bernice Robinson and Emma Reed, and the sprinters Mabel Walker, Lillian Young, Nell Jackson, and Mae Faggs.

Coachman's victory not only advanced America's medal count in London, but also played a role in challenging racial boundaries on the home front as well. When Coachman returned home to Albany, Georgia, the town held a parade and ceremony in her honor, and while the seating was segregated, both white and Black Georgians cheered their hometown hero. The *Chicago Defender* found hope in the ceremony, effusing, "Here was evidence that good impulses were at work and that there was a spark of decency in the leadership. They were afraid to stand up and be true Americans, true lovers of democracy, true Christians but they gave us some reasons to believe the day is going to come when the color line is going to lose its magic in Dixie."[7] Coachman also joined a group of seven Black Olympians to visit the White House. With his crucial reelection vote looming only a few months away and Civil Rights a major plank on his campaign platform, President Harry Truman invited six Black female athletes and double-medalist Harrison Dillard to the White House in October of 1948. As historian Cat Ariail argues, "Coachman and her fellow Black track women served as safe symbols; they showed the president's support for expanding the rights of citizenship to Black Americans without overtly offending white Americans."[8]

THE BLACK MERCURIES ASCENDANT IN HELSINKI

The 1952 Olympics in Helsinki, Finland, were symbolic of a world moving past the events of World War II and into the new era of the Cold War. Helsinki had for a brief time prepared to host the 1940 Olympics, but they were cancelled due to the war. The IOC voted in 1947 to award the 1952 Olympics to Helsinki to atone for the games lost to the war, and in light of the preparations already made to host those games. In another effort to move beyond the Second World War, the IOC invited athletes from Germany and Japan to participate. At the same time, Cold War issues saturated these games, none more important than the decision to invite the athletes of the Soviet Union to participate, which the IOC voted to do in May 1951. The Soviets, despite Western claims that their policies violated Olympic rules of amateurism, wholeheartedly embraced the pursuit of Olympic medals, beginning a fierce rivalry with the United States that persisted throughout the Cold War.

A group of outstanding Black athletes again anchored the American track and field team at the 1952 Olympics in Helsinki, Finland, perhaps none greater than Plainfield, New Jersey's Milt Campbell. It is fair to call Campbell a prodigy; as a youth he excelled in every sport he tried, including football, shot put, hurdles, and even a one-match experiment in wrestling. Campbell was also an outstanding high school swimmer, winning a state championship as part of his school's 200-meter freestyle relay team. So prodigious was Campbell's talent that his high school track coach secured funding to enter him in the 1952 Olympic trials in the decathlon, even though Campbell had never competed in six of the ten events! Amazingly, Campbell finished second in the trials, behind only Bob Mathias, the reigning "world's greatest athlete" and defending decathlon gold-medal winner. With expectations low for the eighteen-year-old schoolboy athlete, Campbell put in one of the most surprising performances of the Helsinki Olympics, winning the silver medal behind only Mathias after training in the ten events for less than a year.

Campbell was only one of many outstanding African American athletes to star at the Helsinki Olympics, including Mal Whitfield, who repeated his gold medal performance in the 800-meters and added a silver in the 4×400-meter relay. Harrison Dillard also returned for his second Olympics, this time as the top qualifier in his best event, the 110-meter hurdles. He took the gold, becoming the first and only athlete in Olympic history to reign as the "World's Fastest Man" and the "World's Fastest Hurdler" by winning both the 100-meter sprint (in London) and the 110-meter hurdles. Again, he also ran with the 4×100-meter relay team, adding a fourth gold medal to his Olympic total and matching his idol, Jesse Owens. Dillard continued breaking records in the years between the Helsinki and Melbourne Olympics, and in 1955 he won the Sullivan Award, the second African American so honored, after Mal Whitfield the previous year.

Americans swept the medals in the 200-meter sprint, led by Seton Hall's Andy Stanfield, one of America's top sprinters from 1948 to 1956. In peak form and the world record holder at that time, Stanfield set an Olympic record of 20.81 seconds, followed by Thane Baker and James Gathers, of Huston Tillotson HBCU in Austin, Texas. Another standout on the track was San Francisco's Ollie Matson, who won the bronze medal in the 400-meters and was part of America's silver medal-winning 4×400-meter relay squad. Matson is especially noteworthy for his long and illustrious football career after the Olympics. He starred in the NFL from 1952 to 1966 and was elected to the NFL Hall of Fame in 1972.

A triumvirate of African Americans starred in the men's long jump competition in Helsinki. Jerome Biffle, a multi-sport athlete at the University of Denver, won the gold medal. A high school football and track star, Biffle enjoyed an undefeated season in the long jump in 1950, earning him acclaim as one of America's finest amateur athletes. However, he was not the favorite in Helsinki. His teammate and fellow African American George Henry Brown from Los Angeles was the world's best long jumper from 1951 to 1953, including an unbeaten streak in 41 consecutive competitions. That streak was broken at the Olympic trials, however, when he finished third behind Biffle and Cornell University's Meredith Gourdine, who took first. In Helsinki, Brown struggled with wet conditions and fouled on all six of his attempts, failing to medal. Brown's struggles left Biffle and Gourdine to vie for the top spot in Helsinki, and the two exchanged impressive jumps right up to Biffle's final leap of 24'10", which bested Gourdine by an inch and a half.

The powerful U.S. boxing squad in Helsinki featured six Black boxers, five of whom won gold. The most prominent in the group was Floyd Patterson, who won gold in the middleweight division before going on to a celebrated twenty-year professional career. Patterson, born in North Carolina and raised in Brooklyn, overcame an adolescence spent engaged in petty crime on the streets to become a multi-sport athlete in high school. His route to the gold in Helsinki was relatively easy, and he won the final match with a first-round knockout. Following his amateur career, Patterson quickly rose through the professional ranks and twice won the heavyweight title.

Norvel Lee of Eagle Rock, Virginia, returned for his second Olympics and won the gold in the light-heavyweight division and was also awarded the Val Barker Trophy as the outstanding boxer at the Olympics. Lee was involved in a number of extraordinary exploits outside of the ring, foremost among them his service with the Tuskegee Airmen during World War II. He was also involved in a landmark Civil Rights case in his hometown of Eagle Rock, after refusing to move to a "Jim Crow" seat in a passenger train car in

1948. He appealed the case several times, eventually winning in a decision by the Virginia Supreme Court in 1949. Charles "Chuck" Adkins of Gary, Indiana won the gold medal in boxing's light-welterweight division. In the final he defeated Viktor Mednov of the Soviet Union on a 2–1 decision, the first Olympic boxing match between the United States and the Soviet Union. Nathan Brooks of Cleveland won the gold in the flyweight division, defeating Edgar Basel of West Germany in the final on a 3–0 decision.

Two boxers from this team, sadly, are noteworthy for their tragic ring-related deaths. Hayes Edward "Big Ed" Sanders, a Navy seaman from Los Angeles, won the gold medal in the heavyweight division after a bizarre gold-medal match in which his opponent, Ingemar Johansson of Norway, was disqualified for failing to engage after dodging Sanders for most of three rounds. After the Olympics, desperate to provide for his family and to satiate the eager boxing world, Sanders took on eight fights in less than nine months. His ninth bout was his last, when on December 11, 1954, his former sparring partner Willie James pummeled Sanders into unconsciousness. "Big Ed" was carried from the ring on a stretcher; emergency surgery to relieve the pressure on his brain was unsuccessful. He died in the operating room.

The sixth African American member of the team, Davey Moore, lost in the quarterfinals of the bantamweight competition and thus failed to medal. He became a household name in the years after the Olympics, first by virtue of a ten-year professional career that included a run as the world featherweight champion. It is Moore's death, however, that cemented his legendary status. Following a 1963 bout with Cuban boxer Sugar Ramos, in which he endured a vicious beating, Moore fell into a coma from which he never recovered. Bob Dylan penned a song in his honor that was a favorite among the folk singers of the day.

Despite a string of injuries, and perhaps showing signs of the debilitating effects of his wartime service, John Henry Davis repeated his gold-medal performance in the heavyweight powerlifting competition at the 1952 Helsinki Olympics. So profound had his dominance grown that the Soviets declined to enter an athlete in the heavyweight division, effectively conceding Davis the gold. Davis' exploits had now garnered truly national attention. He was featured in a story in the popular weekly *Reader's Digest* and was the subject of a fifteen-minute documentary produced by journalist Bud Greenspan, called *The Strongest Man in the World*. The United States Information Agency eventually purchased the film and circulated it around the world as part of a global campaign to counteract Soviet propaganda that depicted the United States as a racist society. Having realized few financial rewards as a celebrated amateur athlete, he "retired" to a long career as a prison guard, passing away from cancer in 1984 at age sixty-three. Finishing second behind Davis was James E. Bradford, a soft-spoken librarian from Washington, D.C. Bradford had the misfortune of spending most of his decade-long weightlifting career competing against some of the greatest lifters ever, notably Davis.

THE TIGERBELLES AND AMERICA'S BLACK FEMALE ATHLETES IN HELSINKI

The crucible of international competition inspired America's Black female athletes to develop an informal support network—mentoring, encouraging, and competing—with more experienced athletes aiding the younger ones with each successive Olympics. Beginning in 1948 with Alice Coachman and proceeding through numerous athletes highlighted by Mae Faggs, Wilma Rudolph, and Wyomia Tyus, they created a pipeline that historian Cat Ariail has dubbed "Passing the Baton."[9] This process of mentorship benefited greatly from the concentration of top athletes at a handful of schools, starting at Tuskegee Institutes and shifting to Tennessee State University (TSU). There, under the tutelage of track coach Ed Temple, the famous "Tigerbelles" became the dominant force in international women's track for some two decades, from the early 1950s through the early 1970s. The TSU squad became so strong that America's top female track stars often confronted stronger competition every day in practice than they faced in any international meet, including the Olympics.

With her medal-winning performance in London, Coachman ascended to first in this line of great Black women athletes. Joining Coachman in London was Mae Faggs, who at age sixteen was just beginning a long and stellar career, which would include medal-winning performances at the next two Olympics. Faggs was raised under difficult conditions in Newark, New Jersey. Like Coachman, with no access to formalized training in her youth, she simply ran on her own or challenged the boys in her neighborhood to races. Eventually, a patrolman scouting in her school for the Police Athletic League noticed the young girl beating all the boys, so he recruited her to race in the league. After just a few years of organized training, Faggs demonstrated abilities so transcendent that her coach, Sergeant John Brennan, began grooming her in the summer of 1947 for the 1948 Olympics, when Faggs was just fifteen. Against long odds, Faggs finished third in the Olympic trials the following summer, behind fellow Black women Audrey

Patterson from Tennessee State and Nell Jackson from Tuskegee, and with a time fast enough to qualify for the Olympics. In that first Olympics, Faggs failed to qualify for the finals, finishing third in her qualifying heat.

Despite missing out on a medal, Faggs drew much from that first Olympic experience. First, the influence of Coachman and the other athletes was profound. "The first person that I think left an indelible impression on me was Alice Coachman," Faggs later said. "Alice was my roommate when we went to Paris on a tour. . . . She was a lady but she persevered and she competed. I liked her very much."[10] Second, for Faggs, traveling to London and other countries opened her eyes to the limitations of life for Black Americans. "It was difficult to come back to being poor after the Olympics," Faggs said. "We stayed at this mansion house, quite different from home. . . . Then I came home and I was a poor, Black person again."[11]

After that initial Olympic experience in 1948, Faggs returned to the United States and quickly became the dominant female runner in the country. Within a few months of the Olympics, she had beaten Audrey Patterson and Nell Jackson, who had bested her at the Olympic trials. Within a year, at the 1949 Indoor Nationals in New York City, she broke the world record at 220 yards and soon held world records in every distance from 60 meters to 220 yards. While Faggs envisioned dominating at the next Olympics—1952 in Helsinki—over the next few years she was overtaken by a basketball player-turned-sprinter, Catherine Hardy from Georgia. Hardy, a basketball star at Fort Valley State College, was encouraged to consider competing in track by her coach, Raymond Pitts. She began competing in 1949, just as Faggs was establishing national dominance and by 1951 was breaking records of her own. At the 1952 AAU National Championships, Hardy defeated Faggs in the 50-yard dash, and the 100- and 200-meter sprints. At the Olympic trials that year, Hardy took first over Faggs in the 200-meters, breaking the American record. Faggs returned the favor in the 100-meters. Thus, the pair was positioned to anchor a strong U.S. women's team in the Olympics, led once again by a cohort of Black athletes.

In Helsinki, both Faggs and Hardy were disappointed in their individual performances. Despite posting one of the fastest times of the Games in her opening heat, Hardy failed to advance past the quarterfinals in the 100-meters. Faggs reached the final but simply did not have the speed of the other competitors in that race, and she finished sixth. With the individual superiority of sprinters from Germany, Great Britain, and especially Australia thus established, it was a stunning upset when the American squad prevailed in the 4×100-meter relay in world-record time. The American team of Faggs, Hardy, Barbara Jones, and Janet Moreau bested the

Australian, German, and British teams on the way to the gold medal, as the favored Australians bobbled a baton exchange and dropped out of contention. In winning the coveted relay, the American sprinters overcame the disappointment of their earlier races.

Upon her return from Helsinki, Faggs was awarded a $100 gift from the Kiwanis Club, a small award with life-changing ramifications. Still embroiled in poverty, Faggs used the money to purchase a train ticket and a few supplies to get her to college at Tennessee State University. She had been recruited by new coach Ed Temple and chose Tennessee State over Tuskegee, because the trip from New Jersey was shorter, and she had concerns about moving into the Deep South of Alabama. Temple got his first star athlete, and the mighty "Tigerbelles" were born. As the only Olympic gold medalist on campus for those first few years, Faggs both basked in her role as the "big star" on campus and served as a mentor for the younger athletes, notably Wilma Rudolph.[12]

BLACK MERCURIES IN MELBOURNE: MEN'S TRACK AND FIELD

When the Olympics opened in Melbourne, Australia, four years later, the impact of the Cold War extended to every corner of the globe. While the athletic spotlight remained focused on the U.S.–Soviet rivalry, matters at the periphery of the Cold War took on heightened significance in Melbourne. The People's Republic of China boycotted the games because Taiwan participated; several nations boycotted because of the ongoing Suez Crisis in the Middle East; and several others boycotted in protest of the Soviet Union's invasion of Hungary. The last issue spilled over into the athletic competition, as perhaps the most memorable event of the Games was the notorious "Blood in the Water" water polo match between the Soviet and Hungarian teams, which grew so violent that it had to be canceled, with Hungary declared the winner as it held the lead when the match was ended.

In the United States, the Civil Rights struggle had taken center stage since the Helsinki Olympics, as evidenced by events such as the 1954 *Brown v. Board* decision, the lynching of Emmett Till in the summer of 1955, and the launching of the Montgomery Bus Boycott in December of 1955. The central role played by Rosa Parks in that event underscored the fact that Black women in America were prepared to demand equality more assertively than ever before. As all Black athletes learned in the late 1950s and 1960s, though, the line between being heralded as an American hero and being scorned as too audacious was a fine one. For the most part, Black athletes—with some exceptions—remained reluctant to engage in public activism, as their access to gainful employment still hinged largely on the sympathy and support of whites, who controlled the administration of athletics.

As they had in London and Helsinki, African Americans on the men's track and field team accomplished significant feats in Melbourne. Most notable was Milt Campbell, who improved on his silver medal finish in Helsinki, winning gold in the decathlon in Melbourne. After the 1952 Olympics, Campbell had returned home to complete his high school degree, was a multi-sport athlete at Indiana University for two years, then served two more years in the U.S. Navy in San Diego. All the while, he trained full-time for the decathlon, and his abilities peaked as the Melbourne Olympics neared. Unfortunately for Campbell, it appeared that he was once again fated to come second to one of the all-time great decathletes, this time Rafer Johnson, a basketball and track star at UCLA. Johnson had not yet reached the heights of greatness he would display in the Rome 1960 Olympics, but he had already broken the world decathlon record as a college freshman in 1954. Indeed, Johnson bested Campbell in the Olympic trials by nearly 200 points and was the clear favorite heading into Melbourne. Campbell mustered one of his best performances in Melbourne, though, and defeated Johnson while also setting an Olympic record with 7,937 points, and the two stood 1–2 on the medal podium.

The men's 4×100m relay team featured two African American runners, Leamon King and Ira Murchison, and two white runners, Bobby Morrow and Thane Baker. Chicago's Murchison was the co–world record holder in the 100-meter sprint from 1955 to 1960 and was one of the favorites to win the gold in Melbourne. Nicknamed the "human Sputnik" for his small stature and extraordinary burst at the start of a race, Murchison struggled in the final and finished fourth. He ran the leadoff leg of the gold medal–winning 4×100-meter relay team. Joining him on that squad was Cal-Berkeley's King, who shared the world record with Murchison at that time. Andy Stanfield, former world record holder in the 200-meters, remained among the world's best through the Melbourne Olympics, where he finished second behind white American Bobby Morrow.

Charles Lamont Jenkins Sr. was a double–gold medal winner in Melbourne, winning both the 400-meter sprint and the 4×400-meter relay. Jenkins surprised in the 400-meters as he had struggled in qualifying rounds, and his Black teammate Lou Jones was the current world record holder and favorite in the event. Jenkins surged to the victory with a strong finish in the final, however, while Jones struggled home in fifth place. Jones joined

Jenkins as part of the gold medal–winning relay team. Another gold medal winner was Lee Quincy Calhoun of Laurel, Mississippi, and North Carolina Central University. Calhoun won the gold medal in the 110-meter hurdles, setting a personal-best time of 13.5 seconds and edging out his white U.S. teammate, Jack Davis, at the line. Josh Culbreath, who served in the Marine Corps from 1956 to 1958, won the bronze medal in the 400-meter hurdles.

In the field events, African American athletes again captured gold in the long jump and high jump. Indiana's Greg Bell, NCAA champion and the top-ranked long-jumper in the world for three years, improved his qualifying distance by more than a foot in the long jump finals, winning the gold over his white teammate John Bennett with a jump of 25'8". Charlie Dumas, originally from Tulsa, Oklahoma, but attending Compton College in 1956, set a world record as the first person to clear seven feet in the high jump at the U.S. Olympic trials in Los Angeles that year. He went on to take gold in Melbourne, setting an Olympic record of 6'11".

BILL RUSSELL AND THE 1956 U.S. BASKETBALL TEAM

Don Barksdale's initial foray in Olympic basketball did not inspire immediate change in the makeup of the U.S. team. In fact, four years later in Helsinki, the United States returned to having an all-white squad. In 1956, however, the U.S. team featured three Black players, including two future Basketball Hall-of-Famers, Bill Russell and his University of San Francisco teammate, K. C. Jones, along with Carl Cecil Cain, who had led the Iowa Hawkeyes to back-to-back Final Fours in 1955 and 1956.

No observer of collegiate basketball in that era could dispute Russell's sheer dominance. Long and lean at 6'9", Russell had redefined the position of center, and indeed redefined the game itself. Far more athletic than most big men of that era, Russell spearheaded an offensive attack that often revolved around the fast break. He was even more imposing on the defensive end, where his shot-blocking and rebounding made him nearly impossible to score on. Building around Russell in the middle, the Dons won back-to-back national titles following the 1955 and 1956 seasons.

The United States swept to the gold medal, winning all nine of its games by an average margin of 53.5 points, a record that still stands today. Along the way, the Americans defeated the Soviet team twice, 85–55 in the semifinals and 89–55 in the gold medal game. The Soviets, despite investing heavily in their basketball program since rejoining the Olympic movement in 1952, and despite adding several players more than seven feet tall, still came up well short of offering a true challenge to the U.S. team. In exhibitions and Olympic competitions, though, U.S. officials kept a close eye on the progression of the Soviet team, which was quickly becoming one of the best in the world. Russell led the team in scoring at 14.1 points per game, with K. C. Jones averaging 10.9 points per game. Cain saw spot duty in only two games, scoring three points. Following his Olympic experience, Russell continued the tradition established by Mal Whitfield and other Black Olympians, participating in a State Department tour of West Africa in 1959 and another of Eastern Europe in 1964.

One other Black athlete of note competed in Melbourne. The U.S. boxing team had historically featured a strong cohort of Black athletes. In Melbourne, there was only one. Jim Boyd, of Rocky Mount, North Carolina, learned to box while stationed at Fort Benning, Georgia, for the U.S. Army. Boyd won the gold medal in the light-heavyweight division in Melbourne before embarking on a star-crossed professional career.

THE TIGERBELLES REIGN TRIUMPHANT IN MELBOURNE

Once again in Melbourne, the "Tigerbelles" anchored the American women's team, and once again they performed admirably. Returning for her third Olympics was Mae Faggs, now the seasoned veteran, joined in Melbourne by five of her Tennessee State teammates along with four other young Black women. The Tigerbelles included Isabel Daniels, Lucinda Williams, Willye White, Margaret Matthews, and sixteen-year-old Wilma Rudolph. Faggs, who by that time had stopped competing in the 100- in order to focus on the 200-meters, again failed to reach the final and later said she had over-trained for the event, leading to exhaustion. Faggs and her teammates Rudolph, Matthews, and Daniels attempted to repeat the remarkable U.S. victory in the 400-meter relay of four years earlier but came up just short, taking the bronze in a photo-finish. The Australians did not drop the baton this time and captured the gold in their home country.

In addition to the bronze medal–winning relay team, Mildred McDaniel took the gold medal in the high jump while setting a new world record. She featured prominently in the mainstream American press after her record-breaking performance, and she and Matthews were honored with a parade in their home town of Atlanta upon their return from Australia. Willye White of Mississippi won the silver medal in the long jump, the first of her five Olympic competitions. Daniels made the final in the 100-meters and was designated as the third-place finisher before a review of the photos determined she was fourth. Rudolph competed but failed to advance to the final in the 200-meters. Also making her Olympic debut in Melbourne was Earlene Brown of Los Angeles, who finished fourth in the discus and sixth in the shot put. A new mother in 1956, Brown struggled to find acceptance in the press like other, more traditionally "attractive" female athletes. Brown, Rudolph, and White all returned in Rome four years later and achieved even greater things.

The Black female Olympians representing the United States in Melbourne were expected to comply with strict conventions in appearance, behavior, and femininity. Especially those training under Ed Temple at Tennessee State University had to follow his mandates under the "Temple Way," including adhering to specific modes of dress and behavior and especially avoiding any situations that might suggest promiscuity. Temple famously stated at one point, "I want foxes, not oxes," a now-notorious phrase that bothered some of his athletes even then.[13] A sociology professor as well as coach, Temple understood that American society would deal even more harshly than he did with those athletes who did not follow his rules. Those who did not adequately fit this mold were not as readily embraced by an America still shuddering from the early confrontations of the Civil Rights era.

The women—as all the athletes—also enjoyed the comforts of life in the athletic village and a foreign country. For a time, they relished the idyllic lifestyle, including nice furnishings and good meals. They also welcomed the opportunity to mingle with other athletes from all over the world. These experiences opened their eyes in a new way to the limitations of their home country. The return home, therefore, was jarring. As Willye White later explained, "Being in Australia was quite an experience. I discovered there were two worlds. There was Mississippi and the other world. [In] the world outside of Mississippi, Blacks and whites socialized together, they danced and ate together, even dated each other. Had I not had the opportunity to experience that, I could have spent the rest of my life thinking that the world consisted of lynching, racism, murder, and cross-burning."[14]

THE 1960 ROME OLYMPICS AND THE DOMINANCE OF AFRICAN AMERICAN ATHLETES

The Cold War was front and center during the Rome 1960 Olympics, even more so than four years previously. Cold War tensions in general had eased somewhat after Dwight Eisenhower assumed the U.S. presidency in 1953 and Nikita Khrushchev had ascended to the premiership in the Soviet Union. Both leaders saw value in lowering the barriers each had established. While the athletes still competed fiercely against each other, there was also a sense of mutual respect and appreciation for the others' accomplishments. Among the signs suggesting a rapprochement was the Cultural Exchange Agreement signed by the two sides in 1958. The agreement paved the way for a host of exchanges between the two nations, including students, scholars, scientists, and athletes. By virtue of this agreement, American and Soviet athletes engaged in a number of high-profile meets and competitions beginning in 1958, most notably the U.S.–U.S.S.R. Dual Track Meets, which featured many intense one-on-one contests between some of the best athletes in the world. As they pointed toward the 1960 Olympics, then, athletes on both sides achieved a greater sense of familiarity with their opponents. Rivalries were born. As but one example, at the celebrated U.S.–U.S.S.R. Dual Track Meet in Moscow in 1958, Rafer Johnson set a world record in the decathlon, besting the Soviet champion Vasily Kuznetsov, who up to that point was the only person to surpass 8,000 points in the event.

By 1960, the prominence of Black athletes on the American Olympic squad had been well established. At the same time, there were still other "firsts" to be achieved. Most notably, for the Rome 1960 Olympics, Johnson became the first Black athlete chosen as captain of the U.S. Olympic team, thus also becoming the first to carry the U.S. flag during the Opening Ceremonies. USOC member Louis J. Wilke explained the decision, "We thought Rafer represented the best in Americanism. We not only felt he was probably the greatest all-around athlete in the country, but also an example of your finest traditions."[15] Beyond his status as a record-breaking athlete, Johnson exhibited many of the qualities that American officials relished. He attended UCLA—Jackie Robinson's university—and was an honors student and student body president there. He had already conducted goodwill tours for the State Department, including a nearly three-month odyssey in 1957, drawing high praise for his athletic prowess as well as his comportment. Finally, Johnson remained largely silent on the growing Civil Rights tumult in America, preferring to focus on his training rather than protesting the mistreatment of African Americans. Johnson put it plainly, saying, "Confrontation was simply not my style."[16] He was, therefore, the ideal candidate to carry the flag.

Not only was Rafer Johnson the "best in Americanism"; he also produced the most riveting individual performance of the games. Following his second-place finish to Milt Campbell in Melbourne, Johnson redoubled his efforts in practice, especially refining the mental aspects of the grueling ten-event, two-day grind of the decathlon. In Rome, Johnson's closest competitor was his friend and UCLA teammate C. K. Yang, who represented the Republic of China, or Taiwan. Yang and Johnson, though friends, battled fiercely, with the lead alternating from one to the other after almost every event. Finally, Johnson established an insurmountable lead after the penultimate event, the javelin, before seizing the gold, and an Olympic record, by running a personal best in the last event, the 1,500-meters. Johnson's achievement made him a hero in America, and he remained a prominent public figure for the rest of his life.

Rafer Johnson was the most celebrated of yet another highly touted group of Black American track athletes to compete in the 1960 Olympics. Ray Norton, an early exemplar of coach Bud Winter's "Speed City" group at San Jose State, arrived in Rome as the favorite in the sprints. Co–world record holder in the 200-meters and world record holder in the 100-yard dash, Norton was on the verge of an historic Olympic trifecta. Unbeknownst to many, though, Norton was struggling with a nagging back injury, the result of a bizarre incident in training when a teammate found a small snake in the grass and twirled it near Norton, who instinctively flinched. The twinge in his back from that moment never quite healed even as he took to the track in Rome, months later. Norton's qualifying times were among the slowest of the finalists, and he finished last in the six-man field. Villanova's Frank Budd, the fifth-place finisher, later set a world record in the 100-yard dash in 1961. He and Norton suffered one more ignominious moment in Rome, as members of the U.S. 4×100-meter relay team, which finished first and appeared to have broken the world record with a time of 39.4 seconds. However, it was determined that Norton had left his box too soon in accepting the baton exchange from Budd, and the team was disqualified.

Norton's disappointment was only one on a day regarded as "Black Thursday" for the U.S. track squad, in which a number of favorites came up short of expectations. In the 800-meters, no American made the final. In the high jump, Boston University's John Thomas, the favorite to win the gold, engaged in a riveting jump-off with his three Soviet rivals, Robert Shavlakadze, Valeriy Brumel, and Viktor Bolshov. At height after height, Thomas watched as the Soviets cleared the bar, forcing him to do the same. Struggling with nerves, with the chill of the evening air, and with long periods of inactivity between jumps, Thomas was not his usually dominant self and finished third, behind Shavlakadze and Brumel. Further down the finishing list, Charles Dumas, who had won the gold medal in Melbourne, finished in a tie for fifteenth place.

Despite the propaganda blow delivered by the three Soviets who had relegated Thomas to a bronze medal on "Black Thursday," the disappointments of that day were not as severe as the press made it seem, and on the whole the track and field squad continued to perform well. Black athletes achieved a sweep in the 110-meter hurdles, with Lee Quincy Calhoun achieving a surprising repeat gold medal, edging out his teammate Willie May, at the time a senior at Indiana University, by .01 seconds to win the gold. Taking the bronze was Hayes Wendell Jones from Starkville, Mississippi.

African American athletes also finished one-two in the men's long jump competition. Ralph Boston, a Tennessee State athlete who went on to notch the remarkable achievement of winning gold, silver, and bronze in the same event over three Olympics, had broken Jesse Owens' world record earlier in the year with a leap of 26'11". His form was a little off in Rome, however, and his jumps were much in kind with the other competitors, making for a close and riveting final. On his last jump, Boston took the lead with a mark of 26'7¾", then watched as all his rivals came within a few inches—but just short—of that distance. His teammate and fellow African American, Cornell's Irvin "Bo" Roberson, came within one-half inch of Boston's mark to take the silver.

Otis Davis, from Tuscaloosa, Alabama, but running for the powerhouse track team at the University of Oregon, earned a surprise double-gold in Rome in the 400-meters and 4×400-meter relay. Davis, whose first sport was basketball, was a late bloomer in track terms, taking up the 400 only after four years in the military and a year of junior college basketball. Still adjusting to the challenges of running the longest sprint, Davis finished third in the Olympic trials, just making the team. Reaching peak form at the perfect time, Davis outpaced a strong field in the 400-meter final, breaking the world record in the process at 44.9 seconds. Davis also anchored the 4×400-meter relay team to the gold medal, in another world-record time of 3:02.37.

Two days after "Black Thursday," Ray Norton returned to the track with a chance at redemption in the 200-meters, along with his teammates Lester "Les" Carney of Ohio University and Stone Johnson of Grambling College. Norton's maladies persisted, though, and he struggled to another last-place finish in the event final, with Johnson just ahead. Les Carney made a surge to the finish but came up short of catching Italian Livio Berruti, who captured the gold.

OTHER EXPLOITS OF THE BLACK MERCURIES IN ROME

The U.S. boxing team in Rome included a strong contingent of Black athletes, with six, including three who won gold medals. Without question, the most attention was paid to the young boxer from Louisville, Cassius Clay. In his final bout, he faced Zbigniew Pietrzykowski of Poland, the bronze medal winner in Melbourne, three-time European champion, and veteran of 233 fights already. The two fought fairly even in the first two rounds, before Ali unleashed a barrage of punches in the final round that left the Polish fighter bloodied. In a unanimous and uncontroversial decision, Ali was declared the gold medal winner.

Two other African American fighters won gold in Rome. Wilbert McClure faced Italian Carmelo Bossi in the light-middleweight gold medal match. Fearing biased judging, which some claimed had impacted previous decisions in bouts featuring American boxers, McClure held nothing back in a final round featuring almost nonstop punching. He secured a 4–1 decision to win the gold medal. Deward "Eddie" Crook faced a similar situation in his gold medal match, against Tadeusz Walasek of Poland. Unable to offer up a clear and defining round like Ali and McClure, Crook instead prevailed in a less one-sided decision. Several other African Americans competed in Rome but did not medal.

Returning to the Olympics after an eight-year hiatus was weight lifter James Bradford, who had finished second behind John Henry Davis in the heavyweight division in 1952. Despite qualifying for the 1956 Olympics in Melbourne, Bradford elected to stay home with his wife rather than travel to the opposite side of the globe for no pay. Qualifying again in 1960, Bradford joined an American team of lifters intent on defeating the Soviets. Victory was not in the cards for Bradford, who finished second again, this time to Soviet Yuri Vlasov, who lifted a world record total.

As it had in 1956, the U.S. basketball team also featured three Black players, once again including a transcendent star in Oscar Robertson and another Basketball Hall-of-Famer in Walt Bellamy. The pair was joined by Robert "Bob" Boozer, who had led Kansas State to the Final Four in 1958 and was already a first-round pick of the Cincinnati Royals. The team is regarded as one of the greatest ever, with four Hall-of-Famers on the court, including Robertson and Bellamy, and white players Jerry West and Jerry Lucas, as well as a Hall-of-Fame coach in Pete Newell. It won all eight of its games in the tournament by a Dream-Team-esque average of more than forty-two points per game. The team itself was elected to the Basketball Hall of Fame in 2012.

   While not seriously challenged in any game, the team did play one game of significance on its way to the gold medal. Midway through the tournament, the Americans faced a Soviet team that had improved greatly in limited international play since World War II. The Soviet team had beaten the Americans in the World Championships in Chile in 1959—albeit a less than all-star American squad. Coach Newell underscored the importance of the game in his pre-game speech to the team, saying, "Guys, this is more than a game. We're talking about a way of life."[17] Instead, the Soviets offered little more than a speed bump of resistance to the mighty American team, which unleashed the backcourt tandem of Robertson and West. The pair led the team in scoring and swiped a string of steals early in the second half to put the game out of reach. The Americans won easily, 81–57, and put to rest for the moment the prospect of the Soviets closing the gap in the sport born and raised on American soil. It would be more than a decade before the Americans lost a basketball game in the Olympics.

WILMA RUDOLPH AND THE TIGERBELLES IN ROME

If Rafer Johnson was the leader of the U.S. Olympic team in Rome and Cassius Clay soon became its most famous alumnus as Muhammad Ali, the unquestioned queen of the Olympics was Wilma Rudolph, who ran her way to three gold medals and international acclaim. Rudolph came to Rome as the favorite to win the 100- and 200-meters along with the 4×100-meter relay; however, she faced a grueling schedule and multiple qualifying heats in each event leading up to the finals. Indeed, she almost fell prey to the misfortune that struck Norton, as the night before her first race, she twisted her ankle stepping in a hole. The sprained ankle responded well to treatment, however, and Rudolph was able to compete in the 100-meter heats the following day, in part because the race was straight rather than around a curve, like the 200. With each successive heat, her times improved, culminating in a majestic final in which she finished five meters clear of the field and broke the world record, running eleven seconds flat. She then proceeded through the process again in the 200-meters. Though her time in the 200-meter final was unremarkable at twenty-four seconds, due largely to the rains that had descended and less than ideal track conditions, she secured her second gold medal.
   Rudolph's greatest challenge lay in the relay, in part because her teammates had struggled in their individual races. None of her fellow sprinters had reached the finals in their events, Martha Hudson and Barbara Jones

Members of the United States women's 4×100-meter relay team, the Tennessee State University "Tigerbelles," standing together during the 1960 Olympics in Rome shortly after capturing the gold medal in the event in world record time. Left to right: Wilma Rudolph, Lucinda Williams, Barbara Jones, and Martha Hudson. *Courtesy of the Library of Congress, Prints and Photographs Division, NYWT&S Collection LC-USZ62-113285*

in the 100-meters, and Lucinda Williams and Ernestine Pollards in the 200-meters. Despite concerns about the strength of the team in comparison to those from the Soviet Union, Germany, and Great Britain, the four Tigerbelles—Hudson, Jones, Williams, and Rudolph—cruised to victory and a new world record of 44.4 seconds. In addition to the Tigerbelles on the track, two of America's foremost Black female Olympians made their second Olympic appearances. Earlene Brown made the finals in the shot put and won the bronze medal. Willye White qualified for her second of five Olympics, making the final in the long jump and finishing sixteenth.

Rudolph was already an accomplished track star—and athlete-diplomat—before the Rome Olympics. After her gold-medal trifecta, though, her fame and prominence achieved heights rarely experienced by a Black American female athlete before. Still, her return home was not entirely positive. As she stated to the *New York Amsterdam News*, "It's going to all but kill me to have to go back home and face being denied this, that, and the other, because I'm a Black American. In America, they push me around because I'm Negro, here in Europe, they push me to the front."[18] She returned to Clarksville, Tennessee, still a city in the grip of Jim Crow. Rudolph attempted to use her considerable clout to encourage change in the city. The parade and party in her honor was to have been segregated, until Rudolph refused to attend unless it was integrated. The celebration became the first significant integrated event in Clarksville's history. Yet even Rudolph's magnetism had its limits. Three years later, when she joined other Civil Rights activists in a sit-in to desegregate the local Shoney's restaurant, the protest proved unsuccessful. In that instance, she was treated as just another Black woman, denied equality in a country still on the leading edge of the Civil Rights Movement.

MUHAMMAD ALI'S GOLD MEDAL

After the Olympics in Rome, America's Black athletes returned home to a nation still mired in Jim Crow but also making fitful progress toward desegregation and equality. Many athletes returning to Southern states found their status as Olympians provided only short-lived solace, if any. As the limelight faded and their lives became more mundane, the Black Mercuries typically returned to life as average Black Americans, fraught with challenges in finding work, making a decent living, finding housing, and at times confronting outright racism.

Cassius Clay struggled with the return to civilian life. He was a champion, with a career of great promise ahead of him, but he was also a Black citizen of Louisville, Kentucky, a city still governed by Jim Crow. For a time, Clay made many comments declaring his faith in the United States. He wore his gold medal everywhere. However, his views evolved in the years after he won that gold medal. While he prospered in those early years of his professional career, he also grew increasingly suspicious of the entourage of white people who always seemed to be pulling at him. Pushed into fights at an alarming rate, hawking all manner of products to boost his (and his backers') endorsement income, and constantly pestered by the media, Clay grew more introverted and searched for deeper meaning in his life. Ultimately, he became enamored with Malcolm X and the Black Muslims, converted to Islam, changed his name to Muhammad Ali, and came to be reviled by many white Americans who had cheered his victory in Rome.

Later in life, Muhammad Ali often told the story that upon his return to Louisville after the Olympics, he was turned away from a local diner even while wearing his gold medal around his neck. So disgusted was he with this treatment that—as he told it—he threw his cherished medal into the Ohio River, forever casting away his allegiance to the red, white, and blue. The story was fiction; biographers have determined that he actually lost the medal, and he concocted a good yarn rather than admit the truth. Yet the story lodged in the American collective conscience, and for decades Ali's chroniclers dutifully recited the myth. The truth, however, was that whether Ali threw away his medal metaphorically or actually, his passionate support for the country had wavered. Between 1960 and 1964, one of the nation's most beloved Black Olympians had spurned the country he once hailed as "the best country in the world."[19] He set the stage for a generation of Black athletes to follow, who were more willing than their predecessors to challenge a nation that often failed to live up to its ideals.

5

BLACK MERCURIES IN THE AGE OF PROTEST

In March of 1964, the African American monthly magazine *Ebony* published a controversial article, written by five-time Olympic medalist Mal Whitfield. The title stated it all: "'Let's Boycott the Olympics: Olympic Champ Asks Negro Athletes to Act." Whitfield declared, "I advocate that every Negro athlete eligible to participate in the Olympic Games in Japan next October boycott the games if Negro Americans by that time have not been guaranteed full and equal rights as first-class citizens." He urged a boycott for two main reasons. First, it was time for Black athletes to fully join in the broader fight for civil rights. Second, in the words of Martin Luther King Jr., Whitfield wrote, "It [was] time for America to live up to its promises of Liberty, Equality and Justice for all, or be shown up to the world as a nation where the color of one's skin takes precedence over the quality of one's mind and character."[1]

Whitfield gave voice to grievances that many of the Black Mercuries, either through their Olympic experience or other international travels, had come to understand. Despite the fact that they were celebrated as champions after defeating athletes from around the world—and especially the Soviet bloc nations—and despite the fact that they were deployed by the State Department to show the world that African Americans fully enjoyed all the benefits of American democracy, in fact Black Americans were not treated as "first-class citizens."

At that time, no athletes accepted Whitfield's invitation to join the wave of Civil Rights protests, and none echoed his call for an Olympic boycott. Whitfield's suggestion of a boycott of the Olympics, however, was a portent of things to come. By 1968, after several summers of racial violence that followed the assassinations of John F. Kennedy, Malcolm X, Martin Luther King Jr., and Robert Kennedy and with the growing militancy of Civil Rights activists and many Black athletes, the call for a boycott took root in a significant way.

THE BLACK MERCURIES FLOURISH IN A PEACEFUL GAMES

The International Olympic Committee had originally awarded the Olympic Games of 1940 to Tokyo; however, those games were never held due to the onset of World War II. At its 1959 convention in Munich, the IOC designated Tokyo as the host city for the 1964 Olympics, in part to account for the 1940 Olympics being cancelled and in part as a gesture welcoming the return of Japan to the peaceful global community. As such, the Olympics became an important symbol for Japan in expunging the awful memories of the war-torn 1930s and 1940s and moving forward into a better future. Aside from the fact that these were the first Olympics from which South Africa was banned due to its policy of apartheid and the accompanying debate about the place of politics in sport, the Tokyo Olympics were scandal-free. For the remainder of the Cold War, that would never be true again.

As had become commonplace, African Americans featured prominently in the sprints in Tokyo. "Bullet" Bob Hayes of Florida A&M (FAMU), a Historically Black University in Tallahassee, Florida, won the 100-meters. Hayes, a man some consider the greatest sprinter of all time, represented a new breed of athlete: a football player with a sprinter's speed rather than a sprinter who played football. He was thickly muscled, and he churned down the track as he ran, arms pumping furiously. Between 1962 and 1964, Hayes never lost a race at 100 yards or 100 meters, and he never lost a race during his collegiate career at FAMU. In Tokyo, Hayes posted the fastest time in each of the qualifying rounds, including a time of 9.9 seconds in the semifinal, which bettered the world record but was wind aided. Hayes drew lane one for the final, an unlucky draw since that lane had been battered by runners in the long-distance races and softened by rain. He also found himself running in borrowed track shoes, the result of an unfortunate prank pulled by the boxer Joe Frazier that caused one of Hayes' own shoes to be left back in his room. The disadvantage only caused Hayes to run harder. He exploded from the blocks and was clear of the field within just a few strides. He streaked to victory in a world record-tying 10.06 seconds, two meters ahead of his closest challenger.

Hayes' dominance showcased even more in the 4×100-meter relay, in which the U.S. team faced a deep field of international teams, seven out of eight of which tied or broke the Olympic record in the event. With America's next two fastest sprinters, Mel Pender and Trent Jackson, out with injuries, the U.S. team relied on substitutes Paul Drayton, Gerry Ashworth, and Richard Stebbins, along with Hayes, Ashworth the only white runner among them. By the time the baton came to Hayes for the anchor run, the U.S. team was in fifth place and trailing the leaders by three meters. Hayes then produced one of the greatest runs of all time in the event, passing the leaders in only fifty meters and pulling ahead to win by three. Hayes' leg was clocked at 8.6 seconds, still the fastest relay leg ever run, and the team broke the world record with a time of 39.0 seconds.

The American team featured several other great sprinters in 1964. Throughout that season, Hayes had been pushed in the 100-meters by Trenton "T .J." Jackson, the nation's top collegiate sprinter that year from the University of Illinois. In Tokyo, Jackson suffered an injury in the same semifinal in which Hayes ran 9.9 seconds, laboring across the line nearly a second slower and compelled to withdraw from the relay. Also competing in the 100-meters was Pender, who was already nearly a decade into military service that saw him complete two tours of combat in Vietnam. Pender had less than a year of experience in running track, and he was only given a few weeks off from his military service to train for the Olympics. Like Jackson, Pender was injured in the semifinals; despite the injury, he ran in the final and finished sixth.

African Americans also took first and second in the 200-meters. Arizona State's Henry Carr, a three-sport star in football, basketball, and track, won the gold medal and set an Olympic record with the time of 20.3 seconds. Finishing second behind Carr was Paul Drayton, star of the Villanova track team, whose greatest exploits came in the years between the 1960 and 1964 Olympics. Also competing in the 200-meters was Richard Stebbins of Grambling, who finished seventh. Drayton and Stebbins were also part of the gold medal-winning 4×100-meter relay team. Carr won a second gold in the 4×400-meter relay, with white teammates Ollan Cassell, Mike Larrabee, and Black runner Ulis Williams. Carr ran the final leg in 44.5 seconds, and the team broke the world record with a time of 3:00.07. Williams of Arizona State, who ran in the individual 400-meters, finished fifth.

Three African Americans competed in the men's high jump in Tokyo. John Thomas made a return appearance and hoped to improve on his bronze finish in Rome. He did that but settled for a silver behind his nemesis, Soviet Union jumper Valeriy Brumel. Both cleared an Olympic record height of 2.18 meters, but Thomas had more misses in the final round. Taking the bronze was John Rambo of Los Angeles, who dominated the sport for a time, often winning meets by taking only a single jump, and at one point holding the world record. In Tokyo, he could not quite match his friend and rival Thomas or Brumel. Ed Caruthers, the great jumper for the University of Arizona, finished eighth.

The long jump featured the return of the gold medalist in Rome, Ralph Boston, facing his rival, Igor Ter-Ovanesyan of the Soviet Union. Since 1960, the two had exchanged world-record jumps several times, with Boston setting a new world record in the Olympic trials. The pair jockeyed back and forth throughout the final round, when Lynn Davies of Great Britain surpassed them both. Boston passed Ter-Ovanesyan on his final jump to take the silver.

The 1964 Olympics saw the debut of one of America's greatest Black Olympians. Willie Davenport achieved a shocking upset at the 1964 Olympic trials when he won the 110-meter hurdles, upsetting five-time national champion Hayes Jones, the bronze medalist in the event at the Rome Olympics and favorite to win in Tokyo, and Blaine Lindgren, a great white hurdler and champion in the event at the 1963 Pan American Games. Born in Troy, Alabama, and raised in Ohio, Davenport joined the military after running track and playing baseball in high school. While stationed in Germany with the military from 1961 to 1963, Davenport trained and honed his form in the hurdles. Davenport failed to medal in the 110-meter hurdles in Tokyo, straining his quadriceps in his semifinal heat and not making the final. He went on to compete in four more Olympics. In 1968, 1972, and 1976 he competed again in the 110-meter hurdles, finishing first, fourth, and third respectively. Then, in 1980, Davenport competed in the Winter Olympics as part of the four-man bobsled team, becoming along with his teammate Jeff Gadley the first Black Americans to compete in the Winter Olympics. He was also only the fourth athlete at that point to have competed in both the Summer and Winter Olympics.

While Davenport did not medal in the 110-meter hurdles in Tokyo, Americans did finish one-two, in one of the most controversial finishes of those Olympics. In the final, Lindgren and Jones led the field, with Lindgren just ahead throughout the race. As they approached the finish, though, Lindgren faltered. Race organizers had added five lines on the track at one-meter intervals in the last five meters before the finish line, to assist with the evolving technology of the photo-finish. Lindgren, mistakenly thinking the first of those lines marked the finish, leaned too soon and stumbled across the line, under the tape. Jones broke the tape first, his chest leading the way over the line. Initially Lindgren was announced as the winner, but as they prepared to take the medal stand, officials told the athletes that Jones was the winner, with Lindgren second, and Soviet hurdler Anatoly Mikhailov third. Jones thus added a gold medal to the bronze he had won in Rome; Lindgren returned home to Utah saddled with disappointment that lingered for the rest of his life.[2]

In Tokyo, Oscar Moore became the first African American man to compete in the 5,000 meters in an Olympics. Moore, an extraordinarily talented and versatile runner who served four years in the U.S. Marine Corps from 1956 to 1960, competed at various times during his career at every distance from 400 meters to the marathon. Left with little supervision and several weeks to train before the Tokyo Olympics, Moore engaged in a few too many of his customary long runs. The overtraining drained him, and Moore finished eighth in his qualifying heat, some thirty seconds behind the pace needed to qualify for the final.

1964 TOKYO: MEN'S BASKETBALL AND OTHER SPORTS

The 1964 U.S. basketball team, anchored by six African American players, once again won the gold medal without much trouble. Prominent Black players on the team included Jim "Bad News" Barnes, the first player taken in the 1964 NBA draft, who played for Coach Don Haskins at Texas Western University; Walt Hazzard of UCLA; Arizona State's Joe Caldwell; Arizona's Lucious Jackson; and "Big George" Wilson, a recent graduate of the University of Cincinnati.

The closest encounter came in a game against Yugoslavia in which Wilson hit two clutch jump shots late in the contest, with the U.S. team leading by only four points. They ended up winning that game by eight points and were not threatened in any other games on their way to the finals. In the gold-medal game, the Americans once again faced their Cold War rivals, the Soviets, who were also undefeated and 8–0 entering the game. The game was close early, but eventually the U.S. team took control and won 73–59. Lucious Jackson was the leading scorer in the game with seventeen points, and Joe Caldwell added fourteen.

Black athletes also featured prominently in the ring, and on the mat in Tokyo. The boxing squad featured three Black pugilists, the best known of whom was heavyweight "Smokin' Joe" Frazier who went on to an illustrious professional career after the Olympics, including a three-year run as the heavyweight champion and a trilogy of memorable fights with his great rival, Muhammad Ali. Frazier was actually defeated in the final match of the Olympic trials by Buster Mathis, but he traveled to Tokyo as a reserve and advanced into action when Mathis broke a knuckle while training. In the main draw, Frazier scored first round knockouts against his first two opponents, then knocked out Soviet Vadim Yemelyanov in the next round, suffering a broken thumb in the process. In the final match, he battled through the thumb injury and prevailed in a 3–2 decision over German Hans Huber to win the gold medal. Charles Brown of Cincinnati won the bronze in the featherweight division, winning his first three matches before losing a 4–1 decision in the semifinals.

The American wrestling team also featured its first Black athletes in Tokyo: Bob Pickens, Bobby Douglas, and Charles Tribble. Pickens, who wrestled and played football at the University of Wisconsin and later the University of Nebraska, was the first to take the mat, in the heavyweight class of Greco-Roman wrestling. Pickens went 1–2 in three matches at the Games, finishing sixth in his division. Douglas, a great collegiate wrestler at Oklahoma State, went 4–1 in five matches in Tokyo but finished fourth and missed out on a medal by virtue of being outpointed by the only man to defeat him, Soviet Nodar Khokhashvili. Tribble, a welterweight who had a stellar amateur career before the 1964 Olympics, fought in only one bout, losing to the eventual gold medalist, Ismail Ogan of Turkey.

Finally, the Americans entered a team of four athletes who called themselves the "Rainbow Team" in the new Olympic sport of judo, added to the competition at the request of the host nation, Japan. The "Rainbow Team" included Jim Bregman, a Jewish American; Ben Nighthorse Campbell, an American Cheyenne who later became a U.S. Representative and U.S. Senator from Colorado; Paul Murayama, a Japanese American; and George Harris, an African American from Philadelphia. Harris enlisted in the Air Force straight out of high school and was introduced to judo as part of his mandatory training at Travis Air Force Base in California. In Tokyo, Harris won his first match but then lost to Soviet Parnaoz Chikviladze, who went on to win the bronze medal.[3]

AFRICAN AMERICAN WOMEN AT
THE 1964 TOKYO OLYMPICS

Aspiring Black female Olympians in the 1960s continued to confront the double marginalization of being both Black and female. Many were raised in small towns or cities where no organized sports were offered for girls. Instead, they competed in all manner of pickup games, either in isolation or against the neighborhood boys and girls. At the same time, this informal brand of competition instilled in some of them a feeling of equality with the other kids, whether white or Black, and it led some to become skilled in a wide array of games and contests.[4]

Wyomia Tyus, raised on a farm in Griffin, Georgia, a small town on the outskirts of Atlanta, grew up competing both with and against her three older brothers in every imaginable contest, from running races, to bike races, marbles, and even boxing. Her brothers, reluctant to accept her in their games at first, soon introduced her as a "ringer" in their pickup basketball games, often to the surprise of neighborhood boys who had not yet been beaten by the girl on the Tyus farm. Similarly, the Tyus children tolerated no racism from those who wanted to play on the vast baseball and football fields they drew up on their land or on the basketball hoops they erected.[5]

Tyus was thus raised in an environment of tough, interracial and inter-gender competition where girls asked no quarter—and gave none—when playing with the boys. These battles of her youth prepared her well for the Olympics, and for the rigors of training at Tennessee State under demanding coach Ed Temple, who recruited Tyus after seeing her as a high school junior at the 1961 Georgia High School championships. Tyus trained with the Tigerbelles for two summers before joining them full-time in 1963. By the summer of 1964, Tyus was running stride-for-stride with the world's elite and was primed for a strong showing in Tokyo.[6]

In order to take the gold in Tokyo, though, Tyus would have to overcome her teammate, Edith McGuire of Atlanta. A year older than Tyus, McGuire was actually the favorite in the 100-meters, having won at that distance in both the U.S.–U.S.S.R. Dual Meet in 1964 and at the Olympic trials. Prior to the Olympics, Frank Litsky of the *New York Times* described McGuire as the "heiress apparent to Wilma Rudolph."[7] In Tokyo, however, it was Tyus who won the gold, with McGuire taking the silver. McGuire took gold in the 200-meters with an Olympic record of 23.05 seconds and was part of the silver medal–winning 4×100-meter relay team.

Tyus was pushed in the sprints by another great Black female runner, Marilyn White. Raised on the other side of the country and in very different circumstances, White nonetheless grew up racing against the boys in her neighborhood more often than the girls. As White described it, "I was a tomboy from when I was little. That didn't mean that I wasn't feminine. It just meant that I enjoyed physical activities."[8] White, shorter and stockier than most of the sprinters, powered her way down the track as quickly as any runner of her generation.

Running beside her rivals in the 100-meters, White was denied a medal only because she was too short to lean effectively at the tape. She finished with an identical time as the second- and third-place finishers but was awarded fourth as they out-leaned her at the finish. White also won silver in the 4×100-meter relay, a disappointing finish for a team that had world-record aspirations. In the final race, the first two baton exchanges went smoothly as the team built a lead, but as White went to give the baton to Tyus, Tyus had to slow down to avoid leaving the box too early. That misstep was enough to open the door for the Polish team to pass her and take the gold.

On the whole, African American women performed stronger on the track than in the field events. A trio of Black women competed in the high jump in Tokyo but did not medal. Estelle Baskerville of Columbus, Ohio, did not make the final round. Terrezene Brown, White's teammate on the Mercurettes, advanced to the finals but finished fourteenth. Eleanor Montgomery, one of the Tigerbelles, cleared 1.71 meters but came up just short of the height necessary to win a medal, finishing eighth. Three Black women also competed in the long jump but did not medal. Willye White had the strongest finish, reaching the final but finishing twelfth. Two others missed making the final round by only a few centimeters. Martha Watson, who was competing in her first of four Olympics, came up six centimeters short of the 6.00 meter qualifying distance; Tigerbelle Joann Grissom missed by nine centimeters. Finally, the matriarch of the women's team competing in her third and final Olympics, Earlene Brown, concluded her Olympic career with a twelfth-place finish in the shot put, struggling to find her footing in the wet conditions.

The 1964 Olympics marked the debut of women's volleyball in the program. One member of that team—and thus the first African American Olympian in the sport—was Verneda Estella Thomas of Chicago. A product of the Chicago Comets amateur track team, Thomas began her athletic career as a high jumper. She won the AAU championship at age seventeen and, for a time, participated in many international meets and tours with the U.S. team. She eventually transitioned to volleyball, where she toured the country and the world as a member of the Chicago Rebels, a barnstorming team created at the Chicago YMCA. On the strength of her performances with that team, Thomas was selected to be a member of the inaugural U.S. team in Tokyo. The team went 1–4 in five matches and failed to win a medal.

1968 AND THE REVOLT OF THE BLACK ATHLETES

While Mal Whitfield and a few others voiced frustration with persistent racial inequality in the United States in advance of the 1964 Tokyo Olympics, a host of Black athletes seriously considered boycotting the 1968 Mexico City Olympics. The intervening years brought changes in attitudes among Black athletes that reflected broader changes among Black Americans more generally. The Civil Rights Movement as coordinated by Martin Luther King Jr. and the Southern Christian Leadership Conference confronted growing challenges from other Black leaders, and new groups formed around more radical and urgent agendas, often ambivalent to the concept of non-violence. Drawing inspiration from Malcolm X and others, such groups embraced the slogan "Black Power," emphasizing Black independence and self-reliance above integration into white-dominated society.

In addition to the change in tone of many Civil Rights leaders, a series of violent and heart-rending events also rocked the nation, forcing even the most optimistic activist to question whether racial progress was actually being made. Most tragic, on April 4, 1968, a white supremacist named James Earl Ray shot and killed Martin Luther King Jr. in Memphis, Tennessee. King's assassination was only one in a cascade of monumental events that rocked the nation—and the world—in the year 1968. Most jarring were the events of June 5, when Democratic candidate Robert Kennedy was mortally wounded as he left his campaign headquarters at the Ambassador Hotel in Los Angeles, hours after winning the California primary. The Olympian Rafer Johnson was at his side and actually wrestled the gun away from the assassin, Sirhan Sirhan. A disheartened nation also watched at the end of August as Democrats convened in Chicago, Illinois, for their national convention. Violence and chaos reigned in the streets of Chicago and at times even unfolded on the floor of the convention, as witnessed by millions on their television screens.

Black athletes confronted their own unique array of challenges, operating in an athletic system controlled by white coaches, administrators, and sponsors. Many Olympians were collegiate athletes or recent graduates, who faced a host of racial concerns on college campuses. Many experienced overt racism in the athletic arena, not only from opposing fans, players, and coaches, but also at times from officials. Even worse, some endured persistent racism from coaches, teammates, or fans at their own universities

In this atmosphere, a group of Black athletes at San Jose State University (SJSU) began to organize under the tutelage of Harry Edwards, a young sociology professor who would soon achieve a PhD from Cornell University. He was also an imposing figure, physically, verbally, and intellectually. Edwards, a former basketball player and discus thrower standing 6'8", adopted the dress and aura of Black Power advocates, usually appearing in a black leather jacket, black beret, and sunglasses; he was a magnetic—and polarizing—figure. In the fall of 1967 at SJSU, Edwards organized a group called the Olympic Project for Human Rights (OPHR), with a boycott of the 1968 Olympics as one of their stated goals. He shared his passion and knowledge with his students and the track cohort at San Jose State, including one of the world's best in the 200 meters, Tommie Smith.

Smith made the first direct public comment announcing the possibility of a boycott of the Mexico City Olympics by Black athletes, following the University Games in Tokyo in the fall of 1967. When asked about the prospect of a boycott, Smith answered, "Yes, this is true. Some Black athletes have been discussing the possibility of boycotting the games to protest racial injustice in America."[9] Arriving home to a media frenzy, Smith and others like Lee Evans, the 400-meter specialist, continued to talk publicly about a possible boycott.

Building around a core of top athletes from the famous "Speed City" track team at San Jose State, Edwards organized a meeting with a group of the nation's top Black athletes in November of 1967 to discuss an Olympic boycott. Leaders at the meeting included Olympic-caliber Black athletes Smith, Evans, John Carlos, and UCLA's basketball star Lew Alcindor. While not unanimous, the athletes broadly supported a boycott of the Olympics. Female athletes, while asked by the media about the potential boycott, were not included in the early discussions. Madeline Manning, the dominant 800-meter runner, voiced her support from a distance, offering, "It would be very difficult to refuse if our people asked this of us."[10]

Both white and Black athletes were divided in their opinions about the boycott movement. Some white athletes were openly supportive, notably the Harvard rowing team who met with Edwards and wore OPHR buttons in solidarity with the Black athletes. Others criticized the protests, in some cases resenting the attention paid to the Black athletes at the expense of white athletes competing in sports that rarely garnered media attention. While many prominent Black athletes supported the boycott—and for a time they were literally the loudest voices in the room—just as many did not support it. Their reasons varied. Most could not stomach the thought of giving up on their dream of competing in the Olympics, a goal they had spent years pursuing. Others resented not being involved in the OPHR. The project had always been centered at San Jose State University and almost exclusively included Black, college, male athletes. The Tigerbelles and other women knew about the meetings and understood what was taking place; however, they were not a part of the meetings and their voices were only heard at the periphery of the movement. Non-college athletes, most notably the boxer George Foreman, stewed over the fact they were excluded from the process. Foreman intended to go to Mexico City and show not only the rest of the world that he was the equal of any man but also his own Olympic teammates.

At the preliminary Olympic trials in Los Angeles in June, a group of twenty-six of the most promising medal hopefuls gathered to discuss the boycott a final time. Half voted for it, half against.[11] Without a unified voice, Edwards and the leaders of the OPHR decided to abandon the idea of a boycott. Instead, the athletes would go to Mexico City with the freedom to protest however they chose.

THE BLACK MERCURIES IN MEXICO CITY

A number of other things weighed on the minds of Black athletes in Mexico City, in addition to the possibility of some sort of protest. The IOC implemented drug and gender testing for the first time in 1968, so all athletes were subjected to greater scrutiny of their bodies and their practices than they were accustomed to. Challenges to amateurism—most notably the "sneaker wars" and under-the-table payments from shoe companies—were also peaking in 1968. However, the high elevation and thin air of Mexico City concerned the athletes the most. While some analysts offered dire predictions of athletes suffering or perhaps even dying, the consensus seemed to be that while some athletes might feel the effects of the thin air more acutely than others, they should be able to compete safely.

Of course, the most indelible image of the Games is the medal stand protest of Tommie Smith and John Carlos, which followed the 200-meter sprint final on the fourth day of the games, October 16. The race played out like many of their previous ones, with the 100-meter specialist Carlos taking an early lead. As they came down the stretch, Carlos slowed just a bit and glanced over his shoulder to see whether Smith was gaining. Indeed, he was. "Tommie Jets" had turned on his customary afterburners for the stretch run, and he blew past Carlos and the other competitors on his way to a world record and the gold medal. Carlos, in easing up, opened the door for Peter Norman, a white Australian, to catch him at the line for the silver. Carlos won the bronze.

On the medal podium, Tommie Smith occupied the top step, Norman the second step to Smith's right, and Carlos the third step to his left. Between

Tommie Smith and John Carlos with their black-gloved fists raised high into the air and heads bowed while on the victory stand during the 1968 Olympic games in Mexico City. Smith won the gold medal in the 200-meter sprint; Carlos won the bronze. Silver medal winner Australian Peter Norman is in front. *Unidentified Artist, 1968, Gelatin silver print, National Portrait Gallery, Smithsonian Institution; acquired through the generosity of David C. Ward.*

the race and the medal ceremony, the men had made some hasty arrangements for their protest, grabbing one pair of black gloves, black scarves and some beads, along with their OPHR pins. Smith and Carlos set their Puma shoes on the podium next to them, their exposed black socks symbolic of the poverty many Black families endure. Norman wore an OPHR pin to show his solidarity with the Black athletes. As the United States national anthem began to play, Smith and Carlos lowered their heads. Smith raised his right arm, Carlos his left, in a "Black Power" salute, revealing the black gloves on each hand. The two continued to raise their fists as they left the field to a mixed reaction from the confused crowd, cheers and yells mingling with boos and whistles.

Avery Brundage, President of the IOC, was enraged at the gesture and issued a warning that any other protests would be met with swift repercussions. The United States Olympic Committee (USOC) suspended Smith and Carlos and forced them to leave the athletic village, though both remained in Mexico City for several days, counseling and encouraging their fellow Black athletes. A number of other athletes delivered gestures of solidarity during their events or on the medal stand, such as wearing black socks, black berets, or giving a "Black Power" salute. However, no other protests matched the profound impact of the one delivered by Smith and Carlos.

The consequences for both of them were indeed severe, as they struggled to find work after the Games in Mexico City. Carlos continued competing for several years after 1968, and both men had tryouts for NFL teams, none of which led to a steady job. It was decades before the track and field power structure softened, and both eventually found coaching positions in addition to their work as local community activists. Over time, these once vilified men came to be celebrated by most Americans as heroic as the national view of racial inequality gradually came to accept what Edwards, Smith, Carlos, and so many others had argued in the 1960s. Today, they are recognized in statues, artwork, and as the recipients of many awards. Such recognition, however, came only after decades of profound suffering. Most notably, students at SJSU launched a movement to memorialize Smith and Carlos, a process resulting in a twenty-foot statue of their medal stand protest erected near the spot where the athletes first met on the SJSU campus. Nearby is a commemorative bench, funded by a $25,000 donation from Harry Edwards himself, honoring the women who had worked with the OPHR. Over time, Edwards came to regret not including women more prominently in the movement, his reluctance to do so born perhaps from his own paternal instincts to protect the women who were doing important work behind the scenes, like his future wife, Sandra Boze Edwards, who later became an attorney advocating children's rights. In the decades since, he has been a passionate advocate for women's rights in addition to racial equality.

RECORDS FALL IN THE THIN AIR OF MEXICO CITY

Concerns about the high elevation and its possible dangerous impact on the athletes dissipated as it actually contributed to a cascade of records in the sprints, hurdles, and field events in Mexico City, many of them set by African American athletes. Most memorably, within a span of only a few minutes on October 18, the sixth day of the Games, two athletes shattered world records so thoroughly that the new marks would stand for decades. Most spectacular was the long jump of Bob Beamon. Beamon entered the Olympics as the favorite in the event, but no one—including Beamon himself—was prepared for the record-shattering leap he unleashed with his first attempt in the final round. Beamon's jump measured 8.90 meters, or 29'2½", nearly two feet farther than the previous record. Two other African Americans competed in the long jump. Participating in his third Olympics, Ralph Boston completed a remarkable trifecta, adding a bronze medal in Mexico City to the gold he had won in Rome in 1960 and the silver in Tokyo in 1964. A third African American, Charlie Mays from Jersey City, New Jersey, made the final round but did not medal.

Fewer than ten minutes after Beamon's incredible leap, Lee Evans shattered another world record, in the 400-meters. Evans, one of the stalwarts of the "Speed City" team from SJSU, had contemplated boycotting his event as a gesture of solidarity with Smith and Carlos. Encouraged to run by his teammates, including Carlos, Evans ultimately decided to run. He took the gold with a time of 43.8 seconds, setting a world record that stood for twenty years. Larry James, who had a stellar collegiate career for Villanova, won the silver, and completing the African American sweep was Ron Franklin from Elizabeth, New Jersey, who took the bronze. On the medal stand, all three athletes wore black berets in support of Smith and Carlos, but they took them off during the playing of the anthem, and they smiled and waved at the crowd. Evans suffered backlash from both sides after the modest gesture of protest; more militant boycott advocates thought he should have done more, and those opposed to the protests thought any gesture was inappropriate.[12] A fourth African American runner, Vince Matthews of the New York Pioneer Club and Johnson C. Smith College in Charlotte, North Carolina, joined the trio two days later to form the 4×400-meter relay team, which won the gold medal and set another long-standing world record.

The historic events of October 18 were only two of many record-setting performances in Mexico City. One of the first events of the Olympics, the 100-meter sprint featured two African American runners from Arkansas who had been dueling for the title of "world's fastest human" for over a year. Jim Hines of Texas Southern University and Charles Greene of the University of Nebraska each had held a share of the world record in the 100 since the 1968 AAU Outdoor Championships, where they both ran heats in 9.9 seconds on the way to finishing one-two in the final, won by Greene. In Mexico City, Greene matched the Olympic record of 10.0 seconds in the semifinals but struggled with a leg injury in the final, which Hines won in 9.95 seconds, a time later declared the official world record as it was the first such time automatically and electronically recorded. Greene labored but managed to finish third for the bronze medal. Mel Pender, the U.S. Army captain returning for his second Olympics, finished sixth. Joining Hines, Greene, and Pender in the 4×100-meter relay was Ronnie Ray Smith, another athlete from SJSU's "Speed City." The all-Black foursome won the gold medal with a world record time of 38.24 seconds.

A promising tandem of African American high jumpers found themselves battling for second place behind one of the revelations of the 1968 Olympics, Dick Fosbury from Oregon State University. Fosbury deployed a novel technique that became known as the "Fosbury Flop" in which he launched himself backward and head-first over the bar. A top contender for several years, he exploded in Mexico City to an Olympic-record jump of 7'4¼". Taking second behind Fosbury was Ed Caruthers, who had finished first at the Olympic trials and hoped to win gold in his second Olympics. Caruthers cleared a personal-best 7'3¼" but brushed the bar on his last attempt at Fosbury's height and settled for second.

A trio of African American runners starred in the 110-meter hurdles, including Willie Davenport and Ervin Hall, who finished one-two. Hall, part of Villanova's deep track squad, set an Olympic record of 13.3 seconds in his semifinal heat. Davenport returned for the second of his five Olympic appearances, this time running in peak form. He matched Hall's Olympic record time in the final to take the gold medal. Leon Coleman, of Winston-Salem State College, ran stride-for-stride with Davenport in their semifinal heat and took fourth in the final.

Three African American men competed in the triple jump, an event that saw the world record broken an astounding five different times in the course of the competition. Art Walker, of Morehouse College and the U.S. Army, was ranked number one in the world heading into the Olympics. He jumped a personal record 17.12 meters in his final attempt—better than the world record distance heading into the Olympics—but amazingly good enough only for fourth place in the competition.

AFRICAN AMERICAN MEN IN THE RING
AND ON THE COURT IN MEXICO CITY

Once again, the Black Mercuries significantly impacted the ring and the court in Mexico City. The United States sent a strong contingent of African American boxers, led by a nineteen-year-old heavyweight from Houston, George Foreman. Foreman may have been the most prominent Black athlete not included in the protest movement, a snub he resented. Those at the forefront of the protests were all college athletes, and Foreman felt they looked down on athletes such as him, who were not college educated. Rather than supporting the protestors, Foreman waved a tiny American flag in the ring after his gold medal bout, a broad grin on his face, a gesture that ingratiated him with many white Americans. Ronald Harris of Kent State University won the gold medal in the lightweight division after winning the AAU title for three consecutive years. Albert Robinson of Oakland, California, dominated his first four matches in the featherweight division before losing a controversial final match to Antonio Roldán of Mexico. Robinson was dominating the fight before being warned by the referee of a potential foul. Moments later, the official called a foul, and Robinson was disqualified, settling for the silver medal.

A trio of African American boxers won bronze medals in Mexico City. Johnny "The Mad" Baldwin of Detroit secured the bronze medal in the light middleweight division, losing only a close decision to Rolando Garbey of Cuba. Alfred Jones of Detroit won his first three matches in the middleweight division, before suffering a close loss in the semifinals to the eventual gold medal winner, Chris Finnegan of Great Britain. Harlan Joseph Marbley of White Oak, Maryland, who compiled an amateur record of 189–5, defeated his first two opponents 5–0 on points before losing a 4–1 decision in the semifinals to the eventual gold medal winner, Francisco Rodríguez of Venezuela.

The U.S. men's basketball team continued their unbeaten streak in the Olympics, defeating Yugoslavia 65–50 in the gold medal game. Once again, a strong cohort of Black players anchored the team, including Calvin Fowler, Spencer Haywood, Charlie Scott, and "Jo Jo" White. All four made the Olympic team in part because of their commitment to playing tough defense, after head coach Hank Iba put them through a grueling tryout process that saw prolific scorers like Pete Maravich of LSU and Calvin Murphy of Niagara missing the cut. Other prominent players like Lew Alcindor of UCLA and Elvin Hayes of Houston opted not to play, meaning that the less-than-star-studded U.S. team faced the real possibility of losing an Olympic game for the first time. Still, the team won most games comfortably, the closest being a five-point victory over Puerto Rico. They did not have to play the favored Soviet team, which lost to Yugoslavia in the semifinal game on the other side of the draw. Haywood, from Trinidad State Junior College, became the youngest player in Team U.S.A. history, at age nineteen. He averaged 16.1 points per game, including a game-high 21 points in the gold medal game. "Jo Jo" White from the University of Kansas was the most prominent player on the team, leading all players with 16.3 points per game. He went on to have a Hall of Fame NBA career, most of which was spent with the Boston Celtics.

Finally, two members of Team U.S.A. in Mexico City were the first Black American athletes to compete in their respective sports, James Kanati Allen in gymnastics and Uriah Jones in fencing. Allen, who was half-Black and half-Cherokee, attended UCLA. He had the highest combined total score for the United States in the team competition, with the team finishing seventh. Jones, born in Harlem, has been called the "Jackie Robinson of fencing" and broke the color barrier with several clubs and in several venues.[13] As he struggled to find support in the sport, he broke through relatively late, competing in Mexico City at the age of forty-three. Jones competed in the team foil competition, finishing with a 1–3 record as part of a losing effort against the team from Great Britain.

AFRICAN AMERICAN WOMEN IN MEXICO CITY

The unquestioned star of the track in Mexico City was Wyomia Tyus, who returned to defend the gold medal she won in the 100-meters in Tokyo. Against a strong field, including two of her African American teammates, Tyus ran a world record time of 11.08 seconds, becoming the first Olympic athlete—male or female—to repeat as winner in the 100-meters. She also competed in the 200-meters, finishing sixth in the final. Tyus added a third gold medal to her career achievements, anchoring the 4×100-meter relay team to victory. The latest in a line of great Black female champions, Tyus moved to California, married a Puma shoe representative with ties to the SJSU program, ran professionally for several years, and eventually raised a family and worked in the Los Angeles Department of Education.

While her name may be less well-known, Margaret Johnson Bailes was a legitimate rival to Tyus in 1968. Born in the Bronx, New York, but raised in the track city of Eugene, Oregon, Bailes rose to stardom as a high schooler. At age seventeen she dominated regional meets and became a force on the national scene. At the 1968 AAU Championships, she defeated the sublime Wyomia Tyus and tied the world record in the 100-meters at 11.1 seconds. At the Olympic trials, she finished second to Tyus in the 100-meters and actually won the 200-meters, ahead of Tyus. Unfortunately, Bailes was stricken with a bout of pneumonia while in Mexico City. While she recovered enough to compete she was not running at full strength. She was bitterly disappointed with a fifth-place finish in the 100 and seventh in the 200, an event she was favored to win. Despite her disappointment, Bailes was determined to run in the 4×100-meter relay and helped the team to a gold medal with a world-record time. Only seventeen years old at the time of the Olympics, Bailes might have gone on to become an Olympic legend; however, she had run her last major race. Already married, within a few months after the Olympics she was pregnant and retired from track at the behest of her husband to raise a family.[14]

Another sprinter, Barbara Ann Ferrell of Los Angeles, also ran in the 100- and 200-meters and the 4×100-meter relay. Ferrell finished second behind Wyomia Tyus in the 100-meters and fourth in the 200-meters. She joined Bailes and Tyus as part of the world record setting 4×100-meter relay team. The fourth runner, Mildrette Netter of Alcorn A&M, had finished fourth in the Olympic trials in the 100- and 200-meters.

Mexico City also saw the beginning of another remarkable Olympic career, that of Madeline Manning (who later raced as Madeline Manning-Jackson and Madeline Manning-Mims). Manning dominated the 800-meters for the year leading up to the Olympics, and while she won the Olympic trials she was not regarded as one of the favorites to take a gold medal by the national media, a slight that motivated Manning during her race. In the final, Manning raced to a gold medal in an Olympic-record 2:00.9, though she insists she could have set the world record and broken the two-minute mark had she not slowed slightly to look for her white teammate, Doris Brown.

1972 MUNICH: "THE MOST BEAUTIFUL OLYMPIC GAMES THAT WERE EVER DESTROYED"[15]

The 1972 Munich Olympics marked a watershed moment; never again would security at the Games be taken lightly. In an attempt to demonstrate to the world that Germany had recovered from the authoritarian era of the Nazi regime and that it was now an open and democratic society, organizers of the Munich Games sought to avoid any appearance of a militarized or heavily armed event. Thus, fences around the facilities were chain link, low, and without barbed wire or other protections at the top; in short, they were easily cleared by would-be intruders. Security personnel were kept to a minimum, with few armed guards, police, or soldiers in the area. The athletes themselves largely ignored security concerns, sharing access passes and opening doors for visitors on the grounds.

In the early morning hours of September 5, eight Palestinian terrorists, lightly disguised in track suits and carrying gym bags loaded with weapons, climbed over the fence and entered the Athletic Village. They sought out the Israeli quarters and launched their attack, killing two Israeli athletes and taking nine more as hostages. Attempts at negotiations failed over the course of the next nineteen hours, and a botched rescue attempt on the tarmac at the Munich airport eventually ended with all nine of the Israeli athletes dead, along with five terrorists and one policeman. For African American athletes—as all Olympians in Munich—the horrific tragedy of the terrorist attack shook their sense of purpose and led many to question whether, in the infamous words of IOC President Avery Brundage, "The Games must go on."[16] Out of respect for the dead and recognition of the gravity of the attack, athletic competitions were postponed for one day, and a memorial service was held the morning after the failed rescue attempt. The competition resumed all too soon.

BLACK ATHLETES AND THE "FORGOTTEN" PROTEST: ACTIVISM AT THE 1972 MUNICH OLYMPICS[17]

The activist spirit among Black athletes of the late 1960s had dissipated somewhat by 1972 but had not completely disappeared. Black athletes noted that conditions had not noticeably improved since their protests in 1968, and some wondered whether they should engage in some kind of protest in Munich. Two athletes chose to do just that . . . sort of. After finishing first and second in the 400-meter race, Vince Matthews, who won the gold medal, and Wayne Collett, who took the silver, stood together on the top of the podium, seemed to turn their back on the American flag, and chatted while the anthem played. Matthews rubbed his chin and scowled and then twirled the gold medal casually around his finger as they stepped down from the podium. Collett appeared to give a Black Power salute as they left the field.

The reaction of the fans was instant; many in the stadium jeered and booed the athletes as they stood on the podium and then walked off the field. The reaction of IOC President Brundage and Olympic officials was nearly as swift; in less than twenty-four hours the pair were kicked off the U.S. Olympic team and banned for life from participating in the Olympics. Even their own family members questioned their actions. Matthews' mother chided him, "You should have stood at attention. You were on top of the world. Now you've knocked yourself down from being on top of the world."[18]

Collett, from Los Angeles, attended UCLA and won numerous collegiate meets and national titles prior to his Olympic experiences. Matthews was from Queens, New York, and rose through the amateur track ranks as part of the New York Pioneer Club. Matthews and Collett were joined in the Olympics by John Smith, Collett's teammate at UCLA and world-record holder in the 440 yards, and Lee Evans, who had smashed the world record in Mexico City and now, as the fourth place qualifier, would compete only in the 4×400-meter relay. In the final, Smith suffered a relapse of a hamstring injury and had to pull up, leaving Matthews and Collett to duel for the gold. Incidentally, Smith's injury along with the expulsion of Matthews and Collett meant that the United States could no longer field a team in the 4×400-meter relay, and thus Evans did not get to compete in his second Olympics. It was Matthews who finished first in 44.66 seconds, followed by Collett and Julius Sang of Kenya, who took the bronze.

In occasional interviews and comments since, the pair has struggled to explain their intent. Their protest was clearly unplanned and lacked the clarity of the unwavering raised, gloved fists of Smith and Carlos four years earlier. Collett later explained that he could not in good conscience sing the words of the national anthem, but he also claimed that, "It wasn't a protest."[19] For Matthews, his nonchalant attitude on the medal podium represented a lifetime of struggles as a Black athlete, especially the four years since his first Olympic experience. In Munich, he sought to atone for what he felt was a meek protest after the relay in Mexico City. There, as part of the gold medal winning 4×400-meter relay team, he and his teammates wore black berets and briefly raised their fists in salute on the medal stand but then stood at attention during the playing of the national anthem. "I always considered what we did a token gesture," he wrote in his autobiography.[20]

While Matthews and Collett, and the controversy surrounding their protest and the subsequent punishment, attracted considerable attention in the press and around the athletic village, it faded from view fairly quickly and ultimately garnered far less attention than the protests of 1968. Their protest suffered from poor timing within the context of the Games. Matthews and Collett's action took place on September 7, two days after the terrorist attacks and among those events just resuming as the world still stood in shock over the horror. As the competition resumed, many athletes found their focus shaken. Matthews and Collett seemed somewhat disinterested in their own protest, so it is possible that they questioned their own purpose on the medal stand in those difficult moments, though they never stated as much. In any case, unlike 1968, their actions did not spark any further protests among Black athletes and have drawn relatively little attention from scholars.

CONTROVERSY ON THE COURT AND IN THE RING IN MUNICH

Among the other athletes to see action on the day play resumed were the basketball players, as Team U.S.A. played a game against Italy the day after the memorial service. Players, both Black and white, questioned whether the game should be played and approached it with lackluster enthusiasm. The U.S. team featured six Black players, more than ever before: Mike Bantom, Jim Brewer, James Forbes, Thomas Henderson, Dwight Jones, and "Easy" Ed Ratleff. Of the group, only Forbes did not go on to have a long and successful NBA career. The 1972 team became the first U.S. team to lose a game in the Olympics, after a run of sixty-three consecutive victories and seven straight gold medals. Complications with building a roster left the 1972 squad without some of the best players in the country, including UCLA center Bill Walton, who disliked the harsh practices run by head coach Hank Iba, his UCLA teammate Swen Nater, who was recovering from an injury, and soon-to-be professional stars such as Julius Erving, Bob McAdoo, Len Elmore, and David Thompson. By 1972, the gap had also closed between the once-dominant Americans and a number of international teams, most notably the Soviets, who had spent the last decade grooming a team built to defeat the Americans. Still, the U.S. team arrived at the final game against the Soviets undefeated at 8–0 and with a chance to continue their long unbeaten Olympic streak.

The end of the game involved one of the most controversial finishes in basketball history. For a variety of disputed reasons, the Soviets were awarded possession three different times with three seconds remaining, with the United States holding a tenuous 50–49 lead. On the third attempt, the Soviets converted a layup to take a 51–50 lead and the gold medal.

American protests of the controversial outcome were not successful. So bitter were American players that they declined to accept their silver medals. Despite the loss, the African American contingent all made valuable contributions to the team, as Bantom, Forbes, Henderson, Jones, and Ratleff all led the team in scoring during at least one game, while Brewer averaged 7.6 points and 7.1 rebounds per game.

African Americans were well represented in the ring and on the mat in Munich, including seven Black boxers (out of eleven weight classes) and one wrestler. Most notably, "Sugar" Ray Seales took the gold in the light welterweight division. Seales, a product of the Tacoma (WA) Boys Club, fought 350 amateur bouts, including victories in the 1971 AAU Championships and 1972 Golden Gloves, before winning gold in Munich. He went on to a prolific professional career of 68 fights, including a trifecta against the legendary "Marvelous" Marvin Hagler, the last of which led to a retinal tear that left Seales legally blind. Other boxing medalists included Ricardo Carreras, who won the bronze medal in the bantamweight division. An Air Force veteran from New York City, Carreras won the inter-service championship three times before fighting in the Olympics. Carreras won four bouts in Munich before a loss in the semifinals to Mexico's Alfonso Zamora. Also winning the bronze was Marvin "Pops" Johnson of Indianapolis in the light-heavyweight division. Johnson entered the Olympics as a two-time Golden Gloves champion and the 1971 AAU National Champion. In Munich, he won his first two bouts easily before being knocked out in the second round by the eventual champion, Soviet Vyacheslav Lemeshev.

Four other Black boxers competed in Munich but did not medal. Among them was light-middleweight Reginald Jones, who was involved in the most controversial decision at these Olympics. Jones, who picked up boxing while serving in the U.S. Navy at Guantanamo Bay, Cuba, twice won the inter-service competition before his Olympic experience. In his second-round bout against the Soviet Valeri Tregubov, Jones battered his opponent nearly to submission by the third round. Tregubov remained on his feet but appeared resigned to defeat as the fighters awaited the judges' decision. Shockingly, the referee raised Tregubov's arm in victory, and Jones was eliminated. It was one of several questionable rulings in the boxing competition and by far the most egregious. Before the Olympics concluded, six boxing judges had been suspended, but the suspensions did nothing to assuage Jones, whose chance at Olympic glory was dashed.

The U.S. roster in team handball included one Black player, Rudolph Matthews. Team handball returned to the Olympic program for the first time since 1936, and the 1972 team was the first for the United States.

Matthews, a talented multi-sport athlete from Woodville, Mississippi, who earned a baseball scholarship to Grambling State University and joined the U.S. Army in 1968, the beginning of a long career in the military. During his service, he discovered the sport of handball and was eventually recruited to join the inaugural U.S. Olympic team. In Munich, Matthews played in all five of America's games and scored ten goals, including the team's first goal in competition. The United States finished in fourteenth place. As a final note, Tyrone Simmons of Detroit became the second African American for the U.S. men's fencing team. Twice a runner-up in the national championships, Simmons competed in the team foil. The team lost both of its matches in pool play and did not advance to the medal round.

THE BLACK MERCURIES: MEN'S TRACK AND FIELD IN MUNICH

The United States had grown accustomed to sending a powerful squad of Black sprinters to the Olympics, and 1972 was no exception. Unfortunately, a tandem of medal hopefuls were denied an opportunity at a medal due to a scheduling mix-up. The 100-meter sprint team included Eddie Hart, Rey Robinson, and Robert Taylor, all three of whom were potential medal-winners. Hart and Robinson had both tied the world record of 9.9 seconds at the Olympic trials, and all three men won their first heats. Black assistant track coach Stanley Wright, who supervised the sprinters at both the 1968 and 1972 Olympics, had been given a schedule indicating that the quarterfinal heats would be held at 7:00 p.m. that evening. However, as they watched races on the television at about 4:15 p.m., they realized what they saw were actually the heats that they were supposed to run. They rushed to the track, arriving just before the third quarterfinal heat, in which Taylor was scheduled to run. Taylor threw off his track suit, stretched quickly, and somehow managed to finish second in the heat, advancing to the semifinals. Unfortunately, Hart and Robinson had been scheduled in the first and second quarterfinal heats, which had already concluded, and they were eliminated. Taylor went on to win the silver medal. A week later, Eddie Hart found some redemption in anchoring the 4×100-meter relay team to the gold medal in world-record time, along with Taylor, Larry Black from North Carolina Central University, and Gerald Tinker from Miami. Robinson was not part of the relay team, and thus left Munich despondent at being denied a chance at a medal. He remained bitter for years after the controversy, and his failure to qualify for the 1976 team only enhanced that bitterness.[21] Black also competed in the 200-meter sprint in Munich, winning the silver behind the great Soviet sprinter Valeri Borzov. Another African American, Larry Burton, placed fourth in the 200-meter final.

The United States once again sent a strong contingent in the men's 110-meter hurdles; three of the top four finishers in the final were African Americans. Rodney "Hot Rod" Milburn, one of the great hurdlers in American history, won the gold and matched the world record in the final. Milburn, from Louisiana and Southern University, set his first world record during an undefeated 1971 season and entered 1972 as a prohibitive favorite to win gold in Munich. At the Olympic trials, however, Milburn uncharacteristically showed some nerves, brushing several hurdles as he struggled to match Willie Davenport, who ran in the lane next to him. Milburn managed to finish third and qualify for the Olympics, where he returned to form. Thomas Hill of Arkansas State and the U.S. Army won the bronze. Davenport, competing in his third of five Olympics, finished fourth.

The United States also sent a strong group of long- and triple-jumpers, most of them African American. In the long jump, Randy Williams of Fresno, California, and USC, had the longest jump of the meet at 8.34 meters in the qualifying round, then secured the gold medal with a leap of 8.24 meters in the final. Paul "Arnie" Robinson, from San Diego State University and a veteran of the U.S. Army, won the bronze medal. On the medal stand, he wore an arm band picturing three bombs with a red line through them, an antiwar symbol. Preston Carrington of Wichita State University leapt 8.22 meters on his only jump in the qualifying round, a distance that would have been good enough for the silver medal in the final round. He could not match that distance, however, finishing fifth in the final. Two African Americans competed in the triple jump but did not medal. Art Walker returned with hopes of improving on his fourth place finish in Mexico City, but he did not qualify for the final round, finishing twenty-ninth. John Craft of Eastern Illinois University finished fifth. Finally, Jeff Bennett of Oklahoma Christian College finished fourth in the decathlon. The smallest athlete in the competition at only 5'8" and 152 pounds, he missed a medal by only ten points with a total of 7,974 points, one of the narrowest margins in Olympic history.

DIVERSITY, AND DISAPPOINTMENT, FOR AFRICAN AMERICAN WOMEN IN MUNICH

By the late 1960s, opportunities for American women to participate in amateur sports were expanding. While the Tigerbelles remained a dominant force in women's sports, particularly track and field, young women around the country found opportunities to train and compete with a variety of local clubs, A.A.U. organizations, or universities, such as Mayor Daley's Youth Club in Chicago and the Atoms Track Club in Brooklyn, New York. The 1972 U.S. Olympic team, which did feature several Tigerbelles such as Willye White and Iris Davis, included women from all parts of the country. The primacy of the Tigerbelles was beginning to decline. The women's team, for the first time in a generation, also failed to include a star African American competitor, as most of the women failed to medal; there was no Wyomia Tyus on the 1972 team.

While it may have lacked the star power of some previous teams, the 1972 women's squad did have experienced competitors. Most notably, long jumpers Willye White and Martha Rae Watson returned for their fifth and third Olympics, respectively. White qualified for the final, but a jump of 6.27 meters was good enough only for eleventh in the final. Watson finished twenty-third and did not make the final. Two other former Olympians returned for the 1972 squad in the 100-meter hurdles (formerly run at eighty meters). Mamie Rallins, who had competed in Mexico City, and Lacey O'Neal, who had competed in Tokyo, both finished seventh in their semifinal heats, failing to advance to the final.

One highlight for the U.S. women was a silver medal finish in the 4×400-meter relay. The relay team included two women who competed in the individual 800-meters, Madeline Manning and Cheryl Toussaint. Manning returned for her second Olympics after having won the gold in Mexico City. She missed qualifying for the final round by .03 seconds, though it would have been an immense challenge for her to medal against a field in which all eight finalists bettered Manning's Olympic record from four years earlier. Toussaint from Brooklyn, New York, finished sixth in her qualifying heat and did not advance. The relay also included Mable Fergerson of Los Angeles, a seventeen-year-old who had broken many high school records, who finished fifth in the individual 400-meters competition.

America's other sprinters similarly came up just short of medaling. The latest in the string of great sprint champions from Tennessee State University, Iris Davis, twice finished fourth in Munich, both times beaten at the line by Cuban runner Sylvia Chivás. Davis was a four-time national champion and a two-time Pan American champion in the 100-meters and several other sprints. She narrowly missed a medal in both the 100-meter individual sprint and the 4×100-meter relay. Barbara Ferrell of the Los Angeles Mercurettes returned for her second Olympics, finishing seventh in the 100-meters and failing to reach the final in the 200-meters. Jackie

Thompson of San Diego, who ran for the Mickey's Missiles Track Club founded by the first African American female Olympic medalist Audrey Patterson, competed in the 200-meters but failed to reach the final round by .04 seconds. Pamela Greene of Denver, Colorado, also competed in the 200-meters but failed to advance out of the heats.

A final athlete warrants mention. Ruth White of Baltimore became the first African American woman to represent the United States in the Olympics in fencing. White, who endured racist taunts and bullying as a child in Baltimore, ultimately found in fencing a refuge from the torment. "When you walked into the fencing salle," she said, "Nobody really cared what color you were. . . . It was like being in heaven."[22] White also found that a childhood spent running to and from school and fighting with her brother had endowed her with traits essential for success in fencing: strong legs and fast reaction time. "I was a very aggressive, very athletic kid," she explained.[23] Success came quickly for her, and she won the senior national championship at age seventeen, in 1969. She won her second national title in 1972, which earned her a spot on the Olympic team. In Munich, she advanced to the second round in the individual event and helped lead the team to seventh place in the team event, its best finish ever to that point.

As the athletes departed from Munich, they could not have known that they had witnessed the passing of an Olympic era. Never again were the Olympics to be treated as a "safe space" in the midst of global turmoil. After 1972, security was always a top priority for Olympic organizers. While the wave of African American protest in the Olympics subsided, global uproar over the South African policy of apartheid would only grow in the following years. A new generation of female athletes rose to the forefront, a development hastened greatly by the implementation of Title IX in 1972, which banned gender discrimination in education programs receiving federal aid. Olympic athletes in the 1970s continued their push for more pay and opportunities after their Olympic careers, and by the end of the Cold War the Olympic movement had largely abandoned its insistence that the athletes remain amateurs. Finally, and most important, America's Olympians joined others from around the world in an era when the Olympics were drawn fully into the realm of international politics, as the next generation saw their Olympic dreams sometimes dashed, sometimes aided, by a pair of Olympic boycotts.

6

BLACK MERCURIES IN THE AGE OF BOYCOTTS

The two men sat motionless on their bikes, eyeing each other with suspicion. It is not uncommon in cycling "sprint" races for the riders to employ all manner of tactics, in an effort to preserve the all-important trailing position as the race moves to its final sprint. But this moment in the semifinal race at the 1984 Los Angeles Olympics seemed almost impossible. The French national champion, Philippe Vernet, pulled to the top of the track, slowed to a crawl, and then stopped. African American cyclist Nelson Vails inched behind Vernet, bunny-hopped his back wheel to nestle up next to him, and stopped as well. For nearly a minute, the two men held their bikes nearly motionless. Aside from the tremble in their muscles, one might think this exercise was easy. At last, in a moment when the Frenchman glanced away, Vails pulled out and began the race in earnest. He gained enough advantage that Vernet was never able to get close until the final, desperate sprint. From a full stop to a top speed over forty miles per hour, with pedals spinning at an incredible rate, Vails held off Vernet in the final stretch, winning the race and earning a spot in the finals. In so doing, Vails was assured of becoming the first African American medalist in Olympics cycling history.

Vails represented a new generation of Black athletes. Raised in the aftermath of the Civil Rights Movement, and with little or no memory of the activist-athletes of the late 1960s, Vails and others became trailblazers in a host of Olympic sports in which Black athletes had made little or no impact before. By the end of the Cold War, African Americans were competing—

and medaling—in Olympic sports such as cycling, fencing, judo, and gymnastics, in addition to sports where they had always excelled, such as boxing, basketball, and track and field. For some, breaking barriers in such sports came at a hard price, as they confronted discrimination, intimidation, and outright racism. For others, it was competing and winning at the highest level that posed the greatest challenge. For all of them, making the Olympics, contending for medals and representing their country continued the long tradition established by the generations of Black Mercuries who had come before, and they joined the process of moving forward as a race and a nation with zeal.

THE BLACK MERCURIES STRUGGLE TO MATCH PREVIOUS HEIGHTS AT THE 1976 MONTREAL OLYMPICS

On May 12, 1970, the International Olympic Committee awarded the Games of the XXI Olympiad (1976) to Montreal, which had hosted a successful World's Fair in 1967, and launched a new Major League Baseball (MLB) franchise, the Expos, in 1969. Coupled with Montreal's heavy French cultural influence, rich history, and European vibe, it seemed an ideal host city. Almost immediately, though, Montreal's Olympic campaign was beset with problems. The initial budget of C$120 million proved far too low. Construction over the following years was stricken by labor issues leading to long periods of inactivity. In the final year, organizers rushed to complete the facilities on time, only barely making it. As the Opening Ceremonies commenced on July 17, 1976, "the Greek athletes who traditionally led the Parade of Nations came up the ramp toward the Olympic stadium to find their way almost blocked by construction workers."[1] The Olympics left Montreal C$1.6 billion in debt, a figure that left city officials hamstrung for decades and took thirty years to pay off.

The Montreal Olympics also ushered in what would become a distressing new trend in Olympic politics: the boycott. Only three weeks before the Opening Ceremonies, twenty-eight African nations announced they would not participate alongside athletes from New Zealand, who had sent their rugby team on a controversial tour of South Africa. The other nations of Africa insisted that no country should tacitly endorse apartheid by sending athletes to compete there. The boycott hurt, not only from the financial perspective as Montreal organizers (already financially strapped as described above) had to refund more than $1 million in unused tickets, but also in the absence of many of the world's top athletes, especially in distance running.

Finally, the boycott also paved the way for other nations to do the same in the future, as would be demonstrated four years later in 1980.

In Montreal, African Americans performed well in track and field but faced a stiff challenge from the Soviet Union and the Eastern bloc teams, which were not only at full strength but also at the height of their state-sponsored doping programs. Some smaller teams rising to prominence in the track world also chipped away at the medal count, as nations such as Jamaica and Trinidad produced medal winners. Americans won nineteen medals in men's track and field: six gold, six silver, and seven bronze. African Americans accounted for more than half of those medals, capturing twelve, including gold in both sprint relays, for which all eight of the runners were Black.

A strong contingent of African American runners in the 400-meters produced three of those medals. Fred Newhouse from Prairie View A&M held the lead for much of the final race in the individual 400-meters, but he was caught down the stretch by Cuban Alberto Juantorena, who broke a streak of five consecutive gold medals for the United States in this discipline. Newhouse took the silver, and Herman Frazier of Arizona State University took the bronze. Maxie Parks of UCLA entered the race as the favorite, having won the Olympic trials, but he finished fifth in the final. Newhouse, Frazier, and Parks teamed with UCLA's Benny Brown to win the gold in the 4×400-meter relay, finishing three seconds clear of the second place team from Poland and third place team from West Germany.

The United States had become accustomed to success in the competition for the "world's fastest human" in the 100-meter sprint. The Montreal Olympics was no exception, as a trio of African American runners posted some of the top times in the preliminary heats. In the final, however, Harvey Glance of Auburn University could do no better than fourth place, and Johnny "Lam" Jones, a football star at the University of Texas, finished sixth. Steve Riddick of Norfolk State had been eliminated after finishing fifth in his semifinal heat. That left the 4×100-meter relay as a chance at redemption for those three, teaming with 200-meters star Millard Hampton and taking the gold in 38.33 seconds over the teams from East Germany and the Soviet Union. Hampton added a silver medal in the individual 200-meter sprint. Dwayne Evans, who had just graduated from high school and not yet started his track career at Arizona State, finished third in that event.

African American athletes added to the U.S. medal count in the hurdling events as well. One of the breakout stars in Montreal was the 400-meter hurdler Edwin Moses from Morehouse College, who had never participated in an international meet prior to the 1976 Olympics. He swept to victory in a world-record time of 47.64 seconds. African American Quentin Wheeler of San Diego State University, who had beaten Moses at the NCAA championships that year, finished fourth. A trio of African American runners also represented the United States in the 110-meter hurdles. Willie Davenport, back for his fourth and final Summer Olympics, won the bronze.

In the field events, Arnie Robinson of San Diego State University, who won the bronze in the long jump in Munich, captured gold in Montreal with a career-best jump of 8.35 meters. Randy Williams of USC, who had won the gold in 1972, finished second behind Robinson. The United States looked to be in contention for a sweep of the medals, but Larry Myricks of Mississippi College broke his foot while warming up for the final and could not compete. James Butts of UCLA added a silver medal in the triple jump, finishing behind the great Soviet jumper Viktor Saneyev, who won his third consecutive gold medal in the event.

The U.S. women's track and field contingent also struggled to match its successes of previous Olympics. A new generation of young women was beginning to show its potential. Title IX, which contributed greatly to the growth of women's college sports, was evidenced in the breadth and variety of backgrounds and training of Olympic athletes, but it had not fully taken hold. It would be a decade or more before the financial and cultural impact of Title IX would produce a truly transformative generation of female athletes. Additionally, the East Germans had implemented a sweeping doping program, which inflated the performance of their athletes.

In the women's 100-meters, West and East Germans swept the medals. Nineteen-year-old Evelyn Ashford, making her Olympic debut, finished fifth. Two Tennessee State Tigerbelles also competed in the 100-meters. Chandra Cheeseborough finished sixth, and Brenda Morehead finished sixth in her semifinal heat and did not make the final. Ashford and Cheeseborough teamed with Martha Watson—competing in her fourth and final Olympics—and Debra Armstrong in the 4×100-meter relay, but they could manage only a seventh place finish as East Germany, West Germany, and the Soviet Union went one-two-three. Cheeseborough and Armstrong also competed in the 200-meters, but both finished sixth in their semifinal heats and failed to qualify for the final.

The U.S. women sent a promising group in the 400-meter sprint, but they came up just short of medaling. Rosalyn Bryant of Chicago set a new U.S. record time in her semifinal heat, but she finished fifth in the final. Sheila Ingram of Washington, D.C., finished sixth, and Debra Sapenter from Prairie View, Texas, finished eighth. Bryant and Ingram were within one-half second of the silver medal. All three medal winners, from Eastern bloc nations, have since come under suspicion of doping. The trio of Americans, joined by Pamela Jiles of Dillard University, hoped for redemption in the 4×400-meter relay. They ran the final in 3:22.81—better than the world record at that time—but still finished nearly three seconds behind the dominant East German squad, settling for silver.

The youngest member of the U.S. women's track squad, while she did not medal, warrants mention. Rhonda Brady, having just completed her junior year of high school in Gary, Indiana, and having turned seventeen the week before the Olympics, competed in the 100-meter hurdles but failed to advance out of her qualifying heat. After high school, she joined the Tennessee State Tigerbelles and would eventually compete in three more Olympic trials, but Montreal was her only Olympic experience. Madeline Manning, at twenty-nine and in her third Olympics, competed in the 800-meters but failed to make the finals.

African American women also competed in the jumping events, where the Tigerbelles continued to exert their influence. Kathy McMillan, who had just graduated from high school in Raeford, North Carolina, and soon to sign with Tennessee State, vaulted from tenth in the qualifying round to second in the final of the long jump. Martha Watson, another Tigerbelle, competed in the long jump in her fourth Olympics but failed to advance out of qualifying, as did Sherron Walker of Cal State–Long Beach.

U.S. BASKETBALL AND BOXERS THRIVE IN MONTREAL

The U.S. boxing squad in Montreal is regarded as one of the best ever, including five gold-medal winners, one silver, and one bronze. They included: Leo Randolph, flyweight; Howard Davis, lightweight; "Sugar" Ray Leonard, light-welterweight; Michael Spinks, middleweight; and Leon Spinks, light-heavyweight. Howard Davis earned the Val Barker Trophy, given to the most outstanding boxer in the tournament. Ray Leonard had the most celebrated professional career of the group, winning titles in five weight classes and battling in some of the greatest fights of the 1980s, against such greats as Thomas "Hitman" Hearns, Marvin Hagler, and Roberto Duran. The Spinks brothers became the first pair of brothers to win gold medals in the same Olympics, and both went on to successful professional careers. Sweetening the gold medal matches was the fact that U.S. boxers swept four matches against their Cold War rivals from Cuba and the U.S.S.R. Heavyweight John Tate did drop his match against a Cuban opponent in the semifinal round, losing to defending Olympic champion Teofilo

Stephenson and settling for the bronze medal. The lone silver medal in the group went to Charlie Mooney, who won his first five matches in the bantamweight division before losing in the final match to Gu Yong-ju of North Korea.

African Americans were well represented in other combative sports in Montreal. Most notably, Allen Coage from New York City won the bronze medal in the heavyweight division in judo, the first American heavyweight to medal in the sport. Coage discovered judo while in high school and later trained for two years in Japan. After Montreal, he went on to a long career in professional wrestling, known by the stage name "Bad News Brown." Lloyd "Butch" Keaser, a two-time All-American at Navy, won the silver medal in 68kg freestyle wrestling, losing to Soviet champion Pavel Pinigin in the final.

For the men's basketball team, Montreal promised the opportunity to avenge the controversial and disheartening loss to the Soviets in Munich. Continuing to suffer from some of the challenges of building a quality roster, most significantly that the best college players typically wanted to sign professional contracts as soon as possible rather than extending their uncompensated amateur careers, the U.S. team was young and lacked international experience. They did reach the final game undefeated at 6–0 but along the way had very close games against Puerto Rico and Czechoslovakia, whom they defeated 95–94 and 81–76, respectively. Awaiting them in the gold-medal game was not the Soviet Union but Yugoslavia, which had beaten the Soviets 89–84 in the semifinals. The Americans dispatched Yugoslavia 95–74 to win the gold, but they disappointingly never faced the Soviets in the tournament. Nine of the twelve players on the U.S. roster were Black, all of whom went on to play in the NBA: Tate Armstrong, Quinn Buckner, Scott May, Kenneth Carr, Adrian Dantley, Walter Davis, Phil Ford, Phil Hubbard, and Steve Sheppard.

Women's basketball, a new sport at the 1976 Olympics, featured a small field of six teams who played a round-robin tournament. The U.S. team fared well, going 3–2 and winning the silver medal. However, no one could match the mighty Soviet team, which crushed the U.S. team 112–77 en route to the gold medal with a 5–0 record while outscoring their opponents by an enormous 158 points. The 1976 squad included four African American women: Lusia Harris, Charlotte Lewis, Gail Marquis, and Trish Roberts. Harris played professionally for several years and actually was selected in the seventh round of the 1977 NBA draft by the New Orleans Jazz, the first and only time a woman has been drafted by an NBA team. She is in both the Naismith Basketball Hall of Fame and the Women's Basketball Hall of Fame.

Peter Westbrook, who eventually became one of the most influential Black fencers in America and established a school that spawned a number of future Black Olympians, competed in his first of five Olympics in the sabre competition in Montreal. Despite a serious ankle injury, he advanced to the elimination round in a very deep field featuring the top six finishers from the Munich Olympics, all of whom returned in 1976. He lost to the eventual silver medalist, Vladimir Nazlymov of the Soviet Union. Nikki Franke of Harlem, New York, and Brooklyn College competed in women's fencing. She qualified again in 1980 then later became the fencing coach at Temple University.

THE 1980 U.S. OLYMPIC TEAM: STOLEN DREAMS

On July 19, 1980, more than 100,000 fans packed the Central Lenin Stadium for the Opening Ceremonies of the Moscow Summer Olympics. Athletes representing eighty-one nations paraded into the stadium, including more than 4,000 men and 1,100 women. The United States team of nearly 500 athletes was absent, along with teams from sixty-four other nations. On December 27, 1979, the Soviet Union had launched an invasion of its neutral neighboring country, Afghanistan. A few weeks later, U.S. President Jimmy Carter announced that he would not support sending a U.S. team to the Summer Olympics in Moscow. Carter explained, "The Soviet Union must pay a concrete price for their aggression."[2] American athletic bodies continued the process of Olympic qualifying, and eventually selected a U.S. Olympic team. Some hoped that the USOC might vote to participate anyway, despite the pressure applied by the Carter administration. However, on April 12, 1980, the USOC House of Delegates voted 1,604 to 797 to support the boycott.

As a final desperate attempt to preserve their Olympic dream, twenty-five American Olympians signed on to a class-action claim against the USOC. The lead plaintiff in the case was African American rower Anita DeFrantz, who had won a bronze medal in the 1976 Olympics and hoped to return in 1980. Their hopes hinged on a recently passed law, the 1978 Amateur Sports Act, that sought to give greater structure to American amateur athletics, resolve long and bitter disputes between governing bodies such as the National Collegiate Athletic Association (NCAA) and Amateur Athletic Union (AAU), and to improve the rosters of America's Olympic teams. On May 16, 1980—just two months from the Opening Ceremonies in Moscow—Judge John H. Pratt dismissed the athletes' claims. The last hopes for the 1980 Olympians to compete in Moscow were dashed. DeFrantz still contends the decision was wrong: "It was up to the athletes to make that decision and no one else had the right to make that decision."[3] For her leadership among the 1980 Olympians, DeFrantz was appointed vice president of the 1984 Los Angeles Olympic Organizing Committee, and in 1986 she became the first African American and first woman to represent the United States as a member of the International Olympic Committee.

The decision to boycott robbed 470 American Olympians of their opportunity to compete, including seventy-one African Americans. Although the 1980 Olympians were recognized with a congressional gold medal and invited to visit the White House, some found the invitation too painful to accept. Thirteen of them were Olympic veterans who had been able to live the Olympic experience before, but the final chapter in their Olympic story went unwritten due to the boycott. For instance, qualifying for the 1980 team brought an end to the storied athletic careers of Madeline Manning Mims, the two-time medal winner who competed in 1968, 1972, and 1976, and Randy Williams, who had won gold in the long jump in 1972 and silver in 1976.

For others, the lure of being able to return in 1984 and compete in the Olympics on American soil proved a powerful motivation to keep competing. Twenty of them returned in 1984 or beyond, including future gold medal winners Carl Lewis and Jeanette Bolden. Perhaps the most remarkable redemption story involved freestyle wrester Chris Campbell of Westfield, New Jersey. A three-time NCAA champion at the University of Iowa, Campbell was the favorite to win gold in Moscow. After the boycott, Campbell retired from competition and embarked on a legal career. Unhappy in that career and convinced he had unfinished business on the mat, he returned to wrestling and qualified for the 1992 Barcelona Olympics, where he won a bronze medal just a month shy of his thirty-eighth birthday. Four athletes achieved the remarkable feat of competing in the Olympics both before and after 1980, including the legendary Edwin Moses, who was in the midst of an unbeaten streak that stretched to 122 races and who won the gold medal in the 400-meter hurdles in both the 1976 and 1984 Olympics.

For thirty-four African American athletes, though, 1980 represented their one and only chance at Olympic glory. Many of them were basketball players or boxers, both disciplines in which lucrative professional careers often followed amateur experience, so a return for a second Olympics was unlikely. Among those who missed their Olympic window were ten African American basketball players, each of whom went on to play for at least five years in the NBA. They included Mark Aguirre, Rolando Blackmon, Sam Bowie,

Michael Brooks, Alton Lister, Rodney McCray, Darnell Valentine, Charles Williams, Martin Wood, and Isiah Thomas. Thomas, a nineteen-year-old freshman at Indiana University in 1980, led the Hoosiers to the NCAA title the following year, and went on to become a twelve-time NBA All-Star and two-time NBA champion. Perhaps such professional success mitigated any bitterness Thomas might have felt about the boycott. He later maintained, "At that time it was made clear to us by the president of the stance he was taking and the country was taking. We wanted to do what was right by our country, so we understood and we all followed through."[4] Thomas, incidentally, brushed with a second chance at the Olympics but did not make the roster of the U.S. "Dream Team" that went to the 1992 Barcelona Olympics.

The 1980 U.S. Olympic women's basketball team included three African Americans, Debbie Miller, LeTaunya Pollard, and Rosie Walker. Opportunities for professional basketball were more limited for women than for men at that time, but each of them played professionally, with Miller and Pollard having long careers in the European leagues. Walker played professionally in the United States for a time then enjoyed a long and successful career in coaching. Pollard and Walker are enshrined in the Women's Basketball Hall of Fame in Knoxville, Tennessee.

Tragically, a plane crash took the lives of twenty-two members of the U.S. National Boxing Team just two months before the Olympic trials in 1980, including thirteen boxers, eight staff members, and team coach Thomas "Sarge" Johnson. The team was traveling to Poland for a series of exhibition bouts, when their plane crashed upon landing in Warsaw on March 14, 1980. Among the boxers who perished was Lemuel Steeples of St. Louis, Missouri, who had a great amateur career and was considered a favorite to medal in Moscow. A handful of fighters had missed that fateful flight and went on to make the team, including James Shuler of Philadelphia, who later won the WBA Light Middleweight title, and Johnny "Bump City" Bumphus, who later became the WBS Light Welterweight champion. The official 1980 U.S. Olympic team included seven African Americans, each of whom went on to professional boxing careers. Other noteworthy members of that team included Bernard Taylor, who amassed an incredible amateur record of 481–8 and as a professional fought three times for the featherweight title, and Donald Curry, who reigned as the WBA welterweight champion from 1983 to 1986.

Many other athletes stricken by the boycott suffered emotionally and physically in the aftermath and did not have a chance to return. Gwen Gardner, who grew up in Los Angeles and became a member of the Los Angeles Mercurettes, finished second in the 400-meters at the 1980 track and field Olympic Trials held in Eugene, Oregon, securing a spot on the team. After the boycott, Gardner picked up work in Los Angeles to make ends meet, including working as a stunt double for a film called *Oklahoma City Dolls* about a women's football team competing against men. In the course of filming, Gardner suffered a broken leg, which set back her Olympic training by two years. Not quite fully up to speed by the 1984 Olympic trials, Gardner finished fifth in the 400-meters; the top four made the team.

Another Olympian who missed his only chance to compete was Ron Galimore, the first African American to make the U.S. gymnastics team. Galimore, from Tallahassee, Florida, won the NCAA championship in the floor exercise as a freshman at Louisiana State University then won the vault as a sophomore. Expanding his range to all six gymnastic events, Galimore made the 1980 Olympic team. "I was so excited and elated that I accomplished something that only six people every four years have the chance to achieve, let alone be the first African American to accomplish that," he expressed later.[5] After the boycott, Galimore lost his direction and slipped into depression. He eventually caught on with the television crew for the 1984 Olympics, assisting as a spotter for the gymnastics telecast. Rejuvenated, he returned to Tallahassee, where he opened a gymnastics center. His only chance at Olympic glory, though, had gone by the wayside.

Galimore's experience was similar to the first African American to make the U.S. women's gymnastics team, Luci Collins. Collins, a sixteen-year-old from Englewood, California, at the time of the Olympic trials, had trained with Russian gymnasts and coaches from a young age in California, so she was both prepared and excited to contend with the best in the world in Moscow. After the boycott, she focused her efforts on qualifying for the 1984 team and competed for the University of Southern California for two years, but her aspirations for an Olympic return were derailed first by injury, then by an eating disorder. She did not try out for the 1984 team. While she never got to compete in the Olympics herself, Collins paved the way for other Black women gymnasts, a number of whom later became American icons.

THE OLYMPICS RETURN TO AMERICAN SOIL: 1984 LOS ANGELES

Four years after the American boycott of the Moscow Olympics, the Games returned to the United States for the first time since 1932. Los Angeles was the only city to submit a serious bid to host the 1984 Olympics, a process held in 1977, less than a year after the 1976 Olympics left the city of Montreal

Decathlon champion Rafer Johnson carrying the Olympic flame at the opening ceremonies of the 1984 games in Los Angeles. Silver medalist in the decathlon in 1956 in Melbourne and gold medalist in the same event four years later in Rome, Johnson was the recipient during his lifetime of many awards and honors for his plethora of achievements both in and outside of sport. *Courtesy of the LA 84 Foundation.*

C$1.6 billion in debt and served as a cautionary tale to potential host cities around the world. The citizens of Los Angeles then passed a referendum denying any public funding to the Olympic enterprise, a vote that dimmed the prospects for a successful Games. However, Peter Uebberoth, the forty-seven-year old travel executive at the helm of the Los Angeles Olympics Organizing Committee, insisted that the L.A. Olympics could survive—and thrive—on funding raised solely from television rights, sponsorship and advertising, and ticket sales. Over time, with the backing of corporations such as Coca-Cola, Xerox, Kodak, and McDonald's, the 1984 Olympics began to take shape, and Americans rallied to support Team U.S.A.

Olympic organizers utilized the multitude of facilities already available in and around the city, and they sought corporate sponsors to foot the bill for the construction of new venues such as the $4 million velodrome, paid for by the Southland Corporation, and a $4 million swimming arena on the campus of the University of Southern California, paid for by McDonald's. In contrast to the bloated Montreal budget, Ueberroth stuck to a streamlined $500 million budget, which ultimately allowed the L.A. Games to present a new paradigm in Olympic profitability to the world.

After the American boycott of the Moscow Olympics in 1980, it seemed likely that the Soviets would return the favor in 1984. Organizers of the L.A. Olympics, and other leaders up to and including U.S. President Ronald Reagan, hoped to give the Soviets no excuse other than to participate. Nonetheless, the Soviets expressed concerns about the safety of their athletes, fans, and support staff. In the end, while their claims were dubious, the Soviets chose to boycott the L.A. Olympics, and they were supported by their Eastern European satellite states and Cuba. Once again, the most important athletic competition on the planet was disrupted by politically driven boycotts. As historian Nicholas Evan Sarantakes explains, "Neither of these political actions served any purpose except to spoil the lives of hundreds of athletes who had given up everything to take part in the Olympic Games."[6]

The games went on without the Soviets, and they became a hyper-patriotic celebration for the United States. The 1984 Olympics were the most-watched television event to that point, and more than six million people attended the events in person. Attendance records were shattered at venue after venue, including more than 100,000 people watching the final soccer match in the Rose Bowl, and a total of more than 385,000 fans over eight sessions of baseball at Dodger Stadium, averaging more than 48,000 per session. Team U.S.A. was by far its largest ever, with 614 athletes competing in all 24 sports. Concerns about smog, traffic, and security at the games never materialized, and the competition was completed with nary a snag.

The unquestioned star of these Olympics was Carl Lewis. Born in Birmingham, Alabama, and raised in New Jersey, Lewis came from an extraordinarily athletic family. His father was a track coach and his mother a hurdler; his older brother became a professional soccer player; and his sister Carol qualified for the 1980 and 1984 Olympics in the long jump. Initially coached by his father, Lewis evolved into an elite high school long jumper in New Jersey then competed at the University of Houston under coach Tom Tellez, where he branched out into the sprints as well. Lewis qualified for the 1980 Olympic team, though he was not yet the best in the world in any discipline. After four more years of training, though, Lewis emerged as the favorite in both the 100-meter and 200-meter sprints, and the long jump at the 1984 Olympics.

Carl Lewis at the start of the 200-meter final during the 1984 Olympics, August 8, 1984. In the race, Lewis won his third gold medal of those Olympics; he won a total of nine gold medals over four Olympics in his career. *Courtesy of the LA 84 Foundation.*

Lewis matched Jesse Owens' remarkable feat from the 1936 Olympics, winning four gold medals, in the 100-meters, 200-meters, long jump, and 4×100-meter relay. The first—and in his own opinion most challenging— was the 100-meters. He was pushed by a strong field, including his U.S. teammates Sam Graddy of the University of Tennessee and Ron Brown of Arizona State University, as well as the Canadian Ben Johnson. Lewis chased down Graddy, who had a great start and led the field at the halfway mark, to secure his first gold, with Johnson taking third. Two days later, Lewis prevailed in the long jump competition, needing only one jump in the finals to secure the gold. Lewis then won the gold in the 200-meters, in Olympic-record time of 19.8 seconds, followed by his University of Houston teammate, Kirk Baptiste, and Thomas Jefferson of Kent State University, who took silver and bronze. His final event was the 4×100-meter relay, and the powerhouse lineup of Lewis, Graddy, Brown, and Calvin Smith cruised to a new world record in 37.83 seconds. No one could have known at the time that Lewis was only just getting started, his four gold medals in L.A. merely representing the first of nine total he would win over four Olympics.

Second only to Lewis in prominence in Los Angeles was Edwin Moses, undefeated in the 400-meter hurdles since 1977. Moses did not falter, taking the gold in 47.75 seconds. For his victory, Moses was named the 1984 co-sportsperson of the year by *Sports Illustrated*, along with the white gymnast Mary Lou Retton. Moses also was universally respected for his steady demeanor, his defense of athletes' rights and compensation, and his outspoken criticism of the growing number of athletes turning to steroids, growth hormones, and other performance-enhancing drugs. Danny Harris, a twenty-year-old from Iowa State University, took silver in the event in a photo-finish over Germany's Harald Schmid. Three years later, Harris ended Moses' ten-year undefeated streak, beating him at a competition in Madrid. Three-time world champion Greg Foster was a heavy favorite in the 110-meter hurdles, but he hesitated at the start of the finals after what he thought was a false start by Finland's Arto Bryggare. He recovered from the slow start to finish second, but he could not catch fellow African American Roger Kingdom of the University of Pittsburgh, who held on for the gold by just three-hundredths of a second, 13.20 to 13.23.

Another star on the track was Alonzo Babers, who won double gold in the individual 400-meters and the 4×400-meter relay. Babers, of Montgomery, Alabama, ran track and played football at the Air Force Academy prior to his Olympic experience. Focusing on track in 1984, he lowered his personal best in each 400-meter heat of the Olympic trials, and then the Olympics, winning the gold in Los Angeles. Antonio McKay of Georgia

Tech finished third, and Sunder Nix of Ball State University finished fifth. The 4×400-meter relay team included Babers, McKay, Nix, and Ray Armstead of Truman State University and won easily in 2:57.91. Earl Jones, a teammate of Carl Lewis on the Santa Monica Track Club, won the bronze medal in the 800-meters.

In addition to Lewis' victory in the long jump, the Black Mercuries achieved a number of successes in the field events. Americans achieved a one-two finish in the triple jump, with Al Joyner of Arkansas State University securing the gold on his first attempt. Mike Conley of the University of Arkansas, who had been favored heading into the meet, finished second behind Joyner. Fellow African American Willie Banks finished sixth. Banks was a crowd favorite, clapping vigorously before his jumps, and laughing and smiling throughout the meet. In 1985, he set the world record in the triple jump at 17.97 meters, which stood for ten years. Future NFL star Michael Carter won the silver medal in the shot put, with a throw only inches behind gold medal winner Alessandro Andrei of Italy.

U.S. BASKETBALL AND BOXING ACHIEVE NEW HEIGHTS AT THE 1984 OLYMPICS

The 1984 U.S. Olympic boxing squad was arguably the greatest ever assembled. The team won medals in eleven out of twelve divisions, including nine golds, one silver, and one bronze. Many members of the team went on to great success in the professional ranks, including Pernell Whitaker and Evander Holyfield, considered among the best of all time. Holyfield, who won the lone bronze medal in the group, was victim of one of the most controversial decisions of the games. He was clearly one of the best boxers in the entire competition, battering his first two opponents before meeting New Zealand's Kevin Barry in the semifinals. He was beating Barry, too, until the referee tried to break up the two boxers as they were in a hold, and Holyfield delivered a knockout blow to Barry's jaw as the referee moved in. Holyfield was given a disqualification for an illegal punch, Barry could not fight in the gold-medal fight, and Yugoslavian Anton Josipović was awarded the gold without having to fight. In an act of sportsmanship—and tacit recognition that Holyfield was the better fighter—Josipović invited Holyfield to join him on the top platform of the medal stand during their ceremony.

Eight of the nine gold medalists were African American. They included Tyrell Biggs, Mark Breland, Steve McCrory, Jerry Page, Frank Tate, Meldrick Taylor, Henry Tillman, and Pernell Whitaker. Taylor, of Philadelphia, was just seventeen when he won the gold medal in Los Angeles. He went on to a professional career that saw him hold world titles in two weight classes, regarded for a time as one of the best "pound for pound" fighters in the world. Whitaker, a member of the International Boxing Hall of Fame, went on to hold championship titles in four weight classes, amassing a professional record of 40-1-1 before losing three of his last four fights.

Two African Americans medaled in other combative sports. Edward Liddie won the bronze medal in the extra lightweight division, becoming the first African American to win an Olympic medal in judo. Liddie achieved an improbable victory in his bronze medal match against Guy Delvingt of France, in which he trailed in the final minute before executing a difficult takedown (called a "yuko"), scoring enough points to win. Gregory Gibson, two-time NCAA champion with the University of Oregon, became the first African American to win a medal in Greco-Roman wrestling, taking silver in the heavyweight division. At the time, Gibson was two years into a twenty-five-year career in the U.S. Marine Corps, during which time he won nineteen Armed Forces wrestling championships.

The U.S. men's basketball team also returned to its former glory, cruising to the gold medal with an 8-0 undefeated record and an average margin of victory of 32.1 points. Coached by the Indiana Hoosiers' combustible Bobby Knight, the team included seven African American players, most notably consensus college All-Americans Sam Perkins, Michael Jordan, Wayman Tisdale, and Patrick Ewing. Joining them on the team were Vern Fleming, Alvin Robertson, and Leon Wood. Wood, who played at Santa Monica Catholic High School and then Cal State-Fullerton, had the privilege of playing point guard for the U.S. Olympic team in his hometown of Los Angeles and led the team with 7.9 assists per game. Most of these players enjoyed successful careers in the NBA, including all-time greats Ewing and Jordan.

The U.S. women's basketball team was just as dominant as the men's team and included six African Americans, some of whom rank among the greatest players of all time. Coached by Pat Summitt of the University of Tennessee, who as a player had competed internationally herself, the team easily won the gold medal, going undefeated at 6-0 and outscoring their opponents by an average of 32.7 points per game. Summitt asserted of her team, without hyperbole, "I think it's the best women's basketball team ever assembled."[7] The star of the team was Cheryl Miller, who had won two national titles while playing for the University of Southern California, and whose brother Reggie became a Hall-of-Fame NBA player. The Riverside, California, native was a favorite among the L.A. fans, and she led the team in scoring, rebounds, steals, and assists. Joining Miller was her USC teammate, Pamela McGee, who had gone 75–0 and won two state titles at Northern High School in Flint, Michigan, before adding two national titles at USC. Making her first of five Olympic appearances was Teresa Edwards of the University of Georgia, who over her long career would become both the youngest and the oldest American basketball gold medal winner. Lynnette Woodard of the University of Kansas was the second-leading scorer on the team. A 1980 Olympian, Woodard returned for the 1984 Olympics before launching a professional career that included a run as the first woman to play for the Harlem Globetrotters and being drafted in 1997 to play in the newly established WNBA. Janice Braxton led Louisiana Tech to two national championships before making the 1984 Olympic team. All five of these women are in the Women's Basketball Hall of Fame, and Woodard is also in the Naismith Basketball Hall of Fame. Also on the team was Illinois State's Cathy Boswell, who went on to a twenty-four-year professional playing career, mostly in Europe, followed by a lengthy coaching career.

Among the most popular sports in Los Angeles was the demonstration sport of baseball. The American team, which lost the final game 6–3 to Japan, has been described as a "dream team" in its own right.[8] All twenty players on the roster were drafted by MLB teams, including three African American players: Arizona State outfielder Oddibe McDowell; UCLA outfielder and Los Angeles native, Shane Mack; and San Diego State outfielder, Chris Gwynn, brother of MLB Hall-of-Famer Tony Gwynn. All contributed meaningfully to the team, notably Shane Mack's home run in a losing effort against Japan in the championship game.

Importantly, African Americans excelled in a number of sports in which they traditionally have been underrepresented. One of the sensations in the velodrome was Nelson Vails, described in the introduction to this chapter and the first African American cyclist to win an Olympic medal. While a popular legend had it that Vails tried out for Olympic cycling because he was so good at his job as a bike messenger in New York City, in fact he competed in bike races from a young age and became a messenger because it suited his skills. He did concede that the job helped his training, because dodging New York City traffic "kept (him) on his toes."[9] Nicknamed "The Cheetah," Vails had become a star in a sport dominated by Europeans, a sport in which he claimed he faced more bias because he was an American than because he was Black. In Los Angeles, notwithstanding the fact some of his chief rivals were absent because of the Eastern bloc boycott, Vails rode the wild cheers of the crowd into the final, where he confronted his U.S. teammate, Mark Gorski. Despite a valiant cat-and-mouse effort to

Cyclist Nelson Vails during the 1984 Olympics. Vails was the first African American cyclist to win an Olympic medal, the silver in the sprint, Aug. 3, 1984. Vails' red helmet is adorned with a decal depicting the New York City skyline, an homage to his home town. *Courtesy of the LA 84 Foundation.*

outwit Gorski, Vails simply could not match the speed and power of his teammate, losing the first two sprints and settling for silver.

Peter Westbrook returned for his second Olympic fencing competition, having competed on an injured ankle in 1976 and missing 1980 due to the boycott. Westbrook, the son of a Japanese mother and African American father, was bullied relentlessly as a child in the streets of Harlem, where he was raised. He became both a fast runner and a good fighter, at times fending off his attackers with sticks. His mother eventually "bribed" Westbrook to join a fencing club, giving him $5 per session to keep him off the streets. After just a few lessons, he stopped taking the money as he grew to love the sport. In Los Angeles, Westbrook had what he described as the greatest victory of his career, over the number two-ranked fencer in the world, Italy's Gianfranco Dalla Barba. Faced with a panel of mostly Eastern European judges who refused to recognize what Westbrook considered legal touches, he fell behind 6–1. The first to score ten would win. Frustrated, Westbrook removed his face shield and refused to continue. He engaged in his protest until a huge crowd gathered on the scene, at which point the intimidated judges had to rule more fairly for the duration of the match. Westbrook overcame the deficit and won the match 11–9 to reach the final round, where he ended up winning the bronze, the first African American fencer to win an Olympic medal.[10] Westbrook was joined on the team by three other African Americans: Peter Lewison, Michael Lofton, and Mark Smith, none of whom medaled.

LOS ANGELES 1984: WOMEN'S TRACK AND FIELD AND OTHER SPORTS

The 1984 U.S. Olympic women's track and field team was its strongest since the heyday of the Tigerbelles in the 1960s. Since the advent of Title IX in 1972, women's sports programs had grown exponentially on college campuses around the country, meaning that more women had greater access to quality training than ever before. California schools, in particular, embraced the new emphasis on women's sports, and powerhouse track programs evolved at colleges such as UCLA, USC, and Cal State-Northridge. The 1984 Olympic team reflected this West Coast trend, represented by some of its strongest competitors such as Florence Griffith and Evelyn Ashford of UCLA and Valerie Brisco-Hooks of Cal State-Northridge.

Finally reaching her true potential in 1984 was Ashford, who cemented her reputation as one of America's great Olympians by winning two gold medals. Ashford first competed in the 1976 Montreal Olympics, finishing fifth in the 100-meters. She was twenty-three years old and at her peak in 1980, when the boycott denied her a chance at three gold medals, as she was among the world's best in the 100-meters and 200-meters. In Los Angeles, Ashford won the gold in the 100 meters with an Olympic-record time of 10.97 seconds and anchored the gold-medal winning 4×100-meters relay, which won the final by the astonishing margin of 1.12 seconds over the second-place team.

Valerie Brisco-Hooks was the closest thing to Carl Lewis in the women's competition, winning three gold medals and setting new Olympic records in each discipline. Brisco-Hooks feared her track career was over when she became a mother in 1982, but she continued training and ultimately came to believe that being a mother made her stronger on the track. First, she won gold in the 400-meters in 48.83 seconds, with American Chandra

Cheeseborough coming second. Next came the 200-meters, which she won in 21.81 seconds, ahead of teammate Florence Griffith. Finally, she anchored the 4×400-meter relay team, which won with ease in 3:18.29, another Olympic record.

A number of outstanding African American sprinters finished behind Ashford and Brisco-Hooks in those events. Alice Brown won the silver in the 100-meters. A fast starter, she also ran the opening leg for the 4×100-meter relay team. A third member of that relay team was Jeanette Bolden of Cal State-Northridge and then UCLA, who finished fourth in the individual sprint. The fourth member of the relay team was Chandra Cheeseborough, one of the Tennessee State Tigerbelles, who had placed sixth in the 200-meters in Montreal and had won the Olympic trials in 1980. She won the silver medal in the 400-meters in Los Angeles and accomplished the remarkable feat of winning gold in both the 4×100-meter and 4×400-meter relays, which were run less than an hour apart. Florence Griffith won the silver in the 200-meters, a hint of the great success she would have four years later in Seoul.

Brisco-Hooks and Cheeseborough finished one-two in the 400-meters, but the other women who competed with them in the 4×400-meter relay had compelling stories of their own, among them the Howard sisters, Sherri and Denean. The two had achieved fame in California when, with their two sisters, they had set the national high school record in the girls' 4×400 yard relay in 1979. Sherri and Denean then both qualified for the 1980 Olympics in the 400-meters, Sherri finishing first and Denean second at the Olympic trials, at ages sixteen and fourteen, respectively. At the 1984 Olympics, the pair both won gold medals in the 4×400 meter relay, with Denean running in the qualifying heat and Sherri running the second leg in the final. Lillie Leatherwood of the University of Alabama finished fifth in the individual sprint, and won gold as part of the 4×400-meter relay, running the lead-off leg. Diane Lynn Dixon from Brooklyn, New York, and Ohio State University won a gold medal as part of the 4×400-meter relay team, running in the qualifying heat but not the final. African American women also performed strongly in the hurdling events and middle distances. Benita Fitzgerald of the University of Tennessee won the gold in the 100-meter hurdles with a time of 12.84 seconds. Judith Brown of Michigan State University won the silver in the 400-meter hurdles, and Kim Gallagher of Philadelphia won the silver medal in the 800-meters.

Like the men, women's performances tended to be stronger on the track than on the field, but there were some notable exceptions. Jodi Anderson won both the long jump and pentathlon competitions at the U.S. Olympic trials in 1980 and had the world's longest jump in 1981. In 1984, she qualified in the new event of the heptathlon but suffered an injury and was unable to complete all the disciplines. She was overshadowed in the event by the great Jackie Joyner, sister of Al Joyner, who won gold in the triple jump. Joyner led heading into the final event, the 800-meter run, and only needed to stay close to the leaders to secure the gold. But Australian Glynis Nunn outpaced her by 2.5 seconds, one half second more than she needed to surpass Joyner for the gold, 6,390 points to 6,385 points. It remains one of the most dramatic finishes in heptathlon history. Joyner also competed in the long jump, finishing fifth. Angela Thacker from the University of Nebraska finished fourth, and Carol Lewis—sister of Carl—finished ninth. She returned four years later and qualified for the 1988 Olympics but did not make the final.

African American women impacted a number of other sports as well. Most notably, three Black women—all from the University of Houston—competed on the silver medal–winning volleyball team. Six-foot-five-inch Flora Jean Hyman, the first woman to earn an athletic scholarship at Houston, played outside hitter and was a stalwart on the U.S. team from 1976 to 1984. In 1986, Hyman collapsed and died during a professional game in Japan from Marfan Syndrome, a heart condition. Rita "The Rocket" Crockett was considered the best athlete on the U.S. team throughout the late 1970s to the early 1980s and reportedly had a forty-two-inch vertical leap. She played professionally in Europe for many years after her Olympic experience. Rose Magers was the starting middle blocker on the team, which made it to the gold medal game but lost to China, 16–14, 15–3, 15–9.

SEOUL 1988: A PEACEFUL BUT TAINTED GAMES

The International Olympic Committee selected Seoul, South Korea, as the host for the 1988 Summer Olympic Games in a vote held on September 30, 1981. The 1988 Olympics were the last of the Cold War era, and the first in a dozen years to feature a (nearly) full complement of nations, as there was no major international boycott. A record 160 nations attended, including all the major powers of both Eastern and Western blocs. For the first time since 1976, American athletes contended with their formidable rivals from the Soviet Union, East Germany, and others in an Olympic games. As a result, the American medal count was far lower in 1988 than the bonanza of 1984, with the United States winning 94 total medals, compared to 132 for the Soviet Union and 102 for East Germany.

While the Cold War was evident in many events, the most memorable rivalry played out between the top two sprinters on the planet, who had been contending with each other for the title of "world's fastest human" for nearly a decade. Carl Lewis, the great American champion, and Ben Johnson, a Black sprinter from Canada, clashed in the men's 100-meter sprint. Both men had been competing at the highest levels since 1980, when the nineteen-year-old Lewis won triple gold at the Pan American Junior Games in Canada, winning the 100-meter and 200-meter sprints and anchoring the victorious 4×100-meter relay. Finishing sixth in that 100-meter final was eighteen-year-old Johnson. For the better part of the next decade, the two would duel in sprint finals all over the world, exchanging world-record times frequently.

Over the course of that decade, Johnson's physique morphed. Once a lean, skinny runner, he evolved into one of the most muscular and sculpted sprinters to ever take the track. His metamorphosis, as we now know and many—including Lewis—suspected at the time, was due in part to a steady program of steroids administered by his coach, Charlie Francis, starting in September of 1981. Lewis was at the top of the track world at the 1984 Olympics, with his four gold medals. Finishing third in the 100-meter final was Johnson, who was closing the gap between himself and the world's best. Johnson defeated Lewis at the 1987 World Championships in Rome, shattering the world record with a sprint of 9.83 seconds. Lewis was determined that things would be different in Seoul. His father Bill had passed away from cancer the previous year. At the funeral, Lewis placed the gold medal he had won for the 100-meters in Los Angeles in his father's hand in the casket. He told his mother, "Don't worry, I'll get another one."[11]

He got his chance in Seoul on September 24, 1988. It was never a contest. Ben Johnson took the lead early and powered down the track, never threatened. He crossed the line two strides clear of the field in a mind-boggling 9.79 seconds, besting his own world record, thrusting his finger in the air with a fierce scowl as he crossed the line. Lewis was visibly despondent three lanes over, shaking his head as he finished second with a personal best 9.92.

Disappointment hung over him during the next few days, even as he won gold in the long jump. Then, three days later, IOC officials announced that Johnson had failed his post-race drug test, as the steroid Stanozolol was detected in his system. Johnson was stripped of his gold medal, and the other competitors all moved up a spot. Lewis was awarded the gold, Linford Christie of Great Britain the silver, and another American, Calvin Smith, the bronze. For its explosive impact on the sport, this race has been called "the dirtiest race in history," as almost every runner in the race—Lewis included—eventually came under suspicion of doping.[12]

With the repercussions of the 100-meter final, Lewis was now again two-for-two in his gold medal quest, with the 200-meters next. But he was disappointed again, this time meeting defeat at the hands of his American friend and teammate Joe DeLoach, 19.75 to 19.79. Like Lewis, the nineteen-year-old DeLoach competed at the University of Houston and then the Santa Monica Track Club. Lewis, DeLoach, and several other American runners were later revealed to have tested positive for banned stimulants during the 1988 Olympics, but they were not punished at that time. Each appealed the findings and claimed the substances were consumed accidentally in dietary supplements or medications, and in such small quantities as to remain legal. The USOC accepted their explanations, and thus far there have been no penalties associated with these positive tests.

There was still hope for a historic three-gold performance for Lewis, with the 4×100-meter relay remaining. The Americans had dominated the event, and with one of the strongest lineups in Olympic history, they seemed assured of gold, especially with Johnson now banned and the Canadians not a factor. The relay is never a sure thing, however, and a botched exchange by the American squad in the semifinals left them disqualified and out of the running for the gold. Lewis, battling adversity throughout the meet, left with two golds and a silver, and perhaps with a new group of fans who witnessed a more humble, gracious side of Lewis in defeat.

Led by Lewis and his African American teammates, the Americans dominated in track and field. The men's track team won gold in all three sprints and both hurdle events, winning multiple medals in each event. While the 100-meters final was thrown into disarray after Ben Johnson's ban, in the final result Calvin Smith was elevated to the bronze and Dennis Mitchell of the University of Florida finished fourth. A quartet of great African American runners formed a dominant group in the 400-meters, led by world-record holder Butch Reynolds, who had topped Lee Evans' twenty-year-old world record at a meet in Zurich, Switzerland, that year with a time of 43.29 seconds. In Seoul, however, Reynolds was not fast enough to beat Steve Lewis, a nineteen-year-old freshman at UCLA. Reynolds appeared to take the first half of the race too easily, letting Lewis extend his lead to six meters, before accelerating to catch Lewis down the stretch. He was a step late, and Lewis took the gold with a time of 43.87 seconds, to Reynolds' 43.93. Fellow American Danny Everett, Lewis' teammate at UCLA, took the bronze in 44.09. This formidable group teamed with Kevin Robinzine of Southern Methodist University in a quest to break the world record in the 4×400 meter relay. They won the gold medal easily and tied the world record in 2:56.16.

African Americans also brought home several medals in the hurdle events. Edwin Moses, now thirty-three and at the end of his Olympic run, was challenged in the 400-meter hurdles by twenty-nine-year-old Andre Phillips of UCLA, who had missed the 1984 Olympic Trials with the flu and had spent his career chasing Moses, yet never beaten him. In Seoul, the two were stride-for-stride through the first eight hurdles, when Moses began to fade. Phillips streaked to victory, with Moses hanging on for the bronze. Kevin Young of UCLA finished fourth. In the 110-meter hurdles, Roger Kingdom returned to defend his Olympic title from 1984, running a blazing 12.98 seconds to repeat as gold-medal winner. Tonie Campbell of USC took third, and Arthur Blake of Florida State finished eighth.

African American men also swept the long jump competition. Carl Lewis defended his title and kept alive an undefeated streak that now extended to fifty-seven meets and would eventually reach sixty-five competitions over ten years. Lewis was pushed in the final by Mike Powell of UCLA, who would later break Bob Beamon's world record, and Larry Myricks, who finally secured an Olympic medal after breaking his foot during the 1976 Olympics then missing the 1980 Olympics due to the U.S. boycott. In general, the American men struggled in the other field events, which were dominated by the Soviets and Eastern Europeans. One exception was the high jumper Hollis Conway of the University of Southwestern Louisiana, who won the silver with a jump of 7'8¾". The triple jumper Willie Banks, the world record holder now at age thirty-three, managed only a sixth place finish.

HIGHS AND LOWS ON THE COURT AND IN THE RING IN SEOUL

After nearly two decades, the U.S. men's basketball team faced the Soviet team in the Olympics for the first time since the controversial 1972 final game in Munich. As important as any player was Georgetown University's John Thompson, the first African American head coach of Team U.S.A. The U.S. team, laden with future NBA stars, cruised through the early rounds of the tournament. Meantime, the Soviet team struggled in the early going, losing their first game and needing overtime to beat Puerto Rico. When the two met in the semifinals, the United States was the clear favorite. The Americans played their worst game in the semifinal; the Soviets played their best. Soviet center Arvidas Sabonis, who played professionally for the NBA's Portland Trail Blazers, dominated the middle, while top American player Danny Manning went scoreless. In the end, the United States fell, 82–76. The Soviets then beat Yugoslavia to take the gold, and the United States defeated Australia to win the bronze. Virtually the entire United States roster was made up of African American players, including Willie Anderson, Stacey Augmon, Bimbo Coles, Jeff Grayer, Hersey Hawkins, Danny Manning, J. R. Reid, Mitch Richmond, David Robinson, and two players both named Charles Smith. As the man who had exerted almost total control over the roster and in-game decisions, Coach Thompson shouldered much of the blame in defeat. His defensive-minded team did not play great defense against the Soviet team, and his reserves lacked the scoring ability needed to lead a comeback. Nonetheless, Thompson carried on a career that ended with his induction into the Naismith Basketball Hall of Fame, and laid the groundwork for a number of future Black assistant and head coaches who would work with the U.S. Olympic team.

The boxing competition in Seoul was mired in controversy. Most visibly, after Korea's Byun Jong-Il lost a 4–1 decision to Bulgarian fighter Aleksander Hristov after being penalized two points for head butts, Korean coaches leapt into the ring and assaulted the referee, and Byun staged a sit-down strike in the ring for sixty-seven minutes. NBC covered the protest in its entirety, at times showing Byun on split screen while airing other events. From that point forward, the judging seemed to favor Korean fighters, at times in glaringly obvious fashion. Several questionable judging decisions worked to the detriment of top African American boxers. Roy Jones won the Val Barker Trophy for the tournament's outstanding boxer, but he did not win the gold medal. In the gold medal match, he battered Korea's Park Si-Hun thoroughly, landing 86 punches to Park's 32. Nonetheless, the judges awarded Park a 3–2 victory, which seemed to surprise even Park. Jones left the arena in tears with a silver medal, the victim of one of the great judging injustices in Olympic history. He went on to a stellar professional career, listed by some as the greatest "pound for pound" boxer of all time. The lesson for other boxers was not to let any match involving a Korean boxer go to the judges, which heavyweight Ray Mercer took to heart when he faced Baik Hyun-Man in a gold medal bout later that night. Mercer knocked out Baik in the first round, securing the gold.

Bouts not involving Korean fighters tended to be less controversial. Kennedy McKinney won the bantamweight gold medal over Hristov, 5–0. Andrew Maynard took the gold over the Soviet Nurmagomed Shanavazov, 5–0. Welterweight Kenneth Gould and lightweight Romallis Ellis both lost decisions in their semifinal bouts to take bronze medals. In a final bit of controversy, super-heavyweight Riddick Bowe lost the gold medal match to future heavyweight champion, Canadian Lennox Lewis. Bowe was penalized for several head butts in a first round that he dominated, then counted out in the second round after a standing eight count, although he appeared able to continue. Lewis may have gone on to win the fight anyway, but U.S. boxing authorities felt Bowe had been robbed.

Questionable scoring was not limited to the boxing ring. One of America's most promising wrestlers also fell victim to poor officiating. Nate Carr of Iowa State University, who had allowed only four points in five matches in 68kg freestyle wrestling, lost a controversial 3–2 decision to Korea's Park Jang-soon in the semifinals. Though he trailed on points, Carr was the more aggressive wrestler, and Park was warned twice for stalling. In the second period, Park retreated outside the circle for a third time, which officials later agreed should have led to a disqualification. Instead, Park was not penalized and won the match, while Carr went on to win the bronze medal. Kenny Monday, a three-time All-American wrestler for Oklahoma State University, was more fortunate. In a dramatic Cold War clash against Soviet Adlan Varayev in the gold medal match at 74kg, Monday managed to score a one-point reversal with three seconds remaining, forcing an overtime period. Moments into the extended time, he threw the Soviet onto his back, ending the match and securing the gold medal.

SEOUL 1988: WOMEN'S TRACK AND FIELD AND OTHER SPORTS

While Americans hung on every result for Carl Lewis, the unquestioned star of these Olympics was Florence Griffith-Joyner—known as Flo-Jo—who captured three gold medals and a silver, and the attention of the global media. Joyner first drew attention at the 1984 Olympics, racing with long, colorful four-inch fingernails. By 1988, Joyner had added considerably to her eye-catching fashions, designing her own clothes and running at times in a white lace bodysuit, at others in brightly colored one-legged track pants. As historian Jennifer Lansbury has described it, "She combined overt expressions of sexuality and speed in ways that seemed to indicate she was unconcerned with stereotypes of the past."[13] Joyner won the 100-meters in 10.54 seconds, several tenths faster than her own world record, although wind-aided. She then won the 200-meters in even more impressive fashion, a world record 21.34 seconds that was comparable to times of some of the best male sprinters. Her third gold came in the 4×100-meter relay, in which she ran the third leg and handed off to the ageless Evelyn Ashford, who chased down her East German rival, Marlies Göhr, to secure the gold. Finally, Joyner ran the anchor leg of the 4×400-meter relay, which became one of the most riveting Cold War confrontations of the Games. The U.S. squad faced the world record–holding team from East Germany and the powerful Soviet team that included the gold and bronze medalists in the individual 400 meters, as well as the silver medalist in the 400-meter hurdles. The Soviets led through the first two legs by a wide margin, until Valerie Brisco-Hooks closed the gap on the third leg and handed the baton to Joyner in a dead heat with the Soviets. Joyner and Olha Bryzhina battled over the final lap, with Bryzhina outlasting Joyner and securing gold for the Soviets. Both teams broke the world record with times of 3:15.17 and 3:15.51, which remain the two fastest women's 4×400-meter relays ever run.

Just as memorable were the performances of Flo-Jo's sister-in-law, Jackie Joyner-Kersee, who won two gold medals, in the long jump and the heptathlon. Joyner-Kersee competed in much of the heptathlon on an injured knee, which especially impacted her in the penultimate event, the javelin. She then ran a personal-best 2:08.51 in the 800-meters to break the world record. Just two days later, in the long jump, Joyner-Kersee found herself trailing midway through the competition. Then, she unleashed a gold medal–winning leap of 24'3½" to shatter her own world record, becoming the first woman to top 24'.

While the U.S. men's basketball team endured a humiliating loss to the Soviets, the U.S. women's basketball team offered some redemption, beating the Soviets in the semifinals then defeating Yugoslavia to secure the gold medal. While not as dominant as the 1984 squad, the 1988 team was also unbeaten and included a number of future Hall of Fame players. There were eight African American players on the team. Katrina McClain and Teresa Edwards, both from the University of Georgia, led the team in scoring with 17.6 and 16.6 points per game, respectively. McClain averaged 10 rebounds per game, and Edwards had 23 steals, each leading the team. Other standout players included Cynthia Cooper, Bridgette Gordon, and Teresa Weatherspoon. Several of these players went on to become stars in the new Women's Professional Basketball Association when it formed in 1996.

Tennis returned as a medal event in Seoul, for the first time since the 1924 Paris Olympics. One of the stars of the sport was African American Zina Garrison, who won a bronze medal in women's singles and a gold in women's doubles. Garrison, from Houston, showed great athletic ability as a child, often beating older kids in an array of games and sports and thriving

in softball, track and field, and tennis. At age ten, she came under the tutelage of John Wilkerson, himself a pioneering Black tennis player. Wilkerson
offered tennis instruction at MacGregor Park in Houston and coached a
number of future professionals, including Garrison. Garrison developed
into one of the best junior players in the world, and at age seventeen,
despite battling bulimia, won both the Wimbledon and U.S. Open junior
titles. In Seoul, Garrison and her white partner Pam Shriver won the gold
medal in doubles, defeating the Czech team in the final match. In singles,
Garrison defeated Shriver to reach the medal round, before losing to world
number one, Germany's Steffi Graf, and earning the bronze medal.

As the Seoul Olympics drew to a close, the Olympics—and the Black
Mercuries—launched into a new era, with significant changes on the hori-
zon. Growing numbers of athletes, such as Edwin Moses and Carl Lewis,
competing in multiple Olympics suggested that the days of the true amateur were waning; the struggles of the U.S. basketball team only hastened
that decline. By the next Olympics, the team would be populated not with
college players, but rather a "Dream Team" of the greatest players of all
time. At the same time, increasingly professional Olympic athletes seemed,
for a time, less connected to the broader race struggle than Black athletes
a generation before. Best exemplified by Carl Lewis and Michael Jordan—
who were among the most recognizable athletes on the planet—these
athletes generally did not use their visibility as a platform for encouraging
societal change, as Bill Russell, Wilma Rudolph, and others had done. Ben
Johnson's disgrace signaled a new focus on drug testing, which would grow
far more prominent in the decades to come, and Johnson was only the first
of many athletes who would see medals stripped away after failing a drug
test. The massive security presence in Seoul, mingled with a few minor
instances of protest, stood as stark reminder that at every Olympics security would be the foremost concern. Finally, as the athletes departed from
Seoul, Soviet and American rivals stared across the Iron Curtain for the last
time. The Cold War, which had dominated global diplomacy for forty years,
was at an end. By 1992, the contending athletes were living in a new world.

7

BLACK MERCURIES IN THE IMMEDIATE POST–COLD WAR PERIOD

In 1990, Gail Devers, the great African American sprinter and hurdler from UCLA, was diagnosed with Graves disease and underwent radioactive iodine treatment therapy followed by thyroid hormone treatment therapy. As a result of the treatments, she suffered from vision problems, swollen and blistered feet, could barely walk, and was threatened with amputation. Miraculously, Devers eventually recovered and raced her way into post–Cold War Olympic glory, along with an impressive array of other African American athletes who fenced, swam, boxed, and yes, ran their way into sporting history. For Devers and her teammates, however, it was a decidedly different world that was clearly reflected in the most significant and impactful mega-sporting event. Dramatic political changes took place across the world toward the end of 1989 and beginning of 1990 that greatly impacted the summer Olympic Games. The fall of the Berlin Wall in November of 1989 resulted in the German team being united once again for Olympic competition in 1992, and the International Olympic Committee (IOC) invited athletes from newly independent and other reunified countries to participate in the world's most important mega sporting event. In February of 1990, recently appointed president of South Africa F. W. de Klerk began the process of ending apartheid by lifting the ban on the African National Congress and releasing Nelson Mandela and other political prisoners. South Africa's abandonment of apartheid resulted in its being invited to participate in the 1992 Olympic Games, something not allowed since the 1960 Games in Rome. The end of the Cold War and elimination of apartheid in South Africa combined with a host of other factors to usher in three Summer Olympic Games staged in Barcelona 1992, Atlanta 1996, and Sydney 2000 that were enormously elaborate, expensive, and commercial events that made clear the increased globalization of sport and importance that nations attached to hosting the Games and ensuring that they came off without any economic and political disruptions. Tellingly, these three Summer Games were devoid of the boycotts that characterized previous Olympics, included outstanding and memorable athletic performances, saw the expansion of sports offerings, and were fraught with political and racial symbolism.

Transformative during this period—not unexpected, considering the continued commercialization of the Games—was the addition of professional athletes into Olympic competition. For the United States, it could send its very best athletes to the Games to compete against those from other countries who, in some cases, had for years been amateurs in name only. The official entry of professionals into the Games, however, provided further evidence of the commodification of African American athletes as well as the fissure within the Black community as to what role those athletes had in the larger civil rights struggle and their level of responsibility in speaking out against inequality and racial discrimination. Some prominent individuals in the African American community chastised Black athletes for refusing to voice their concerns about racial issues, contending that they had been rendered silent on such matters out of fear of jeopardizing their careers and the large amount of money they had accumulated. Importantly, in lodging their criticisms Black commentators frequently harkened back to the active role played by African American athletes in the civil rights movement of the 1960s, pointing specifically to the courage shown by Tommie Smith and John Carlos via their Black Power salute on the victory stand in Mexico City in 1968 as well as other outspoken African American athletes such as Muhammad Ali, Bill Russell, Kareem Abdul-Jabbar, and Jim Brown. As always, African American athletes of the post–Cold War period, Olympians and non-Olympians alike, were faced with the almost impossible task of reconciling individual ambition with group loyalty and commitment to civil rights issues.

BURNING UP THE TRACK IN BARCELONA

Barcelona, hometown of then IOC president Juan Antonio Samaranch and the second largest city in Spain as well as capital of the autonomous community of Catalonia, was selected in October of 1986 to host the 1992 Summer Olympics. By all measures, the Games were extraordinarily successful with over 9,300 athletes representing 169 countries competing in an expanded slate of sports. African American men and women athletes made significant contributions to the U.S. overall medal count in Barcelona. Not unexpectedly, their major contributions were in track and field, the sport in which they had always been most prominent and would continue to be so to the present day. As has always been the case, however, it was in the sprints and jumping events rather than endurance events that they were most dominant. Carl Lewis, although past his prime and not the dominant athlete who had matched the legendary Jesse Owens' four-gold medal winning performance in the 1984 Games in Los Angeles and garnered two golds and a silver in the Seoul Olympics in 1988, was, along with the great sprinter Evelyn Ashford, the seasoned veteran of the group. He failed to qualify for the 100 and 200 meters but captured his third of four Olympic gold medals in the long jump in Barcelona and anchored the 4×100 gold medal winning relay team. In the long jump, he outdueled his long-time rival Mike Powell, the UCLA star, with a leap of 28'5¼", more than an inch farther than Powell's best mark. In addition to his gold medal victory over Powell in the long jump, Lewis furthered his already legendary status by anchoring the U.S. gold-medal-winning 4×100 relay team. The team, which also included in the finals UCLA's Michael Marsh, University of Houston's Leroy Burrell, and University of Florida's Dennis Mitchell, smashed the world record with a time of 37.40.

As great as the performances turned in by Lewis in the long jump and by him and his teammates in the 4×100 meter relay, they constituted a small fraction of the outstanding contributions made by African American men to the U.S. track and field team in Barcelona. Michael Marsh added another gold medal to his collection by capturing the 200 meters, winning over silver medalist Frankie Fredericks of Namibia and bronze medalist Michael Bates, a University of Arizona track and field and football star. Quincy Watts, another track and field and football star from USC, captured gold in the 400 meters by beating UCLA star and Olympic teammate Steve Lewis who won silver and Samson Kitur of Kenya who won bronze. Kevin Young of UCLA captured gold in the 400-meter hurdles in world record time over silver medalist Winthrop Graham of Jamaica and bronze medalist Kriss Akabusi of Great Britain. The University of Mississippi's Tony Dees won the silver medal in the 110-meter hurdles, and capturing bronze medals were Morgan State University's Jack Pierce in the same event, Arizona State University's Johnny Gray in the 800 meters, and

Dennis Mitchell in the 100 meters. Mitchell's loss in the 100 meters came at the hands of two of the world's great sprinters, silver medalist Frankie Fredericks of Namibia and gold medalist Linford Christie, the redoubtable Jamaican-born athlete from Great Britain who at the age of thirty-two became the oldest man to win the event in Olympic competition. The U.S. 4×400 meter relay team provided one of the most memorable performances in the running events in Barcelona. The team, which consisted in the finals of Seton Hall's Andrew Valmon, Quincy Watts, Steve Lewis, and Baylor University's Michael Johnson, captured the gold medal and in the process smashed the world record with a time of 2:55.74. Rounding out the medals for African American men in track and field were those captured in the field events. In addition to Carl Lewis's victory in the long jump, Mike Conley, the outstanding University of Arkansas athlete, captured the gold in the triple jump over Baptist College's (Charleston, SC) Charles Simpkins; Mike Powell, as previously mentioned, came in second to Lewis in the long jump with Ohio State University's Joe Greene winning the bronze; and the University of Louisiana at Lafayette's Hollis Conway taking the bronze in the high jump.

African American women, although not garnering the number of medals as their male counterparts, had some outstanding performances in track and field in Barcelona. One of the stars of the Games was Gwen Torrence, the great University of Georgia sprinter who would win multiple world titles and Olympic medals during her long career. In Barcelona, she captured the gold medal in the 200 meters and ran on the U.S. silver medal 4×400 meter relay and gold medal 4×100 meter relay teams. In the 4×400 relay, she competed in the finals alongside Natasha Kaiser of the University of Missouri, Jearl Miles of Alabama A&M University, and Rochelle Stevens of Morgan State University for a silver medal, placing second to the Unified Team and ahead of Great Britain. In the 4×100 relay, Torrence joined in the finals Louisiana State University's Esther Jones, the University of Texas's Carlette Guidry, and the great UCLA sprinter Evelyn Ashford, to take first place over the Unified Team and Nigeria, earning Ashford her third Olympic gold medal in the event. UCLA's phenomenal Gail Devers added greatly to the overall performances of African American women in track and field in Barcelona by capturing the gold medal in the 100 meters. Having contracted Grave's Disease just two years earlier that necessitated both radioactive iodine treatment and thyroid hormone replacement therapy, Dever's victory, a photo finish in which she was timed at 10.82 and silver medalist Juliet Cuthbert of Jamaica at 10.83 and bronze medalist Irina Privalova of the Unified Team at 10.84, was that much more remarkable because of her health issues and helped make up for her hitting the final hurdle and coming fifth in the 100-meter hurdles race in which she was heavily favored. Other outstanding performances were turned in by University of Tennessee's LaVonna Martin who won silver in the 100-meter hurdles, Cal State University, Los Angeles's Sandra Farmer-Patrick who captured silver in the 400-meter hurdles, and UCLA's Janeene Vickers who took bronze in the same event. Finally, Jackie Joyner-Kersee, the East St. Louis native and UCLA star, won a bronze medal in the long jump and her second Olympic gold medal in the heptathlon. She beat out second place finisher Irina Belova of the Unified Team and third place finisher Sabine Braun of Germany for the gold medal in the grueling seven events that make up the heptathlon.

FROM HEAVY EVENTS TO GYMNASTICS AND BEYOND

African American athletes distinguished themselves in other sports in Barcelona besides track and field. In boxing, the United States generally performed poorly in Barcelona, capturing just three medals in the Games, which was the lowest total since the 1956 Olympics in Melbourne. The mediocre performance by U.S. boxers renewed the long debate about the proper training of Olympic pugilists and raised the question once again whether the boxers qualifying for the Games should be allowed to use their own personal trainers rather than those assigned to them by USA Boxing. Notwithstanding these circumstances, the three boxers who made it to the victory stand in Barcelona were legendary Mexican American fighter Oscar de La Hoya who captured the gold medal in the lightweight division; African Americans Chris Byrd who garnered the silver medal in the middleweight division, and Tim Austin who captured the bronze medal in the flyweight division. Byrd, a Flint, Michigan, native who began training at age five in his father's Joe Byrd Boxing Academy, came close to garnering the top prize, losing only to the great Cuban pugilist Ariel Hernandez in the championship bout 12:7. Byrd would go on to a highly successful professional career, capturing the WBO heavyweight championship in 2000 over then undefeated Ukrainian boxer Vitali Klitschko and the IBF heavyweight title in 2002 over Evander Holyfield. His career totals as a professional were 41 wins (22 by knockout), 5 losses, and 1 draw. Austin, fighting in the very competitive flyweight division, came in third to gold medalist Choe Chol-su of North Korea and silver medalist Raul Gonzalez of Cuba. A talented southpaw known as the "Cincinnati Kid," Austin had captured both the 1990 and 1991 National Golden Gloves Championships prior to Barcelona and at the professional level won the IBF Bantamweight Title in 1997 from Mbulelo Botile, a title he would defend nine times until losing to Rafael Marquez in an eighth-round technical knockout in 2003.

Another African American duo would enjoy even greater success in wrestling. Kevin Jackson, a three-time All-American at Louisiana State University before the school dropped its wrestling program and later a NCAA runner-up at Iowa State University, captured the gold medal in the 82 kg division (181 pounds) by defeating Elmadi Zhabrailov of the Unified Team 3–0 in the final round. Three years after his victory in Barcelona, Jackson captured gold medals in both the World Championships and Pan American Games. Jackson's teammate Kenny Monday also achieved much success in Barcelona. A three-time All-American at wrestling powerhouse Oklahoma State University and gold medalist in the 74kg division (163 pounds) in the 1988 Seoul Games, Monday captured the silver medal in the 74kg division in Barcelona, being defeated in the final round 3–0 by Park Jang-soon of South Korea.

In gymnastics, Takoma Park, Maryland, native Dominique Dawes and Betty Okino, born in Uganda to a Ugandan father and Romanian mother, captured bronze medals for the United States in the women's team competition. In volleyball, Tonya (Teee) Williams, a three-time All-American from the University of Hawaii, Nigerian-born Ruth Modupe-Lawanson, an excellent player from Fresno State University, and Tara Cross-Battle, an outstanding athlete from Long Beach State University, all made important contributions to the bronze medal won by the U.S. women's team. In Barcelona America's "National Pastime" of baseball officially debuted as a medal sport in the Olympic Games. The U.S. team came in a disappointing fourth in the standings but managed nonetheless a 5–2 record against high-quality squads from around the world. The USA Baseball Collegiate National Team represented the United States in Barcelona since only amateurs were allowed to participate in the sport in the Olympic Games at the time. The roster included four African Americans who made significant contributions to the team and would go on to successful professional careers on the diamond.

ONE "DREAM TEAM" AND ANOTHER BRONZE

In basketball competition in Barcelona, African American women and men had decidedly different experiences and results from one another. The

U.S. women, who were seeking their third straight gold medal in Olympic competition, were loaded with a talented roster that included, with the exception of Suzie McConnell of Penn State University, all Black players from predominantly white universities. This was not unexpected as it was merely a reflection of the continued funneling of a large number of outstanding African American women athletes into basketball and to a lesser extent track and field, at predominantly white universities as a result of Title IX legislation in 1972. Unfortunately, they are decidedly underrepresented in all other sports at those institutions, which is made quite clear in Olympic competition.

Although playing well in most contests and finishing with an overall record of 4–1, the U.S. women had to settle for a bronze medal behind the Unified Team that won gold and China that took the silver. The team started well, scoring a lopsided 111 to 55 victory over Czechoslovakia with Cynthia Cooper of the University of Southern California leading the way with eighteen points and seven other players scoring in double digits. In the second contest, the team beat China 93–67 with Medina Dixon of Old Dominion University scoring nineteen points and the University of Texas's Clarissa Davis and Auburn University's Vickie Orr supporting her with fourteen points each. The team finished pool play with a resounding 114–59 victory over Spain with Dixon again leading the way with twenty-eight points. Unfortunately, in the semifinals, the U.S. women lost a close contest to the Unified Team 73–79, negatively impacted by poor shooting from the field as well as the free throw line. As a result, the Unified Team would go on to a gold medal with a win over China, while the United States had to settle for the bronze with a close 88–74 semifinal victory over Cuba.

The experience of the U.S. men's basketball team in Barcelona could not have been more different from that of their female counterparts. On April 8, 1989, the International Basketball Federation (FIBA) at its World Congress in Munich, Germany, voted overwhelmingly (56–13) to allow professional players, including those from the National Basketball Association (NBA), to participate in the Olympic Games. As a result of the FIBA's historic decision, USA Basketball formed a committee to choose the twelve players to represent the United States in Barcelona. The committee, headed up by University of Kentucky athletic director and 1984 Olympic team assistant coach C. M. Newton, included notable college coaches P. J. Carlesimo of Seton Hall and Mike Krzyzewski of Duke as well as such NBA executives as Jack McCloskey and Rod Thorn. Shunning the tryouts that had traditionally been the method of selecting team members, the committee chose the 1992 U.S. Olympic basketball squad based on the recent performances of

NBA and college players. The committee announced, with much anticipation and fanfare, the first ten members of the team on an NBC selection show on September 21, 1991. Those players were legendary Black NBA stars Magic Johnson, Charles Barkley, Karl Malone, Patrick Ewing, David Robinson, Scottie Pippen, and Michael Jordan, and white NBA greats John Stockton, Larry Bird, and Chris Mullin. Added to the team shortly thereafter was the outstanding Black Portland Trail Blazers' player Clyde Drexler and Christian Laettner, the excellent white collegiate player who had led Duke University to back-to-back NCAA championships and garnered national player of the year honors.

Not unexpectedly, the selection of what has famously become known as the "Dream Team," a name first used on the February 18, 1991, cover of *Sports Illustrated* that featured African American stars Jordan, Ewing, Johnson, Malone, and Barkley, was not without controversy. Some players, most notably Malone, expressed concerns about competing with Johnson who famously announced on November 7, 1991, that he had contracted the HIV virus. Those fears were eventually assuaged, no doubt partly a result of the fact that no players competing alongside or against Johnson suffered any ill effects during the memorable 1992 NBA All-Star Game in which he garnered MVP honors in spite of not participating in any regular season games that year. The most notable player left off the "Dream Team" was the outstanding Black Detroit Pistons' player Isiah Thomas, a twelve-time All-Star and member of two NBA championship teams. The snub supposedly resulted from a feud between Thomas and Eastern Conference rivals Jordan and Pippen from the Chicago Bulls. Other accomplished players left off the team were African Americans Dominique Wilkins of the Atlanta Hawks, Tim Hardaway of the Golden State Warriors, and Michael Adams of the Denver Nuggets. Notwithstanding those players and a few others, the "Dream Team" was made up of an extraordinary group of athletes. Jack McCallum of *Sports Illustrated* claimed years later that it was "arguably the most dominant squad ever assembled in any sport" and compared it to "Johnny Cash at Folsom Prison, the Allman Brothers at the Fillmore East, and Santana at Woodstock."[1] The "Dream Team" overwhelmed Angola in their first game 116–48 and then went on to successive victories over Croatia, Germany, Brazil, Spain, Puerto Rico, Lithuania, and then Croatia again to capture the gold medal. The team scored over 100 points in each of their eight contests and defeated their opponents by an average of 43.8 points.

The legacy of the "Dream Team" is difficult to assess with any certitude. For many of the players themselves, however, the chance to compete in Barcelona was the greatest and most impactful basketball experience of their lives. Magic Johnson noted that playing on the "Dream Team was the greatest moment of my life in terms of basketball, bar none."[2] IOC President Juan Antonio Samaranch believed "the most important aspect of the games has been the resounding success of the basketball tournament, as we've witnessed the best basketball in the world. The Palau d' Esports de Badalona has become the mecca of the sport."[3] There also seems little question that the success and accompanying attention garnered by the "Dream Team" contributed to the global spread of the sport. It is no coincidence that there were just 23 international players representing 18 countries in the NBA at the start of the 1991 season and by the 2012 season there were 74 international players representing 35 countries in the NBA. Foreign-born athletes had been inspired by the greatest basketball players in the world who as a collective were elected to the FIBA Hall of Fame in 2017 and will always be remembered for their dominating performance in Barcelona's one and only Olympic Games.

At the same time, an indication of the rapidly expanding commercialization of the Olympic Games, and sport more generally for that matter, was on full display among the basketball team in Barcelona. While on the medal stand with the rest of the "Dream Team," Michael Jordan, Nike's most famous pitchman, draped an American flag over his shoulder to conceal the Reebok logo on his warm up suit. An obvious attempt to protect his economic interests, members of the African American community heavily criticized Jordan and increasingly lodged biting assessments of him as the most famous and highly paid Black professional athlete for not using his public platform to speak out about racial justice and inequality. Two observers castigated Jordan for his lack of commitment to social justice, Black sportswriters Shaun Powell and William Rhoden. Both chided the legendary Chicago Bulls' player unmercifully by juxtaposing his actions on the medal stand in Barcelona with the Black Power salute of Tommie Smith and John Carlos in Mexico City in 1968. Powell, like Rhoden deeply troubled by the apathy of many Black athletes at the time toward larger racial issues and ambivalent more generally about the impact of sport on the African American community, wrote that when Jordan placed the American flag over the Reebok logo in Barcelona "he was literally covering his own assets." In Mexico City, "Carlos and Smith raised a fist and spoke for those without a voice back home, Jordan struck a pose for the almighty dollar."[4] Rhoden was even more unsparing in his criticism of Jordan. The Black gloves of Smith and Carlos "symbolized the mounting anger, frustration, and fury of so many African Americans, impoverished, brutalized, and marginalized in the world's greatest democracy," wrote Rhoden. Exactly "twenty-four years later, Jordan made a 'stand' of his own on the medal ceremony at an Olympics game. Jordan's 'protest' underlined the thickness of his blinders and revealed where his heart lay."[5]

ALI AND THE "AUDACIOUS PERFECTION OF IT"

In 1996, Atlanta hosted what are often referred to as the Centennial Olympic Games in commemoration of the first modern Games held 100 years before in Athens. Although Athens was the sentimental choice to host the Games because of this fact, the IOC eventually selected Atlanta because of its supposed excellent infrastructure and facilities, promises to utilize funding generated solely through the private sector, potential to realize large television revenues, civil rights history, and reputation for racial harmony that the city's mayor Andrew Young and other municipal leaders were anxious to showcase. Much of the above was questionable and in some respects simply not true, but the Atlanta Committee for the Olympic Games (ACOG), headed up by its CEO and president Billy Payne, who was a former University of Georgia football player, was also able to convince the IOC, U.S. Olympic Committee (USOC), and National Olympic Committees (NOCs) of the many benefits that would result from the Games. The 1996 Olympics in Atlanta actually turned out to be one of the most extravagant in history with over half a billion dollars being spent on the Games by the city of Atlanta, the federal government, the state of Georgia, and the various municipalities that hosted sporting events.

One torch ceremony in the history of the modern Olympic Games stands out from the rest and took place in Atlanta. In a stirring and glorious moment in Olympic history, Muhammad Ali, the legendary heavyweight champion and sporting icon now suffering from Parkinson's disease, energized the whole world when he suddenly appeared on the platform at the far end of the Olympic stadium and lit the flame at the opening ceremonies of the 1996 Games in Atlanta. It was a moment marked by great symbolism and transition. Materializing unexpectedly on the platform inspired millions as Ali, who captured gold at the 1960 Games in Rome and was once demonized for his membership in the Nation of Islam and for refusing to enter military service, had been transformed along the way into a beloved figure admired for his principles and willingness to sacrifice his freedom for his religious beliefs. To Janet Evans, the multiple gold medal–winning swimmer from the United States who had the honor of handing the torch to Ali, the moment was a defining one. For Ali "to stand there in front of the world" noted Evans in 2015, "and inspire even more young people like myself, to be and do and accomplish anything we want to do, it was an epiphany for me."[6] Noted sportswriter George Vecsey of the *New York Times* wrote that having Ali light the cauldron "was a stroke of genius that transformed a very nice ceremony into a celebration, a block party. I was sitting with a black male colleague and a white female colleague, and when we saw Ali shining on that platform, we exchanged high-fives at the audacious perfection of it."[7]

The "stroke of genius" of having Ali light the cauldron almost did not come off. The evidence indicates that Billy Payne as president of the Atlanta Committee for the Olympic Games initially pushed to have Evander Holyfield light the Olympic flame. Payne's choice made perfect sense as Holyfield was a hometown hero who had captured multiple heavyweight boxing titles and engaged in legendary fights against the likes of Mike Tyson, Lennox Lewis, Riddick Bowe, and Larry Holmes. NBC executive Dick Ebersol, however, thought otherwise, lobbying Payne and other committee members to pick Ali to do the honors. Ebersol remembers telling Payne that "Muhammad Ali may be, outside of perhaps the Pope, the most beloved figure in the world."[8] Payne, for his part, responded by noting, "Where we're from, he's [Ali] perceived as a draft dodger."[9] Ultimately, Ebersol successfully made his case. The only thing left to do was to ask Ali if he was willing and capable of lighting the cauldron despite his considerable physical challenges but with his usual confidence, the legendary boxer answered in the affirmative.

BLACK MAN WITH THE GOLDEN SHOES

Ali's poignant and memorable lighting of the Olympic torch foreshadowed some great sports performances in Atlanta, many of them achieved by African American men and women athletes. They garnered an assortment of medals in track and field, breaking records in a number of events. On the men's side, Carl Lewis won gold in the long jump with a leap of 27'10½" to become at the time, along with sailor Paul Elvstrom and discus thrower Al Oerter (later matched by swimmer Michael Phelps), only the third Olympian to win the same event four times. He beat out James Beckford of Jamaica who won the silver and the Black Ohio State star Joe Greene who captured bronze in the event for the second straight Olympic Games. Unfortunately, a bit of luster was taken off Lewis's gold when he became embroiled in a controversy a few days later involving the U.S. 4×100 meter relay team. Lewis demanded to be put on the team even though he had not participated in the mandatory relay training camp. To Lewis's chagrin, head coach Erv Hunt denied the request and the U.S. team, made up in the finals of Texas Christian University's Jon Drummand, University of Kentucky's Tim Harden, UCLA's Michael Marsh, and University of Florida's Dennis Mitchell, ended up second to the gold medalists from Canada who were anchored by the great Donovan Bailey, the Jamaican-born winner of the 100 meters in Atlanta in a new world record time of 9.84.

The controversy surrounding the U.S. 4×100 meter relay team did not diminish the other great athletic performances by African American men in track and field in Atlanta. In the running events, Allen Johnson of the University of North Carolina beat out his U.S. teammate Mark Crear from the University of Southern California for the gold in the 110-meter hurdles in a new Olympic record of 12.95. In one of the great individual performances in Olympic history, Baylor University's Michael Johnson, wearing his famous gold Nike racing spikes and running in his very unorthodox but highly recognizable upright stance, became the only athlete to capture gold in both the 200 and 400 meters in the same Olympics. In the 200-meters, he beat runner-up Frankie Fredericks of Namibia and bronze medalist Ato Boldon of Trinidad and Tobago in a new world record of 19.32. In the 400-meters, he captured gold by defeating silver medalist Roger Black of Great Britain and bronze medalist Davis Kamoga of Uganda in a new Olympic record of 43.49. For his accomplishments, the "hyper-rational, hyper-commercial, ram-rod straight king of US athletics," had become "the face of the Games" and one of the most recognizable people in the world.[10] When asked on *The Charlie Rose Show* a few weeks after the Games what he was thinking about at the moment he achieved victory on the track in Atlanta, Johnson noted that he "thought about how in 1992 when I didn't win an individual Olympic Gold medal and now I finally did it. Now I don't have to go through the rest of my career being afraid that I'd finish my career and people will say that 'he was the greatest two hundred and four hundred meter runner ever, but he never won an Olympic Gold Medal.'"[11]

Drawing less attention but noteworthy in its own right was the University of Arkansas's Calvin Davis's bronze medal in the 400-meter hurdles and the gold medal by the U.S. 4×400-meter relay team, which included in the finals Santa Monica Track Club's Lemont Smith, Salinas (CA) High School star Alvin Harrison, Georgia Tech's Derek Mills, and University of Iowa's Anthuan Maybank, over the silver medalists from Great Britain and bronze medalists from Jamaica. Importantly, Johnson was originally scheduled to be a member of the U.S. 4×400-meter relay team but was unable to do so

Michael Johnson winning the 200-meters in a new world record time of 19.32 at the 1996 Olympic Games in Atlanta. The victory was historic in that Johnson became the only man to win both the 200-meter and 400-meter (accomplished days earlier) races in the same Olympic Games. *Courtesy of the Associated Press.*

because of a strained muscle he suffered in the 200-meter final, preventing him from capturing his third gold medal in Atlanta.

In the field events, besides Lewis's gold in the long jump, Texas State University's Charles Austin won gold in the high jump in an Olympic record of 7'8" over silver medalist Artur Partyka of Poland and bronze medalist Steve Smith of Great Britain; Kansas State University's Kenny Harrison captured gold in the triple jump with a new Olympic record of 59'3" over silver medalist Jonathan Edwards of Great Britain and bronze medalist Yoelbi Quesada of Cuba. The University of Idaho's Dan O'Brien became the first Black athlete since Rafer Johnson to win the decathlon with 8,824 points over silver medalist Frank Busemann of Germany and bronze medalist Tomas Dvorak from the Czech Republic. Tellingly, O'Brien and those athletes who captured the decathlon title in subsequent Olympic Games, irrespective of color, never realized the attention and adulation of Johnson, a result perhaps more than anything else of an event that has lost its luster over the years because of its incompatibility with the current emphasis on specialization in sport and all aspects of society.

In the women's running events, Florida State University's Kim Batten added to the U.S. medal count by taking second place in the 400-meter hurdles, beating out her teammate Tonja Buford-Bailey of the University of Illinois who captured bronze. UCLA's Gail Devers won her second consecutive Olympic gold medal in the 100-meters in a photo finish over Marlene Ottey of Jamaica and teammate Gwen Torrence of the University of Georgia, and then teamed in the finals with Torrence, Stanford University's Chryste Gaines, and USC's Inger Miller (daughter of Jamaican sprint star Lennox) to capture the title in the 4×100-meter relay over the silver medalists from the Bahamas and bronze medalists from Jamaica. The U.S. women also captured gold in the 4×400-meter relay. The team, which included in the finals Morgan State University's Rochelle Stevens, Arizona State University's Maicel Malone-Wallace, Clemson University's Kim Graham, and Alabama A&M University's Jearl Miles, outran the silver medalists from Nigeria and bronze medalists from Germany. The only U.S. woman to be victorious in a field event in Atlanta was Jackie Joyner-Kersee. At the latter stage of her remarkable career and dropping out of the heptathlon in Atlanta because of an injury, Joyner-Kersee won bronze in the long jump with a leap of 22'11½", being edged out in a heavily contested event by gold medalist Chioma Ajunwa of Nigeria and Fiona May of Italy who won silver.

INCHING THEIR WAY INTO OTHER SPORTS

Like four years earlier in Barcelona, African American men and women athletes distinguished themselves in other sports in Atlanta besides track and field. Boxer David Reid of Philadelphia, dubbed "The American Dream," captured a rare gold medal in boxing for the United States with a come-from-behind one punch knockout over Alfredo Duvergel of Cuba in the light-middleweight division. Gathering bronze medals for the United States in boxing were Floyd Mayweather Jr. in the featherweight division, Trenton, New Jersey's Terrance Cauthern in the lightweight division, Texas's Rhoshii Wells in the middleweight division, Chicago's Nate "The Snake" Jones in the heavyweight division, and Orlando, Florida's Antonio Tarver in the light-heavyweight division. Mayweather Jr. would become the most famous of these boxers, capturing several professional titles and being named the "fighter of the decade" for the 2010s by the Boxing Writers

Association of America. In freestyle wrestling, Townsend Saunders, who had captured an NCAA title at Division II California State University, Bakersfield before transferring to Arizona State University where he became a two-time All-American, captured the silver medal in the 149-pound class in an extraordinarily exciting match against Vadim Bogiev. Tied 1–1 in regulation, the two wrestlers went eight minutes of overtime without scoring, but Bogiev was declared the winner as a result of two passivity calls against Saunders.

In baseball, the U.S. team fared better than they had in Barcelona, taking the bronze medal behind Cuba who captured the gold medal and Japan who took the silver medal. The only African American on the twenty-man squad was Jacque Jones, the University of Southern California star who had a .395 batting average, .921 slugging percentage, and scored twelve runs to lead the team in that category. In softball, catcher Gillian Boxx, a three-time All-American from the University of California, Berkeley, made important contributions to the U.S. historic women's gold medal in a sport that was being held for the first time in Olympic competition. Although not generating the attention of her more famous teammates such as Mexican American Lisa Fernandez and whites Michelle Granger, Laura Berg, and Dot Richardson, Boxx was a steady presence behind the plate and hit .250 for the tournament with a slugging percentage of .384. In soccer, the U.S. women's gold medal–winning team included four African Americans: Goal keeper Brianna Scurry of the University of Massachusetts at Amherst, reserves Staci Wilson of the University of North Carolina and Saskia Johnson-Webber of North Carolina State University, and alternate Thori Staples Bryan of North Carolina State University. The very talented Scurry played every minute of all five matches and gave up only three goals for the United States. As it turned out, this was in many ways just the beginning for Scurry as she led the U.S. women to the 1999 World Cup title in front of 90,000 fans at the Rose Bowl in a legendary overtime match against China and another gold medal in the 2004 Olympics in Athens.

In gymnastics, Jair Lynch captured silver in the parallel bars to become the first African American man to win an individual Olympic medal in gymnastics. Lynch, an impressive individual by any measure, is the son of a Trinidadian father who took his PhD in political science and economics from Harvard University and a mother from Bogota, Colombia, who worked for a number of years as an economist for the Organization of American States. Taking a degree in civil engineering and urban design from Stanford University, Lynch was nominated for a Rhodes Scholarship following his graduation. After the Games in Atlanta, Lynch served from

2004 to 2012 on the United States Olympic Committee (USOC) Board of Directors and was as a member of groups from the District of Columbia in 2001 and 2014 that put in bids to host the Summer Games. The extraordinarily gifted Dominique Dawes followed up her outstanding performance in Barcelona with an even better one in Atlanta. She helped capture the first Olympic gold medal for the U.S. women in the team all-around competition and won an individual bronze medal in the floor exercise. The gold in the team all-around was captured by the U.S women famously known as the "Magnificent Seven," a talented group of gymnasts that included Dawes, Shannon Miller, Dominique Moceanu, Kerri Strug, Amy Chow, Amanda Borden, and Jaycie Phelps. The most memorable performance by a "Magnificent Seven" member and one etched firmly in historical memory was Strug's sticking the landing in the vault to secure the gold medal in spite of being injured.

RECOMMITTING TO BASKETBALL DOMINANCE

In basketball, both the U.S. women and men's teams performed superbly. After a disappointing performance in Barcelona as well as at the 1994 World Championship, USA Basketball recommitted itself, both financially and organizationally, to putting the best women's team on the floor as they possibly could. With the NBA "exploring a business model for professional women's basketball" and "willing to put some money behind the USA women's team as a marketing 'project'" (a success considering the WNBA began play in 1997), USA Basketball hired coach Tara VanDerveer away from Stanford University for the year and implemented a program in which the team would train together over an extended period of time like others around the world.[12]

With a roster filled "with veteran players such as Teresa Edwards, who had been playing for years in anonymity overseas, and young guns such as Leslie [Lisa] and Dawn Staley, who were best known for their NCAA resumes and were about to break through on another level," the U.S. women's team prepared for Olympic competition with twelve months of extensive training that included "a 22-game college tour that introduced the team to the country" and a series of exhibition games in seven countries.[13] It paid off. Competing in front of an average 25,320 fans per game and a total of 202,556 during the eight games they played, the U.S. women's team, certainly the most popular of any previous women's Olympic basketball teams with nine of the twelve members of the squad made up of African

American players, breezed through the competition on its way to the gold medal. Playing its first two games in front of sold-out crowds at Morehouse College, one of Atlanta's legendary Historically Black Colleges and Universities, the United States beat Cuba in its opening contest 101–84 and never looked back. In the gold medal game in the Georgia Dome, the team was pitted against Brazil, a team that was also 7–0 in the tournament and had defeated the United States in both the 1991 Pan American Games and 1994 World Championship. This time would prove far different. The U.S. women jumped out to an immediate lead, hitting 71.9 percent of their shots in the first half and ultimately winning 111–87. For the game, the U.S. team shot an Olympic record 66.2 percent from the field.

The U.S. men's basketball team, while certainly not drawing the attention and volume of media coverage realized by the "Dream Team" four years earlier, featured a roster of just one white player, the Utah Jazz's John Stockton, and eleven African American players, including returning veterans from the 1992 squad (in addition to Stockton) Charles Barkley, Karl Malone, Scottie Pippen, and David Robinson. Gone were Michael Jordan who chose not to play, Larry Bird and Magic Johnson who were both retired, Christian Laettner who was not gifted enough to be on the team, Chris Mullin and Clyde Drexler whose best days were behind them, and Patrick Ewing whose skills had begun to deteriorate. The 1996 team was coached by Lenny Wilkens, the great Providence College and Saint Louis Hawks' point guard chosen to both the NBA's 50th and 75th Anniversary Teams, the NBA's all-time winningest coach until being passed for that honor in 2019 by the San Antonio Spurs' Gregg Popovich, and a member of the Naismith Memorial Basketball Hall of Fame. Only the second African American in history to be head coach of the U.S. men's Olympic basketball team, the other being Georgetown's John Thompson in 1988, Wilkens is a member of a very select group of Blacks who have been selected for head coaching or upper-level administrative positions in the Olympic hierarchy and sport more generally, for that matter.

With Wilkens at the helm, the U.S. 1996 men's basketball team overwhelmed their opponents with an 8–0 record to win another gold medal. The U.S. men won all their games by substantial margins and received major contributions from every member of the team. In the gold medal game, the U.S. men defeated Yugoslavia 95–69 behind David Robinson's twenty-eight points and seven rebounds, and the Indiana Pacers' Reggie Miller's twenty points and Anfernee Hardaway's seventeen. The contest was marked by a halftime celebration in which the U.S. men's team presented Muhammad Ali with a gold medal to replace the one he had "lost" following his victory in the light-heavyweight division at the 1960 Rome Olympics. A decision made by the IOC, the ceremony was a memorable occasion for the players who crowded around and hugged the "People's Champ" as the theme to *Superman* was booming in the background and spectators were chanting his name over and over again. In hindsight, the ceremony was thick with irony since the great Black heavyweight champion who had spoken out about racial inequities during the height of the civil rights movement and sacrificed the best years of his boxing career on account of his religious beliefs was being showered with love by a generation of younger African American athletes reluctant to fight back against racial oppression. It would be many years later following the killing of many innocent Black men and the subsequent Black Lives Matter movement that African American athletes began exhibiting a more Muhammad Ali–like conviction to racial matters and realization of the power they had to collectively effect change because of their elevated status in the African American community.

BLACK ATHLETES AND RACIAL SYMBOLISM "DOWN UNDER"

In a narrow vote, the IOC selected Sydney, Australia, as the site for the 2000 Olympic Games over Beijing, partly a result of Sydney's intention to involve smaller Oceania countries as hosts and utilize recovered toxic waste-lands as sporting venues as well as Human Rights Watch's efforts to "stop Beijing" because of its atrocious record on human rights. As in Barcelona in 1992 and Atlanta in 1996, the opening ceremony in Sydney was elaborate and fraught with much symbolism. It was also controversial. In the lead up to the Olympics it was apparent the Aboriginal community, not dissimilar to the disputes evident among African Americans surrounding the 1968 Mexico City Games, was divided as to how their lives should be portrayed during the Games, with the more radical elements of the community call-ing for protests (when not calling for a boycott of the Games) and deeply troubled that their culture would be exploited by Olympic organizers, while the more moderate elements of the community envisioned the Games as an important step toward reconciliation that had officially begun with the federal government's creation in 1991 of the Council for Aboriginal Rec-onciliation. This necessitated an opening ceremony that would obscure the abhorrent separation of Aboriginal children and their families while at once displaying the racial progress that had taken place in the country. In the end, the moderates won out as indicated by an opening ceremony that celebrated the history of Australia, particularly the singular yet little known contributions of the Indigenous people who inhabited the continent. A particularly poignant moment was the lighting of the Olympic Flame which was brought into the stadium by legendary Australian middle-distance runner Herb Elliott who had captured gold in the 1,500 meters at the 1960 Rome Olympics. In a celebration of 100 years of women's participation in the Olympic Games, Elliott next passed it for a final relay to former Australian Olympic medalists beginning with sprinter Betty Cuthbert and then in succession sprinter Raelene Boyle, swimmer Dawn Fraser, sprinter Shirley Strickland, swimmer Shane Gould, and hurdler Debbie Flintoff-King who brought the torch through the stadium before handing it off to the great Aboriginal sprinter Cathy Freeman who lit the cauldron and later cemented her place in Olympic lore by capturing gold in the 400 meters.[14]

DRUG SCANDALS GALORE ON THE TRACK

Sydney witnessed many great performances by athletes from around the world and the usual mix of surprises and poignant Olympic moments. One of the most impressive all-around performances was by Marion Jones, the great African American sprinter from the University of North Carolina. Jones astonished the track and field world by capturing gold medals in the 100-meters, 200-meters, and 4×400 meter relay and bronze medals in the long jump and 4×100 meter relay. Unfortunately, in one of the more protracted and sordid episodes in sports history, Jones was ultimately disqualified from all five events after admitting to taking performance-enhancing drugs. For years refusing to confess she had taken steroids, even though Victor Conte, infamous founder of the Bay Area Laboratory Co-Operative (BALCO), had admitted in 2004 to injecting her with performance-enhancing drugs and providing her instructions as to how she could do it herself, Jones finally admitted on October 5, 2007, to lying to federal agents under oath about her drug use. On December 12, 2007, the IOC formally stripped Jones of her Olympic medals from Sydney and barred her from participating in any capacity at the 2008 Games in Beijing. The disgraced Jones was sentenced to six months in prison and has encountered serious financial difficulties as a result of the loss of endorsement deals, court costs, and poor economic decisions. Importantly, Jones was just one of the most notorious of the more than twenty athletes to get entangled in the famous scandal in which Conte provided a special concoction of performance enhancing drugs to athletes prepared by Illinois chemist Patrick Arnold and dispersed by California trainer Greg Anderson. Other athletes snared in the scandal included Jones' ex-husband, shot putter C. J. Hunter, who apparently blew the whistle on Jones' use of drugs to federal investigators; sprinter Tim Montgomery, a former boyfriend of Jones and father of her first child; Bill Romanowski, a white professional football player; Jason Giambi, a white professional baseball player; and, most importantly Barry Bonds of the San Francisco Giants whose ties to BALCO and Anderson specifically generated the most damning publicity. Following a federal investigation of the laboratory that commenced in 2002, BALCO's doors were shut. Conte, Arnold, and Anderson all spent time in prison, and Bonds, while never punished by Major League Baseball, has failed to be inducted into the Baseball Hall of Fame because of his supposed use of performance-enhancing drugs and ties to the scandal. The BALCO episode is especially noteworthy because of the contrasts in punishment meted out to Black athletes relative to their white counterparts snared in the scandal, a difference that would be seriously questioned in future Olympic Games.

As a result of Jones' disqualification from the five events in which she medaled, only one African American woman athlete medaled in an individual track and field event in Sydney. Melissa Morrison-Howard, the outstanding track star from Appalachian State University, prevented the shutout in individual competitions by taking the bronze medal in the 100-meter hurdles. African American women had a better time of it in the relays, although Jones's guilty plea and ultimate conviction of using steroids jeopardized the medals awarded to both the gold medal–winning 4×400 relay and bronze medal 4×100 relay teams. Because Jones participated in the finals of both relays, the medals awarded to the other team members, including those women who only participated in the preliminaries and semi-finals, were initially taken from them by the IOC and not given back until that decision was overturned in 2010 by the Court of Arbitration for Sport. This meant that the women's gold medal-winning 4×400 relay squad, made up in the finals of Alabama A&M's Jearl Miles Clark, University of North Carolina's Monique Hennagan, University of North Carolina's LaTasha Colander, and alternate Andrea Anderson of UCLA, were not punished for the lack of judgment exercised by their more famous teammate and the same thing held true for the bronze medal–winning 4×100 relay squad made up in the finals of Stanford's Chryste Gaines, USC's Torri Edwards, University of Texas's Nanceen Perry, and alternate Passion Richardson of the University of Kentucky.

There was just as much drama and controversy in Sydney involving African American men on the U.S. track and field team. Although realizing

Marion Jones (left) with Australia's Cathy Freeman after capturing the gold medal in the 200-meter run at the 2000 Olympic Games in Sydney. Some seven years later the IOC formally stripped Jones of all the medals she won in Sydney for her use of performance-enhancing drugs. *Courtesy of the Associated Press.*

more total medals than their female counterparts, suspected drug use and doping scandals also marred the performances of African American men in track and field at the 2000 Olympic Games. Ironic considering what had happened on the women's side of the ledger, the U.S. men's 4×400 meter relay team, which included in the finals Salinas (CA) high school stars Alvin and Calvin Harrison, St. Augustine College's (Raleigh, NC) Andrew Pettigrew, and Baylor University's Michael Johnson, originally captured the gold medal over the silver medalists from Nigeria and the bronze medalists from Jamaica. However, on July 18, 2004, the International Association of Athletics Federations (IAAF) announced that the Court of Arbitration of Sport ruled that St. Augustine College's Jerome Young, who had competed in the heats and semi-final of the 4×400 meter relay, was ruled ineligible to compete in Sydney, banned permanently from athletic competition, and had the results from all his events negated since being found guilty of a doping offense on June 26, 1999. Young was not the only one to suffer the consequences of his actions as the entire 4×400 relay team were stripped of their gold medal, resulting in Nigeria, Jamaica, and Bahamas all being moved up one slot on the medal board. On July 22, 2005 the Court of Arbitration of Sport reversed the decision and restored the original order of finish, contending that no team could be disqualified for a doping offense committed by a member who did not participate in the finals. Unfortunately, this was not the end of the sordid and protracted story. In June 2008, Andrew Pettigrew, after being identified as a user of steroids by Trevor Graham, member of Jamaica's 1988 silver medal winning 4×400 relay team, former coach, and critical whistleblower in the Balco Scandal, admitted in U.S. court that he had used performance-enhancing drugs and agreed to return his gold medal. As a result, on August 2, 2008, the IOC once again stripped the gold medal from the U.S. 4×400 relay team and four years later confirmed the reordering of medals.

African American men fared better in other track and field events in Sydney, although clouds of suspicion always hung over the athletes in the sport during an era in which performance-enhancing drugs were obviously so prevalent. The U.S. 4×100 relay team, which included in the finals the University of Florida's Bernard Williams, Norfolk State University's Brian Lewis, University of Kansas's Maurice Greene, and Texas Christian University's Jon Drummond, captured gold by defeating Brazil who garnered the silver medal and Cuba who took bronze. In April of 2008 the *New York Times* reported Greene had paid Mexican discus thrower Angel Guillermo Heredia Hernandez $10,000, which Hernandez said was in payment for performance-enhancing drugs, and in 2014 Drummond was banned from the sport until 2022 for encouraging and transporting performance-enhancing drugs to sprinter Tyson Gay whom he had coached. In the individual running events, Greene captured the 100 meters in a winning time of 9.87, and Angelo Taylor of Georgia Tech captured one of his three gold medals in Olympic competition by triumphing in the 400-meter hurdles over Hadi Al-Somaily of Saudi Arabia and Llewellyn Herbert of South Africa. Michael Johnson repeated as the Olympic gold medalist in the 400 meters and cemented his reputation as one of the greatest athletes in Olympic track and field history by defeating silver medalist Alvin Harrison of the United States and bronze medalist Greg Haughton of Jamaica. Terrence Trammell of the University of South Carolina won the silver medal in the 110-meter hurdles, sandwiched between Anier Garcia of Cuba and Mark Crear of the University of Southern California. Unfortunately, only one medal was captured by an African American male in the field competitions, but it was a historic triumph. Lawrence Johnson of the University of Tennessee became the first African American to medal in the pole vault in Olympic competition by capturing silver in the event, just behind his U.S. teammate Nick Hysong of Arizona State who won the gold. It was just one of the highlights of Johnson's remarkable career that also included 4 NCAA titles and a gold in the 2001 World Championships. Important from a symbolic standpoint, it helped dispel the notion that Blacks were incapable of success in an event that had always been categorized as a "technical" discipline requiring a rare combination of commitment, hard work, and intelligence.

BLACK ATHLETIC EXCELLENCE FOUND IN DIFFERENT PLACES

African American athletes added to the U.S. stash of medals in the 2000 Games in Sydney in an assortment of other sports. Danielle Victoria Slaton, a three-time All-American at Santa Clara University, was the youngest member of the U.S. women's soccer team that took the silver medal in Sydney, losing a heartbreaking final match to Norway. (Brianna Scurry was on the squad but did not get any minutes because of weight and other health issues.) Venus Williams captured the singles title in tennis and, along with her younger sister Serena, garnered another gold medal in doubles. Anthony Ervin, the outstanding athlete from the University of California, Santa Barbara who was born to a father of Black and Indian descent and a Jewish mother, became the first African American to capture gold in an individual swimming event by winning the 50-meter freestyle. He would also win a silver medal as part of the U.S. 4×100 freestyle relay team. Travis Sentell "Gookie" Dawkins, Marcus Jensen, and Ernie Young all contributed to the success of the gold medal–winning baseball team. The three players, all of whom had Major League experience, took advantage of the 2000 decision by the International Baseball Association to open up the Olympic Games to professional athletes. Because the Olympic Games are always held during the Big League season, however, the standard practice of USA Baseball is to fill its roster with Minor League players, some of whom are former Major Leaguers.

Also contributing to the medal count in Sydney were Dominique Dawes and Tasha Schwikert, who were members of the U.S. gymnastics team that was belatedly awarded a bronze medal in the all-around competition in 2010 after China was stripped of the medal by the IOC when it was determined that one of its team members, Dong Fangxiao, was underage at the time of competition. Far less known at the time than Dawes, the other African American on the team, who was participating in her third Olympic Games and had already won a gold and two bronze medals, Schwikert's selection to the squad was controversial as she placed ninth at the Olympic trials and was originally in Sydney only as an alternate. Even so, she performed admirably and outshined many of her more famous teammates in Sydney.

Perhaps most importantly, Schwikert, the daughter of an African American father and white mother who both worked as croupiers in Las Vegas, became arguably the most prominent and recognizable gymnast in the United States following the Games in Sydney. Although the career trajectory of Olympians in many sports necessitates that they initially hone their skills in intercollegiate athletics, Schwikert, who first became a national team member at the age of thirteen, joined the UCLA gymnastics team after an ankle injury prevented her from competing in the 2004 Games in Athens. She competed for UCLA from 2004 to 2008 and twice won the NCAA all-around championship as well as a silver medal in floor exercise, and gold, silver, and bronze in the uneven bars. Her accomplishments were so prodigious that in 2007 she was nominated along with three other gymnasts for the Honda Sports Award, given annually to the outstanding female athletes in intercollegiate athletics in twelve different sports. Sadly, Schwikert was one of the many women gymnasts abused by former national team doctor Larry Nasser, who is now serving 175 years in a prison outside Orlando, Florida. In an inclusive interview with ABC News in 2018, Schwikert announced she had been abused by Nasser hundreds of times between 2000 and 2005, the first time when she was sixteen and training at the now infamous Karolyi Ranch in Huntsville, Texas.

Just as in Atlanta in 1996, African American athletes also added to the U.S. medal count in Sydney in boxing. Pugilist Ricardo "Slicky Ricky" Williams of Cincinnati, Ohio, was clearly not "slick" enough and captured a silver medal in the light welterweight division, while Clarence "Untouchable" Vinson of Washington, D.C. was not quite "untouchable" and garnered a bronze medal in the bantamweight division. Finally, Jermaine Taylor, a native of Little Rock, Arkansas, captured the bronze medal in the light middleweight division, losing to Yermakhan Ibraimov of Kazakhstan when the referee stopped the contest in the fourth round. Of the four U.S. boxing medalists from Sydney, it was Taylor who had the longest and most successful professional career in the sport. Sadly, his life also reflects the troubling and downward spiral that has too often befallen pugilists outside of the ring. An extraordinarily gifted boxer who began fighting at age thirteen, Taylor began his professional career just a year after the Games in Sydney and won his first twenty-five bouts over such talented pugilists as former WBA middleweight champion William Joppy and former IBF light-middleweight titlist Raul Marquez. A watershed event in Taylor's professional boxing career took place on June 16, 2005, when he defeated Bernard Hopkins in a split decision for the Undisputed Middleweight Championship at the MGM Grand in Las Vegas, Nevada. In a rematch on December 3, 2005, held at the Mandalay Bay Resort and Casino in Las Vegas, Taylor defeated Hopkins in a unanimous decision with all three judges scoring the fight 115–113 in his favor. Taylor parlayed his success in the ring and good looks into other professional opportunities, including modeling for *GQ*, *Vogue*, and Everlast. These opportunities were offset by several legal problems and run-ins with the police, incidents that resulted from mental health issues seemingly caused by damage inflicted on Taylor in the ring, particularly his October 17, 2009, loss to undefeated Armenian-German champion Arthur Abraham at the Super Six World Boxing Classic in Berlin in which he was hospitalized with a severe concussion and suffered short-term memory loss.

BASKETBALL AND ANOTHER JOHNSON IN THE HOUSE

As significant and noteworthy as the individual boxing performances were by Williams, Vinson, and Taylor, they paled in comparison to the gold medal–winning women's and men's basketball teams in Sydney that were made up largely once again and continue to be so to the present-day of African American players. The women's team, coached by Nell Fortner of Purdue and with great talent led by holdovers from the 1996 team, the Sacramento Monarchs' Ruthie Bolton, Teresa Edwards (who was in semi-retirement after the folding of the American Basketball League in 1999), the Los Angeles Sparks' Lisa Leslie, the Washington Mystics' Nikki Mc-Cray, the Charlotte Sting's Dawn Staley, and the Houston Comets' Sheryl Swoopes, played an extended exhibition schedule like they had four years earlier. It was apparent they would be formidable in Sydney. The team sailed through its exhibition games with a record of 38–2, demolishing different opponents with a high-powered offense and smothering defense and all-around great play. They duplicated it in the Olympic tournament, amassing a record of 8–0 while averaging 81 points a game, holding their opponents to 59.3, and defeating host Australia in the final game despite having only eleven players because of the inability to replace Chamique Holdsclaw, the youngest member of the squad who had gone down with a stress fracture to her right foot. Importantly, the victory in Sydney was the swan song for Edwards who first played on the women's national team in 1984 in Los Angeles as a twenty-year-old and then in the next four Olympic Games, capturing four team gold medals and a bronze and amassing a total of 2,008 points for USA Basketball.

The U.S. men's team also won gold in Sydney but did not dispatch their opponents with the same ease as their female counterparts. An all-Black team led by white coaches Rudy Tomjanovich of the Houston Rockets, Larry Brown of the Philadelphia 76ers, and Gene Keady of Purdue University, and African American Tubby Smith of the University of Kentucky, the Olympic men's basketball team was loaded with talented athletes, ranging from highly skilled youngsters such as Vince Carter of the Toronto Raptors and Kevin Garnett of the Minnesota Timberwolves to more veteran players such as Tim Hardaway of the Miami Heat and Gary Payton of the Seattle Supersonics. Their road to gold, however, was not as easy as expected considering the team's talent level and experience. One big reason for this fact was the continued globalization of basketball and the increased popularity, and vastly improved play among various countries around the world that threatened the U.S. dominance of the sport. In their third game, for instance, the U.S. men beat Lithuania 85–76. A close contest throughout, the nine-point win was the narrowest margin of victory for the U.S. men since NBA players began participating in the Olympic Games in 1992. The team rebounded with a decisive 102–56 victory over New Zealand, which was making its first appearance in Olympic competition, and then followed up with a 106–94 triumph over France with Keven Garnett scoring nineteen points and snaring eleven rebounds and Antonio McDyess of the Denver Nuggets tallying twenty points and collecting eleven rebounds. In the semifinals, the team once again faced Lithuania and eked out an 85–83 victory but only after rallying in the final ninety seconds and surviving a desperation three-point shot by Lithuania's Sarunas Jasikevicius as the buzzer sounded.

Finally, an intriguing personal story involving two African American athletes emerged out of the Games in Sydney. Although not medaling, Jennifer Johnson Jordan teamed with another African American, Annett Davis, to place fifth in the beach volleyball competition. It was a historic accomplishment considering the white-dominated culture of beach volleyball in the United States and made all that more fascinating by the family backgrounds of the two players, especially Johnson Jordan. The daughter of Olympic hero Rafer Johnson and niece of Rafer's brother Jimmy, a member of the Pro Football Hall of Fame, Johnson Jordan followed in their footsteps by becoming an outstanding UCLA athlete, competing on the women's indoor volleyball team from 1991 to 1995. One of her teammates was Davis, the daughter of former NBA player Cleveland Buckner, who also enjoyed a stellar career as a member of the Bruins indoor volleyball squad. Shortly after graduating, Johnson Jordan and Davis began their professional beach volleyball careers together and in 1997 became the first African American team to play for a championship on the professional beach volleyball tour at the Cybergenics Open in Orlando, Florida. They lost the match to Karolyn Kirby and Nancy Reno but went on to win major titles, including the AVP Sunkist Michigan Open in 1999. A year later they occupied their biggest stage yet on Bondi Beach in Sydney, two young African American women from California competing for Olympic gold with Rafer Johnson in attendance and proudly rooting on his daughter and her teammate.

In all, African American athletes contributed significantly to the United States medal count in Sydney just as they had in Barcelona in 1992 and Atlanta in 1996. Those contributions, however, were generally confined to a limited number of sports just as in past Olympic Games. Like the institution more generally, African American athletes, because of tradition and a variety of social, cultural, and economic factors, were heavily concentrated in some sports and underrepresented in others. This circumscribed number of sports would never completely be eliminated, but gradually individual Black athletes appeared more frequently in other traditionally white-dominated sports in the next three Summer Olympic Games that were staged in Athens in 2004, Beijing in 2008, and London in 2012. It was cause for some optimism and no doubt partly a result of efforts to attract and train minority athletes in Olympic sports as well as the impact of the increased commercialization of the Games and concomitant embrace of professionals who welcomed the opportunity to participate in the world's most important mega-sporting event. In the quest for victory, however, African American Olympians got caught up in the drug scandals permeating high-level sport, which tarnished reputations, negatively impacted commercial appeal, and, in some cases, effectively terminated careers in sport. This was a chance some were willing to take in a mega-sporting event that had long ago ceased to be a celebration of gentleman sportsmen displaying manly virtues and embodying a balanced physical, moral, and spiritual approach to life.

8

BLACK MERCURIES DURING THE AGE OF GLOBALIZATION

The games held in Athens in 2004, Beijing in 2008, and London in 2012 confirmed that the summer Olympics had evolved into a spectacular mega-sporting event involving thousands of athletes from around the world who trained diligently in the hopes of representing and bringing honor to themselves and their respective countries. Like their immediate predecessors, the three cities spent billions on infrastructure and facilities and seemingly tried to outdo one another regarding the quality of the sporting venues, media coverage, Olympic village, and opening and closing ceremonies. The sheer costs of the games were astronomical. Beijing serves as the best example. The amount spent on the games in Beijing has been estimated at US$40–44 billion, the only games exceeding that amount being the 2014 winter Olympics in Sochi, which was priced at over US$51 billion. As a basis of comparison, the estimated cost for Athens in 2004 was US$2.9 billion and London US$15 billion.

The Black Mercuries competing in the increasingly globalized games of 2004, 2008, and 2012 certainly lived in a far different world than that occupied by John Baxter Taylor, George Poage, Alice Coachman, Jesse Owens, Mal Whitfield, and the other early African American athletes who graced the Olympic stage. In the United States, legal segregation no longer existed, a Black meritocratic middle class seemingly thrived, fantasies of a post-racial America flourished, and the election of a Black president made history. In spite of these changes, these three Olympic Games clearly substantiated that African American athletes still confronted racialist thinking, deep-seated stereotypical notions, and systematic obstacles to full participation in sport. It was reflected in the type of media coverage they received, obstacles they faced accessing certain sports, the continued assertion that Black success in sport was biologically determined, and persistent struggles they encountered in securing coaching and other upper administrative positions in sport. However, through sheer grit, good fortune, and talent, African American athletes, men and increasingly more women, navigated the racial realities of American culture to achieve success in sports in which they were either not closely identified or received relatively little Olympic media coverage. Black Mercuries were still most prominent in basketball and track and field, but a select number continued to find their way into sports their pioneering Olympic predecessors would have found unimaginable.

FAILING TESTS, CONTINUED ATHLETIC SUCCESS

Athens outbid Rome, Cape Town, Stockholm, and Buenos Aires to host the Olympics in 2004. Although over twenty athletes were disqualified for failing tests for performance-enhancing drugs and the judging of gymnastics and fencing was surrounded by controversy, an all-time high 201 National Olympic Committees were represented in Athens with over 11,000 athletes competing in 28 different sports. The 101 medals garnered by the United States in Athens could not have been reached without the contributions made by African American athletes. Three of the more important of these athletes were swimming's Maritza Correia, softball's Natasha Watley, and boxing's Andre Ward. Correia, originally from Puerto Rico, grew up in Tampa, Florida, and competed for the University of Georgia. She became the first African American woman to capture a swimming medal in the Olympic Games when she participated in the preliminaries of the 4×100 meter freestyle relay in which the U.S. women finished second to take the silver medal. Correia would go on to win multiple medals in the World University Games, Pan American Games, and World Championships before retiring in 2008 because of injuries.

Watley, a supremely talented and accomplished athlete, garnered numerous honors in her outstanding career at UCLA, including being selected first-team All-American four times and receiving in 2003 the Honda Sports Award as the nation's best softball player and Honda-Broderick Cup as the nation's best female athlete. Having the distinction of being one of the first two African Americans on the U.S. national softball team to

Softball's Natasha Watley celebrating with her U.S. teammates. The UCLA star was an outstanding player on both the U.S. 2004 gold-winning team in Athens and 2008 silver-medal winning team in Beijing. She also played several years of professional softball. *Courtesy of USA Softball.*

participate in the Olympics—sharing the distinction with the biracial Taira Flowers, an outstanding utility player from UCLA—Watley hit over .450 in the Aiming for Athens tour in preparation for the 2004 games. At the games themselves, Watley, a slick-fielding shortstop as well as great hitter and base stealer, helped the team to its third straight gold medal through superlative play in the field, at the plate, and on the bases. In the team's nine games, which included a 5–1 victory over Australia (the only run scored against the U.S. women in the entire tournament in Athens, just one reason that some have anointed them "The real dream team") in the gold medal game with Lisa Fernandez on the mound, Watley stole five bases to break the Olympic record, had a batting average of .400, and led the U.S. squad in at-bats and hits. A year after the games in Athens, Watley embarked on a successful nine-year professional career only to be interrupted by her preparation for and participation in the 2008 games in Beijing.

Andre Ward, one of only two U.S. fighters to win a medal in Athens (the other being African American pugilist Andre "The Matrix" Dirrell from Flint, Michigan, who captured the bronze medal in the middleweight division), had an outstanding boxing career at both the amateur and professional levels of competition. Born in San Francisco to an African American woman and Irish American man, Ward's life as a boxer began at the age of nine when he began training at the U.S. Karate School of the Arts in Hayward, California. One of the most important people in his life proved to be his godfather Virgil Hunter who began to care for him after his parents fell victim to drug abuse. Hunter became his mentor, taught him the intricacies of the sport, and served as Ward's trainer throughout the duration of his boxing career. As an amateur, Ward boasted an impressive record of 115 wins and 5 losses, including such titles as the Under 19 National Championship, United States Amateur Middleweight Champion, United States Amateur Light Heavyweight Champion, and 2004 Olympic gold medalist in the light heavyweight division. His march to Olympic gold in Athens began with a second round 17–9 decision over Italy's Clemente Russo and then a quarterfinal 23–16 victory against Russia's Evgeny Makarenko, 17–15 semifinal defeat of Uzbekistan's Utkirbek Haydarov, and 20–13 triumph over Magomed Aripgadjiev of Belarus in the gold medal match. Ward turned professional shortly after his Olympic triumph and went undefeated in thirty-two fights, good enough to eventually be elected to the International Boxing Hall of Fame.

GATLIN LEADS THE WAY

Great performances of other African American athletes in track and field complemented the outstanding achievements of Correira, Watley, and Ward. In the men's competition, both running and field events resulted in many outstanding performances. The talented Justin Gatlin, a great sprinter who enjoyed a very long and successful yet tumultuous career in the sport, led the way for the men in the running competitions. A native of Pensacola, Florida, Gatlin competed for two years at the University of Tennessee where he won multiple NCAA titles in the 100 and 200 meters. The International Association of Athletics Federations (IAAF) banned him from international competition following his freshman season after testing positive for amphetamines. About a year later, he left the university to pursue a professional career in the sport. In 2003, his first year as a professional, Gatlin captured his first of many world championships in the 60 meters in Birmingham, England. A year later in Athens, he captured a gold medal in the 100 meters, a bronze medal in the 200 meters, and a silver medal as a member of the U.S. 4×100 meter relay team. In the 100 meters, Gatlin ran a personal best of 9.85 in narrowly defeating second-place finisher Francis Obikwelu of Portugal and his U.S. teammates Maurice Greene who finished third and Shawn Crawford who came in a close fourth. In the 200 meters, he finished third behind Crawford who won gold and Bernard Williams who captured silver to complete a U.S. sweep in the event. In the 4×100-meter relay Gatlin combined with his teammates Crawford, Greene, and Auburn University's Coby Miller in the finals to take the silver medal behind the gold medalists from Great Britain and in front of the third-place team from Nigeria. Two years after his multiple medal–winning performance in Athens, Gatlin was initially banned by the U.S. Anti-Doping Agency for testing positive for performance-enhancing drugs, a ban later reduced to four years because of his cooperation with doping authorities. He began a successful comeback in 2010, culminating in a bronze medal in the 100 meters in the 2012 games in London, a silver medal in the 100 meters in the 2016 games in Rio de Janeiro, and several world championships.

The outstanding performances by Gatlin and his teammates in the 100-meters, 200-meters, and 4×100 meter relay were accompanied by impressive victories in Athens by other African American men track and field athletes. Terrence Trammell from the University of South Carolina took his second straight silver medal in the 110-meter hurdles, losing to the gold medalist from China Liu Xiang who broke the world record in the event in a time of 12.91. The United States swept the 400 meters just as they had the 200 meters with Otis Harris of the University of South Carolina taking silver and Derrick Brew of Louisiana State University taking bronze in a race won by their white teammate Jeremy Wariner of Baylor University.

The gold medal by Wariner in the 400 meters, and his subsequent triumphs in other Olympic and world track and field competitions, generated enormous attention and revived age-old conversations about race and sport performance. As an outstanding white runner, the Baylor University star challenged the persistent stereotype of Black athletic determinism and the more recent speculation (and fear) about the supposed exit of white athletes from highly organized sport most famously outlined in the 1997 *Sports Illustrated* article, "Whatever Happened to the White Athlete?" Not unexpectedly, comments about Wariner varied widely. Some observers correctly noted that Wariner's success resulted from a combination of physical talent and hard work and determination, positive character traits possessed in abundance by Black Mercuries but downplayed historically by a sporting public imbued with the racist belief of African Americans as lazy and devoid of serious ambition. Other observers countered that Wariner had turned to performance-enhancing drugs in order to defeat naturally superior Black sprinters. Still others simply refused to accept that Wariner was white, contending that he must be of mixed blood that could not be detected from his unpigmented physical appearance. Wariner's own mother fed into this argument, proffering that she had "some Cherokee blood in her ancestry and believes that's where Jeremy got his speed."[1]

Discussions about mixed blood aside, Wariner followed his victory in the 400-meters by combining in the finals with Otis Harris, Derrick Brew, and his Baylor University teammate Darold Williamson to capture gold in the 4×400-meter relay in dominating fashion, beating the second-place team from Australia and third-place team from Nigeria by some five seconds. Dwight Phillips of Arizona State University defeated his U.S. teammate John Moffitt from Louisiana State University and third place finisher Joan Lino Martinez of Spain in the long jump with a leap of 28'2¼". Finally, Bryan Clay from Azusa Pacific College in California took the silver medal in the decathlon, scoring 8,820 points, which was 95 points more than bronze medalist Dmitriy Karpov of Kazakhstan and just 73 points fewer than the total amassed by gold medalist Roman Sebrle of the Czech Republic.

African American female athletes in track and field could not match the number of medals captured by their male counterparts in Athens. In fact, it was a mediocre Olympic year for African American women in the sprints and a dreadful one in the field events (no medals were won by U.S. women in the field events). Sheena Johnson-Tosta of UCLA finished a disappointing fourth in the 400-meter hurdles. Shelia Burrell of UCLA finished in the same position in the heptathlon, losing by just 128 points to bronze medalist Kelly Sotherton of Great Britain. Marion Jones, in events that certainly would have been included in the 2007 ban she incurred for performance-enhancing drugs, finished fifth in the long jump competition and was involved in an unsuccessful baton exchange with teammate Lauryn Williams from the University of Miami that resulted in the disqualification of the U.S. women in the 4×100-meter relay. Monique Hennagan of the University of North Carolina finished fourth, Dee Dee Trotter of the University of Tennessee finished fifth, and Sanya Richards-Ross finished sixth in the 400-meters. In spite of these disappointments, Hennagan, Trotter, Richards-Ross, and Monique Henderson of UCLA teamed up in the finals to capture the gold medal in the 4×400-meter relay. Joanna Hayes of UCLA won the gold medal in the 100-meter hurdles in a new Olympic record of 12.37 over silver medalist Olena Krasovska of Ukraine and her U.S. teammate Melissa Morrison-Howard of Appalachian State University. Lauryn Williams captured the silver medal in the 100-meters and Allyson

Felix of the University of Southern California garnered the silver medal in the 200-meters, the first of her Olympic record eleven medals during a remarkable career that has spanned some two decades.

DIFFERING LEVELS OF SUCCESS ON THE HARD COURT

The disappointment of African American women athletes in track and field in Athens could not have been any greater than that experienced by the 2004 U.S. men's basketball team. For the first time since 1992 when NBA players began participating in the Olympic Games, the U.S. men's team, consisting of an all-Black squad, did not come home with gold. Beginning Olympic competition with an embarrassing 73–92 loss to Puerto Rico, the U.S. men ended tournament play with a 5–3 record and took the bronze medal behind Argentina who captured gold and Italy who won the silver.

Much speculation took place following the games attempting to explain the poor performance of the U.S. men's basketball team in Athens. There is little question, though, that one of the reasons for the poor showing stemmed from the fact that the best NBA players simply chose not to participate in the games. Kobe Bryant was still embroiled in his trial on sexual assault charges. Some players, including both Jermaine O'Neal and Shaquille O'Neal, were exhausted from the NBA playoffs, and others were reluctant to travel to Athens because of projected safety issues and health concerns. The final roster was young and very inexperienced and never established any chemistry on or off the court. Co-captained by the Philadelphia 76ers' electric shooting guard Allen Iverson and San Antonio Spurs' center Tim Duncan, the team had six players who were under the age of twenty-four, including LeBron James of the Cleveland Cavaliers who was only nineteen and Carmelo Anthony of the Denver Nuggets who was just twenty. The team was coached by Larry Brown, the well-traveled sixty-three-year-old white coach of the Detroit Pistons who had a difficult time communicating with his players and convincing them to play his style of basketball. He was despised by some players, especially Stephon Marbury of the New York Knicks who noted that his time on the 2004 Olympic team was the "worst 38 days of my life."[2] The feeling was mutual. When Brown found out Marbury had complained about his coaching style to ESPN reporter Chris Sheridan, he told assistant coach Gregg Popovich he wanted "Stephon Marbury off the team. Now. Put him on a plane and send him back home."[3] Well known at the time, of course, was that the hard-nosed Brown would also have ongoing public spats with Iverson, the co-captain of the 2004 team and mercurial young talent who bucked authority at every turn. Ultimately, Brown's difficulties with Marbury in Athens, and with Iverson more generally, cannot be divorced from the deep cultural divide in the NBA at the time among players, fans, and coaches based on race and generational differences.

Ultimately, as bad as the experience was for the U.S. men's basketball team in Athens, something good came out of it. In 2005, veteran white NBA executive Jerry Colangelo was named director of USA Basketball, and he immediately began changing the culture of the organization and the process for how players were selected to the team. History has clearly shown that the hiring of Colangelo was a brilliant decision as the U.S. men have won four straight gold medals in Olympic basketball. Colangelo retired from his position as director of USA Basketball following the 2020 games in Tokyo and has since been replaced by Grant Hill, the great African American player from Duke, member of the 1996 USA basketball team, and son of former Yale and NFL star Calvin Hill.

The U.S. women's basketball team, by all accounts and certainly in comparison to the men's team, experienced great success in Athens. Coached by Van Chancellor of the Houston Comets and including such African American stars as Lisa Leslie of the Los Angeles Sparks, Dawn Staley of the Charlotte Sting, and Sheryl Swoopes of the Houston Comets, the U.S. women went 8–0 in Athens to capture their third straight gold medal in Olympic competition. They crushed many of their opponents, beating New Zealand in their opening contest 99–47, took out South Korea in their third game 80–57, and defeated Greece in the quarterfinals 102–72. In the gold medal game, the U.S. women outlasted Australia 74–63. Among the more notable aspects of the basketball tournament in 2004 was that it would be the last Olympic Games for both Staley and Swoopes, two players who had been mainstays and prominent contributors to the U.S. women's national team for many years. For Staley, it marked the end of a fifteen-year playing career for USA basketball and the ninth time she would be part of a gold medal–winning team in international competition. She is now the highly successful head coach of the women's basketball team at the University of South Carolina and recently guided the U.S. women to the gold medal in the 2020 games in Tokyo.

Lastly, Briana Scurry, along with two other outstanding African American players, Shannon Boxx of the University of Notre Dame and Angela Khalia Hucles of the University of Virginia, would contribute to the U.S. women's second gold medal in Olympic soccer competition. Frequently remembered as the last Olympic Games for legendary national team members Mia Hamm, Joy Fawcett, and Julie Foudy, the U.S. women marched through the tournament with great performances from a number of players and beat Brazil in the final game to capture the top spot. Boxx played in all six games, scoring one goal and assisting on another. Hucles appeared in two games during the tournament. Scurry, whose father passed away just two months prior to the games, had an outstanding tournament in what would be her last Olympic Games.

ONE WORLD, ONE DREAM, MORE THAN ONE SPORT

The official motto of the 2008 Olympic Games in Beijing, "One World, One Dream," reflected the hope of moving forward toward a unified world devoid of conflict and imbued with the Olympic spirit.[4] A noble and worthwhile dream to be sure, the motto was merely one aspect of the marketing of a very expensive Summer Olympic Games that cost by some accounts over $40 billion. The games themselves, which included participation of 10,942 athletes from 204 National Olympic Committees in 28 sports, was chock-full of great performances and the shattering of Olympic and world records. The United States won the most total medals (36 gold, 39 silver, 37 bronze) with 112, China followed with a total medal count of 100 (48 gold, 22 silver, 30 bronze), and Russia came in a distant third with 60 total medals (24 gold, 13 silver, 23 bronze). African American athletes made their presence known in Beijing with some outstanding performances. While Michael Phelps was shattering Olympic and world records in the pool and garnering international attention because of his exploits, Cullen Jones' membership on the U.S. gold medal–winning 4×100 meter relay team in Beijing was extraordinarily important symbolically with significant practical implications. An African American born in New York City who spent his formative years in Irvington, New Jersey, and competed at the intercollegiate level for North Carolina State University, Jones swam the third leg on perhaps the Olympic Games' most famous race that saw Jason Lezak chase down the talented Frenchman Alain Bernard in dramatic fashion on the final leg to capture gold in world record time in an event that the United States had not won in twelve years. It was not the first time an African American had captured gold in Olympic swimming. That distinction goes to Anthony Ervin who won gold in Sydney. However, Jones' involvement in such a highly publicized event in an overwhelmingly white sport that had always reflected the white fears about Black bodies and race mixing, not to mention the ludicrous myth of the inability of African Americans to float let alone move through the water, seemingly resonated far more deeply with people than Ervin's accomplishments, a fact also perhaps accounted for because Ervin could easily pass for white and the larger public identified him as Jewish.

The press portrayed Jones as a racial pioneer, and he seemed comfortable with the moniker, pleased to serve as a role model for other African American swimmers and committed to encouraging minority participation in the sport. Evidence of this has been his steady involvement with "Make a Splash," serving as an ambassador for an organization founded in 2007 to prevent drownings (Black children drown at a three-time higher rate than white children with some 70 percent of African Americans not knowing how to swim) and provide free swimming lessons to underprivileged children as well as his impact on the next generation of elite swimmers from minority populations. Simone Manuel, the outstanding Stanford University swimmer who would become the first African American woman to win an individual gold medal in the Olympic games by capturing the 100-meter freestyle in Rio de Janeiro, noted shortly after her historic victory that the two people who had inspired her most were Maritza Correia and Cullen Jones. Olympic swimming champion and NBC sports analyst Rowdy Gaines recently told Nick Zaccardi of NBC Sports that he had probably taken over fifty trips with Jones on "Make a Splash" trips. "I don't think there's any question, at least up to date now," noted Gaines, "that Cullen has certainly made the biggest impact on the African American community and the Black community in general in the sport of swimming. There are trailblazers, but nobody has made the overall impact of Cullen."[5]

While Cullen Jones was making history in the pool, other African American athletes, some little known and others household names, were contributing to the U.S. medal count in a limited range of sports. Shannon Boxx and Angela Khalia Hucles were once again members of the U.S. women's soccer team in Beijing. They both added a great deal, as did Asian Pacific and University of Hawaii star Natasha Kai, to the gold medal garnered by the U.S. women in the 2008 games, Boxx playing every minute of all five contests in Beijing, and Hucles scoring four goals in the tournament, two of them in the semi-final game against Japan. Hucles has been equally accomplished in her post-athletic career, serving, among other things, as President of the Women's Sports Foundation from 2015 to 2017 and continuing as a member of the Advisory Board for *You Can Play*, a campaign focused on overcoming homophobia in sports.

Natasha Watley and Tairia Flowers played once again on the U.S. women's softball team in Beijing. Although the women ended up losing the gold medal to Japan in the final game 1–3, Watley had another great tournament, hitting .321 and leading the team in at-bats and stolen bases. (Softball and baseball were eliminated as permanent Olympic offerings because of their supposed lack of global popularity and difficulty in attracting the sports' top players and would not be included again in the games until 2020 in Japan on a one-time only basis.) Outfielder Dexter Fowler helped the U.S. baseball team win a bronze medal in Beijing. The only African American on the team, Fowler only hit for a .250 batting average but had a slugging percentage of .429 and played flawlessly in centerfield. He has gone on to a successful Major League career with several different clubs. Venus and Serena Williams would capture their second of three Olympic doubles titles by defeating Anabel Medina Garrigues and Virginia Ruano Pascual of Spain in straight sets 6–2, 6–0.

Randi Miller shared the bronze medal in women's freestyle wrestling in the 137-pound class with Yelena Shalygina of Kazakstan. Fighting out of Granite City, Illinois, the 5-foot, 139-pound Miller would be named in 2008 the U.S.A. Female Wrestler of the Year and U.S. Olympic Committee Female Wrestler of the Year. She has since made a successful transition to mixed martial arts. Deontay Wilder, the outstanding fighter from Tuscaloosa, Alabama, known affectionately as "The Bronze Bomber" in obvious reference to the Joe Louis moniker "The Brown Bomber," shared the bronze medal in the men's heavyweight division with Osmay Acosta of Cuba. An extraordinarily powerful puncher, Wilder has enjoyed a very successful professional career, holding the World Boxing Council heavyweight title from 2015 to 2020. He has a record of 42 wins, 2 losses, and 1 tie in 45 fights with all but one of his victories coming by knockouts. The U.S. women would capture the silver medal in indoor volleyball, losing to the gold medalists from Cuba 0–3 and defeating the bronze medalists from China 3–2. Contributing to the success of the team were the five African Americans on the roster: Kimberly Marie Glass of the University of Arizona, Danielle Scott-Arruda of Long Beach State University, Ogonna Nnamani of Stanford University, Tayyiba Haneef-Park of Long Beach State University, and Kim Willoughby of the University of Hawaii. Of this group, perhaps the most impressive post-volleyball career is that of Nnamani. The oldest daughter of Nigerian immigrants who came to the United States for better educational opportunities, she took her doctorate in medicine from the University of California San Francisco School of Medicine and is now a resident in plastic and reconstructive surgery at Harvard Medical School.

In fencing, African American siblings Keeth Smart and Erinn Smart from Brooklyn, New York, made history in Beijing by capturing silver medals in

Keeth Smart and his younger
sister Erinn both captured
medals in fencing at the 2008
Olympic games in Beijing,
Keith a silver medal on the
sabre team and Erinn a silver
medal for the foil team. The
two siblings first learned the
sport at the Peter Westbrook
Foundation in New York City.
Courtesy of USA Fencing.

the traditionally white sport. Keeth took silver as part of the U.S. men's sabre team that lost out on the gold medal to the squad from France. Erinn captured silver as a member of the U.S. women's foil team that finished second to the gold medalists from Russia. Tellingly, both brother and sister were introduced to and trained in the sport at the Peter Westbrook Foundation that began in 1991. Started by its namesake Peter Westbrook who captured the bronze medal in the individual sabre event at the 1984 Olympic Games in Los Angeles, the foundation was established to teach the sport to inner-city youth as well as to coach life skills and foster both character development and academic expertise. It has proven to be enormously successful, developing world-class fencers from minority populations who have gone on to successful post-athletic careers. There are no better examples of this than Keeth and Erinn Smart. Keeth Smart took his MBA from Columbia University and at the time of this writing was working for Chelsea Piers Fitness, while his sister Erinn earned her MBA at the Wharton School of Business at the University of Pennsylvania and is currently the Director of Strategic Partnerships at the Meredith Corporation.

BATTLING THE JAMAICANS AND CONTINUED HOOP DOMINANCE

As always, many of the medals garnered by African American athletes in Beijing took place in track and field. Beginning in 2008 in Beijing and continuing through the 2020 games in Tokyo, however, they encountered in the highly prized sprint races the extraordinarily talented Jamaicans led by the magnificent Usain Bolt. The tall (6'5"), athletically gifted, and charismatic "Lightning Bolt" mesmerized the sporting world in Beijing by first capturing the gold medal in the 100-meters in the world record time of 9.69 in spite of slowing down toward the finish line after looking back and recognizing that he had overwhelmed his opponents. Four days later he won the gold medal in the 200-meters in another world record time of 19.30, thus becoming the first person to hold the world record in both the 100- and 200-meters at the same time. Remarkably, Bolt would follow up his great performance in Beijing by winning both the 100- and 200-meter races in London in 2012 and Rio de Janeiro in 2016, a feat never before accomplished and not likely to be duplicated any time soon. Bolt, whom historian David Goldblatt correctly notes garnered "admiration, riches, and love" through "his charming treatment of volunteers and helpers and his fabulously choreographed post-race celebrations, from the archer (poised to fire an arrow skywards from an imaginary bow) to the dance-hall moves he puts on with such aplomb," was joined in Beijing by a cadre of other great Jamaican sprinters and a seemingly endless number of others in subsequent Summer Olympic Games.[6]

Not unexpectedly, the dominance of the Jamaicans in the sprints caused much speculation as to the reasons for their success, reminiscent in many ways of the debate that began in earnest in the 1930s regarding the great performances on the track of Jesse Owens and other African American athletes. Some conjectured that the extraordinary success of the Jamaicans resulted from performance-enhancing drugs while others speculated it had to do with genes, the drive to escape poverty, and even the consumption of yams that supposedly have chemical properties identical to testosterone. Richard Moore, the individual who has delved most deeply into the phenomenon, argues in his *The Bolt Supremacy: Inside Jamaica's Sprint Factory* that the most compelling explanation for the success of Jamaican sprinters has to do with the country's extraordinary culture of athletics, specifically the highly competitive secondary-school sports programs culminating in the popular week-long inter-school contest known as the "Champs" and Kingston sports clubs filled with expert coaches and sponsorship opportunities.[7] Importantly, some of the Jamaican runners have been part of the wave of international student-athletes who have competed in college sport at major universities in the United States, only to represent their native countries in Olympic competition. They have all the opportunities of other college student-athletes with the notable exception of being able to take advantage of the NCAA's recent decision allowing college student-athletes to profit from the commercial use of their name, image, and likeness (NIL).

Ultimately, African American athletes withstood the "Jamaican sprint factory" and competitors from other countries reasonably well in Beijing, gathering several medals with some outstanding performances. In the 100-meters, Florida State University's Walter Dix had to face off against an extraordinarily strong field and performed admirably, taking third with a personal best of 9.91 behind silver medalist Richard Thompson, the talented Louisiana State University runner representing Trinidad and Tobago, who posted a personal best of 9.89 and Bolt in his world record time of 9.69. In the 200-meters, Shawn Crawford of Clemson University captured the silver medal and Dix the bronze medal behind Bolt, but only after the original second place finisher Churandy Martina of Netherlands Antilles and third place finisher Wallace Spearman of the United States had both been disqualified for running out of their lanes. In the 110-meter hurdles, David Payne of the University of Cincinnati won the silver medal, and David Oliver of Howard University garnered the bronze medal in an event captured by world record–holder Dayron Robles of Cuba. The United States swept the 400-meter hurdles with Georgia Tech's Angelo Taylor capturing gold, the University of Florida's Kerron Clement winning the silver, and Saint Augustine University's Bershawn Jackson taking the bronze. It was a comeback of sorts for Taylor who had finished fourth in the semifinals four years earlier in Athens after having captured gold in the event in Sydney in 2000. The United States also swept the 400-meters, with LaShawn Merritt of Old Dominion University capturing the gold medal with a personal best time of 43.75 and a record margin of victory of 0.99 over his white teammate Jeremy Wariner who came in second and David Neville of Indiana University who finished third. The victory had to be particularly satisfying for Merritt because of his intense rivalry with Wariner who had won all the major championships in the 400-meters since 2014. The triumph proved to be no fluke as Merritt followed it up with a victory over Wariner at the 2008 International Association of Athletes Federations final which gave him four wins over his arch rival that year. Unfortunately, as would befall many track athletes during the era, Merritt was suspended in 2010 for testing positive for performance-enhancing drugs, originally for two years but eventually lowered to twenty-one months and was out of the sport until mounting a comeback in 2011 and capturing a bronze medal in the 400 meters in the 2016 games in Rio de Janeiro. It was sweet redemption for Merritt who pulled up lame with a hamstring injury in a qualifying heat of the 400-meters four years earlier in the London Olympics.

Merritt collected another gold in Beijing as a member of the United States' victorious 4×400-meter relay team. Consisting in the finals of Merritt, Wariner, Georgia Tech's Angelo Taylor, and Indiana University's David Neville, the team beat the second-place finishers from the Bahamas and third place finishers from Great Britain in a new Olympic record of 2:55.39. Finally, Bryan Clay followed up his silver medal in the decathlon in Athens in 2004 with a gold medal in the event in Beijing. The son of an African American father and Japanese mother who was raised in Hawaii, Clay won by 240 points, which was the largest margin in the decathlon since 1972 when Mykola Avilov of the Soviet Union beat his teammate Leonid Lytvynenko by an astonishing 419 points. Clay accumulated 8,791 points, silver medalist Andrei Krauchanka of Belarus totaled 8,551 points, and bronze medalist Leonel Suarez came in at 8,527 points at the end of the grueling two-day and ten-event competition in Beijing to determine the "World's Greatest Athlete." For his accomplishments, Clay was featured, along with white gymnast Nastia Liukin, on a special Olympic Wheaties box and also given the USA Track and Field Jesse Owens Award and named *Track and Field News* US Athlete of the Year.

African American women athletes performed only slightly better in track and field in Beijing than they had in Athens in 2004. In Athens they garnered a total of five medals, four in individual events and one in team competition while in Beijing they captured a total of six medals, five in individual competitions and one in team competition. Like their male counterparts, they had to battle a very talented group of Jamaican runners who dominated the sprints. The Jamaican women swept the 100-meters, with Shelly-Ann Fraser and Sherone Simpson, both coached by the legendary Stephen Francis from the Kingston club called MVP, finishing one and two respectively and another silver medal going to Kerron Stewart, coached by Glen Mills of the Racers, the other prominent club in Kingston. In the 200-meters, Stewart captured the bronze, her Jamaican teammate Veronica Campbell-Brown the gold for the second consecutive Olympics, and Allyson Felix of the University of Southern California capturing silver.

The one African American woman who captured an individual gold medal in track and field in Beijing was UCLA's Dawn Harper who defeated runner-up Sally McLellan of Australia and bronze medalist Priscilla Lopes-Schliep of Canada in the 100-meter hurdles in a personal best time of 12.54. The favorite to win the race was LoLo Jones who was leading all the runners until hitting the ninth hurdle and finishing in seventh place. Jones, who competed for Louisiana State University and has described her heritage as a mixture of French, African American, and Norwegian, had one of the more publicized athletic careers punctuated by many successes and an equal number of disappointments and heartaches. Much of the attention she received, perpetuated by various cultural forces, resulted from her multi-racial beauty, an American obsession that has always revealed a bias against those who look less stereotypically Black. The media, in much the same way they were preoccupied with the mixed-race background of President Barack Obama, seemingly focused as much on her physical appearance as they did on her athletic abilities, which were formidable. As a college athlete, Jones won multiple NCAA indoor and outdoor championships, was a six-time Southeastern Conference champion, and an eleven-time All-American. She also took gold medals in the 60-meter hurdles at both the 2008 and 2010 World Indoor Championships as well as gold medals in the 100-meter hurdles at the 2008 and 2010 International Association of Athletics Federations World Championships and 2015 Championships sponsored by the North American, Central American, and

Caribbean Athletic Association (NACAC). Unfortunately, in spite of her outstanding athletic abilities and many championships, Jones, the woman of mixed French, African American, and Norwegian heritage embraced by so many, was chided for her inability to capture the prestigious title of Olympic champion. In addition to her terribly disappointing performance in Beijing, Jones had failed to qualify for the 2004 games in Athens in the 100-meter hurdles and fell out of medal contention with a very disheartening fourth place finish in the finals of the 100-meter hurdles in the 2012 London games.

Besides Dawn Harper's (now Dawn Harper-Nelson) victory in the 100-meter hurdles, another rare highlight for African American women in track and field in Beijing took place in the 4×400 meter relay. Consisting in the finals of holdovers from the 2004 squad, Monique Henderson and Sanya Richards-Ross and newcomers Allyson Felix and Mary Wineberg from the University of Cincinnati, the team was victorious over the second-place team from Russia and third-place team from Great Britain. The medal order changed in 2016, however, when Russia was disqualified after it was determined that one of its team members, Tatyana Firova, had tested positive for performance-enhancing drugs. This meant that the original fourth place team from Jamaica was catapulted into the silver medal position. In addition to the gold in the 4×400-meter relay, Sheena Tosta of UCLA took the silver medal in the 400 meter hurdles, losing to gold medalist Melaine Walker of Jamaica who won the race in the Olympic record time of 52.64 and ahead of the Great Britain's Tasha Danvers who took the bronze medal. In an event fraught with drug issues, Hyleas Fountain of the University of Georgia originally placed third in the heptathlon but was eventually awarded the silver medal since the initial second place finisher Lyudmyla Blonska of Ukraine was disqualified after testing positive for performance-enhancing drugs (she was given a lifetime ban since it was her second offense). The original fourth-place finisher Tatyana Chernova was moved to the third-place spot when Blonska was disqualified, but in 2017, ironically enough, she was stripped of her medal after it was determined she had tested positive for drug use. Chernova's bronze medal for finishing third in the race was then awarded to Kelly Sotherton, which was significant since it gave the outstanding athlete from Great Britain her second consecutive bronze medal in Olympic competition. The gold medalist in the heptathlon in Beijing was Blonska's teammate Nataliya Dobrynska who won with a personal best of 6,733 points. The final individual medal garnered by an African American woman in the track and field competition in Beijing was by Richards-Ross. She captured the bronze medal in the 400-meters, losing to Shericka Williams of Jamaica who won the silver medal and Christine Ohuruogu of Great Britain who took home the gold medal in the time of 49.62.

Unlike the 2004 games in Athens, both the U.S. men and women basketball teams came home with gold medals from Beijing. The men's squad, an all-Black contingent sometimes referred to as the "redeem team" so as to rectify its poor Olympic performance four years earlier and coached by the legendary Mike Krzyzewski of Duke University, sailed through the tournament in Beijing with a record of 8–0 and very large margins of victory in most of those contests.[8] The U.S. women's basketball team was tasked with continuing their winning ways in Beijing rather than redemption. They completed the task with a dominating performance, winning eight contests by an average margin of victory of 37.6 points a game. The team, coached by Anne Donovan who had been a member of four previous Olympic squads as both a player and an assistant coach, included three white and nine African American players with much experience at the collegiate and professional levels of competition. Included on the team was the very talented and highly decorated Lisa Leslie, along with such other veterans as the Detroit Shock's Katie Smith, Indiana Fever's Tamika Catchings, Houston Comets' Tina Thompson, Seattle Storm's Sue Bird, and Phoenix Mercury's Diana Taurasi. Although having little time to train together, the U.S. women sailed through the tournament, beating the Czech Republic in their first game 97–57, closing out the preliminary round with a dominating victory over New Zealand 96–60, and overwhelming Australia 92–65 for the third straight time in the Olympic gold medal game. Tellingly, the games in Beijing would be the final Olympics for both Leslie and Smith, two prominent and long-time members on the U.S. women's team. Leslie captured four gold medals during her Olympic career, and Smith three during her extended tenure on the team.

AFRICAN AMERICANS IN THE RING
AND ON THE MAT IN LONDON

The city of London, hoping to "inspire a generation" of younger people to engage in sport, outbid Moscow, Madrid, Paris, and New York City to host the games in 2012.[9] The initial frontrunner was Paris, but London would eventually be awarded the games, partly through the efforts and influence of two-time Olympic gold medalist Sebastian Coe who was chairman of the London Organizing Committee of the Olympic and Paralympic Games (LOCOG). The games, while marred like many of the previous Olympics with disqualifications for drug use both before competitions and retroactively, were characterized by many great athletic performances in a variety of sports. Included among those standout performances were those completed by such outstanding African American athletes as pugilist Claressa Shields who captured a gold medal in the middleweight division in the boxing tournament. Competing in a sport that officially became part of the Olympic program in London (women's boxing had previously appeared as an exhibition sport in the 1904 Olympics in London), Shields' story is an inspirational one, a classic tale of someone raised in impoverished circumstances who through hard work and perseverance rises to the top of her profession. Born in Flint, Michigan, in 1995, Shields came from a broken home, her father spending several years in prison and her mother plagued by years of addiction problems. Fortunately, she would be taken in by Jason Crutchfield, a local resident and boxing expert who would become her coach and trainer and guide her through the first seven years of her career. In 2011 Shields captured the middleweight title in the National Police Athletic League Championships, her first victory in an open-division tournament. Buoyed by this early victory and others, Shields, at only seventeen years of age, earned a spot on the U.S. Olympic team the following year and scratched her way to the gold medal by first defeating Anna Laurell of Sweden in the quarterfinals 18–14, demolishing Marina Volnova of Kazakhstan in the semifinals 29–15, and overcoming thirty-four-year-old Nadezda Torlopova of Russia in the finals 19–12. She repeated as the Olympic gold medalist in the middleweight division four years later in Rio de Janeiro and then embarked on a highly successful professional boxing career. Importantly, Shields, who has waged publicized battles against gender inequality in boxing, and sports more generally, is expected to have her life story told in a forthcoming sports biopic directed by Rachael Morrison titled *Flint Strong*. Based on the PBS documentary of her life that premiered on August 2, 2016, titled *T-Rex: Her Fight for Gold*, Shields will be played by actress and singer/songwriter Ryan Destiny with Jason Crutchfield being played by rapper and actor Ice Cube.

Also enjoying a very successful 2012 Olympic games, but like Shields, not receiving the adulation he deserved, was African American wrestler Jordan Burroughs who captured the gold medal in the 163-pound weight division in London. Born in Camden, New Jersey, Burroughs participated in football, track and field, and wrestling as a student at Winslow Township High School, but ultimately concentrated on wrestling largely because of his relatively small size. He was twice New Jersey state champion as well as regional champion and in his senior year (2006) was the National High School Coaches Association National champion. He continued his wrestling career at the University of Nebraska where he was Big 12 Champion in 2008 (149 pounds), 2009 (157 pounds), and 2011 (165 pounds), and NCAA champion in 2009 (157 pounds) and 2011 (165 pounds). In the games in London, Burroughs won his opening match against Francisco Soler of Puerto Rico and then followed with a victory over Matt Gentry of Canada. In the semifinals, he defeated two-time world champion Denis Tsargush of Russia and in the finals eked out a 1–0 victory over the highly regarded Sadegh Goudarzi of Iran for the gold medal.

THE "LIGHTNING BOLT" COULD NOT OBSCURE FELIX'S GREATNESS

Not unexpectedly and just as in Beijing, Usain Bolt and the other talented sprinters from Jamaica dominated the 100- and 200-meter sprints in the track and field competitions in London. In the 100 meters, Bolt bested his teammate Yohan Blake, who finished second, and the United States' Justin Gatlin, who took third. Bolt led a Jamaican sweep of the 200-meters, taking gold in the event with his teammates Blake and Warren Weir finishing second and third respectively. Although the "Jamaican sprint factory" garnered a voluminous amount of publicity, perhaps nothing mesmerized and made the hometown crowd prouder than the gold medals captured by Mo Farah in both the 5,000- and 10,000-meter runs. The Somalia-born refugee, who fled to Great Britain at the age of eight to escape his country's ruthless civil war, brought spectators to their feet in the Olympic stadium for his triumphs in the two races and much praise from notable citizens around the world. The British took special delight in Farah's victories because they served to convince themselves of the specialness and progressive nature of their culture. The triumphs of the practicing Muslim from Somalia in the most important mega-sporting event in the world was extraordinarily significant representationally to the host country as noted by British historian and commentator Dominic Sandbrook shortly after Farah's victories: "What better symbol could there be of a united, inclusive country in the post-imperial age? What better advert for British identity: confident and colour-blind?"[10]

The triumphs of Farah and the Jamaican sprinters did not obscure the memorable performances of African American track athletes in both the running and field events in London. The University of Tennessee's Aries Merritt captured the gold medal in the 110-meter hurdles over second place finisher Jason Richardson of the University of South Carolina and third place finisher Hansle Parchment of Jamaica, who would win the same event eight years later in the 2020 Tokyo Olympic Games. Christian Taylor of the University of Florida garnered the gold medal in the triple jump over his college teammate Will Claye, who took the silver, and Fabrizio Donato of Italy, who captured the bronze medal. The final gold medal won by an African American man in track and field went to Ashton Eaton, the outstanding University of Oregon athlete who took the gold medal in the decathlon over white teammate Trey Hardee of the University of Texas, who took the silver medal, and Leonel Suarez of Cuba, who garnered his second consecutive Olympic bronze medal in the event. Other outstanding medal-winning performances in London were Kansas State University's Erik Kynard's silver medal in the high jump; Will Claye's bronze medal in the long jump; Jackson State University's Michael Tinsley's silver medal in the 400-meter hurdles; and the silver medal by the 4×400-meter relay team that included as members the University of Southern California's Bryshon Nellum, Florida State University's Joshua Mance, University of Florida's Tony McQuay, and Georgia Tech University's Angelo Taylor. In an unfortunate turn of events, the U.S. 4×100-meter relay team, which originally took silver in the event, was forced to give up its medal in 2015 because of the suspension of Tyson Gay for testing positive for performance-enhancing drugs.

The performances of African American women in track and field were far better than four years earlier in Beijing. Leading the way was the University of Southern California's Allyson Felix who captured gold in the 200-meters, 4×100-meter relay, and 4×400-meter relay. Her victory in the 200-meters was over second-place finisher Shelly-Ann Fraser-Pryce of Jamaica and her U.S. teammate Carmelita Jeter from California State University, Dominguez Hills who came in third to win the bronze medal. Felix's gold medal in the 4×100-meter relay final, which was won in the world record time of 40.82 over the silver medalists from Jamaica and bronze medalists from Ukraine, was completed with teammates Jeter, Tianna Madison of the University of Tennessee, and Bianca Knight of the University of Texas. Felix's gold medal in the 4×400-meter relay final was captured along with teammates DeeDee Trotter of the University of Tennessee, Francena McCorory of Hampton University, and the University of Texas' Sanya Richards-Ross who easily beat the silver medalists from Jamaica and bronze medalists from Ukraine. Richards-Ross, in addition to her gold medal as part of the 4×400-meter relay team, captured a second gold in the 400-meters, defeating Christine Ohuruogu of Great Britain who won the silver medal and her relay teammate Trotter who garnered the bronze medal. (Ross is now, among other things, a track and field analyst for NBC and worked in that capacity for both the 2016 and 2020 Olympic Games.) Dawn Harper of UCLA, the lone African American woman to win an individual gold medal in Beijing, captured the silver medal in the 100-meter hurdles, beaten out for the gold medal by Sally Pearson of Australia who won the event in a new Olympic record of 12.35 and ahead of her Black teammate Kellie Wells of Hampton University who finished third.

Jeter won her third medal in the games by placing second in the 100-meters, finishing behind Fraser-Pryce who captured her second consecutive Olympic gold medal in the event and ahead of Fraser-Pryce's Jamaican teammate Veronica Campbell-Brown. Lashinda Demus of the University of South Carolina garnered a silver medal in the 400-meter hurdles, losing to first place finisher Natalya Antyukh of Russia and beating out Zuzana Hejnova of the Czech Republic who won the bronze medal. Unlike the Beijing Games four years earlier, African American women also made their presence felt in the field events with Brigetta Barrett of the University of Arizona capturing a silver medal in the high jump behind gold medalist Anna Chicherova of Russia and ahead of third place finisher Ruth Beitia of Spain, and Brittany Reese of the University of Mississippi winning the gold medal in the long jump over silver medalist Yelena Sokolova of Russia and bronze medalist Janay DeLoach of Colorado State University.

CULLEN CONTINUES HIS WINNING WAYS, GABBY DESERVED MORE

In addition to track and field, there were outstanding performances by a select number of African Americans in London in soccer, swimming, gymnastics, and fencing. Soccer's Shannon Boxx represented the United States in Olympic competition for the last time and was joined by another African American on the team, Sydney Rae Leroux, an exceptional athlete who played collegiately at UCLA. Boxx announced prior to the games in London that she had lupus and then just seventeen minutes into the opening game against France suffered a hamstring injury that would sideline her for most of the tournament. After extensive rehabilitation, Boxx recovered in time to play all ninety minutes in the final game against Japan in which Carli Lloyd scored two goals to clinch the gold for the U.S. women. One observer claimed that Boxx's gutty performance in London made her "a global symbol of toughness."[11] LeRoux, born to a white Canadian mother and African American father, was the youngest player and most prominent reserve on the U.S. women's soccer team who won the gold medal in London. She has gone on to a successful professional career, currently playing for the Orlando Pride in the National Women's Soccer League (NWSL). She parlayed her success on the soccer field into several endorsement deals and commercial ventures. In 2013, for instance, Leroux and teammate Alex Morgan were featured in a Nike commercial with several other prominent athletes. The following year, she became the first female endorser for the sports drink company BODYARMOR.

As it turned out, Cullen Jones' performance in swimming in Beijing in 2008 was merely a preview of what he would accomplish in the pool in London. Armed with much confidence and part of a U.S. team stacked with great talent (United States captured thirty-one medals to runner-up China's ten and third place finisher France who had seven), Jones would take the silver medal in the 50-meter freestyle, silver in the 4×100 freestyle relay, and gold in the 4×100 medley relay. In the 50-meter freestyle, Jones came in second to Florent Manaudou of France and just ahead of Cesar Ciele of Brazil to win the silver medal. In the 4×100 medley relay, Jones captured gold as an alternate on the team and combined with Michael Phelps, Nathan Adrian, and Ryan Lochte to take the silver medal in the 4×100 freestyle relay. The U.S. team was denied its second consecutive Olympic gold in the latter event by France which got a tremendous anchor leg from Yannick Agnel. Jones' third medal in London was gold, swimming the preliminary heat in the 4×100 medley relay won by the United States over the second-place finishers from Japan and third-place finishers from Australia.

Tellingly, Jones was joined on the U.S. swim team in London by two other African American swimmers, the previously mentioned Anthony Ervin and Lea Neal, a seventeen-year-old from Brooklyn, New York. Ervin, who as a nineteen-year-old had captured gold in the 50-meter freestyle and silver in the 4×100 freestyle relay in the 2000 Sydney Games, had mounted a comeback and qualified for the finals in the 50-meter freestyle in London. Unfortunately, although performing well in London, he finished a disappointing fifth in the race won by Jones. Neal captured bronze as part of the women's 4×100 relay team. Competing alongside Missy Franklin, Jessica Hardy, and Allison Schmitt, the U.S. women lost to Australia who captured gold and the Netherlands who garnered the silver. Following the games in London, Neal competed for the powerful Stanford University swim team for four years, capturing eight NCAA championships. She would capture a silver medal in the 4×100 relay in the 2016 games in Rio de Janeiro.

African American women would also find success in gymnastics in London. Kyla Ross, born in Honolulu to a mother of Filipino and Puerto Rican descent and father who was part African American and part Japanese, was a member of the U.S. women's gymnastics team as was Gabby Douglas, the outstanding African American athlete from Virginia Beach, Virginia. Ross and Douglas, along with McKayla Maroney, Aly Raisman, and Jordyn Wieber, made up the squad affectionately referred to as the "fierce five" for their resiliency and recognition of the gold medal they captured in the team all-around competition.[12]

Without question, the most famous of the "fierce five" was Douglas. Her great performances in London and appeal as a Black person in a traditionally white sport garnered Douglas much attention and media coverage. As the only member of the team to participate in all four events of the all-around competition, Douglas contributed mightily to the victory of the "fierce five" over the runner-up team from Russia and bronze medalists from Romania. Douglas followed up her stellar performance in the team all-around competition by capturing the gold medal in the individual all-around over silver medalist Viktoria Komova and her Russian teammate Aliya Mustafina who won the bronze medal, in order to become the first African American to ever win the event. She earned many honors for her accomplishments in London and took advantage of her sudden fame by giving countless interviews, making television appearances, and engaging in numerous other projects seemingly nonstop until being overshadowed four years later by another Black phenomenon—Simone Biles. For instance, the Associated Press named Douglas the 2012 Female Athlete of the Year, she was featured alongside her teammates on the *Sports Illustrated* Olympic Preview issue, a picture of her standing on the Olympic podium with her gold medal appeared on special boxes of corn flakes, she released her autobiography *Grace, Gold, and Glory: My Leap of Faith* (2012), and Lifetime aired *The Gabby Douglas Story* (2014).

Unfortunately, Douglas, in spite of her sterling performance in London, could never escape the complicated nature of racialist thinking and deep-seated stereotypical notions of Black femininity experienced by African American women over the years. In spite of her great Olympic achievements and accompanying honors that followed, it was obvious the world was not prepared to anoint her "America's Sweetheart" as was the case for the white Mary Lou Retton, who captured the women's all-around gymnastics title at the Los Angeles Games in 1984. One example of this was Douglas's inability to secure endorsement deals comparable to her white teammate Aly Raisman, whom she had defeated for the all-around title.

Douglas also came under intense fire via the internet for an assortment of perceived offenses, including failing to smile enough, failing to show adequate support for her teammates, failing to place her hand over her heart during the playing of the national anthem, and failing to style her hair "appropriately." The latter criticism, which was particularly vicious and hurtful, came largely from members of the African American community who were "publicly disciplining" Douglas for neglecting to conceal the natural texture of her hair.[13] Black writer Renee Martin cogently points out that Douglas, like other well-known African Americans such as Viola Davis, Rihanna, and Zahara Jolie-Pitt, was shamed and pilloried for her "refusal to conform to the socially-imposed behavior and appearance standards for Black women." What is especially painful about the criticism of Douglas, explains Martin, is that it calls to mind an earlier time when Blacks were encouraged to champion their identities as a way to counter white racism. In this instance, writes Martin, "pride is being employed not to encourage self-love, but rather to suggest a lack of personal dignity and accountability. Where Afros once represented a rejection of white supremacy, today, Gabby's nappy edges and kinky kitchen mean a failure to perform Blackness in a way which uplifts the race."[14]

MAYA, VENUS, AND THE STRONG CONTINGENT OF BLACK WOMEN OLYMPIANS

Fencer Maya Lawrence of Teaneck, New Jersey, whose mask perhaps shielded her from the abuse experienced by Douglas as well as harmful blows to her face and head, followed the outstanding performances of fellow African Americans Keeth Smart and Erinn Smart in Beijing with her own outstanding performance in London. Introduced to fencing at Teaneck High School and ultimately coached there by her mother Pamela, Lawrence enjoyed a distinguished academic and athletic career at Princeton University after matriculating to the famous Ivy League institution following graduation from Teaneck High School. She earned All-American honors and was named All-Ivy in fencing during her four years at Princeton while at once being an honors student with a dual major in political science and African American studies. She followed up her undergraduate student days at Princeton by taking a master's degree in English as a second language at Teachers College, Columbia University in 2007 and continuing to train in fencing, first under her college coach Michel Sebastiani while teaching at the Princeton Day School and also in New York City before deciding to hone her talents in the sport under coaches in Paris. In London, Lawrence along with U.S. teammates Courtney Hurley and Kelley Hurley, sisters from the University of Notre Dame, and another Princeton University graduate, Susie Scanlon, captured a bronze medal in team epee, losing out to the gold medalists from China and silver medalists from South Korea. After the games, Lawrence returned to Paris where she currently works as a marketing specialist.

The performance of Maya Lawrence was complemented by other great athletic achievements by African American women in tennis, volleyball, and basketball, three sports that did not have to wait every four years to be recognized by the sporting public. In tennis, Serena Williams, who less than three weeks earlier had won her fifth Wimbledon championship, overwhelmed Maria Sharapova of Russia to capture the gold medal. Held at the famed All-England Club in Wimbledon, the site of all the tennis matches for the 2012 games, Williams dispensed of Sharapova while only losing one game in the process. Williams then joined her sister Venus to win the doubles in straight sets over Andrea Hlavackova and Lucie Hradecka of the Czech Republic. Tellingly, similar to the story of Gabby Douglas, Williams' victory over Sharapova in London and in most of their other head-to-head matches did not correspond to more endorsement deals for Williams like her athletically inferior and less accomplished white Russian rival. In fact, for eleven straight years, Williams earned far less in endorsements than Sharapova, largely a result of Williams' inability to meet white standards of beauty. It's only in the last several years, argues sociologist and sport studies scholar Scott N. Brooks, that Williams' endorsements have kept pace with her accomplishments on the court as she has moved "beyond the gendered tag of female athlete," has "benefited from the myth of natural black athleticism," and is now appreciated for "her physical strength and abilities and her black femininity."[15]

In addition to their contributions in tennis, Black women made major contributions to the U.S. silver medal–winning indoor volleyball team in London. Although losing out on the gold medal to Brazil, the U.S. women's volleyball team in London was remarkable in a number of ways, including the diverse backgrounds of its players. Among the members of the team, for instance, were Danielle Scott-Arruda, a Black American-Brazilian player born in Baton Rouge who played on five U.S. Olympic teams; African American Destinee Hooker from the University of Texas; Tayyiba Haneef-Park, born to a Muslim father who was a great star at Long Beach State, and also a member of the U.S. women's team in Beijing; Logan Tom, the Stanford University star of Chinese-Hawaiian descent; Megan Hodge who was born in the Virgin Islands and played at Penn State; Hawaiian-born Tamari Miyashiro who competed for the University of Washington; and Foluke Atinuke Akinradewo, the outstanding player who had the distinction of competing on the U.S. women's silver medal–winning team in London, the bronze medal–winning team in Rio de Janiero in 2016, and the gold medal–winning team in Tokyo in 2020 as well as holding citizenship in the United States, Nigeria, and Canada. These women, along with their equally talented teammates, went 5–0 in pool play, beating in order South Korea, Brazil, China, Serbia, and Turkey. In the quarterfinals they defeated the Dominican Republic and in the semifinals beat South Korea. Unfortunately, Brazil atoned for their loss to the United States in pool play by beating them in the finals.

The U.S. women's basketball team, while not as diverse as the volleyball squad, included nine African American players on its twelve-person roster. This included Seimone Augustus of the Minnesota Lynx, Swin Cash of the Chicago Sky, Tamika Catchings of the Indiana Fever, Tina Charles of the Connecticut Sun, Sylvia Fowles of the Chicago Sky, Asjha Jones of the Connecticut Sun, Maya Moore of the Minnesota Lynx, Angel McCoughtry of the Atlanta Dream, and Candace Parker of the Los Angeles Sparks. They were joined by Olympic mainstays Sue Bird of the Seattle Storm and Diana Taurasi of the Phoenix Mercury as well as Lindsay Whalen of the Minnesota Lynx. Not unexpectedly, deep in talent, experienced, and coached by the legendary Geno Auriemma of the University of Connecticut, the U.S. women dominated their opponents and captured their fifth consecutive Olympic gold medal.

While the U.S. women's basketball team captured their fifth consecutive Olympic gold medal in London, the U.S. men captured their second consecutive title. Coached by Duke University's Mike Krzyzewski, the team was once again loaded with great NBA players. With the exception of Kevin Love of the Minnesota Timberwolves, the team was made up entirely of African American players, including Tyson Chandler of the New York Knicks, Kevin Durant of the Oklahoma City Thunder, LeBron James of the Miami Heat, Russell Westbrook of the Oklahoma Thunder, Devon Williams of the Brooklyn Nets, Andre Iguodala of the Philadelphia 76ers, Kobe Bryant of the Los Angeles Lakers, James Harden of the Oklahoma City Thunder, Chris Paul of the Los Angeles Clippers, and Anthony Davis of the New Orleans Hornets. The U.S. men plowed through their opponents, averaging 116 points per game and won by an average margin of 32.1 points per game.

Like the games in Athens in 2004 and Beijing in 2008, African American men and women made major contributions to the success of the U.S. Olympic team in 2012 in London. As was the case of the two previous games and the upcoming ones in 2016 in Rio de Janeiro and Tokyo Games in 2020, African American athletes excelled in those sports in which they had always been most dominant (i.e., basketball and track and field) and found some success, extraordinarily so in selected cases, in those sports traditionally considered the prerogative of whites. Perhaps most significantly, the Olympic Games would continue to provide an especially important venue for African American women athletes, and women athletes more generally for that matter, to showcase their skills to a worldwide audience. The globalization of the games and enormous media coverage afforded them provided a singular opportunity to witness the athletic exploits of African American women in sports of a more aesthetic nature such as gymnastics, those associated with country clubs such as tennis and swimming, and those most often associated with men such as boxing and wrestling. It was, for example, in 2012 that the world was first introduced to gymnastics' Gabby Douglas and boxing's Claressa Shields, 2016 that the world was first introduced to swimming's Simone Manuel, water polo's Ashleigh Johnson, and gymnastics' Simone Biles, and 2020 that the world was first introduced to soccer's Crystal Dunn and wrestling's Tamyra Mensah-Stock. Much more needs to be done, of course, to see that African American women find their way into more sports in greater numbers and to increase the likelihood they can be respected for their athletic achievements rather than being disparaged for their physical appearance.

9

BLACK MERCURIES SHINE IN RIO AND TOKYO

Black Mercuries were similar to many others in questioning whether the games in Rio de Janeiro and Tokyo could be pulled off successfully and without serious incidents. Serious questions abounded about Rio de Janeiro's ability to stage the world's most important mega-sporting event because of the fear that athletes, officials, and others attending the games would be negatively impacted by the recent outbreak of the Zika virus in Brazil, the heavily polluted waters of Guanabara Bay, and the high crime rate in the city. Compounding these issues was the volatile political environment in Brazil resulting from the alleged corruption committed by the government of President Dilma Rousseff and by the fact the country was facing a debilitating economic recession. Questions as to whether Tokyo could successfully pull off the Olympics in 2020 had to do with how athletes, officials, and others attending the games would be kept safe during the worldwide COVID-19 pandemic. Many observers, including most notably health experts, were so alarmed by the continuing spread of the disease that they were calling for the cancellation of the games in Tokyo. Fortunately, with some careful planning, ingenuity, and adjustments made to infrastructure and scheduling of events, the games in Rio de Janeiro and Tokyo went off remarkably well, without any major controversies.

Importantly, the games in Rio de Janeiro and Tokyo took place amid a horrendous refugee crisis, a growing activism among African American athletes and their white allies in the United States, and a global right-wing counter-attack to social justice initiatives. In the years spanning the games, African American athletes, from a variety of sports at different levels of competition, exhibited a renewed racial consciousness propelled by, among other things, the death of innocent Black men at the hands of police and the subsequent Black Lives Matter movement. A watershed event indicating a renewed racial awareness took place in 2016 when Black San Francisco 49ers' quarterback Colin Kaepernick began taking a knee rather than standing for the national anthem in protest of police brutality. He was brutally criticized for his "silent gesture" and battered with a shower of negative press and vitriol from seemingly all segments of society.

Kaepernick's protests, which resulted in him being blackballed by the National Football League and suffering the loss of his football career, contributed to a national dialogue on race as evident in the replication of his national anthem protests as well as an assortment of personal statements by Black and white athletes, collective action by teams and organizations, town hall meetings, and pointed conversations and debates with government leaders about racial inequality and police brutality. His protests also served to inspire other athletes, many of them Olympians, to speak out about racial inequality and issues ranging from unequal pay, transgender rights, and concern for mental health issues. These protests, in turn, resulted in heightened and feverish criticism from conservatives on the right who saw them as "a manifestation of the ascendancy of liberal cultural values in public life."[1] This sense of alienation on the part of the American right became particularly acute leading up to and during the Tokyo Games, with conservative commentators taking verbal shots at Olympians for their stands on social issues rather than applauding them as representatives of the United States. In *VOX*, Zack Beauchamp cogently wrote that "when conservatives see American athletes representing values at odds with their vision for the country, they don't back Team USA in the name of patriotism—they turn on the icons of the nation itself."[2] One can only speculate on the number of protests and level of rancor that would have been directed at socially conscious Olympic athletes if the Tokyo Games had been held as originally scheduled in the summer of 2020 when Donald Trump was still president.

A BRILLIANT BLACK GYMNAST IN "A NEW WORLD"

The games in Rio de Janeiro featured more than 11,000 athletes from 207 nations competing in 28 different sports. Particularly notable among this group were ten athletes commonly known as the Refugee Olympic Team (ROT). In the years immediately prior to the games in Rio de Janeiro, a highly publicized and disastrous refugee crisis saw thousands of refugees and immigrants cross the Aegean Sea in dinghies in an effort to get to Europe and realize a better life. In 2015, the worst year of the refugee crisis, more than 8,000 people, including hundreds of children, perished in capsized boats and shipwrecks. Not unexpectedly, this calamitous situation generated much alarm and brought forth a plethora of individuals and groups who offered ways to assuage it, including the IOC who announced in March of 2016 that it was going to select five to ten refugee athletes to participate in the games in Rio de Janeiro who "will act as a symbol of hope for refugees worldwide and bring global attention to the magnitude of the refugee crisis."[3] Originally identifying forty-three potential candidates to be members of the ROT, the IOC ultimately selected ten athletes representing three sports (track and field, swimming, and judo) with each of the athletes being hosted by a particular National Olympic Committee. The ROT was treated like the other Olympic athletes in Rio de Janeiro, staying in the Olympic Village, walking in the opening and closing ceremonies, and provided with coaches and other technical needs. Not unexpectedly, while generally enjoying a great experience in Rio de Janeiro, no one from the ROT medaled in the games.

Olympic observers anticipated that the United States, China, and Great Britain would bring home the majority of medals in Rio de Janeiro, which would prove to be the case. At the team level, the United States enjoyed a very successful Olympics, with African American men and especially African American women having many highly publicized breakout performances. If there is one individual performance that stands out among all the rest, it is that of gymnast Simone Biles. A classic and poignant success story, Biles was one of four siblings born in Columbus, Ohio, to a single mother who was unable to take care of the children. After spending some three years in and out of foster care, Biles and the other three children were taken in by their maternal grandfather and his second wife in the Houston suburb of Spring, Texas. In 2003 the couple officially adopted Biles and her younger sister, offering the two children a stable home life that would allow them to flourish. A turning point in Biles' life took place in 2005 at the age of eight when she began formal training in gymnastics at Bannon's Gymnastics in Houston under Aimee Boorman. Recognizing her prodigious talent and enthusiasm for the sport, Boorman worked tirelessly in honing Biles' gymnastics skills and in 2011 entered her in the American Classic in Houston where she placed first on vault and balance beam, third all-around, fourth on floor exercise, and eighth on uneven bars. This initial success would be duplicated many times over during the next five years. In 2012 Biles competed in the US National Championships where she placed first on vault, third all-around, and sixth on floor exercise, balance beam, and uneven bars. Her performance garnered her a place on the US Junior National team selected by the legendary coach and administrator Marta Karolyi. In 2013, 2014, and 2015 Biles captured the all-around titles and multiple medals in individual events at the US National Championships, and captured silver medals in all four individual events.

   In 2016, Biles, only four feet eight inches in height, cemented her place as the greatest gymnast in the world. She started the year by capturing the all-around title at the Pacific Rim Championships, followed it up with yet another all-around title at the US National Championships, and then closed out the season with an epic performance in the Olympic Games in Rio de Janeiro. Joined on the USA National team by Gabby Douglas, Madison Kocian, Laurie Hernandez, and Aly Raisman, all of whom had signature moments in the games, Biles captured gold medals in the team competition, individual all-around, vault, and floor exercise, and bronze medals in the balance beam. Team USA, coached by Aimee Boorman who had been with Biles from the very beginning of her career, captured the gold medal in the team competition over second-place finisher Russia and third-place finisher China, with Biles contributing an all-around score of 61.833 on all four events. Biles took her second gold medal in the individual all-around event over her teammate Raisman, who captured the silver medal, and Aliya Mustafina of Russia who won the bronze medal. She captured her third gold medal in the vault, beating out silver medalist Maria Paseka of Russia and bronze medalist Giulia Steingruber of Switzerland. Her string of gold medals was temporarily halted in the balance beam, an event in which she garnered the bronze medal, finishing behind her teammate Laurie Hernandez, who captured the silver medal, and Sanne Wevers of the Netherlands, who won the gold medal. Biles recovered very nicely in the floor exercise, the final gymnastics event in the games, by capturing the gold medal over teammate Aly Raisman who won the silver medal and Amy Tinkler of Great Britain who garnered the bronze medal. All told, Biles' four gold medals in Rio de Janeiro was the most ever captured by a United States woman in one Olympic game and the first time it had happened since Ecaterina Szabo of Romania accomplished the feat in Los Angeles in 1984.

PRINCETON AND STANFORD CAPABLY REPRESENTED IN RIO

Besides Biles, two other African American women athletes who had break-out performances at the 2016 games were water polo's Ashleigh Johnson of Princeton and swimming's Simone Manuel of Stanford. Although not draw-ing the enormous amount of attention given Biles, both women garnered symbolically important victories in Rio de Janeiro in sports historically occupied almost entirely by whites. Johnson, raised by her Jamaican-born mother Donna in Miami, is a goalkeeper who has been one of water polo's most dominating players at every level of competition. In 2016 she became the first African American, and notably the only non-Californian, to make the United States women's water polo team and contributed mightily to the second consecutive Olympic gold medal garnered by the very talented squad. She led all goalkeepers in Rio de Janeiro with a very impressive fifty-one saves out of a total of seventy-nine shots on the way to the United States gold medal over Italy who captured the silver medal and Russia who took the bronze medal. Tellingly, Johnson's positive approach and personality belie the enormous pressure and responsibility she felt as a Black woman in a predominantly white sport. Like other African American athletes down through the years, she confronted stereotypical notions regarding race and the seemingly inevitable feeling of not being welcomed in an aquatic space dominated by whites. In comments posted on the United States Olympic and Paralympic Museum website, Johnson noted that when she began her career in the sport people would ask her timeworn questions that "implied I didn't belong" such as "Can Black people float?" or "Black people don't swim, how come you know how?" These inquiries, noted Johnson, "put a lot of pressure on me when I was younger to either act like race wasn't something that was part of my reality or absolutely crush the expectations that people had for me."[4]

Like Johnson, Simone Manuel had an outstanding performance in Rio de Janeiro. Born in Sugar Land, Texas, she complemented her outstanding career at Stanford and many medals she won at the World Championships and Pan Pacific Championships by capturing gold medals in Rio de Janeiro in the 100-meter freestyle and 4×100-meter medley relay and silver medals in the 50-meter freestyle and 4×100-meter freestyle relay. With her victory in the 100-meter freestyle (a tie with Canada's Penny Oleksiak) she became the first African American woman to capture an individual gold medal in an Olympic swimming competition. In the process, Manuel became an im-portant representational figure for the African American community while

Ashleigh Johnson in action for the United States women's water polo team. Considered by many the greatest goalkeeper in the world, Johnson helped lead the United States women to gold medals in both Rio de Janeiro in 2016 and Tokyo in 2020. *Courtesy Jeff Cable/USA Water Polo*

at once potentially helping shatter the myth that Blacks were incapable of swimming. As a result of her heroics in Rio de Janeiro, Manuel also received many honors and awards, including the 2017 USA Swimming's Golden Goggle Award as outstanding swimmer and the 2018 Honda Sport Award as outstanding swimmer. None of this, however, alleviated the pressure she felt as a prominent Black athlete in a sport where there were so few people her color and in a world in which inequality and hatred still existed. Immediately following the games in 2016 and with even more frequency as the Black Lives Matter movement crystallized, Manuel voiced her frustration about the limited involvement of Blacks in the sport she loved as well as the responsibility she felt she owed to the African American community because of her status as an Olympic champion. At times, her comments were also tinged with the not-so-subtle criticism of the racialist thinking and belief in biological determinism that still pervaded the United States. One interesting example of this was the statement she made shortly after her victories in Rio de Janeiro to the Associated Press that was reprinted in *The Christian Science Monitor.* "I would like there to be a day where there are more of us and it's not just Simone, the Black swimmer," noted Manuel, "because the Black swimmer makes it seem like I'm not supposed to be able to win a gold medal or I'm not supposed to be able to break records and that's not true because I work just as hard as anybody else."[5]

REPEAT PERFORMANCE FOR THE WORLD'S GREATEST ATHLETE

The important victories of Ashleigh Johnson and Simone Manuel were complemented by another gold medal in boxing by Claressa Shields as well as many excellent performances by African American women in track and field. Shields repeated as Olympic boxing champion in the middleweight division by defeating Nouchka Fontijn of the Netherlands. In track and field, African American women had one of their better Olympic performances, both in running and field events. They and other athletes were no doubt helped by the fact no Russians competed in track and field in Rio de Janeiro. Caught up in the drug scandal permeating high-level sport, the 68 Russian track and field performers who qualified to compete in the 2016 games were denied the opportunity, not included among the 271 of 389 Russian athletes cleared to participate by a three-person IOC panel. As it turned out, the Russians were fortunate since the World Anti-Doping Agency had originally recommended to the IOC that all their athletes be banned from participating in the 2016 games.

Allyson Felix had an excellent performance in Rio de Janeiro, increasing her overall number of Olympic medals to nine by capturing a silver medal in the 400-meters and gold medals in both the 4×100-meter and 4×400-meter relays. In the 400 meters, Felix garnered the silver medal in a very memorable race, losing to Shaunae Miller of the Bahamas who dove over the finish line to capture the victory. In the 4×100 meter relay, the United States team, which included in addition to Felix the University of Tennessee's Tianna Bartoletta, University of Oregon's English Gardner, and University of Southern Mississippi's Tori Bowie, had to overcome some controversy on their way to the gold medal. During the semi-finals, Felix dropped the baton when trying to hand off to Gardner and initially the team was disqualified from the event. After an appeal by the United States and a review of the film of the race, it was determined that Kauiza Venancio of Brazil had bumped Felix while she was trying to pass the baton so the team was given an opportunity to complete a solo run the following day to qualify for the finals. They ran the requisite time to qualify for the finals and went on to capture the gold medal over the silver medalists from Jamaica and bronze medalists from Great Britain. In the 4×400 meter relay, the United

States team was stacked with great talent, consisting of Felix, Courtney Okolo of the University of Texas, Natasha Hastings of the University of South Carolina, and Phyllis Francis of the University of Oregon. The field was full of other equally skilled teams, however, including Jamaica who was the reigning world champion and Great Britain who had the fastest time of the year in the event. As it turned out, the United States was up to the task. With Felix running a marvelous anchor leg, they captured the gold medal, defeating Jamaica who garnered the silver medal and Great Britain who took the bronze medal.

Felix and her relay teammates had plenty of help from other African American women in track and field in Rio de Janeiro. Tori Bowie added to her gold medal in the 4×100-meter relay by taking the silver medal in the 100-meters and the bronze medal in the 200-meters. Clemson University's Brianna Rollins led a sweep of the 100-meter hurdles, capturing the gold medal over teammates Nia Ali of the University of Tennessee who garnered the silver medal and Kristi Castlin of Virginia Tech who won the bronze medal. The performance was significant in that it was the first time in Olympic history that United States women had swept a track and field event. The United States women did not sweep the 400-meter hurdles but performed extraordinarily well in the event, with Dalilah Muhammad of the University of Southern California capturing the gold medal and Ashley Spencer of the University of Texas winning the bronze medal. High hopes were pinned on sixteen-year-old high school sensation Sydney McLaughlin to also capture a medal in the event, but her fifth place finish in the semifinals failed to qualify her for the finals. In addition to the running contests, African American women would take home medals in the field events in Rio de Janeiro. Tianna Bartoletta took home her second gold medal of the games by winning the long jump with a leap of 23'6¼" inches to beat her teammate Brittney Reese of the University of Mississippi who captured the silver medal and Ivana Spanovic of Serbia who came in a distant third. In the shot put, Michelle Carter from the University of Texas captured the gold medal in the event on her very last toss of the competition. Carter, the daughter of Michael Carter, silver medalist in the shot put in the 1984 Olympic games, three-time NFL All-Pro, and member of three San Francisco 49ers Super Bowl champion teams, beat two-time defending Olympic gold medalist Valerie Adams of New Zealand. The victory by Carter was significant in that she became the first athlete from the United States to win the shot put since women began competing in it in 1948 and only the second woman from the United States since Earlene Brown's bronze in the 1960 games in Rome.

African American men garnered fewer medals than their women counterparts in Rio de Janeiro but yet had some outstanding performances in both running and field events. In one of the more impressive accomplishments, the great University of Oregon athlete Ashton Eaton repeated as the gold medalist in the decathlon in Rio de Janeiro. Born in Portland, Oregon, to a Black father and white mother, Eaton first moved with his mother to La Pine, Oregon, and then later to Bend after she and Eaton's father had divorced. Eaton participated in a variety of sports during his childhood, but he eventually began to focus more intently on track and field, excelling in the sport by capturing the state championship in both the 400 meters and long jump while at Mountain View High School. Receiving few scholarships, Ashton ultimately found his way to the University of Oregon where he concentrated on the decathlon. He competed for the first time at the international level in 2009 at the World Championships in Berlin where he finished eighteenth in the decathlon with 8,061 points. In 2012, Eaton captured the gold medal in the decathlon with 8,869 points in the London Olympics. Three years later at the World Championships in Beijing he broke his own world record in the decathlon with 9,045 points, surpassing the 9,039 points he had scored at the US Olympic trials in 2012. In the 2016 Olympic games in Rio de Janeiro Eaton repeated as the gold medalist in the decathlon, becoming only the third Olympian to win consecutive titles in the event, the other two being the United States' Bob Mathias in 1948 and 1952 and Great Britain's Daley Thompson in 1980 and 1984. Eaton captured the gold medal with 8,893 points, beating the silver medalist Kevin Mayer of France who accumulated 8,834 points and the bronze medalist Damian Warner, a Black Canadian who scored 8,666 points in the competition.

Although Eaton's second gold medal in the decathlon in Rio de Janeiro was historic, there were several other great performances in track and field by African American men in the 2016 games. Two of those performances were by Jeff Henderson of Stillman College and Christian Taylor of the University of Florida. Henderson captured the gold medal in the long jump with a leap of 27'5.9", barely edging South Africa's Luvo Manyonga who jumped 27'5.5" and third place finisher and defending champion Greg Rutherford of Great Britain. It was the first Olympic victory captured by a United States athlete in the event since Dwight Phillips won gold in Athens in 2004. Taylor repeated as Olympic triple jump champion in Rio de Janeiro with a leap of 58'7", beating out his teammate Will Claye from the University of Florida, who won his second consecutive silver medal in the event with a jump of 58'3" and Dong Bin of China who garnered the bronze

Ashton Eaton celebrating after winning the gold medal in the decathlon at the 2016 Olympic Games in Rio de Janeiro. He captured his first gold medal in the event at the 2012 Games in London. *Courtesy of the Associated Press.*

medal with a leap of 57'8". Kerron Clement of the University of Florida captured the gold medal in the 400-meter hurdles, outdueling Boniface Tumuti of Kenya who won the silver and Yasmani Copello of Turkey who garnered the bronze medal.

Paul Chelimo, born in Kenya and ultimately gaining United States citizenship through the Military Accessions Vital to National Interest (MA-VNI) program, captured a silver medal in the 5,000 meters behind Great Britain's legendary Mo Farah (who also repeated in the 10,000 meters) and ahead of third place finisher Hagos Gebrhiwet of Ethiopia. Also representing the United States in the event were two other foreign-born athletes. Somali-born Hassan Mead, who had an outstanding career at the University of Minnesota, failed to medal in the event as did Kenyan-born runner Bernard Lagat who had enjoyed, like other Kenyan-born athletes such as Henry Rono and Michael Kosgei, a highly successful career at Washington State University. Of these athletes, it was Lagat who had the most success on the Olympic stage, capturing a bronze medal in the 1,500-meters in 2000 in Sydney and silver medal in the 1,500-meters in 2004 in Athens while representing his native Kenya.

Justin Gatlin, the controversial sprinter from the University of Tennessee, won his fifth and final medal in Olympic competition by finishing second to the extraordinarily talented Jamaican Usain Bolt and ahead of Andre De Grasse of Canada in the 100-meters. LaShawn Merritt of Old Dominion University captured the bronze medal in the 400-meters behind gold medalist Wayde van Niekerk of South Africa, who shattered the world record in the event with a time of 43.03, and silver medalist Kirani James of Grenada. Finally, the United States 4×400-meter relay team, which included Merritt, Tony McQuay of the University of Florida, Gil Roberts of Texas Tech University, and Arman Hall of the University of Florida, captured the gold medal by defeating the second-place finishers from Jamaica and the third-place finishers from the Bahamas.

BASKETBALL GOLDS CONTINUE TO MOUNT FOR THE UNITED STATES

As expected, African American men and women would contribute significantly to the success of the United States basketball teams in Rio de Janeiro. The United States men's team, an all-Black squad coached again by Duke University's Mike Krzyzewski, captured their third consecutive Olympic gold medal, finishing with an 8–0 record and extending their winning streak to twenty-five games in Olympic competition. The roster was relatively young and inexperienced, with ten of the twelve players on the United States team participating in the Olympic Games for the first time. It was, however, a deeply talented squad with great chemistry and selflessness that was on display in every game of the tournament. All told, in winning the gold medal, the United States men averaged 100.9 points per game and won by an average margin of 22.5 points per game. They also led the twelve tournament teams in most statistical categories, including points scored, blocked shots, steals, rebounds averaged, and three-point percentage. Individually, the team was led in scoring by Kevin Durant of the Golden State Warriors, who averaged 19.4 per game, and Carmelo Anthony of the New York Knicks, who averaged 12.1 per game. Tellingly, this was the fourth and final time Anthony would be a member of the United States men's basketball team; he would finish his Olympic career with three gold medals and a host of records.

The United States women's basketball team outdid their male counterparts if one uses the number of consecutive gold medals in Olympic competition as the criteria. While the men garnered their third consecutive gold medal in Rio de Janeiro, the women captured their sixth consecutive gold medal without seriously being challenged by other teams in the tournament. Coached again by the legendary Geno Auriemma of the University of Connecticut, the United States women's team included five white and seven African American players of varying levels of experience. Of the seven African American players, Brittney Griner of the Phoenix Mercury was a first time member of the team, Tina Charles of the New York Liberty, Angel McCoughtry of the Atlanta Dream, and Maya Moore of the Minnesota Lynx were playing for the second time on the team, Seimone Augustus and Sylvia Fowles of the Minnesota Lynx were on the team for the third time, and Tamika Catchings of the Indiana Fever was on the team for the fourth time. Of the five white players, Elena Delle Donne of the Chicago Sky and Breanna Stewart of the University of Connecticut were on the team for the first time, Lindsay Whalen of the Minnesota Lynx for the second time, and Sue Bird of the Seattle Storm and Diana Taurasi of the Phoenix Mercury were members of the team for the fourth time. The makeup of the final roster was not without controversy. One athlete conspicuous for her absence on the final roster was Candace Parker, the outstanding player from the Los Angeles Sparks who contributed significantly to the success of the team in 2008 in Beijing and again in 2012 in London. Being left off the squad was terribly hurtful to Parker and surprised and angered many observers, a decision never explained by the USA Basketball selection committee. For her part, Parker poignantly noted in 2018 that "I wouldn't be able to represent USA Basketball anymore."[6]

The Parker situation aside, the United States women's basketball team plowed through their opponents in Rio de Janeiro with great efficiency, exhibiting an unmatched degree of skill and teamwork and determination. In the final, the United States women defeated Spain 101–72 behind double-digit scoring from several players. Overall, they established tournament records for field goal percentage, free throw percentage, assists, three pointers attempted, and field goals made. The team ended the tournament in Rio de Janeiro with a forty-nine-game win streak and an extraordinary overall record of 66–3 since the first time they competed in the Olympic games in 1976 in Montreal. On an individual level, Taurasi led the team in scoring with 15.6 points per game, Griner in rebounding with 5.9 rebounds per game, and Bird in assists with 4.4 per game. With the victory, Griner had the distinction of becoming the tenth woman player to capture a FIBA World Championship, a WNBA title, an Olympic gold medal, and an NCAA championship.

CHALLENGING STEREOTYPES BY WEARING A HIJAB

The United States women's volleyball team did not reach the heights of its counterpart in basketball, having to settle for a bronze medal rather than gold in Rio de Janeiro. Their third-place finish, however, would not have been possible without the three African American athletes on the team. Penn State's Alisha Glass, University of Texas's Rachael Adams, and Stanford University's Foluke Akinradewo would all contribute to the third-place finish of the United States women's volleyball team in the 2016 Olympic Games. Glass, named USA Volleyball Female Indoor Athlete of the Year in both 2013 and 2014, was selected the best setter in Rio de Janeiro. Adams, two-time American Volleyball Coaches Association All-America first-team selection in 2010 and 2011, ranked eleventh in scoring with 84 points and third in blocking with 0.56 per set in Rio de Janeiro. Akinradewo (now Akinradewo Gunderson), who holds citizenship in Canada, Nigeria, and the United States, is considered by many as the best middle blocker in the world, and it showed in Rio de Janeiro. She started all eight games, scored a total of 104 points, selected along with Milena Rasic of Serbia as the best middle blocker of the tournament, and was named to the 2016 Olympic Games Volleyball Dream Team.

Other medals garnered by African Americans in Rio de Janeiro came in tennis, boxing, wrestling, and fencing. Venus Williams, in a rare instance not to be playing alongside her younger sister Serena, teamed up with Rajeev Ram, the veteran player of Indian heritage, to take the silver medal in the mixed doubles tennis competition. In boxing, Shakur Stevenson, the outstanding boxer from Newark, New Jersey, enjoyed a great tournament in Rio de Janeiro and was one of the favorites to win it all. Unfortunately, he had to settle for the silver medal, losing the final match 1–2 to Cuban boxer Robeisy Ramirez who had captured the gold medal in the flyweight division four years earlier in London. In freestyle wrestling J'den Cox, the outstanding grappler from Missouri who captured three NCAA titles and two World Championships, shared the bronze medal in 2016 in the light heavyweight division with Sharif Sharipov of Azerbaijan. His one loss in Rio de Janeiro was in the semifinals by a score of 1–2 to Selim Yasar of Turkey who lost in the finals to gold medalist Abdulrashid Sadulaev of Russia and would capture another Olympic gold in the heavyweight division four years later in Tokyo.

Finally, African American fencers continued to distinguish themselves in Olympic competition. In Rio de Janeiro, three African Americans, Myles Chamley-Watson, Daryl Homer, and Ibtihaj Muhammad, all garnered medals on behalf of the United States. Chamley-Watson, born in London and of Jamaican, British, Irish, and Malawain descent, had an outstanding career at Penn State University before capturing a bronze medal in the team foil competition in Rio de Janeiro. Homer, like Chamley-Watson an immigrant to this country, was born in St. Thomas and moved with his family at the age of five to New York City. He was another disciple of Peter Westbrook, joining the legendary fencer's foundation where he initially learned and honed the skills the sport required. He had a highly success-ful career at St. John's University before garnering the silver medal in the individual sabre competition in Rio de Janeiro, the first fencer from the United States to medal in the event since Westbrook took home the bronze in Los Angeles in 1984. Muhammad garnered far more media attention than Chamley-Watson and Homer, and so many other Olympians in Rio de Janeiro, for that matter. Born in Maplewood, New Jersey, Muhammad was yet another member of the Peter Westbrook Foundation and like Maya Lawrence was an outstanding student-athlete, named three times an All-American fencer at Duke University and graduating from the school with a dual major in International Relations and African American Studies. The skills Muhammad exhibited at Duke University were on full display in Rio de Janeiro where she won a bronze medal in the team sabre competition.

The enormous media attention Muhammad received in Rio de Janeiro had less to do with the medal she won and more to do with the fact she won it wearing a hijab. A devout Muslim whose parents had initially searched out sports that would allow her to compete while wearing the veil required by her religion, Muhammad became the first woman to compete in an Olympic games wearing a hijab. Heightening the attention Muhammad received for wearing a hijab in Rio de Janeiro had much to do with the fact that it took place during the 2016 presidential campaign when highly controversial comments were being made about immigration, including Donald Trump's call for temporarily banning all Muslim immigrants from the United States. None of this discussion was lost on Muhammad and the representational role thrust upon her as a Muslim woman competing in the most important mega-sporting event in the world. Besides having harsh words for Trump, expressing the view that if it was up to him "America would be white, and there wouldn't be any color and there wouldn't be any diversity," she told the British Broadcasting Company prior to the games in Rio de Janeiro that she was "excited to challenge the stereotypes and misconceptions about Muslim women. I want to show people that we can not only be on any Olympic team, but on the U.S. Olympic team which is the strongest of the world's teams."[7]

"UNITED BY EMOTION," AND THE "BRAVE GOAT"

The world was certainly "united by emotion," as indicated by the official motto of the Tokyo Olympics but far less united in their opinions as to whether the games should be held. As COVID-19 continued to cause severe illness and result in thousands of deaths, a serious debate ensued with some observers arguing that the games should be cancelled while others suggested postponement. On March 2, 2020, the Tokyo Organizing Committee of the Olympic and Paralympic Games (TOCOG) announced that the games would go on as planned. Almost immediately, the announcement received pushback from countries who were concerned about the health and safety of athletes, coaches, officials, and their support staff, and media expected to participate in the games. Both Australia and Canada made clear on March 23, 2020, that they would not send their athletes to the games unless they were postponed to the following year. One day later, the TOCOG and IOC made a joint announcement indicating that the games would be delayed "beyond 2020 but not later than summer 2021," expressing the view that the Tokyo Olympics "could stand as a beacon of hope to the world during these troubled times."[8] Finally, on March 30, 2020, the TOCOG and IOC got more specific, stating that they had determined the games would be held on July 23, 2021, beginning with the opening ceremony, and ending with the closing ceremony on August 8, 2021.

The Tokyo Games, which continued to use the moniker "Tokyo 2020" for ongoing branding and marketing purposes and adopted strict biosecurity protocols, began with the opening ceremony in the newly built National Stadium. Some 11,656 athletes participated in the Tokyo Olympics from thirty-three different sports. The games featured for the first time the sports of surfing, karate, sport climbing, and skateboarding; fifteen new events in existing sports such as the popular 3x3 basketball; and mixed gender events in the decidedly different sports of track and field, swimming, triathlon, shooting, judo, tennis, archery, and table tennis. The United States captured 113 total medals, with many of those won by African American athletes.

Again, no African American garnered more attention than gymnast Simone Biles. In contrast to Rio de Janeiro, however, this time the attention she drew had less to do with her gymnastics performance. To the astonishment and disappointment of the sports world, on July 27 Biles pulled herself out of the team competition. At first, it was assumed she had taken herself out of the competition because of some physical ailment, but it was soon announced it was for mental health reasons. Biles, referred to as the "darling of the Tokyo games," told reporters that the Olympics had exacted an emotional toll on her and "I have to focus on my mental health."[9] Not unexpectedly, there were some who were highly critical of Biles, voicing very personal and cruel comments that were reminiscent of those directed at tennis star Naomi Osaka when she pulled out of the French Open and Wimbledon to concentrate on her mental health. Conservative commentator Mike Walsh tweeted of Biles: "We now have decorated Olympic athletes quitting in the middle of competition because they're sad. What an absolute embarrassment."[10] British broadcaster and television personality Piers Morgan noted that Biles "calls herself the Greatest of All-Time but no GOAT would quit . . . Get back out there, Simone."[11]

The cruel comments by Walsh, Morgan, and a few other right-wing pundits were countered by an overwhelming show of support and empathy for the troubled gymnast. Sportswriters, health experts, broadcasters, and others vehemently voiced their concern and appreciation for Biles' decision, noting the constant stress she had faced as the world's greatest gymnast and as a Black woman in a white sport who had lived both through a childhood in and out of foster care as well as the more recent sexual abuse suffered at the hands of the ghastly medical doctor Larry Nassar. Among those immediately coming to Biles' defense were current and former athletes who could identify with the enormous pressure and emotional strain she had experienced. The most prominent of these athletes was Michael Phelps, the legendary swimmer and highly decorated Olympic champion. An athlete who had been very public about his own emotional health issues and a long-time advocate of mental well-being, Phelps noted, in one of the regular features he did during the Tokyo games with NBC's Mike Tirico, that Biles' withdrawal from the team competition "broke my heart" and added that he hoped "this is an opportunity for us to jump on board, and to even blow this mental health thing even more wide open."[12] Phelps' hopes, fortunately enough, were realized, with various individuals and groups capitalizing on the courage shown by Biles amid the emotional toll resulting from COVID-19, to continue fighting with even more urgency and determination the battle that had already emerged in athletics and the larger society against the stigma associated with mental health issues. In large measure, Biles' actions transcended gymnastics, helping bring to the fore the importance of maintaining emotional well-being and seeking help for mental problems without fear of being shamed or denigrated for doing so.

CUT FROM A DIFFERENT CLOTH

A decidedly different kind of African American athlete in Tokyo who helped bring attention to mental health issues was Raven Saunders, the outspoken shot put champion from the University of Mississippi by way of Southern Illinois University. After placing fifth in the shot put competition at the 2016 Olympic games in Rio de Janeiro, Saunders took silver in the event in Tokyo behind the gold medalist Gong Lijiao of China and ahead of the bronze medalist Valerie Adams of New Zealand. As successful as she has been as one of the world's great shot putters, it has been off the track where Saunders has garnered much of her attention and notoriety. An openly gay athlete, Saunders has struggled over the years with her mental health, reaching a point in 2018 in which she contemplated ending her life. Fortunately, she chose life instead and checked into a mental health facility and ultimately committed to using her platform to speak out about her personal struggles and assist others in realizing better emotional well-being and finding ways to eliminate the stigma attached to mental illness. Just two months prior to the Tokyo games, Saunders appeared in "Out of the Dark," a mini-documentary series sponsored by the media organization Well Beings that featured the stories of people who have suffered the pangs of mental illness. Saunders' episode detailed her mental health journey and was aptly titled, "An Olympic Athlete Takes on Depression."[13]

Saunders did not just fight against the stigma of mental illness but also actively supported the Black Lives Matter movement and the struggles of underrepresented people, a commitment that would eventually place her in the cross hairs of the IOC. Following the medal ceremony in Tokyo for the top three finishers in the shot put and playing of the Chinese national anthem in honor of winner Gong Lijiao, Saunders raised her arms high above her head and crossed them in the shape of an X while still on the platform. In explaining the crossing of her arms on the medal stand, she told Craig Melvin of NBC that "I'm a black female, I'm Queer and I talk about mental health awareness—I deal with depression, anxiety and PTSD, a lot—so for me personally, I represent being at that intersection. I decided to use my platform to speak up for all those people, for anyone who represents any part of or any one of those groups, this medal is for [them]."[14] Although the United States Olympic and Paralympic Committee (USOPC) defended her gesture, the International Olympic Committee (IOC) debated what, if any, actions should be taken against Saunders since its admittedly less stringent Rule 50, which allows athletes "to make gestures on the field, provided they do so without disruption and with respect for fellow competitors," still bars demonstrations on the medal platform.[15] Tellingly, the IOC stopped its investigation of Saunders' "X protest" on August 4, 2021, after hearing of the death of her mother in Charleston, South Carolina. "The IOC obviously extends its condolences to Raven and her family," noted IOC spokesman Mark Adams. "You will, I hope, fully understand that given these circumstances, the process at the moment is fully suspended for the time being."[16]

As to why the IOC has yet to reopen the investigation of Saunders' medal stand display is open to speculation. It is probably the case, however, that while in principle Saunders violated Rule 50 by demonstrating on the medal stand, the IOC had difficulty in differentiating her protest from the several others by athletes in Tokyo that were apparently completed "without disruption and with respect for fellow competitors."[17] In reality, how dissimilar was Saunders' protest from that of Costa Rican gymnast Luciana Alvarado who took a knee, placed her left hand behind her back and raised her right fist high in the air after her floor routine in tribute to the Black Lives Matter movement; or the Australian women's soccer team that displayed an Indigenous Flag prior to their first game in support of their Aboriginal teammates Lydia Williams and Kyah Simon; or captain of the German women's field hockey team Nike Lorenz who wore a rainbow-colored armband (evidently granted permission to do so prior to the games by the IOC) to indicate solidarity with the LGBTQ community? In spite of her courage and forcefulness, Saunders carefully adhered to the proscribed code of behavior expected of an Olympic athlete by respectfully standing at attention with eyes fixated on the flag while the national anthem of the gold medalist was being played. Unlike the bowed heads and raised fists of Tommie Smith and John Carlos while on the victory stand in Mexico City in 1968 or the refusal of Vince Matthews and Wayne Collett to stand at attention with eyes on the flag while on the medal platform in Munich in 1972, Saunders fulfilled her role as a "signifier of Olympism" during the highly scripted ritual that was the medal ceremony by solemnly standing motionless in honor of the supposed sacredness of the games.[18]

ALLYSON FELIX'S LEGACY, MCLAUGHLIN'S EMERGENCE, RICHARDSON'S CRUEL FATE

Importantly, the silver medal garnered by Saunders in the shot put was one of nine individual and three team medals (three gold, five silver, four bronze) captured by African American women in Tokyo in track and field. Capturing much of the media attention, not just for what she did in Tokyo but also for what she accomplished over the course of her long career, was Allyson Felix. Despite running the second slowest qualifying time, she took bronze in the 400-meters, a race won by Shaunae Miller-Uibo with Marileidy Paulino of the Dominican Republic finishing second. The bronze was Felix's tenth medal in Olympic competition which tied her with Carl Lewis as the most decorated United States track and field athlete in the history of the games. The tie did not last long because the following day Felix, along with Sydney McLaughlin of Dunellen, New Jersey, Dalilah Muhammad of USC, and Athing Mu of Texas A&M combined to win the gold medal in the 4×400-meter relay, beating out Poland and Jamaica, who finished second and third respectively, a fitting end to a marvelous career for Felix who garnered a total of eleven Olympic medals to make her the most decorated United States track and field athlete in the history of the modern games.

Two African American women teammates of Felix on the 4×400-meter relay team who also garnered much media attention and praise for their performances in Tokyo were Mu and McLaughlin. Young, talented, hardworking, and with interesting backgrounds, Mu and McLaughlin were the two African American women who captured individual gold medals in Tokyo. The nineteen-year old Mu, the second youngest of seven children born in Trenton, New Jersey, to parents who had emigrated from South Sudan, first garnered international attention in 2018 when she finished first in the 800-meters in the Pan American U20 Athletes Championships in Costa Rica and second in the 800-meters at the Youth Olympic Games in Buenos Aires. The following year she broke the United States record for women in the 600-meters at the USA Indoor Track and Field Championships with a time of 1:23.57. In Tokyo, Mu won gold in the 800-meters over Keely Hodgkinson of Great Britain who garnered the silver and Mu's teammate Raevyn Rogers who took the bronze.

McLaughlin is a prodigious talent from a family of outstanding athletes. Born in New Brunswick, New Jersey in 1999, her father was a three-time All-American at Manhattan College and a semi-finalist in the 400-meters at the 1984 United States Olympic trials and her mother was a 2:12 half-miler at Cardinal O'Hara High School in Tonawanda, New York. In the Tokyo games, she shattered her own world record in the 400-meter hurdles with a time of 51.46, defeating teammate Dalilah Muhammad who garnered the silver medal in a personal best time of 51.58 and bronze medalist Femke Bol of the Netherlands who broke the European record for the event with a time of 52.03.

Other African American women track and field athletes in Tokyo would also achieve some notable successes. Kendra Harrison from the University of Kentucky won a silver medal in the 100-meter hurdles, losing to the gold medalist Jasmine Camacho-Quinn of Puerto Rico and ahead of the bronze medalist Megan Tapper of Jamaica. Brittney Reese of the University of Mississippi took the silver medal in the long jump behind Malaika Mihambo of Germany who won the gold medal and ahead of the bronze medalist Ese Brume of Nigeria. Gabrielle Thomas, a Harvard University graduate, took the bronze medal in the 200-meters behind the gold medalist Elaine Thompson-Herah from Jamaica and silver medalist Christine Mboma from Namibia. Thomas would join forces with Javianne Oliver of the University of Kentucky, Teahna Daniels of the University of Texas, and white teammate Jenna Prandini of the University of Oregon to take the silver medal in the 4×100 meter relay, crossing the finish line behind the gold medalist from Jamaica and ahead of the bronze medalist from Great Britain. Finally, in one of the nine gender-blended events in Tokyo, Kendall Ellis of the University of Southern California and Kaylin Whitney of East Ridge High School joined with two Black male teammates Vernon Norwood of Louisiana State University and Trevor Stewart of North Carolina A&T to take the bronze medal in the mixed 4×400-meter relay behind the gold medalists from Poland and silver medalists from the Dominican Republic.

Unfortunately, the United States was without the services in Tokyo of yet another outstanding African American woman athlete who could have potentially come home with an Olympic medal based on her past performances on the track. In fact, we will never know how Sha'Carri Richardson, the outstanding sprinter from Louisiana State University, would have fared in the 100-meters since she was disqualified from competition for a month (and for all intents and purposes the games because of the length of the disqualification) shortly after winning the event at the U.S. Olympic trials for testing positive for marijuana use. In one of the biggest stories leading up to the games, Richardson, who first drew national attention in 2019 by capturing the 100-meters in the NCAA Championships in a time of 10.75 and was expected by many to be in medal contention in the event in Tokyo, was forced to become a spectator for using a drug that is legal in some states and includes no ingredients known to improve athletic performance. She admitted that she had used the drug, but only as a way to cope with the death of her mother one month earlier. She also initially accepted the punishment without any apparent bitterness but called out Olympic and anti-doping officials after Russian figure skater Kamila Valieva was allowed at the 2022 winter games in Beijing to compete despite testing positive for a banned substance. "The only difference I see," said Richardson in comparing her situation to that of Valieva, "is I'm a black young lady." Jerry Brewer,

Black columnist for the *Washington Post*, astutely wrote that "Sha'Carri Richardson is guilty of coping, not doping. In the rigid and unfocused system governing Olympic athletes, she is treated as a cheater nonetheless, all for making the rash decision to use marijuana to soothe her stress and manage the trauma of learning—from a reporter—that her biological mother was dead." Importantly, Brewer went on to note that the outdated policy of the U.S. Anti-Doping Agency puts it "at odds with many states in this country that have legalized marijuana or loosened restrictions" and in the case of Richardson "robbed a 21-year-old of her joy during a difficult time and reintroduced us to the long, racist history of cannabis being used as a tool to demonize Black people."[19]

African American men had all their athletes available but did not enjoy the overall level of success in track and field in Tokyo as their female counterparts. In fact, they did not garner any gold medals in individual events and had just one in team competition. In spite of the many disappointments, there were some memorable performances by African American men in the more prestigious track and field events in Tokyo. Fred Kerley of Texas A&M ran a personal best of 9.84 to capture the silver medal in the much-anticipated 100-meter behind the first-place winner Marcell Jacobs of Italy and ahead of bronze medalist Andre De Grasse of Canada. Kenny Bednarek of Indian Hills Community College ran a personal best of 19.68 to take the silver medal in the 200-meters, a race won by De Grasse, with Noah Lyles of the United States finishing in third place. This was one of the more disappointing races for the United States in Tokyo as Lyles, the T.C. Williams High School (Alexandria, Virginia) graduate who shunned college for a lucrative professional career, came into the event with the fastest time of the year and reigning world champion. Paul Chelimo of the University of North Carolina at Greensboro took the bronze medal in the 5,000-meters, finishing behind Joshua Cheptegei of Uganda and Mohammed Ahmed of Canada. Grant Holloway of the University of Florida won the silver medal in the 110-meter hurdles behind gold medalist Hansle Parchment of Jamaica and ahead of bronze medalist Ronald Levy of Jamaica. Rai Benjamin of the University of Southern California took the silver medal in the 400-meter hurdles, losing out to gold medalist Karsten Warholm of Norway who broke the world record in the event and edging out the bronze medalist Alison dos Santos of Brazil. Three days later, Benjamin teamed up with Michael Cherry of Louisiana State University, Michael Norman of the University of Southern California, and Bryce Deadmon of Texas A&M University to win the gold medal in the 4×400-meter relay ahead of the silver medalists from the Netherlands and bronze medalists from Botswana. The victory was redemption of sorts for the United States whose 4×100-meter relay team failed to advance to the finals, a performance that the legendary Carl Lewis called a "clown show" and "total embarrassment."[20]

GOLD IN BOTH THE 5×5 AND 3×3 TOURNAMENTS

The United States men's basketball team was anything but an embarrassment in Tokyo. Once again made up of all-Black players, the team marched to its fourth straight Olympic gold medal in spite of less than optimal circumstances. To a great extent, what the United States men's basketball team had to endure and the adjustments they had to make prior to and during the games in Tokyo serve as an instructive case study of the deleterious impact of COVID-19. Because of the delayed NBA season, the United States men only had a four-day training camp in Las Vegas. Not unexpectedly considering the limited time they had to practice together, they lost their first exhibition game against Nigeria and followed with another loss to Australia. The team was scheduled for a rematch with Australia that same week, but the game was canceled because of a coronavirus scare. Shortly thereafter the dominoes seemed to fall as the Washington Wizards' Bradley Beal was dropped from the team and placed into health and safety protocols after testing positive for COVID-19, the Cleveland Cavaliers' Kevin Love withdrew from the squad because of a lingering right calf injury, and the Chicago Bulls' Zach LaVine could not travel to Japan on the team plane because he was in close-contact quarantine. While quickly able to fill its roster by adding the San Antonio Spurs' Keldon Johnson and the Phoenix Suns' JaVale McGee, three of the team's most prominent players, the Milwaukee Bucks' Jrue Holiday, the Phoenix Suns' Devon Booker, and the Milwaukee Bucks' Khris Middleton, arrived in Japan less than twenty-four hours before the team's first game because of their participation in the NBA finals.

Considering these circumstances, it is not surprising the United States men struggled early in the tournament, losing their initial contest to France 83–76, their first defeat in Olympic competition since 2004. The loss was a big disappointment, but the team, coached by the San Antonio Spurs' Gregg Popovich and led by the Brooklyn Nets' Kevin Durant, made changes to their lineup and won all their remaining games to capture the gold medal. The victory brought forth the usual celebrations but also a visible sense of relief from both players and Olympic officials because of the very high expectations of the United States basketball team. Damian Lillard, a point guard and integral part of the team, perhaps best expressed the sentiments of many people associated with the gold medal squad when he noted after the tournament that "I think it's more joy than relief, but definitely some relief. . . . It's like we have to get it done, so finally getting there and pulling it off in the gold medal game you can only exhale."[21]

The United States women's basketball team as usual breezed through the competition in the Tokyo Games. Coached by Dawn Staley, the only African American woman in history to head up the team, the squad was loaded with talent, consisting of three white and nine Black players who had excelled at the college and professional levels of competition. It was dominated by five former University of Connecticut players that included Sue Bird (Seattle Storm), Tina Charles (Washington Mystics), Napheesa Collier (Minnesota Lynx), Breanna Stewart (Seattle Storm), and Diana Taurasi (Phoenix Mercury). The seven other members of the squad consisted of the University of Texas's Ariel Atkins (Washington Mystics), Louisiana State's Sylvia Fowles (Minnesota Lynx), Baylor University's Brittney Griner (Phoenix Mercury), Notre Dame University's Skyler Diggins-Smith (Phoenix Mercury), Duke University's Chelsea Gray (Las Vegas Aces), Notre Dame University's Jewell Loyd (Seattle Storm), and the University of South Carolina's A'ja Wilson (Las Vegas Aces). In their first game, the United States women defeated Nigeria 81–72 and won their next two contests, first defeating Japan 85–69 and then beating France 93–82. In the quarterfinals, the United States women walloped Australia 79–55, defeated Serbia 79–59 in the semi-finals, and in the finals devastated Japan for the second time in the tournament 90–75.

In addition to capturing the gold medal in the traditional 5x5 basketball contest, the United States women, in contrast to the men's team which stunningly did not even qualify for the tournament, would be victorious in the inaugural 3x3 tournament in Tokyo. The team, consisting of two white players Stephanie Dolson (University of Connecticut/Chicago Sky) and Kelsey Plum (University of Washington/Las Vegas Aces) and two Black stars Allisha Gray (University of South Carolina/Dallas Wings) and Jackie Young (Notre Dame University/Las Vegas Aces), lost just one contest in the tournament, finishing with a record of 8–1 and final game victory over Russia 18–15 for the gold medal

NOT THE MOST VISIBLE OLYMPIC SPORTS, BUT CRUCIAL NONETHELESS

African American women athletes would also make significant contributions to the United States medal count in other individual and team sports in Tokyo. Ashleigh Johnson once again led the United States women's water polo team to another gold medal, blocking eleven of fifteen shots in the final game against Spain. Four African Americans, Crystal Dunn (University of North Carolina/Portland Thorns), Adrianna Franch (Oklahoma State University/Portland Thorns), Casey Krueger (Florida State University/Chicago Red Stars), and Lynn Williams (Pepperdine University/North Carolina Courage), all made contributions to the bronze medal won by the United States women's soccer team in Tokyo. Dunn was the only person from the United States to start all six games in Tokyo and played all but sixteen minutes in the tournament. The United States women's gold medal–winning indoor volleyball team received important contributions from African American players Foluke Akinradewo-Gunderson (Stanford University/Hisamitsu Springs), Chiaka Sylvia-Ogbogu (University of Texas/Eczacibasi VitrA), Haleigh Washington (Penn State University/Igor Gorgonzola Novara), and Jordan Thompson (University of Cincinnati/Eczacibasi VitrA).

Both African American women and men experienced success in wrestling and boxing in Tokyo. In women's wrestling, Tamyra Mensah-Stock of the United States became the first African American to capture a gold medal in the event by defeating Blessing Oborududu of Nigeria in the finals of the 68-kilogram division (light heavyweight) 4–1. Born in Chicago, Illinois, but raised in Katy, Texas, the talented wrestler with a magnetic personality, whose father had immigrated to the United States from Ghana at the age of thirty, sailed through the competition in Tokyo. It did not come as a surprise considering Mensah-Stock's enormous success at Wayland Baptist University and in international competition, including capturing gold medals at the 2019 World Wrestling Championships and 2019 and 2020 Pan American Championships. Importantly, Mensah-Stock was obviously cognizant of the historical significance of her victory in Tokyo. Mensah-Stock noted how proud she was to have wrestled a Black African woman in the finals considering her father's birth and upbringing in Ghana, and the racial implications of two Black women competing for the biggest title in the world. "I'm like, oh my gosh, look at us representing," explained Mensah-Stock. "You're [Oborududu] making history, I'm making history."[22]

Boxer Oshae Jones did not reach the same level of success in Tokyo as her United States teammate Mensah-Stock. The Toledo native, however, had an impressive performance in the 2020 Olympics, capturing the bronze medal in the welterweight division that was won by Busenaz Surmeneli of Turkey, with Gu Hong of China taking second place. The performance of Jones, coached by her father Otha "Big O" Jones Jr. and her brother Roshawn out of the Soul City Boxing Gym in Toledo, must have been all that much sweeter for her, not just for the fact she was the only woman from the United States to medal in boxing in Tokyo but because two months prior to the games she was forced to escape a fire that destroyed her home and all her personal belongings that went with it.

Of the three medals garnered by the United States in men's boxing, African Americans won two of them. Duke Ragan, an outstanding boxer from Cincinnati, Ohio, was one of those men. A very talented fighter, the 5'5" Ragan captured silver medals in the bantamweight division at both the 2017 World Championships and 2019 Pan American Games before turning professional in July of 2020. He won all four of his professional fights, the last one a unanimous decision over Charles Clark in Tulsa approximately five months prior to competing in the Tokyo games. Taking advantage of the 2016 ruling allowing professionals to participate in Olympic competition, Ragan proved different than many of his counterparts in that he risked injury and willingly submitted to amateur rules to represent the United States in the 2020 games. Ragan's second place finish in Tokyo was significant in that it meant he was the first professional boxer to win a medal for the United States in Olympic competition.

Keyshawn Davis, a professional boxer from Norfolk, Virginia, was the other African American to win a boxing medal in Tokyo. Known as "The Businessman" because of his family's boxing gear company DB3 and taking his inspiration from fellow Norfolk native Pernell "Sweet Pea" Whitaker, a gold medalist in the lightweight division in the 1984 games in Los Angeles who died tragically at the age of fifty-five by an automobile while crossing a street in Virginia Beach, Davis had a similar run as Ragan in his march to the silver medal in Tokyo. Fighting in the same weight division as his hero Whitaker, Davis lost in the gold medal bout to Andy Cruz of Cuba 1–4. Davis's defeat was not entirely unexpected since the twenty-six-year old Cruz had amassed a record of 105 victories and just eight losses over his amateur career.

African American athletes contributed, moreover, to the silver medals won by both the United States women's softball and men's baseball teams in Tokyo. The first time the two sports were held in the Olympic Games since 2008, the path to the silver medals for the two teams was very similar with both of them losing their respective gold medal games to Japan by a score of 0–2. There was, however, one significant difference between the two teams. Those African Americans on the women's team, which only included former University of Florida All-Americans Kelsey Stewart and Michelle Moultrie, involved themselves in the Black Lives Matter movement and efforts to make their sport more inclusive. One classic example of Stewart's commitment to the movement took place one year prior to the games in Tokyo. On June 23, 2020, owner Connie May of the Scrap Yard Fast Pitch, an independent women's professional softball team located in Conroe, Texas, in which Stewart and at least one other African American, Kiki Stokes, were members, tweeted a photo of players standing at attention with hands on their hearts with the caption "Everyone Respecting the Flag" (in obvious reference to the protests lodged by Black athletes) and tagged President Donald Trump among others. Stewart, noting that she was motivated and "inspired to use my voice" by basketball stars Natasha Cloud and LeBron James, was livid with May for being so "insensitive to what's going on with the Black Lives Matter movement" and immediately sent a message to her teammates explaining that "I personally would not play for this organization again."[23] Banding together behind Stewart, the entire team quit Scrap Yard Pitch and formed their own club, This is Us Softball. Tellingly, Stewart believed that the postponement of the Tokyo games was a blessing in disguise because it gave her an opportunity to use her platform and speak out on behalf of the younger generation of Black girls. "I was fortunate growing up that softball was in the Olympics consistently," said Stewart, "and I saw Natasha Watley and realized, wow, I can be just like her. Now, I have my platform and I can really thrive in that."[24]

In all, considering the pandemic and the constraints it fostered, the Black Lives Matter movement, and political turmoil around the world, in many ways it was surprising that the Tokyo Games went off as smoothly as they did. The games will certainly be remembered for some great athletic performances in a number of decidedly different individual and team sports. The United States, while experiencing its share of disappointments like any other country during Olympic competition, performed well in Tokyo, garnering many medals and breaking a number of records in the process of doing so. African Americans, by almost any measure, had a highly successful Olympic Games, bringing home medals in sports in which they have traditionally been most closely identified but others as well. Of all the African American athletes in Tokyo, none of them garnered as much media attention as Simone Biles for her decision to withdraw from the gymnastics competition for mental health reasons. Her courageous choice to make public her struggles with psychological problems brought worldwide attention to the stigma attached to mental health issues and the danger in not seeking help from trained professionals in an effort to overcome them. Biles' actions, coming as they did during the Olympic games, was a reminder once again that one of the best ways to illuminate larger societal issues and problems is to disrupt in some manner the sacred institution of sport, especially on the world stage at the Olympic Games. Only time will tell what disruptions, if any, will take place in Paris in 2024 and how African American athletes will fare in the prestigious and globally important sporting event that returns to "The City of Light" for the first time in one hundred years. If history is any indication, however, Black Mercuries will show up in force in Paris, distinguish themselves through great athletic performances, and proudly represent the United States irrespective of the racial realities at home and abroad.

NOTES

INTRODUCTION

1. David Marannis, *Rome 1960: The Olympics that Changed the World* (New York: Simon & Schuster, 2008), 34.

CHAPTER I

1. "Negro Athletes Are Making Good," *Indianapolis Freeman*, August 12, 1916, p. 7.

2. Edwin Bancroft Henderson, *The Negro in Sports*, rev. ed. (Washington, D.C.: The Associated Publishers, Inc., 1949; orig. 1939), 12.

3. "Some Race Doings," *Cleveland Gazette*, August 1, 1891, p. 1.

4. Gregory Bond, "George Coleman Poage," Oxford American Studies Center database, https://oxfordaasc-com.ezaccess.libraries.psu.edu/view/10.1093/acref /9780195301731.001.0001/acref-9780195301731-e-37662?rskey=xWXwcw &result=1.

5. "Colored sprinter" from "Fine Outlook for the Games," *Louisville Courier-Journal*, August 28, 1904, sec. 3, p. 3. "Colored man" from "Olympic Games to Begin Today," *Louisville Courier-Journal*, August 29, 1904, p. 6; "Colored runner" from "Student Waller's Run," *Wisconsin State Journal*," August 30, 1904, p. 5. "Negro" from "Modern Sprinters Strive to Break the Records of the Ancients," *St. Louis Republic*, August 31, 1904, p. 5; "Colored boy" from "Wisconsin Athletes in

Olympic Games at World's Fair," Chippewa Falls (Wisconsin) *Herald-Telegram*, September 1, 1904, p. 3.

6. Charles J. P. Lucas, *Official Report of the 1904 Olympic Games* (New York: Spalding, 1905), 78.

7. Henderson, *The Negro in Sports*, 69.

8. Lucas, *Official Report of the 1904 Olympic Games*, 78.

9. "Olympic Games Begin To-Day at St. Louis World's Fair," *Philadelphia Inquirer*, August 29, 1904, p. 6; "Olympic Games to Begin To-Day," *Louisville Courier-Journal*, August 29, 1904, p. 6; "Louisville Boy May Win Event," *Louisville Courier-Journal*, August 31, 1904, p. 4; "Fine Outlook for the Games," *Louisville Courier-Journal*, August 28, 1904, sec. 3, p. 3.

10. John P. Davis, "The Negro in American Sports," in *The American Negro Reference Book*, ed. John P. Davis (Yonkers, NY: Educational Heritage, 1966), 781; Peter M. Bergman, *The Chronological History of the Negro in America* (New York: Harper & Row, 1969), 344.

11. John M. McGuire, "St. Louis' Homegrown Games," *PD: St. Louis Post-Dispatch Sunday Magazine*, July 22, 1984, p. 7.

12. James Page, *Black Olympian Medalists* (Englewood, CO: Libraries Unlimited, 1991), 109.

13. Bill Mallon, "Olympic Games," in David K. Wiggins, ed., *African Americans in Sports* (Armonk, NY: Taylor & Francis Group, 2003), 264–67.

14. George R. Matthews, *America's First Olympics: The St. Louis Games of 1904* (Columbia: University of Missouri Press, 2005), 146.

15. Bond, "George Coleman Poage."

16. "Will Compete in Olympic Games," *Cleveland Leader*, August 1, 1904, p. 6.

17. "No Color Line in A. A. U. Sports," *Indianapolis Freeman*, December 14, 1907, p. 6.

18. "The Olympic Games," *Outlook*, July 25, 1908, p. 636.

19. "Negro Athlete Dead in Philadelphia," *Augusta (Georgia) Chronicle*, December 3, 1908, p. 5.

20. "Great Tribute Paid to Dead Athlete," *Philadelphia Inquirer*, December 4, 1908, p. 11.

21. "Race Questions at the Olympics," *Independent*, July 25, 1912, p. 214.

22. Edward Bayard Moss, "America's Olympic Argonauts," *Harper's Weekly*, July 6, 1912, pp. 11–12; Edward Bayard Moss, "America's Athletic Missionaries," *Harper's Weekly*, July 27, 1912, pp. 8–9.

23. "Along the Color Line," *The Crisis*, August 1912, 166.

24. "Doings of the Race," *Cleveland Gazette*, July 20, 1912, p. 2.

25. "Howard Drew Manly!" *Cleveland Gazette*, February 8, 1913, p. 3.

26. Ibid.

27. "Athletics an Entering Wedge," *Chicago Defender*, August 2, 1913, p. 7.

28. "No Color Line Is Being Drawn in Track Athletics," *Indianapolis Freeman*, August 9, 1913, p. 7.

29. Untitled, *Savannah Tribune*, March 15, 1913, p. 4.

30. Raymond E. Maddox, "Our World Famous Athlete Who Makes Friends," Oakland *Western Outlook*, April 10, 1916, p. 3.

31. Cover shot of Drew, *The Crisis*, July 1915, front cover.

32. Lucian B. Watkins, "Go!," *The Crisis*, January 1916, 143.

33. "Jim Thorpe Says," *Cleveland Gazette*, May 22, 1920, p. 2.

34. Clifton Harby Levy, "With Fin, Foot, and Wing," *Popular Science Monthly*, July 1918, 106.

35. Henderson, *The Negro in Sports*, 12.

CHAPTER 2

1. American Olympic Association, "Minutes of the Quadrennial Meeting of the American Olympic Association," Willard Hotel, Washington, D.C., November 22, 1922, State Department Records Division, Record Group 59, Box 5069, National Archives and Records Administration II, College Park, Maryland.

2. "Sol Butler Wins Honors in France: Leads the World in Broad Jumping Contest," *Chicago Defender*, June 28, 1919, p. 11.

3. Harry Keck, "Years of Training Make Earl Johnson Runner," *Pittsburgh Gazette Times*, August 10, 1920, sec. III, p. 7.

4. Ibid.

5. Robert E. Butler, "National A.AU. Ends with Johnson Winner: Camp Upton Star Takes Five-Mile Junior Title," *Chicago Defender*, September 28, 1918, p. 9.

6. Keck, "Years of Training Make Earl Johnson Runner."

7. "Expects to Win," *Chicago Defender*, July 17, 1920, p. 9.

8. "Billy Morris, Well Known Athlete, Sails for Europe," *Philadelphia Tribune*, July 31, 1920, p. 5.

9. Tommy Holmes, "Sam Mosberg and the '20 Olympics," *Brooklyn Daily Eagle*, April 29, 1948, p. 19.

10. "Benny Ponteau Wins Amateur Lightweight Championship," *New York Age*, December 11, 1920, p. 7.

11. P. J. Philip, "Landon Sets New Olympic Record in High Jumping," *New York Times*, August 18, 1920, pp. 1, 17.

12. Jack Moakley, "Coach Praises Landon," *Chicago Daily Tribune*, August 18, 1920, p. 12.

13. "Sol Butler Hurt," *Chicago Defender*, August 21, 1920, p. 6.

14. Ibid.

15. Jack Moakley, "Shea Fails to Show His Pre-War Form," *Pittsburgh Gazette-Times*, August 21, 1920, p. 7.

16. "Ted" Hooks, "The Sporting World from All Angles," *New York Age*, September 18, 1920, p. 6.

17. Ibid.

18. Ibid.

19. "Athletics and Steel Employees," *Wall Street Journal*, February 27, 1922, p. 2.

20. "In the Wake of the News: Negroes in Athletics," *Chicago Daily Tribune*, September 9, 1923, A1.

21. "The Sportive Realm," *Pittsburgh Courier*, September 15, 1923, p. 6.

22. "Earl Johnson Makes Great Showing," *Norfolk New Journal and Guide*, January 14, 1922, p. 1.

23. "The Sportive Realm."

24. P. Bernard Young Jr., "Sportboard Reflections," *Norfolk New Journal and Guide*, March 1, 1924, p. 4.

25. "Hubbard, Hussey and Johnson Win Berths," *Norfolk New Journal and Guide*, June 21, 1924, p. 5.

26. "Four Negro Athletes Are among the United States Olympics Representatives," *New York Age*, June 21, 1924, p. 1.

27. P. Young Jr., "Reflections," *Norfolk New Journal and Guide*, June 14, 1924, p. 4.

28. "Fay Says," *Chicago Defender*, June 21, 1924, p. 8.

29. W. Rollo Wilson, "Eastern Snapshots," *Pittsburgh Courier*, June 28, 1924, p. 7.

30. J. M. Howe, "'Sport Sidelights': Race Claiming," *Philadelphia Tribune*, June 28, 1924, p. 11.

31. Matthew Lundeen, "Hurdling Race: The Story of Charles Brookins," February 28, 2017, https://www.goiowaawesome.com/iowa-hawkeyes-olympic-sports/2017/02/1191/draft.

32. E. B. Henderson, "Edward Orval Gourdin," *Messenger: New Opinion of the Negro*, March 1, 1927, p. 86.

33. DeHart Hubbard's Olympic Letter, Manuscript Collections at Cincinnati Museum Center, http://library.cincymuseum.org/aag/documents/hubbardletter.html.

34. "Earl Johnson and Teammates Outrun by Willie Ritola," *Philadelphia Tribune*, July 12, 1924, p. 8.

35. P. Bernard Young Jr., "Sportboard Reflections," *Norfolk Journal and Guide*, July 12, 1924, p. 4.

36. Roscoe Simmons, "The Week," *Chicago Defender*, July 19, 1924, p. 13.

37. "Earl Johnson Is First American in 10,000 Meter," *Chicago Defender*, July 19, 1924, p. 8.

38. "Johnson Wins Third Place in Olympic Marathon Race," *Pittsburgh Courier*, July 19, 1924, p. 6.

39. "Olympic Winner," *Chicago Defender*, July 19, 1924, sec. 1, p. 9.

40. Ted Carroll, "Our Boys in the Olympics," *Pittsburgh Courier*, July 26, 1924, p. 6.

41. "Johnson Wins Third Place in Olympic Marathon Race."

42. Simmons, "The Week."

43. "Should Welcome Negro Olympic Members," *New York Age*, July 19, 1924, p. 6.

44. DeHart Hubbard, "The Color Line," *Pittsburgh Courier*, December 26, 1925, p. 13.

45. Henderson, *The Negro in Sports*, 52.

46. "Fay Says," *Chicago Defender*, July 28, 1928, part 1, p. 9.

47. W. Rollo Wilson, "Sports Shots," *Pittsburgh Courier*, August 11, 1928, sec. 2, p. 6.

CHAPTER 3

1. Henderson, *The Negro in Sports*, 59.

2. Ed Harris, "Billy Morris, Penn's Olympic Trainer: Visions Colored Youths Dominant in His Fifth Olympiad Trip," *Philadelphia Tribune*, February 6, 1936, p. 12.

3. Frederick W. Rubien, ed., *Report of the American Olympic Committee: Games of the Xth Olympiad* (New York: American Olympic Committee, 1933), 76.

4. "Olympic Prospects Primed for Final Test," *Norfolk New Journal and Guide*, July 16, 1932, p. 13.

5. Bill Gibson, "Hear Me Talkin' to Ya," *Baltimore Afro-American*, July 30, 1932, p. 15.

6. Max J. Bond, "Sun-Kissed Olympic Village, Melting Pot Of World, Is Rare Sight," *Pittsburgh Courier*, August 6, 1932, A4.

7. Chester L. Washington, "Smashing Records and Racial Barriers!" *Pittsburgh Courier*, July 30, 1932, A1.

8. Ibid.

9. "Tydia Pickett May Lose Olympic Spot," *Chicago Defender*, July 30, 1932, p. 8.

10. Gladys Jamieson, "Olympic Daze," *Norfolk New Journal and Guide*, August 20, 1932, p. 12.

11. Randy Dixon, "Tolan Defeats Olympic Aces in Fast Race," *Philadelphia Tribune*, August 4, 1932, p. 1.

12. Chester L. Washington, "'Sez 'Ches,'" *Pittsburgh Courier*, July 23, 1932, A5.

13. Grantland Rice, "The Sportlight," *Atlanta Constitution*, August 2, 1932, p. 7; Grantland Rice, "The Sportlight," *Atlanta Constitution*, August 4, 1932, p. 9.

14. "Will Rogers Remarks," *Los Angeles Times*, August 4, 1932, A1.

15. Gladys Jamison, "Metcalfe Is Idol of Olympic Village, and Oh! So Modest," *Norfolk New Journal and Guide*, August 6, 1932, p. 12.

16. "Negro Athletes Dominate Olympic Meeting," *Norfolk New Journal and Guide*, August 13, 1932, p. 12.

17. Charles Isaac Bowen, "Writer Summarizes Doings of Bronze Sports Heroes," *Atlanta Daily World*, August 17, 1932, p. A5.

18. Thomas J. Anderson, "Eddie Tolan Wins 100 Meter Olympic Classic," *New York Amsterdam News*, August 3, 1932, p. 1.

19. "Third Negro Wins Olympic Championship," *Atlanta Daily World*, August 18, 1932, p. 5.

20. Jamieson, "Olympic Daze," p. 12.

21. "'Tolan Day' Observed by State of Michigan for Eddie," *Atlanta Daily World*, September 9, 1932, p. 5.

22. "Metcalfe Day," *The Crisis*, November 1932, p. 360.

23. "Tolan Ponders Futility of Fame after His Long Search for a Job," *New York Times*, January 24, 1933, p. 24.

24. Chester L. Washington, "Sez 'Ches,'" *Pittsburgh Courier*, December 24, 1932, A5.

25. "City of Detroit Will Put Eddie Tolan to Work Soon," *Chicago Defender*, December 24, 1932, p. 9.

26. "Tolan Ponders Futility of Fame After His Long Search for a Job."

27. "Mich. Daily Pictures Tolan 'Victim of Race Prejudice,'" *Norfolk New Journal and Guide*, February 4, 1933, p. 12.

28. Frank Lett Sr., "The Sports Front: A Memorial to a Great Star," *Michigan Chronicle*, February 11, 1967, B18.

29. John Kieran, "On Your Mark for the Olympic Games!" *New York Times Sunday Magazine*, July 26, 1936, p. 16.

30. American Olympic Committee, *Fair Play for American Athletes* (New York: A.O.C., 1935).

31. F. M. Davis, "Sports Snapshots: Forget about the Olympic Boycott," *Baltimore Afro-American*, December 28, 1935, p. 20.

32. "9 Colored Athletes Score 63 Individual Points for America in Olympic Games," *Norfolk New Journal and Guide*, August 15, 1936, p. 14.

33. Dean Cromwell, with Al Wesson, *Championship Techniques in Track and Field* (New York: Whittlesey House, 1941), 6.

34. Charles D. Snyder, "The Real Winners in the 1936 Olympic Games," *Scientific Monthly* 43 (October 1936), 372–74.

35. "Olympic Stars Get Welcome of City," *New York Times*, September 4, 1936, p. 21.

36. "America's Negro Auxiliary," *Cleveland Call and Post*, August 13, 1936, p. 6.

37. "Joe Louis and Jesse Owens," *The Crisis*, August 1935, 241.

38. Charles H. Williams, "Negro Athletes in the Eleventh Olympiad," *Southern Workman* 56 (1937): 58–59.

39. Ed Harris, "Billy Morris, Olympic Trainer, Home Again, Calls Jesse Owens Best Yet," *Philadelphia Tribune*, September 3, 1936, p. 12.

CHAPTER 4

1. Frank Litsky, "Mal Whitfield, Olympic Gold Medalist and Tuskegee Airman, Dies at 91," *New York Times*, November 20, 2015, B14.

2. Joseph M. Sheehan, "Whitfield is First Negro to Gain the Sullivan Trophy in Amateur Athletics," *New York Times* December 31, 1954, 19.

3. Foreign Service Despatch, from AMEmbassy, Tehran, December 22, 1954, CU Collection, Group 2, Series 3, Box 93, Folder 93-8 "MC 468, Whitfield, Malvin, Track & Field, 1954-1967."

4. Frank Litsky, "Harrison Dillard, 96, World's Best Hurdler in the 1940s, Dies," *New York Times*, November 18, 2019: D, 7.

5. Lansbury, 52.

6. Sam Lacy, "Looking 'Em Over," *Afro-American*, July 15, 1944, 15, as cited in Cat Ariail, *Passing the Baton: Black Women Track Stars and American Identity* (Urbana: University of Illinois Press, 2020), 17.

7. "Brave Effort," *Chicago Defender*, September 18, 1948, as cited in Louis Moore, *We Will Win the Day: The Civil Rights Movement, the Black Athlete, and the Quest for Equality* (Santa Barbara, CA: Praeger, 2017), 117.

8. Cat M. Ariail, *Passing the Baton: Black Women Track Stars and American Identity* (Urbana: University of Illinois Press, 2020), 45.

9. Ibid.

10. John C. Walter and Malina Tida, eds., *Better than the Best: Black Athletes Speak, 1920–2007* (Seattle: University of Washington Press, 2010), 44.

11. Ibid, 45.

12. Ibid, 50–52.

13. As quoted in Ariail, *Passing the Baton*, 85.

14. As quoted in Ariail, *Passing the Baton*, 111.

15. As quoted in Thomas, *Globetrotting*, 115.

16. As quoted in Thomas, *Globetrotting*, 118.

17. Rome 1960, 236

18. "Olympic Girl Champ Dreads Coming Home," *New York Amsterdam News*, September 10, 1960, as cited in Moore, *We Will Win the Day*, 131, and Ariail, *Passing the Baton*, 148.

19. As quoted in Thomas, *Globetrotting*, 122.

CHAPTER 5

1. Mal Whitfield, "'Let's Boycott the Olympics': Olympic Champ Asks Negro Athletes to Act," *Ebony* 19:5 (March 1964), 95.

2. Doug Robinson, "Stolen Gold: Utahn Placed First but Had to Settle for Silver," *Deseret News*, August 7, 2008, www.deseret.com/2008/8/7/20268044/stolen-gold -utahn-placed-first-but-had-to-settle-for-silver.

3. Elliott Denman, "George Harris, 77, Judo Great," *Philadelphia Inquirer*, January 12, 2011. https://www.inquirer.com/philly/obituaries/20110112_George_Harris__77__judo_great.html.

4. An Olympian's Oral History: Wyomia Tyus, part 1, the Early Years. LA 84 Foundation. https://digital.la84.org/digital/collection/p17103coll11/id/601/rec/7.

5. Ibid.

6. Ibid.

7. Frank Litsky, "Miss McGuire Excels in Track," *New York Times*, August 9, 1964, S1.

8. An Olympian's Oral History: Marilyn White. LA 84 Foundation. https://digital.la84.org/digital/collection/p17103coll11/id/661/rec/66.

9. Harry Edwards, *The Revolt of the Black Athlete* (New York: Free Press, 1969), 42; Pete Axthelm, "Boycott Now—Boycott Later," *Sports Illustrated*, February 26, 1968, 25.

10. "Cause for Alarm," *Sports Illustrated*, September 25, 1967, 11.

11. Ibid, 73.

12. Frank Murphy, *The Last Protest: Lee Evans in Mexico City* (Kansas City: WindSprint Press, 2006).

13. Frank Litsky, "Uriah Jones 2nd, 75, a Pioneer for Black Fencers in the U.S.," *New York Times*, July 4, 2000: B, 7.

14. Curtis Anderson, "The Forgotten Champion," *The Eugene Register-Guard*, May 11, 2008, https://www.thefreelibrary.com/The+forgotten+champion.-a0179256502.

15. From a Munich daily, cited in Jørn Hansen, "The Most Beautiful Olympic Games That Were Ever Destroyed," in Vida Bajc, ed., *Surveilling and Securing the Olympics: From Tokyo 1964 to London 2012 and Beyond* (London: Palgrave-Macmillan, 2016), 144.

16. Allen Guttmann, *The Games Must Go On: Avery Brundage and the Olympic Movement* (New York: Columbia University Press, 1984), 254.

17. David K. Wiggins, "Vince Matthews, Wayne Collett, and the Forgotten Disruption in Munich," *Journal of African American History* (Spring 2021): 278–303.

18. Vince Matthews with Neil Amdur, *My Race Be Won* (New York: Charterhouse, 1974), 353, as quoted in David K. Wiggins, "Vince Matthews, Wayne Collett, and the Forgotten Disruption in Munich," *Journal of African American History* (Spring 2021), 285.

19. Matthews with Amdur, 362, as quoted in Wiggins, "Vince Matthews," 286.

20. Matthews with Amdur, 340, as quoted in Wiggins, "Vince Matthews," 286.

21. Randy Harvey, "Forgive and Forget: After 21 Years, Sprinters Leave Past Behind and Make Their Way in Teaching Others," *Los Angeles Times*, November 29, 1993. https://www.latimes.com/archives/la-xpm-1993-11-29-sp-62209-story.html.

22. Kristen Henneman, "Olympian Ruth White Found Freedom in Fencing," usafencing.org, (February 27, 2017). www.usafencing.org/news_article/show /762992-olympian-ruth-white-found-freedom-in-fencing.

23. Ibid.

CHAPTER 6

1. Jack Todd, "The 40-Year Hangover: How the 1976 Olympics Nearly Broke Montreal," *The Guardian*, July 6, 2016. https://www.theguardian.com/cities/2016 /jul/06/40-year-hangover-1976-olympic-games-broke-montreal-canada.

2. Tom Caraccioli and Jerry Caraccioli, *Boycott: Stolen Dreams of the 1980 Moscow Olympic Games* (New York: New Chapter Media, 2008), 65.

3. Ibid, 155.

4. Ibid, 123.

5. Ibid, 227.

6. Nicholas Evan Sarantakes, *Dropping the Torch: Jimmy Carter, the Olympic Boycott, and the Cold War* (New York: Cambridge University Press, 2011), 259.

7. *Games of the XXIIIrd Olympiad Los Angeles 1984 Commemorative Book* (Los Angeles: International Sport Publications, Inc., 1984), 90.

8. Ross Newhan, "A Silver Lining: Talented '84 U.S. Baseball Team Didn't Get the Gold, but the Sport Proved to be an International Winner," *Los Angeles Times*, July 22, 1992. https://www.latimes.com/archives/la-xpm-1992-07-22-sp-4198-story .html.

9. Nelson Vails, interview with William Miles, *Black Champions*, Miles Educational Film Productions, Inc., February 13, 1985, Washington University Film and Media Archive, http://repository.wustl.edu/concern/videos/ff3659006.

10. Peter Westbrook, interview with William Miles, *Black Champions*, Miles Educational Film Productions, Inc., February 14, 1985, Washington University Film and Media Archive, http://repository.wustl.edu/concern/videos/w6634779n.

11. *Seoul Calgary 1988*: The Official Publication of the U.S. Olympic Committee (Sandy, UT: Commemorative Publications, 1988), 31.

12. Richard Moore, *The Dirtiest Race in History* (London: Bloomsbury Publishing, 2012).

13. Lansbury, *A Spectacular Leap*, 214.

CHAPTER 7

1. NBC News, Today's Guest Spot: Dream Team, July 13, 2012, https://www .nbcnews.com/news/world/todays-guest-spot-dream-team-flna880260.

2. The Midfield, "Dream Team," August 13, 2017, p. 4. https://themidfield.com /best-nba-moments/the-dream-team-1992-olympics/.

3. USA Basketball, Dream Team Celebrates 25th Anniversary of Golden Olympic Run, July 26, 2017. https://www.usab.com/news-events/news/2017/07/dream-team-25th-anniversary.aspx.

4. Shaun Powell, *Souled Out? How Blacks Are Winning and Losing in Sports* (Champaign, IL: Human Kinetics, 2008), 32–33.

5. William C. Rhoden, *Forty Million Dollar Slaves: The Rise, Fall, and Redemption of the Black Athlete* (New York: Crown Publishers), 2006, 216–17.

6. Nick Zaccardi, "Janet Evans Relives 1996 Olympic Torch Handoff to Muhammad Ali," NBC Sports, October 2, 2015, p. 4, https://olympics.nbcsports.com/2015/10/02/muhammad-ali-janet-evans-1996-olympics-torch-relay-atlanta/.

7. George Vecsay, "Muhammad Ali Turns Vulnerability into Strength at '96 Olympics," *The New York Times*, June 10, 2016, p. 2, https://www.nytimes.com/2016/06/11/sports/muhammad-ali-turns-vulnerability-into-strength-at-96-olympics.html.

8. Cindy Boren, "The Iconic Moment Muhammad Ali Lit Olympic Flame in Atlanta Almost Didn't Happen," *Washington Post,* June 4, 2016, p. 1, https://www.washingtonpost.com/news/early-lead/wp/2016/06/04/the-iconic-moment-muhammad-ali-lit-olympic-torch-in-atlanta-almost-didn't-happen/.

9. Ibid.

10. David Goldblatt, *The Games: A Global History of the Olympics* (New York: W.W. Norton, 2016), 362–63.

11. John Finkel, *1996: A Biography—Reliving the Legend-Packed, Dynasty-Stacked, Most Iconic Sports Year Ever* (New York: Diversion Books, 2021), 179.

12. Michelle Smith, "1996 U.S. Women's Basketball Team Paved Way for Future Generations," ESPN, August 1, 2016, p. 2–3, https://www.espn.com/wnba/story/_/id/17196071/1996-us-women-basketball-team-paved-way-future-generations.

13. Ibid.

14. For a description of the Sydney games see: Darren Arthur, "Life as a Sydneysider When 'The Greatest Show on Earth' Came to Town," ESPN, September 15, 2020, https://www.espn.com/olympics/story/_/id/29882534/sydney-2000-olympic-games-my-personal-journey.

CHAPTER 8

1. John Meyer, "Dashing New Hero," *The Denver Post*, May 7, 2016, p. 3, https://www.denverpost.com/2007/05/12/dashing-new-hero/.

2. Eddie Maisonet, "The Miseducation of the 2004 U.S. Men's Olympic Basketball Team," *Bleacher Report*, September 5, 2017, p. 2, https://bleacherreport.com/articles/2731575-the-miseducation-of-the-2004-us-mens-olympic-basketball-team.

3. Ibid., p. 5.

4. Howard W. French, "Beijing's Unofficial Olympic Slogan," *New York Times*, March 13, 2008, https://www.nytimes.com/2008/03/13/world/asia/13iht -letter.1.11035484.html.

5. Nick Zaccardi, "As Cullen Jones Leaves Olympic-Level Competition, His Mission Is Amplified," *NBC Sports*, July 2, 2020, p. 5–6, https://Olympics.nbc sports.com/2020/07/02/Cullen-jones-swimming/.

6. David Goldblatt, *The Games: A Global History of the Olympics* (New York: W.W. Norton & Company, 2016), 409.

7. Richard Moore, *The Bolt Supremacy: Inside Jamaica's Sprint Factory* (New York: Pegasus Books, 2017). For Moore's initial discussion of the "Champs," see chapter 2, "The Wellspring."

8. Yash Matange, "This Date in NBA History (August 24): Team USA 'Redeem Team' Defeats Spain in Gold Medal Game at Beijing Olympics in 2008," *Sporting News*, August 23, 2021, https://www.sporting news.com/au/nba-history-aug-24 -team-usa-redeem-team-defeat-Spain-gold-medal-game-Beijing-plympics-2008 /py64kbru91bn1/soc201a21bb.

9. Gemma Cairney, "Get Inspired: Did the London Olympics Inspire a Generation?" BBC, https://www.bbc.com/sport/get-inspired/23738916.

10. David Goldblatt, *The Games: A Global History of the Olympics*, 415.

11. Michael Rodio, "Shannon Boxx: Lupus No Obstacle to Gold Medals," Strong of Heart, University of Notre Dame, 2012, https://strongofheart.nd.edu/profiles /shannon-boxx-2012/.

12. Meredith Cash, "Where Are They Now? The 'Fierce Five' US Women's Gymnastics Team That Won Gold at the 2012 London Olympics," *Insider*, July 29, 2020, https://www.insider.com/the-fierce-five-usa-women's-gymnastics-team -2020-7.

13. Renee Martin, "The Real Reason People Keep Making Fun of Gabby Douglas' Hair," *Establishment*, August 17, 2016, p. 7, https://medium.com/the-establishment /the-real-reason-people-keep-making-fun-of gabby-douglas-hair-124fffc1fb14.

14. Ibid.

15. Scott N. Brooks, "Serena Williams: The Cost, Benefit of Being a Strong Black Female Athlete," *Global Sports Matters*, August 20, 2018, p. 4, https://globalsport matters.com/culture/2018/08/20/serena-williams-cost-benefit-being-strong-black -female-athlete/.

CHAPTER 9

1. Zack Beauchamp, "The Anti-American Right: Rooting Against Olympians, Scoffing at Capitol Police, Broaching Civil War–Meet Today's Conservative Movement," VOX, August 3, 2021, p.4, https://www.vox.com/22600500/olympics-conser vatives-simone-biles-anti-american.

2. Ibid.

3. International Olympic Committee, "IOC Refugee Olympic Team Rio 2016, https://olympics.com/ioc/refugee-olympic-team-rio-2016.

4. United States Olympic and Paralympic Museum, "Ashleigh Johnson: First Black Athlete to Make U.S. Olympic Women's Water Polo Team," N.D., pp. 2–3, https://usopm.org/ashleigh-johnson-was-the-first-black-athlete-to-become-a-member-of-the-u-s-womens water-polo-team/.

5. Story Hinckley, "How Simone Manuel Just Made Olympic History," *The Christian Science Monitor*, August 12, 2016, p. 5, https://www.csmonitor.com/How-Simone-Manuel-Just-Made-Olympic-history.

6. Matt Ellentuck, "Candace Parker Says She Won't Play Team USA Basketball Anymore. You Can't Blame Her," *SBNATION*, April 25, 2018, p. 1, https://www.sbnation.com/wnba/2018/4/25/17277018/candace-parker-usa-basketball-olympics-is-a-nah.

7. Cindy Boren, "Muslim American Fencer to Donald Trump: 'I Don't Have Another Home,'" *Chicago Tribune*, August 8, 2016, p.1, https://www.chicagotribune.com/sports/olympics/ct-ibtihaj-muhammad-donald-trump-20160808-story.html.

8. International Olympic Committee, "Joint Statement from the International Olympic Committee and the Tokyo 2020 Organizing Committee," March 24, 2020, p. 3 https://olympics.com/ioc/news/joint-statement-from-the-international-olympic-committee-and-the-tokyo-2020-organising-committee.

9. Sara M. Moniuszko, "'That Solidified Me Being Brave': Simone Biles Most Powerful Statements About Mental Health," *USA Today*, October 21, 2021, p. 1, https://www.usatoday.com/story/life/health-wellness/2021/08/03/simone-biles-wins-bronze-her-most-powerful-mental -health-quotes/5452785001/.

10. Myron B. Pitts, "Myron B. Pitts: Shots at Simone Biles Are Uncalled-For; A Step Back in Discussing Mental Health," *Fayetteville Observer*, July 29, 2021, p. 1, https://www.fayobserver.com/story/opinion/2021/07/29/myron-b-pitts-ugly-shots-simone-biles-uncalled-for-show-lack-progress-discussing-mental-health/5398749001/.

11. Ibid., pp. 1–2.

12. NBC Washington, "It Broke My Heart: Michael Phelps Reacts to Simone Biles Withdrawal," July 27, 2021, p. 2, https://www.nbcwashington.com/news/sports/tokyo-summer-olympics/it-broke-my-heart-michael-phelps-reacts-to-simone-biles-withdrawal/2746920/.

13. Julianne McShane, "Olympian Raven Saunders Looks Toward Tokyo, With a Focus on Mental Health," *NBC News*, May 17, 2021, p. 1, https://www.nbcnews.com/news/nbcblk/olympian-raven-saunders-looks-tokyo-focus-mental-health-rcna936.

14. Danielle Abreu, "Olympic Officials Suspend Investigation Into Raven Saunders' 'X' Protest," *NBC Bay Area*, August 5, 2021, p. 3, https://www.nbcbayarea.com/news/sports/tokyo-summer-olympics/what-raven-saunders-x-protest-means-and-why-the-ioc-is-investigating/2617264/.

15. Danielle Abreu, "Olympic Officials Suspend Investigation Into Raven Saunders' 'X' Protest," *NBC Bay Area*, August 5, 2021, p. 5, https://www.nbcnews.com/news/nbcblk/olympian-raven-saunders-looks-tokyo-focus-mental-health-rcna936.

16. Ibid., p. 2.

17. Ibid., p. 5.

18. David K. Wiggins, "Vince Matthews, Wayne Collett, and the Forgotten Disruption in Munich," *The Journal of African American History*, 106 (Spring 2021), p. 287.

19. Jerry Brewer, "An Outdated Policy Brought Sha'Carri Richardson More of What She Was Trying to Avoid: Pain," *Washington Post*, July 3, 2021, p. 1, 2, https://www.washingtonpost.com/sports/olympics/2021/07/03/shacarri-richardson-outdated-policy-wada-olympics-doping/.

20. Christine Brennan, "Carl Lewis on US Men's 4×100-Meter Relay Failure: It Was a 'Clown Show' that Was 'Totally Avoidable,'" *USA Today*, August 6, 2021, p. 1, https://www.usatoday.com/story/sports/olympics/2021/08/04/carl-lewis-us-relay-failure-reach-olympic-final-clown-show/54944100001/.

21. Mike Decourey, "Damian Lillard Had to Step Back So Team USA Could Move Forward in Quest for Olympic Gold Medal," *Sporting News*, August 7, 2021, p. 8, https://www.sportingnews.com/us/nba/news/damian-lillard-team-usa-olympic-gold-medal/v7al8ohxfnmh18c162kcqyoan.

22. Bill Chappell, "Tamyra Mensah-Stock Becomes 1st U.S. Black Woman to Win Wrestling Gold," NPR, August 3, 2021, p. 2, https://www.npr.org/sections/tokyo-olympics-live-updates/2021/08/03/1024247363/tamyra-mensah-stock-first-u-s-black-woman-to-win-wrestling-gold-tokyo-olympics.

23. Sidney Shaw, "Kelsey Stewart on Making Softball More Inclusive," *Just Women's Sports*, July 13, 2020, p. 3, https://justwomenssports.com/kelsey-stewart-on-making-softball-more-inclusive/.

24. Ibid., pp. 5–6.

A BIBLIOGRAPHIC ESSAY
ON SOURCES

This survey does not pretend to list every source on the fascinating history of race and African American experiences at the Olympics. With that standard caveat out of the way, we offer a list of primary and secondary sources that most influenced our history of *Black Mercuries*.

PRIMARY SOURCES FROM THE BLACK PRESS

Much of the material for this book is rooted in extensive explorations of primary sources including newspapers and magazines, many of which over past three decades have been digitized—a blessing for researchers. Black newspapers from the 1890s forward include a trove of Olympic details. The *Philadelphia Tribune, New York Amsterdam News, New York Age, Baltimore Afro-American, Chicago Defender*, and *Pittsburgh Courier* are rich sources with national readerships that numbered in the tens and even hundreds of thousands. Less well-known Black dailies and weeklies also provide information on Black Olympians, including the *Indianapolis Freeman, Cleveland Gazette, Cleveland Call and Post, Chicago Broad-Axe, Washington Bee*, Oakland, California's *Western Outlook*, Los Angeles' *California Eagle*, and Detroit's *Michigan Chronicle*. The Black press in the South, particularly in the segregation era from the 1890s through the 1960s, provides a unique vantage. Among the key newspapers we used are the *Atlanta World, Norfolk New Journal and Guide, Savannah Tribune, Louisiana Weekly* (New Orleans), and *Houston Observer.*

African American journals and magazines also offered rich sources, in particular the *Before the Second World War*, the NAACP's flagship magazine, *The Crisis: A Record of the Darker Races,* and the *Messenger: New Opinion of the Negro,* stand out. A Black Southern journal offered two excellent surveys of Black Olympians in the 1930s by a leading African American promoter of physical fitness, Charles H. Williams. See, "Negro Athletes in the Tenth Olympiad," *The Southern Workman* 61 (November 1932): 449–460; "Negro Athletes in the Eleventh Olympiad," *Southern Workman* 66 (February 1937), 45–59. In 1945, *Ebony* (a monthly) and in 1951 *Jet* (a weekly) began publishing glossy illustrated compendiums for large, national Black readerships, covering the Olympics extensively through the early twenty-first century.

Of course, the white press covered racial issues and Black Olympians extensively, from local dailies to national mass-circulation outlets including the *New York Times, Time, Newsweek,* and many other publications. A rich reservoir of materials with a digitally searchable archive can be found in the most popular American sports magazine, *Sports Illustrated,* which began publication in 1954 and has devoted sustained attention to both race and the Olympics.

BLACK OLYMPIANS IN THE THEIR OWN WORDS

Autobiographies of Black Olympians also provide rich insights into their experiences. Some of the most famous Black Mercuries have contributed illuminating autobiographies. That list includes Jesse Owens, with Paul Neimark, *Jesse: The Man Who Outran Hitler* (New York: Ballantine Books, 1978); Mal Whitfield, *Beyond the Finish Line* (Washington, D.C.: Whitfield Foundation, 2002); Rafer Johnson and Philip Goldberg, *The Best That I Can Be: An Autobiography* (New York: Doubleday, 1998); and Michael Johnson, *Slaying the Dragon: How to Turn Your Small Steps to Great Feats* (New York: Harper, 1996).

Athletes at the center of the 1968 protests have told their stories, including Tommie Smith with David Steele, *Silent Gesture: The Autobiography of Tommie Smith* (Philadelphia: Temple University Press, 2007); John Carlos with Dave Zirin, *The John Carlos Story* (Chicago: Haymarket Books, 2011); and Bob Beamon and Milana Walter Beamon, *The Man Who Could Fly: The Bob Beamon Story* (Columbus, MS: Genesis Press, 1999). The legacy of the 1968 "revolt" on future games emerges in two fascinating biographies, Vince Matthews with Neil Amdur, *My Race Be Won* (New York: Charterhouse, 1974); and Eddie Hart with Dave Newhouse, *Disqualified: Eddie Hart, Munich 1972, and the Voices of the Most Tragic Olympics* (Kent, OH: Kent State University Press, 2017).

Another 1968 gold medalist provides a fascinating view of the Olympic struggles not only of Black athletes but also of women competitors from her distinctive perspective as a Black woman in Wyomia Tyus and Elizabeth Terzakis, *Tigerbelle: The Wyomia Tyus Story* (New York: Akashic, 2019). Black women, including Tyus, have contributed some of the best Olympic autobiographies. See Wilma Rudolph, *Wilma: The Story of Wilma Rudolph* (New York: New American Library, 1977); and Jackie Joyner-Kersee with Sonja Steptoe, *A Kind of Grace: The Autobiography of the World's Greatest Female Athlete* (New York: Warner Books, 1997). The Tennessee State "Tigerbelles" coach contributed his perspective in Ed Temple with B'Lou Carter, *Only the Pure in Heart Survive: Glimpses into the Life of a World Famous Olympic Coach* (Nashville: Broadman Press, 1980).

Don Barksdale, the first Black Olympian on a basketball team, emerges in his own words in Ron Thomas, *They Cleared the Lane: The NBA's Black Pioneers* (Lincoln: University of Nebraska Press, 2002). The brilliant player who led the U.S. team to basketball gold in 1956 has penned a memoir acclaimed as one finest sport autobiographies ever written, Bill Russell and Taylor Branch, *Second Wind: The Memoirs of an Opinionated Man* (New York: Random House, 1979). A multiple gold-medalist offers perspectives on the challenges of African Americans to break into swimming in Anthony Ervin and Constantine Markidis, *Chasing Water: Elegy of an Olympian* (New York: Akashic Books, 2016). Two stellar Black gymnasts offer their accounts in Gabrielle Douglas with Michelle Burford, *Grace, Gold, and Glory: My Leap of Faith* (Grand Rapids, MI: Zondervan, 2012); and Simone Biles with Michelle Burford, *Courage to Soar: A Body in Motion, A Life in Balance* (Grand Rapids, MI: Zondervan, 2016).

ARCHIVAL MATERIALS

Several archives include not only clip files of newspaper and magazine stories but also official reports, government documents, and illuminating correspondence that shed light on the history of African American Olympians. Among the repositories we visited, several stand out. The United States Olympic Committee Archives in Colorado Springs, Colorado, and the National Archives and Records Administration II facility in College Park, Maryland, have extensive holdings on the subject. The LA84 Foundation Archives in Los Angeles contains records not only on the 1932 and 1984 Olympics, but also information on the broader history of the Olympic movement, including all of the official U.S. Olympic reports since 1920. Official AOC reports for the period from 1896 to 1912 were published as volumes in the Spalding's Athletic Almanac series and are widely available in libraries and online archives.

LA84 also houses an outstanding oral history collection of American Olympians including several from Black athletes. Additional repositories with African American Olympian interviews can be found at the University of Texas at Austin Luther H. Stark Center 1968 Oral History collection. Two websites, "The History Makers" (https://www.thehistorymakers.org/), and "Black Champions" (http://repository.wustl.edu/admin_sets/bchamps), offer more interviews. For printed collections of oral histories, John C. Walter and Malinda Iida, *Better Than the Best: Black Athletes Speak, 1920–2007* (Seattle: University of Washington Press, 2010) is outstanding.

AFRICAN AMERICANS IN THE OLYMPICS—A BRIEF HISTORIOGRAPHY OF ACADEMIC EXPLORATIONS

A variety of secondary sources survey the participation of African American athletes in the Olympics. The original historical chronicle of Black athletes in American history, Edwin Bancroft Henderson, *The Negro in Sports* (Washington, D.C.: The Associated Publishers, Inc., 1939), provides excellent material on Olympians. A revised addition of his work appeared in 1949, and a recent third edition was published in 2014. Henderson also produced one of the earliest histories of Black Olympians, "The Negro in the Olympic Games," *Negro History Bulletin* 15 (December 1951): 43–44.

Other comprehensive histories of African American athletes devote considerable attention to Black Olympians. Among the best, listed chronologically, are Arna W. Bontemps, *Famous Negro Athletes* (New York: Dodd, Mead, 1964); Arthur Ashe Jr., *A Hard Road to Glory: A History of the African American Athlete*, 3 vols. (New York: Amistad, 1993); David K. Wiggins, *Glory Bound: Black Athletes in a White America* (Syracuse: Syracuse University Press, 1997); David K. Wiggins and Patrick B. Miller, *The Unlevel Playing Field: A Documentary History of the African American Experience in Sport* (Urbana: University of Illinois Press, 2003); and David

K. Wiggins, *More Than a Game: A History of the African American Experience in Sport* (Lanham, MD: Rowman & Littlefield, 2018).

A chronological account of encyclopedias and compendiums that cover Black Olympians includes John P. Davis, ed., *The American Negro Reference Book* (Yonkers, NY: Educational Heritage, 1966), Peter M. Bergman, ed., *The Chronological History of the Negro in America* (New York: Harper & Row, 1969), Lonnie G. Bunch and Louie Robinson, *The Black Olympians, 1904–1984: July 22, 1984–January 15, 1985* (Los Angeles: California Afro-American Museum, 1984); James Page, *Black Olympian Medalists* (Englewood, CO: Libraries Unlimited, 1991), and Bill Mallon, "Olympic Games," in David K. Wiggins, ed., *African Americans in Sports* (Armonk, NY: Taylor & Francis Group, 2004). The best collections of Black biographies include many chronicles of Olympians, including the earliest pioneers. See *The African American National Biography*, Henry Louis Gates Jr. and Evelyn Brooks-Higginbotham, editors-in-chief (New York: Oxford University Press, 2008) and the very useful Oxford African American Studies Center database available online through many research libraries.

ACADEMIC WORKS ON BLACK MERCURIES

Among the broader histories of the Olympics, those that provide the most insightful glimpses into African American experiences at the games include Allen Guttmann, *The Olympics: A History of the Modern Games*, second ed. (Urbana: University of Illinois Press, 2002); Alfred Erich Senn, *Power, Politics, and the Olympic Games* (Champaign, IL: Human Kinetics, 1999); Mark Dyreson, *Crafting Patriotism for Global Domination: America at the Olympic Games* (London: Routledge, 2009); and David Goldblatt, *The Games: A Global History of the Olympics* (New York: W.W. Norton & Company, 2018).

On the racial and ethnic dynamics of American nationalism at the Olympics, see several articles by Mark Dyreson: "Return to the Melting Pot: An Old American Olympic Story," *Olympika* 12 (2003): 1–22; and "Globalizing the Nation-Making Process: Modern Sport in World History," *International Journal of the History of Sport* 20, no. 1 (March 2003): 91–106. On racial stereotypes and racialized science emerging out of the Olympics, see Mark Dyreson, "American Ideas about Race and Olympic Races from the 1890s to the 1950s: Shattering Myths or Reinforcing Scientific Racism?" *Journal of Sport History* 28, no. 2 (summer 2001): 173–215; and David K. Wiggins, "'Great Speed but Little Stamina': The Historical Debate over

Black Athletic Superiority," *Journal of Sport History* 16 (summer 1989): 158–185. For an insightful transnational perspective, see Robert G. Weisbord, *Racism and the Olympic Games* (London, Routledge, 2015).

ACADEMIC STUDIES OF PIONEERS, 1896–1936

On race in the earliest period of the modern Olympics, see Mark Dyreson's contributions, including *Making the American Team: Sport, Culture and the Olympic Experience* (Urbana: University of Illinois Press, 1998); "Region and Race: The Legacies of the St. Louis Olympics," *International Journal of the History of Sport* 32, no. 14 (August 2015): 1697–1707; "Playing for a National Identity: Sport, Ethnicity and American Political Culture," *Proteus* 11 (fall 1994): 39–43; and "Melting Pot Victories: Racial Ideas and the Olympic Games in American Culture during the Progressive Era," *International Journal of the History of Sport* 6, no. 1 (May 1989): 49–61. On African American athletes including the earliest Olympians see the outstanding work by Gregory Bond, "Jim Crow at Play: Race, Manliness, and the Color Line in American Sports, 1876–1916," PhD dissertation, University of Wisconsin–Madison, Department of History, 2008. On the Joseph Stadler controversy, see George R. Matthews, *America's First Olympics: The St. Louis Games of 1904* (Columbia: University of Missouri Press, 2005).

For interpretations of how race shaped projections of American nationalism at Olympics in the 1920s, see James E. Odenkirk, "Sol Butler: The Fleeting Fame of a World-Class Black Athlete," in *Before Jackie Robinson: The Transcendent Role of the Black Sporting Pioneers*, Gerald R. Gems, ed. (Lincoln: University of Nebraska Press, 2017), 139–154; Mark Dyreson, "Selling American Civilization: The Olympic Games of 1920 and American Culture," *Olympika* 8 (1999): 1–41; and Mark Dyreson, "Scripting the American Olympic Story-Telling Formula: The 1924 Paris Olympic Games and the American Media," *Olympika* 5 (1996): 45–80. For a reflection on Charles Brookins, "passing," and genealogy, see Matthew Lundeen "Hurdling Race: The Story of Charles Brookins," February 28, 2017, https://www.goiowaawesome.com/iowa-hawkeyes-olympic-sports/2017/02/1191/draft.

On African Americans at the 1932 Los Angeles games, see David Welky, "Vikings, Mermaids, and Little Brown Men: U.S. Journalism and the 1932 Olympics," *Journal of Sport History* 24 (spring 1997): 24–49; Sean Dinces, "Padres on Mount Olympus: Los Angeles and the Production of the 1932

Olympic Mega-Event," *Journal of Sport History* 32 (summer 2005): 137–166; Jeremy White, "The Los Angeles Way of Doing Things: The Olympic Village and the Practice of Boosterism," *Olympika* 11 (2000): 79–116; Mark Dyreson, "Marketing National Identity: The Olympic Games of 1932 and American Culture," *Olympika* 4 (1995): 23–48; and Mark Dyreson and Matthew Llewellyn, "Los Angeles Is *the* Olympic City: Legacies of 1932 and 1984," *International Journal of the History of Sport* 25, no. 14 (December 2008): 1991–2018.

On African American experiences at the "Nazi" Olympics see David K. Wiggins, "The 1936 Olympic Games in Berlin: The Response of America's Black Press," *Research Quarterly for Exercise and Sport* 54 (September 1983): 278–292; John Gleaves and Mark Dyreson, "The 'Black Auxiliaries' in American Memories: Sport, Race, and Politics in the Construction of Modern Legacies," *International Journal of the History of Sport*, 27, nos. 16–18 (November/December 2010): 2893–2924; and Deborah Riley Draper and Travis Thrasher, *Olympic Pride, American Prejudice: The Untold Story of 18 African Americans Who Defied Jim Crow and Adolf Hitler to Compete in the 1936 Berlin Olympics* (New York: Atria Books, 2020). On Jesse Owens in particular see William J. Baker, *Jesse Owens: An American Life* (New York: Free Press, 1986); Jeremy Schaap, *Triumph: The Untold Story of Jesse Owens and Hitler's Olympics* (Boston: Houghton Mifflin, 2007); Mark Dyreson, "Jesse Owens: Leading Man in Modern American Tales of Racial Progress and Limits," in *Out of the Shadows: A Biographical History of the African American Athlete*, David K. Wiggins, ed. (Fayetteville: University of Arkansas Press, 2006): pp. 111–132.

ACADEMIC STUDIES OF RACE AT THE COLD WAR OLYMPICS, 1948 TO 1988

Damion Thomas provides the essential starting point for understanding the racial dynamics of Cold War sport in *Globetrotting: African American Athletes and Cold War Politics* (Urbana: University of Illinois Press, 2012). Other essential texts on race and Cold War Olympic history include Louis Moore, *We Will Win the Day: The Civil Rights Movement, the Black Athlete, and the Quest for Equality* (Lexington: University Press of Kentucky, 2021); and Toby C. Rider, *Cold War Games: Propaganda, the Olympics, and U.S. Foreign Policy* (Urbana: University of Illinois Press, 2017). The outstanding anthology on Cold War sport, edited by Toby C. Rider and Kevin B. Witherspoon, *Defending the American Way of Life: Sport, Culture, and the Cold War* (Fayetteville: The University of Arkansas Press, 2018), includes several essays on race and the Olympics, including Cat Ariail, "'One of the Greatest Ambassadors that the United States has Ever Sent Abroad': Wilma Rudolph, American Athletic Icon for the Cold War and Civil Rights Movement," and Kevin B. Witherspoon, "'An outstanding representative of America': Mal Whitfield and America's Black Sports Ambassadors in Africa." Joseph M. Turrini provides a fascinating overview the changing economic and social dynamics of American track and field in the Cold War era, including the racial parameters of these struggles, in *The End of Amateurism in American Track and Field* (Urbana: University of Illinois Press, 2010).

A robust literature on the emergence of Black women in Olympic track and field in the second half of the twentieth century has developed recently. See Jennifer H. Lansbury, *A Leap: Black Women Athletes in Twentieth-Century America* (Fayetteville: The University of Arkansas Press, 2014); Cat Ariail, *Passing the Baton: Black Women Track Stars and American Identity* (Urbana: University of Illinois Press, 2020); Maureen M. Smith, *Wilma Rudolph: A Biography* (Westport, CT: Greenwood Press, 2006); Rita Liberti and Maureen M. Smith, *(Re)Presenting Wilma Rudolph* (Syracuse: Syracuse University Press, 2015); and Susan K. Cahn, *Coming on Strong: Gender and Sexuality in Twentieth-Century Women's Sport* (New York: Free Press, 1994).

Histories of specific Cold War Olympics detail the racial dimensions of these contests. On the 1960 Rome Games see David Maraniss, *Rome 1960: The Summer Olympics that Stirred the World* (New York: Simon & Schuster, 2008); and Randy Roberts and Johnny Smith, *Blood Brothers: The Fatal Friendship of Muhammad Ali and Malcolm X* (New York: Basic Books, 2016).

On the 1968 Mexico City Olympics and the "Revolt of the Black Athlete," see Harry Edwards, *The Revolt of the Black Athlete*, fiftieth anniversary ed. (Urbana: University of Illinois Press, 2018; orig. 1968); Douglas Hartmann, *Race, Culture, and the Revolt of the Black Athlete: The 1968 Olympic Protests and Their Aftermath* (Chicago: University of Chicago Press, 2003); Amy Bass, *Not the Triumph but the Struggle: The 1968 Olympics and the Making of the Black Athlete* (Minneapolis: University of Minnesota Press, 2002); Kevin Witherspoon, *Before the Eyes of the World: Mexico and the 1968 Olympics* (DeKalb: Northern Illinois University Press, 2008); and David K. Wiggins, "'The Year of Awakening': Black Athletes, Racial Unrest and the Civil Rights Movement of 1968," *International Journal of the History of Sport* 9, no. 2 (1992): 188–208. See also Simon Henderson,

Sidelined: How American Sports Challenged the Black Freedom Struggle (Lexington: University Press of Kentucky, 2013); Harry Blutstein, *Games of Discontent: Protests, Boycotts, and Politics at the 1968 Mexico Olympics* (Montreal: McGill-Queen's University Press, 2021); Frank Murphy, *The Last Protest: Lee Evans in Mexico City* (Kansas City: WindSprint Press, 2006); and Richard Hoffer, *Something in the Air: American Passion and Defiance in the 1968 Mexico City Olympics* (New York: Simon & Schuster, 2009). On the spillover of Black activism to the Munich games in 1972 see David K. Wiggins, "Vince Matthews, Wayne Collett, and the Forgotten Disruption in Munich," *Journal of African American History*, 106, no. 2 (spring 2021): 278–303.

On the boycotts of the 1980s, see Tom Caraccioli and Jerry Caraccioli, *Boycott: Stolen Dreams of the 1980 Moscow Olympic Games* (Washington, D.C.: New Chapter Press, 2008); Nicholas Evan Sarantakes, *Dropping the Torch: Jimmy Carter, the Olympic Boycott, and the Cold War* (Cambridge: Cambridge University Press, 2011).

ACADEMIC STUDIES OF RACE AND THE OLYMPICS IN THE POST COLD WAR U.S., 1990s TO THE PRESENT

Linking the Olympics to the rise of modern global "mega-events" that provide stages for displaying representations of nations, economic systems, social ideologies, and even racial categories emerges as one of the more interesting developments in recent Olympic historiography. Inspired by Maurice Roche's *Mega-Events and Modernity: Olympics and Expos in the Growth of Global Culture* (London: Routledge, 2000), several recent studies offer insights on the "long" history of the Olympic movement since its origins in the 1890s while concentrating on analyses of post–Cold War Olympics from 1992 to the present. These studies touch on how race impacts recent Olympic mega-events, in particular by marketing harmonious visions of racial equity and the suppression of dissenting viewpoints. See in particular, three works by Jules Boykoff, *Power Games: A Political History of the Olympics* (London: Verso, 2016); *Celebration Capitalism and the Olympic Games* (London: Routledge, 2019); and *Activism and the Olympics: Dissent at the Games in Vancouver and London* (New Brunswick, NJ: Rutgers University Press, 2014). In a similar vein, see also John Peter Sugden and Alan Tomlinson, *Watching the Olympics: Politics, Power and Representation* (London: Routledge, 2012); and John Horne, *Leisure, Culture and the Olympic Games* (London: Routledge, 2016).

On the global impact of the African American stars of basketball "dream teams" see Walter LaFeber, *Michael Jordan and the New Global Capitalism* (New York: Norton, 1999); and Jack McCallum, *Dream Team: How Michael, Magic, Larry, Charles, and the Greatest Team of All-Time Conquered the World and Changed the Game of Basketball* (New York: Ballantine Books, 2013). For broader histories of Olympic basketball, women's and men's, see Pamela Grundy and Susan Shackelford, *Shattering the Glass: The Remarkable History of Women's Basketball* (Chapel Hill: University of North Carolina Press, 2005); and Carson Cunningham, *American Hoops: U.S. Men's Olympic Basketball from Berlin to Beijing* (Lincoln: University of Nebraska Press, 2010).

For recent assessments of post–Cold War racial fault-lines in American society that include ruminations on Black Olympians in broader critiques of racial dynamics, see Shaun Powell, *Souled Out? How Blacks Are Winning and Losing in Sports* (Champaign, IL: Human Kinetics, 2008); William C. Rhoden, *Million Dollar Slaves: The Rise, Fall, and Redemption of the Black Athlete* (New York: Crown, 2007); and two Howard Bryant books, *The Heritage: Black Athletes, A Divided America, and the Politics of Patriotism* (Boston: Beacon Press, 2018); and *Full Dissidence: Notes from An Uneven Playing Field* (Boston: Beacon, 2020).

DOCUMENTARY FILMS

Lonnie Bunch's 1984 exhibition for the Los Angeles Olympics also produced a documentary directed by Bunch that included segments of early "pioneers," *The Black Olympians 1904–1984: Athletics and Social Change* (1984). In a similar vein, *Black Olympians: A Golden Legacy*, directed by Mark White (1996), chronicled African American Olympic achievements as Atlanta hosted the games. The best treatment of the brightest American superstar is *Jesse Owens*, in the American Experience series, directed by Laurens Grant (2012). An excellent account of the "Black Auxiliary" who accompanied Owens is *Olympic Pride, American Prejudice*, directed by Deborah Riley Draper (2016). A trio of documentaries focuses on the dramatic racial narratives from Mexico City, *Fists of Freedom: The Story of the '68 Summer Games*, directed by George Roy (1999); *Salute*, directed by Matt Norman (2008); and *With Drawn Arms*, directed by Glenn Kaino and Afshin Shahidi (2020). *The Queen of Basketball*, directed by Ben Proudfoot (2021), recounts the now-forgotten story of basketball pioneer Lusia Harris. Of course, Bud Greenspan's legion of Olympic documentaries feature a variety of popular racial narratives, including the totemic *Jesse Owens Returns to Berlin* (1966).

MUSEUMS AND PUBLIC HISTORY DISPLAYS

The "Sports Gallery" at the National Museum of African American History and Culture in Washington, D.C., highlights Black Olympians in its interpretations. The "Nazi Olympics" at the Holocaust Memorial Museum, also in the nation's capital, showcases the role of the "Black Auxiliary" in the Berlin games. The Missouri History Museum in St. Louis exhibits artifacts from the 1904 Olympics at which the first African American participated. The LA84 Foundation in Los Angeles routinely houses exhibits and posts online displays related to African American Olympians, related not only to the 1932 and 1984 Games but to other eras as well. The Atlanta History Center includes extensive displays showcasing the 1996 Olympics. The recently opened United States Olympic and Paralympic Museum in Colorado Springs contains extensive exhibits that feature aspects of the African American experience in the games.

INDEX

Page references for figures are italicized.

ABOUT THE AUTHORS

David K. Wiggins is professor emeritus of sport studies at George Mason University. The author of many books, book chapters, and scholarly articles, his publications center primarily on the interconnection among race, sport, and American culture. Included among his books are *Glory Bound: Black Athletes in a White America* (1997), *The Unlevel Playing Field: A Documentary History of the African American Experience in Sport* (2003), and *More Than a Game: A History of the African American Experience in Sport* (2018). He is currently editor-in-chief of *Kinesiology Review* and past president of the North American Society for Sport History.

Kevin B. Witherspoon is the Dr. Benjamin E. Mays Endowed Chair in the Department of History and Philosophy at Lander University in Greenwood, South Carolina. He is the author of many articles, chapters, and books, most of which focus on the intersection of race, culture, and sport in the Cold War era. His books include *Before the Eyes of the World: Mexico and the 1968 Olympics* and *Defending the American Way of Life: Sport, Culture and the Cold War*, co-edited with Toby Rider of Cal State-Fullerton, both of which won the North American Society for Sport History (NASSH) Annual Book Award.

Mark Dyreson is professor of kinesiology, affiliate professor of history, and co-director of the Center for the Study of Sports in Society at Pennsylvania State University. He has published numerous articles, chapters, and books on the history of sport, including *Making the American: Sport, Culture, and the Olympic Experience* (1998) and *Crafting Patriotism for Global Dominance: America at the Olympics* (2009). He is a past president of the North American Society for Sport History, a fellow of the National Academy of Kinesiology, and has served as a managing editor and senior special projects editor for the *International Journal of the History of Sport* as well as the co-editor of the Sport in Global Society: Historical Perspectives book series for Routledge Press.